MW01040028

Texas Gardening the Natural Way

THE COMPLETE HANDBOOK

TEXAS GARDENING THE NATURAL WAY

The Complete Handbook

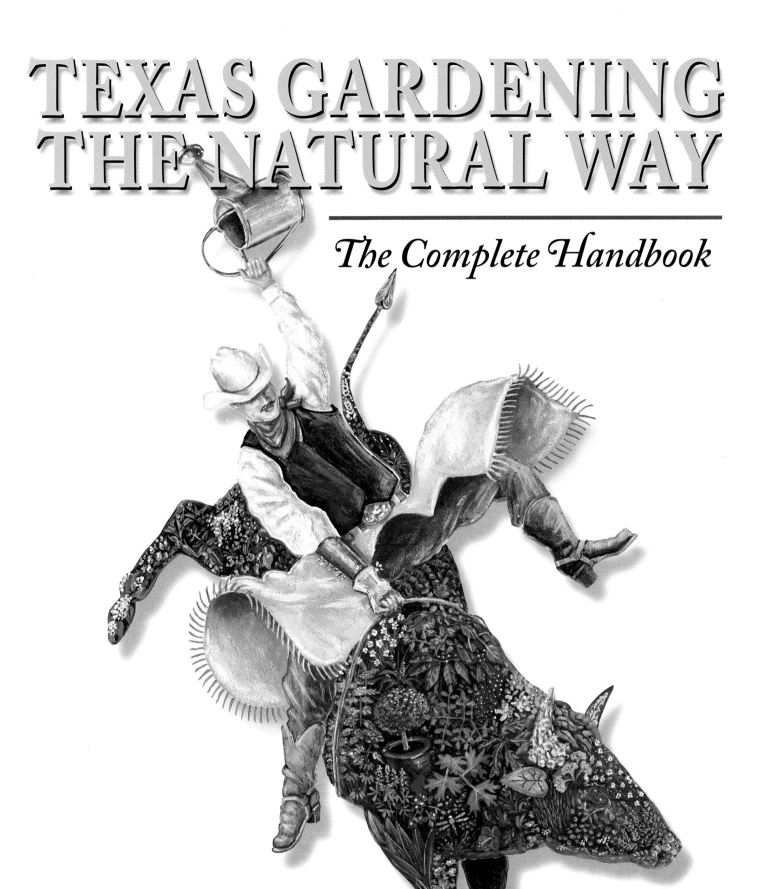

BY HOWARD GARRETT

Illustrations by Chris Celusniak

UNIVERSITY OF TEXAS PRESS AUSTIN

Copyright © 2004 by Howard Garrett
All rights reserved
Printed in China

First edition, 2004

Requests for permission to reproduce material from this work should be sent to
Permissions, University of Texas Press, Box 7819, Austin, TX 78713-7819.

∞ The paper used in this book meets the minimum requirements of
ANSI/NISO Z39.48-1992 (R1997) (Permanence of Paper).

Library of Congress Cataloging-in-Publication Data

Garrett, Howard, 1947–
Texas gardening the natural way : the complete handbook / by Howard Garrett.
      p.   cm.
ISBN 0-292-70542-5 (hardcover : alk. paper)
1. Organic gardening—Texas—handbooks, manuals, etc.   I. Title.

SB453.5 .G424   2004
635'.0484'09764—dc21   2002154909

To Tracy Fields

For many years my assistant,
forever my friend

Contents

Introduction

I came to Dallas with my new wife, Judy, in 1970, after graduating with a Bachelor of Science degree from Texas Tech University in 1969 and completing a short stint in active duty with the U.S. Marine Corps reserves. My first job in Dallas was with Club Corporation of America (CCA) as a laborer. The idea was to learn the golf-course design and management industry from the bottom up and ultimately become a golf-course architect. That way I could use my degree in landscape architecture.

It was there at Brookhaven Country Club in Farmers Branch that I found my true interest—landscape design. It was a much better fit than the labor and mechanical problems of the superintendent's life. Not to mention that those pesticides just didn't interest me and that I began to question other things. Even before my organic epiphany, I started looking at things in a different way. Instead of planting only evergreens, live oaks, hollies, and azaleas, I started asking about and even using deciduous plants and natives as well. I also watched different companies plant trees and noted some significant differences in planting techniques that seemed to work better. By paying attention to Naud Burnett, Cody Carter, and, later, Carl Whitcomb and my own projects, I developed the tree-planting recommendations that are found in this book.

The total organic change began in 1985, when our daughter, Logan, was born. It was at that point that I decided to look into the nonchemical method of gardening. At nine months, she started walking, picking up things, and tasting those things. Why it doesn't hit every parent, I don't understand, but it hit me hard. I wanted no more toxic chemicals around my little girl. I had no idea at that point what an organic program was, so the learning process began. My education consisted of reading tons of books on the subject and learning from personal interviews with people like Beth Bittinger, John Dromgoole, Malcolm Beck, and other vegetable-garden specialists. Converting their techniques to landscaping was easy, and I'm still curious today why so few in the industry use organic programs. Beth was a very special part of my learning curve. It was her enthusiasm and help that connected me with others in the industry who could help me. I had no idea that at the time she was dying of leukemia.

In the late 1980s, there were stores in the Dallas/Fort Worth area that carried organic products. There were only two organic stores in the entire state—Garden-Ville in Austin and in San Antonio. Now there are more than 600 retail stores in Texas that sell a complete line of products for organic gardening and pest control. Over 60 of those stores are 100 percent organic—offering no synthetic pesticides or fertilizers at all. Those numbers are growing, and Texas has the bragging rights of being far ahead of any other state in the country in the spread of stores offering organic solutions. Many of these same stores have also gotten on board the native plant bandwagon. Several commercial sites around the state are now on total organic programs. The most notable is Frito Lay's national headquarters in Plano. It has been under my organic specifications and consultation since 1990.

Unfortunately, there are still many who not only don't believe in organic methods, they have worked hard to try to talk people out of even giving it a try. I call these people organiphobes. They actually come from two camps, those who actively oppose the organic approach and want it to fail and those who unwittingly go along with the toxic chemical recommendations of others. Some of those people do it out of laziness; others are afraid to go against the grain and take on some responsibility.

If you follow my plant recommendations and the management recommendations in this *Complete Handbook,* it will be crystal clear that the Natural Way works better and is the only way.

Texas Gardening the Natural Way

THE COMPLETE HANDBOOK

Horsemint and coreopsis

CHAPTER 1

Texas Gardening Fundamentals

There's only one way for responsible, health- and environment-conscious Texans to garden. Only one way, that is, if you want the best production, the lowest cost, and the most environmentally responsible approach. Just like choosing the best-adapted and most-appropriate plants, the election to use organic techniques simply works better.

ADVANTAGES OF ORGANIC GARDENING

Organic gardening is better in every way. Let's look at the issue first from the critics' viewpoint. Some of the arguments against the Natural Way are as follows:

1. *Organic products smell bad.* Some do and some don't. However, a total organic program can be done with products that have no offensive odor. Even the most odoriferous natural products don't reek as much as toxic chemicals such as Orthene, malathion, diazinon, and others.
2. *No scientific proof.* A growing body of scientific evidence shows that the organic products are safer and that organically grown food is healthier than food grown with neurotoxins and synthetic fertilizers. Although grant money from chemical companies still greatly overshadows the organic industry, organic research and data from several universities do exist—and are growing.
3. *Plants can't tell the difference between synthetic chemical and organic fertilizers.* The truth is simple. Plants can definitely tell the difference. Plants do much more than just absorb solutions of basic molecules. They also take in entire bacteria and other large chunks of organic matter. The large pieces contain not only the basic chemical elements, but also enzymes, compounds, microorganisms, and other properties.

1

Toxic chemicals to eliminate from use include synthetic fertilizers as well as pesticides. Fungicides are as bad as or worse than insecticides, miticides, and herbicides. Weed-and-feed fertilizers are worst culprits of all.

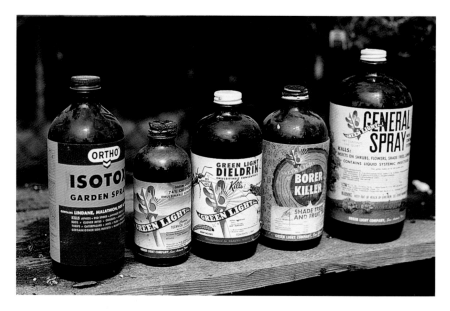

4. *Organic programs cost too much.* Organic programs are cost effective, especially when all costs are considered. Organically maintained plants require fewer applications of fertilizer, have fewer insect and disease problems, and have to be watered less. Organic plants are also more tolerant of extreme weather conditions, both hot and cold. Plants have to be replaced less often, and under organic management, beds never have to be removed and replaced with "fresh" soil. Besides, health is more valuable than anything.

5. *Organic pesticides are more dangerous than the synthetic ones.* Totally false. First of all, organic gardeners no longer recommend or use rotenone, sabadilla, nicotine sulfate, and other highly toxic organic products. The reason is that all pests can be controlled with totally nontoxic food products like pepper, garlic, cornmeal, cinnamon, seaweed, and citrus.

And from a strictly positive viewpoint:

1. *Restoring the environment.* Organic gardening techniques and products improve and support natural ecosystems. They work with nature's laws and systems and don't contaminate the soil, water, and air. Toxic chemical fertilizers and pesticides, on the other hand, do contaminate the soil, water, and air. Organic products improve the soil and the environment in general, with every application. All the synthetic chemical products do is keep sick plants alive artificially.

2. *Productivity of the land.* Organic fertilizing and soil building creates nutrient-rich soil by increasing the carbon and mineral content, reduces or eliminates erosion and soil compaction, and increases the quality of the plant growth year after year.

3. *Organic food tastes better.* Chefs and homeowners across the country are converting to organically grown ingredients because clean plants from healthy soils produce more flavorful and more nutritious fruits, herbs, and vegetables. Organic foods allow true flavors to come through.

4. *It is more fun to garden organically.* There's no worry about spilling products on yourself or concern about having sprays drift onto you, the kids, the pets, or the wrong plants. The best part is—it gets better every year. As the soil health improves, so do plant roots and the plants' overall immune systems, foliage, flavor, and fruit productivity, as well as the beauty of your garden.

PRACTICAL LANDSCAPE DESIGN

Landscape design is the thoughtful arrangement of structures, paving, and plants for the use of people. Whether you hire a landscape architect or design your garden yourself, the process is the same. Arrange the elements in your mind, then on paper to be functional, fun, flexible, and fitting for your family. Be open-minded, continue to learn and make changes where improvement is needed, and don't be limited by your first ideas.

1. Forget the Rules

Creativity is much more important than following a pattern or set of rules established by someone else. It's your home. "Framing the front door," for example, is one of the often-stated goofy rules. Why not, for example, hide the front door for more privacy or for a more interesting arrival experience? "Foundation planting" is another old rule that has lost its use. Grass or ground cover against the base of the house can in many cases be more appropriate than a straight row of shrubs. Sometimes a stone or concrete path against the base of the house solves maintenance and drainage problems, and the closest plantings start three feet away from the structure. See the point? The only rules are those that are self-inflicted. Learn from the experience of others, but don't let their input control what you do.

Instead of rules, set goals for yourself, your family, and your property. What's more important? Decoration or function? My personal goals are privacy, shade, and a feeling of being a part of the landscape. The look of the garden, especially from the street, is not high on my personal priority list. In that context, trees are more important than all other landscape design elements put together. With proper planting and care, trees set the feel or the character of the garden and become more beautiful and valuable every year. If a budget is limited or has to be cut, cut anything but the trees. A simple landscape of graceful trees, grass, a little native ground cover, and a few tough perennials is hard to beat. Don't waste money on unnecessary improvements, such as an expensive fence, when you plan to cover it with plants.

Consider the long-term maintenance during the planning stage. Choose native and well-adapted plants. Maintenance problems are built in from the beginning when unadapted plants are used.

2. Be Flexible

Don't be concerned about having to make changes. My own home gardens have changed many times through the years because of new ideas. Thinning your landscape or removing certain plants allows other materials more room to breathe and grow. In many new gardens, the lack of mature trees allows ample full sun for flowering plants, which must be replaced with shade-loving plants as trees mature. Don't fret about moving plants or replacing them if you've goofed, or if you simply changed your mind, or if the growth of the garden dictates changes. Landscape design is a continual learning experience. Those who think they have figured it all out are doomed to mediocrity. Homeowners should continue to experiment with alternate possibilities and new ideas. Gardens are dynamic and ever changing, as are true designers and gardeners. Successful landscaping is more of a journey than a destination.

3. Assume You're Wrong and Always Improve

The design stage is very simple: sketch something on paper as quickly as possible. Then, no matter whether the sketch is good or bad, the editing and refining process can begin. Most rough drafts should end up in the trash can. Get something down on paper, assume it's wrong, and try again. If it really is good, you'll come back to it. Don't be afraid to admit an idea doesn't work. On the other hand, don't be afraid to use your good ideas. While you're testing new ideas, you're learning. Massage the good ideas into better ones, and then groom and improve the details of the plan.

With all that trial-and-error philosophy duly noted, what do I consider good planning and good design? Successful landscape design is pleasing to the eye, is comfortable, functions as needed, requires moderate care, and costs only a little more than you had planned. Try my techniques for the design of landscape gardens, herb gardens, courtyards, commercial projects, and vegetable gardens. A garden has at least two lives—the first when it is installed, the second when the trees mature and shade the ground. When the trees are young, the majority of the shrubs, ground covers, and grasses must be those that thrive in the full sun. Later, as the trees grow and mature, the situation changes. Shade becomes the order of the day, and the low plants and understory trees must be shade tolerant. Natives and introduced plants can and should be used together. Biodiversity is an important aspect of proper design and proper horticulture.

Trees

Trees are the first consideration. Statistics show that landscaping is the only home improvement that can return 200 percent or more of the original investment. The most important single element of that investment is the trees. In addition to adding beauty, trees create the atmosphere or feel of a garden. They invite us, shade us, surprise us, house wildlife, create backgrounds and niches, inspire and humble us. Trees increase in value as they grow and save energy and money by shading our houses in the summer and by letting the sunshine through for warmth in the winter.

Choosing the correct tree for a specific spot is not just an aesthetic decision but an important investment decision as well. The critical consideration in selecting a tree for a particular site is not how pretty you think the tree will look growing in that particular spot, but rather how the tree will like that particular spot. Understanding the horticultural needs of a tree is essential. Plant hardiness and adaptability are major considerations here. Plant selection and arrangement are only successful if the plants are happy in their new locations. The individual entries on each species in the tree section of this book should provide the needed details.

There are two categories of trees: shade and ornamental. Shade trees are the large structural trees that form the skeleton of the planting plan and grow to be 40' to 100' tall. They are used to create the outdoor spaces, block undesirable views, and provide shade. This category includes the oaks, elms, ashes, pecans, and other long-lived trees.

Trees, if used properly and not simply scattered all over the site, function as the walls and roofs of our outdoor rooms. Of all the plants, shade trees provide the greatest long-term value, so their use should be carefully considered and given a large percentage of the landscape budget.

Ornamental trees are those used for aesthetics, to create focal points, and that grow to be 8' to 30' tall. Trees such as crabapple, hawthorn, and crape myrtle are used primarily for their spring or summer flower color. Others, such as yaupon or wax myrtle, are used for their evergreen color or berries. Some, such as Japanese maple and witch hazel, are used for their distinctive foliage color and interesting branching characteristics.

Shrubs

Shrubs should be selected on the basis of what variety will grow best in the space provided. If more than one variety will work, this decision becomes subjective based on the desire for flowers, interesting foliage, fall color, and so on. However, horticultural requirements should be the prerequisite and have priority over aesthetic considerations. Tall-growing varieties are used for background plantings and screens. Medium-height shrubs are used for flower display or evergreen color. Dwarf varieties are used for masses and interesting bed shapes or as a transition between ground covers and medium-height shrubs. Some shrubs have extremely large leaves, others small, fine-textured foliage. The color of shrub foliage also ranges from light to dark greens and from variegated to red or purple foliage. Some shrubs flower dramatically, and others offer only foliage color.

Ground Covers

Ground-cover plants are low-growing, vinelike, and grasslike materials that are primarily used to cover large areas of ground. They are best used where grass won't grow and for creating interesting bed shapes. Ground covers are usually the best choice in heavily shaded areas. Often the ground covers become the last phase of the permanent garden installation and are planted after the trees have matured to shade the ground. Ground covers can also be used to reduce the area of grass. Once established, these plants will be less time consuming and less costly to maintain.

Vines

Vines are usually fast-growing plants that twine or cling to climb vertically on walls, fences, posts, or overhead structures. They are used for quick shade; vertical softening of walls, fences, and other surfaces; or colorful flower display. Vines are an inexpensive way to have lots of greenery and color in a hurry. They are also quite good in smaller spaces where wide-growing shrubs and trees would be a problem.

Herbs

Herbs make wonderful landscape plants and should be used more in ornamental gardens even if gourmet cooking or herbal medicine is not in the plans. The traditional definition of *herb* is a herbaceous plant that is used to flavor foods, provide medicinal properties, or offer up fragrances. My definition of a herb is a plant that has a use other than landscaping and looking pretty. In other words, most plants are also herbs. Herbs fall into several categories—trees, shrubs, ground covers, annuals, and perennials—and are therefore distributed throughout the pages of this book.

Flowers

Flowers are an important finishing touch to any fine garden. Everyone loves flowers. Annuals are useful for that dramatic splash of one-season color, and the perennials are valuable because of their faithful return to bloom year after year. Since replacing annual color each year is expensive, annuals should be concentrated to one or a few spots rather than scattering them all about. The perennial flowers can be used more randomly throughout the garden.

Grasses

Grass plantings should be kept to a minimum. They should be selected based on proposed use. Grasses should also be selected based on horticultural requirements. For example, large sunny areas that will have active use should use common Bermudagrass or buffalograss. Shady, less-used areas should use St. Augustine. Areas that will not have much water should use buffalograss. Areas that need a smooth, highly refined surface should use the hybrid tifgrasses. Several varieties of zoysia are now available that are supposed to be faster growing and more tolerant of wear and tear. We'll see.

Xeriscaping

Xeriscaping, a term that comes from the Greek word *xeros* for "dry," is a landscaping concept that uses less water than traditional landscaping by choosing plants that are drought tolerant and by using horticultural techniques that use water most efficiently. The basic points are as follows:

1. *Plan and design the garden carefully.* It all starts there.
2. *Soil improvements.* Add organic matter to the soil before planting to help the soil retain water. For sloped sites, reduce water runoff with terraces and retaining walls.

My dad mulching with pine needles in Pittsburg, Texas. This is especially appropriate if your garden has pine trees.

3. *Limit the grass areas.* Plant ground covers or add hard surface areas like patios, decks, or walkways. Use drought-tolerant grass.
4. *Choose low-water-using trees, shrubs, flowers, and ground covers.* Many need watering only in the first year or two after planting. Native plants are important.
5. *Use efficient irrigation.* Install drip or trickle irrigation systems for those areas that need watering. These systems use water efficiently and are available from commercial garden centers. *Note:* I don't like drip irrigation. It is too hard to monitor and can be wasteful.
6. *Effective use of mulches.* Use mulches like pine needles or shredded bark or leaves in thick layers. This keeps soil moist, smothers weeds, and prevents erosion. Do not use pine bark.
7. *Sensible maintenance.* Properly timed pruning, fertilizing, pest control, and weeding will preserve your landscape's beauty and water efficiency.

Xeriscaping is very similar to the organic program except that its proponents don't usually push the importance of natural fertilizers and nontoxic pest controls. Not enough for me, anyway.

Design Mistakes
Some of the worst design mistakes I see on both residential and commercial properties are:

1. Choosing plants that require too much care.
2. Choosing plants that cannot grow in the site's soil.
3. Failure to allow for proper drainage and circulation.
4. Failure to mulch bare soil.
5. Planting too many plants of the same type.
6. Using grass in highly shaded areas.
7. Choosing ill-adapted plants.

PLANTING TECHNIQUES

Soils

Understanding soils is a critical part of successful plantings. Soils in Texas are as varied as the people, with a huge range of terrain, soil types, and climate. Texas has seashore, wetlands, swamps, forests, deserts, grasslands, hills, and mountains. Although the state can be divided into various geological and climatic areas, there is a common basis for organic gardening. The sandy soils of East Texas have certain advantages and deficiencies, and the black clay soils of North Texas do as well. Both can be converted into balanced healthy soil.

Basically, the black and white soils, black clay on top of white limestone rock, are deficient in two things—air and organic matter. Bringing these soils into a healthy condition is relatively easy. It is done by stimulating biological activity with a variety of techniques and products, depending on the budget. These include physical aeration, deep-rooted plants, manure, humates, compost and other organic fertilizers, volcanic rock sands and powders, sugars such as molasses, and natural mulches.

Sandy soils, on the other hand, are usually deficient in everything but sand. They have greater porosity and a higher water-percolation rate. The same approach and the same tools are used, just more and more often until the sand can hold organic matter and nutrients. Once healthy soil is achieved, it can be kept healthy with the Basic Organic Program.

Some people consider pH to be an important factor in soil preparation, watering, and plant selection. The truth is that pH is more an indicator than a controlling factor. Some plants, like azaleas, gardenias, blueberries, and pin oaks, like low pH soils of 5.5–6.2. Many others can stand high pH soils of 6.5 and higher. It could be argued that the texture of the soil is more important. PH can be affected with several amendments. Sodium and potassium will make the soil more alkaline (higher pH), and other amendments such as iron and organic matter will tend to lower pH, or make it more acid. Sulfur is the best tool to use to lower the pH quickly, and high-calcium lime is the best for lowering it.

Railroad ties are toxic and should never be used around herbs or food crops.

Treated lumber and timber, particularly CCA (copper-chromated arsenic) should never be used, especially around food crops.

Raised Beds

Raised beds are often used to improve drainage, for aesthetic reasons, or for ease of maintenance. Wood should not be used for the walls. If there

Malcolm Beck with shredded native cedar mulch—the very best choice

are enough toxic chemicals in the wood to keep it from rotting, it will be far too toxic to be around plants, especially food crops. If there are not enough toxic chemicals in the wood, the wood will rot away quickly. Either way, wood is a bad investment.

Acceptable materials for walls include natural stone, concrete wall systems, poured concrete, or cinder blocks. Cinder blocks are the most economical and easiest to install. If placed with the holes up, the blocks can be filled with paramagnetic sand, such as lava, to help hold the blocks in place and improve plant growth.

Detoxing Contaminated Soil

If your soil has been contaminated with petroleum products, pesticides, treated lumber, or other toxins, it can be cleaned up. After removal of the unwanted material, drench the area with NORIT activated carbon. Mix it with water per the instructions and pour into the soil. NORIT is also sold as GroSafe. It is the only activated-carbon product that will do the job. No other products are ground fine enough to instantly tie up toxic contaminants. Next, drench the area with Garrett Juice plus 2 oz. of orange oil or d-limonene per gallon. Then, for beds, add about 4" compost, lava sand at 80 lbs. per 1,000 sq. ft., Texas greensand at 40 lbs. per 1,000 sq. ft., and horticultural cornmeal at 20 lbs. per 1,000 sq. ft. Organic fertilizer should also be added at 10 lbs. per 1,000 sq. ft. This bed preparation will be sufficient for most ornamentals, herbs, and food crops. Specialty crops like roses, gardenias, and camellias need even greater quantities of the same ingredients. Poorly adapted plants like azaleas and rhododendrons need even more soil improvements. If you are thinking about trying to grow those, create raised beds of 50 percent compost and 50 percent shredded hardwood bark or shredded native cedar. Mix in about 10 lbs. of Texas greensand per cubic yard of material. Mix it thoroughly and moisten completely before placing in the bed. The Azalea Society recommends a 50/50 mixture of fine pine bark and peat moss, but if you use my method and the organic program, the beds won't need to be rebuilt every seven years or so. For grass areas, the improvements aren't as important. Light applications of dry molasses and volcanic rock are usually enough.

When to Plant

In general, the ideal time to plant trees, shrubs, and spring-blooming perennials is fall; second best is anytime in the winter; third is the spring; last is the heat of summer. Planting in the fall or winter offers roots a chance to start growing before the foliage emerges in the spring. Most plants can be planted any month of the year. They will usually be more happy in the soil than in the black plastic pots sitting above ground in the nursery.

Hot part of summer: When transporting plants in an open vehicle, cover to protect the foliage from the sun and wind and keep the root ball moist. Always dampen the planting beds prior to planting.

Freezing weather: Don't leave plants out of the ground during extreme cold without protecting the roots from possible freeze damage. Store plants in sunny areas prior to planting. Always keep the plants moist and mulched during freezing weather. Once in the ground, plants will normally survive a freeze.

Mild weather: The mild weather can make you forget to keep containers or newly planted material moist, so check often but do not overwater.

Planting Seeds Outdoors

Seeds should be broadcast at the proper spacing, and the soil should be firmed by using the back of a hoe or a board, giving the seeds good soil contact. Seeds can then be covered with a very thin layer of earthworm castings or screened compost. There are exceptions to this rule under individual plant entries.

The seedbed should be watered gently and kept moist until the small seedlings come up. The watering should then be cut back to the proper watering schedule and amount for each particular plant species. For small gardens, an effective technique to improve germination is to cover the seeded area with moist burlap, which serves to shade and keep the seedbed evenly moist. Remove the burlap to save and reuse after the seeds have sprouted. Gentle watering is essential to minimize displaced or washed-away seed.

Thinning is a controversial subject. Ruth Stout, a gardening author and mulch proponent, says that thinning is unnecessary. The small plants she leaves always have good production. Many other gardeners believe in removing some of the seedlings so the remaining seedlings have plenty of space for the root systems and top to grow. With wide spacing, the roots will go deeper. Thinning can be done by pulling a rake through the seedbed when the seedlings are about an inch tall. Thinning can also be done by hand by clipping the seedlings with scissors. Edible seedlings or sprouts can be used in salads.

Starting Seeds Indoors

Most seeds need a constant warm temperature, about room temperature (not of the garage but of the living room), to germinate. Most seeds don't need light to germinate and can be put on top of the refrigerator or in other out-of-the-way places. Newspaper or plastic sheets or lids can be put over the flats or pots to help maintain the constant temperature and moisture level. The windowsill is a poor place to germinate seeds because of temperature fluctuations. Windowsills are hot places on sunny days and often too cold at night.

Seed flats should be checked daily. After sprouts emerge, remove the covering. To prevent seedlings from leaning toward the light, turn the pots or flats around at least every two days. If the seedlings don't get enough light, they'll stretch and get weak and spindly. Very few species can recover from legginess.

Water the seedlings gently. If you cover your flats and trays, the soil will stay moist until you remove the covering. After that, check the soil several times a day with your fingers. If it is dry, add water. Plants near heaters, vents, or on top of the refrigerator will dry out quickly and may need water more than once a day. Seedlings are delicate and shouldn't be over- or harshly watered. They can easily collapse under the weight of the water. Water gently around the edge of the container or at the base of each plant.

Some gardeners prefer bottom watering. Fill a sink or other container with 2" of water and put your flats or pots in water until it seeps up into the surface of the soil. Some gardeners oppose this method because it tends to keep the soil too wet and pushes out the oxygen. We prefer watering from above.

Organic fertilizer can be added to the soil after seedlings are about an inch tall. Earthworm castings and compost are very gentle and may be the best choices for young plants. Garrett Juice can be added to the watering at 2 oz. per gallon. Even though it is primarily a foliar-feeding material, it is also an excellent mild fertilizer for the soil.

Seedlings need to be hardened off for a week or so outdoors to acclimate to outdoor temperatures before being transplanted into their final place in the garden. Introducing young plants to an outdoor environment should be done gradually on a mild day. Plants should be left in partial shade and protected from wind for a few hours the first day, then given a little more exposure time each day. It normally takes three or four days to accustom young plants started indoors to direct sunlight outdoors. In a week or so, the plants can stay out all day in the full sun. Seedlings can be moved back indoors during the transition period if the weather changes abruptly. If all this sounds like a lot of trouble, it is, but it's worth it for your ultimate vegetable, herb, or flower production.

Planting Transplants

Flats or pots always need to have a good soaking before they are taken outdoors. Before planting, we like to soak the plants in a bucket of water with seaweed until they are saturated. Using Garrett Juice in the water is also a good technique. Plant roots should be sopping wet and planted into a moist bed.

Installation Mistakes

Some of the worst installation mistakes I see on both residential and commercial projects are:

1. Failure to mulch beds.
2. Planting plants (especially trees) too low.
3. Failure to provide proper drainage.
4. Planting trees in small, smooth, or glazed-wall holes.
5. Planting ill-adapted plants.
6. Staking and wrapping trees unnecessarily.

Planting Trees, Shrubs, Ground Covers, Vines, Flowers, and Other Plants

See specific plant chapters for detailed instructions.

BASIC ORGANIC PROGRAM

Using natural techniques makes gardening easier and more enjoyable. Change and new ideas of any kind always seem harder and more complicated, but the Natural Way really is better in every way, even from an economic standpoint. Another important point is that it all gets easier and better every year. And there is no having to replace worn-out beds ever. For those of you who are new to the Natural Way of thinking and for those of you who are veterans, here's my latest version of the Basic Organic Program. The more we learn, the simpler the program gets.

Build the Organic Matter
Increase the health of the soil by using compost, earthworm castings, and organic fertilizers to increase the organic matter. Mulch all plantings. Maintain an organic mulch layer on the bare soil year-round. Avoid all synthetic fertilizers that contain no organic matter. These fake fertilizers not only don't build soil health, they decrease it with every application.

Build the Mineral Content
Balance the minerals in the soil by applying rock powders or sands that provide the major nutrients and trace minerals needed by plants to be healthy. Volcanic rock materials are especially important because they provide much more than minerals. The best choices include lava sand, Texas greensand, soft rock phosphate, granite sand, zeolite, basalt, and natural diatomaceous earth.

Encourage Biodiversity
Healthy gardens, farms, and ranches need a mix of plants and animals. Monocultures of plants are often very productive for a while but later succumb to insects and diseases. Examples include the Irish potato blight, Dutch elm disease, and more recently oak wilt here in Texas. Monocultures lack the genetic diversity to respond to changing environmental threats and become sitting ducks for parasites, predators, and pathogens. Stop using all products that do damage to the life in the soil. Encourage life.

Use Adapted Plants
Planting well-adapted plants is the most important step. Unless you select adapted plants, it doesn't matter whether your program is organic or toxic. The best choices are the natives, but the well-adapted introductions and naturalized plants are also good.

Add Molasses
Sugar, especially in the form of molasses, is an effective soil amendment. These carbohydrates are food for the beneficial microorganisms. Using sugar heavily should not be done on a continuing basis, but it is highly effective in the early stages of the program. Small amounts of molasses are effective long-term and are often found in quality organic liquid and dry fertilizers.

Healthy Soil: creating a forest floor–like transition of mulch, compost, topsoil, and subsoil is important for the proper growth of all plants.

Two important organic amendments—lava sand (left) and dry molasses (right)

Plant Properly

Prepare beds for ornamentals or food crops by scraping away existing grass and weeds. Toss the material into the compost pile. Spraying herbicides first is an unnecessary, contaminating waste of money and time. Next add a 4"–6" layer of compost, lava sand, or other volcanic material at 40–80 lbs. per 1,000 sq. ft., organic fertilizer at 20 lbs. per 1,000 sq. ft., wheat/corn/molasses amendment at 30 lbs. per 1,000 sq. ft. and till to a depth of 3" into the native soil. Excavation and additional ingredients such as concrete sand, peat moss, foreign soil, and pine bark should not be used. They are a waste of money and can hinder plant growth.

More compost is needed for shrubs and flowers than for ground cover. Add Texas greensand at 40–80 lbs. per 1,000 sq. ft. to black and white soils and high-calcium lime at 50–100 lbs. per 1,000 sq. ft. to acid soils. Decomposed granite is an effective amendment for most soils. It can be used up to 100 lbs. per 1,000 sq. ft.

Remove container-grown plants from their pots, rake the loose soil off the top of the ball, soak the root balls in water with Garrett Juice added, and set the plants in the new beds at a level slightly higher than the surrounding grade. Remove the cloth and excess soil from the top of balled and burlapped plants. Cut or tear bound roots of container-grown plants. In all cases, plant wet root balls into moist soil.

Mulch the Bare Soil

Mulch all shrubs, trees, ground covers, and food crops with 2"–5" of shredded native tree trimmings to protect the soil from sunlight, wind, and rain; inhibit weed germination; decrease watering needs; and mediate soil temperature. Other natural mulches can be used, but avoid Bermudagrass hay because of possible herbicide residue.

Feed the Soil (Fertilization)

Apply organic fertilizer two or three times per year. Foliar-feed during the growing season by spraying turf, tree and shrub foliage, trunks, limbs, and soil at least monthly with Garrett Juice or other organic blends. Add volcanic sand such as lava sand, dry molasses, and humate to the soil the first few years.

There are many problems with synthetic fertilizers, but one of the biggest problems is that they contain no organic matter and therefore no carbon. Soil microorganisms must have this carbon energy source, and if it is not provided, the microbes will take it from the soil. That causes soil health reduction with every fertilizer application.

Organic fertilizers nourish and improve the soil with every application. As opposed to synthetic fertilizers, they help the soil because they do not create high levels of salts and nitrates in the soil, which kill or repel beneficial soil organisms. Organic fertilizers release nutrients slowly and naturally. All components in an organic fertilizer are usable by the plants; there are no useless or toxic fillers as in many synthetic fertilizers.

Decomposed granite (left),
Texas greensand (right)

Results of Logan's school science project—
garlic grown from cloves in a growth
chamber
(A) Potting soil only
(B) Potting soil plus compost
(C) Potting soil, compost, and lava sand

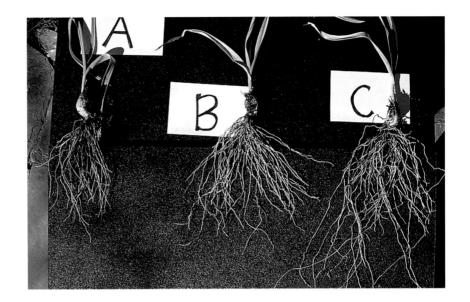

The nitrogen-phosphorus-potassium analysis (N-P-K) printed on bags of fertilizer by law is basically irrelevant in an organic program. Feeding the soil and plants with nothing but nitrogen, phosphorous, and potassium is like feeding your kids nothing but cheese. Soil and people need a balance of vitamins and minerals. For some unknown reason, fertilizer recommendations continue to emphasize these three nutrients, with special emphasis on high levels of nitrogen. A standard obsolete recommendation is a ratio of 3-1-2 or 4-1-2, such as 15-5-10 or 16-4-8. Compost, the most natural fertilizer in the world, has an analysis of less than 1-1-1 in most cases.

A large percentage of synthetic nitrogen applied to the soil will be leached out, and the amount that does reach the plant is harmful. Fast-acting artificial fertilizer creates weak, watery cells, a condition that invites insects and diseases. Harsh synthetic fertilizer slows or even stops the activity of microflora and microfauna such as beneficial bacteria, algae, fungi, and other microorganisms. Harsh fertilizers also cause damage to macroorganisms such as earthworms, millipedes, centipedes, and other beneficial organisms that are extremely important to the natural processes in the soil.

High-nitrogen fertilizers can also cause severe thatch buildup in lawns by forcing unnatural flushes of green growth. That's why mechanical thatch-removal programs are often recommended for chemically maintained lawns. Organic lawn-care programs take care of thatch problems naturally as the living microorganisms feed on the grass clippings and other dead organic matter.

High-nitrogen fertilizers such as 15-5-10 (or even higher) are still being recommended by many in the farming, ranching, and landscaping business. I've made the same recommendations myself in the past, but those amounts of nitrogen, phosphorous, and potassium are unnecessary and even damaging to soil health.

When soil is healthy, microbes in it will produce and release nutrients during the decomposition process. The microbiotic activity releases tied-

Rain is the best irrigation. Overhead sprinklers are second best, and drip irrigation is the third best choice although it can be cost effective and efficient in row crops.

up trace elements such as iron, zinc, boron, chlorine, copper, magnesium, molybdenum, and others, which are all important to a well-balanced soil.

The most important product in an organic program is organic material, which breaks down into organic matter or humus during the decomposition process. Humus reduces down further into humic acid, other beneficial acids, and mineral nutrients.

Organic fertilizers are better than artificial products because they are the derivatives of plants and therefore contain most or all of the trace elements that exist in growing plants. Synthetic fertilizers do not have this rounded balance of mineral nutrients.

In addition, organic fertilizers are naturally slow release and provide nutrients to plants when they need them. Synthetic fertilizers glut the plants with nutrients immediately after application, or soon thereafter, which is usually at the wrong time.

Fertilizer requirements for trees, shrubs, vines, and ground covers:
Fertilize all shrubs and ground covers with an organic fertilizer at 15–20 lbs. per 1,000 sq. ft. Apply three times per year, in February, June, and September. For specific techniques, see individual plant entries.

Fertilizer requirements for turf:
Fertilize all turf areas with an organic fertilizer at 15–20 lbs. per 1,000 sq. ft. Apply three times per year, in February, June, and September.

Water Wisely

I won't waste much of your time here, but rather will assume that you know what a garden hose and a sprinkler look like. I'll also assume you understand how to use them. The key to watering correctly is common sense. Water enough to keep the plants happy and no more. All of the organic amendments will reduce watering requirements.

On drip irrigation—I'm not a fan. It is probably necessary in some agricultural situations, but I really don't trust drip systems for several reasons. They are always in the way and easy to tear up because they are partially or completely hidden. Rodents eat holes in the lines, and the material wears out and rots.

The reason all that's important is that when drip-irrigation lines crack or spring a leak in any way, the water floods some areas and leaves other areas dry. Even if there are no failures and leaks, water naturally seeks the path of least resistance and produces uneven moisture in the soil. Since you can't see where the water is going with a drip system, roots can rot or dry out completely and die before you realize there is a problem.

What's a better way to go? Sprinkle the plants from above. The water is visible, you can monitor it more easily, and there is much less chance of disaster.

Does water on the foliage cause disease problems? Well, it rains at night and that doesn't seem to be a big problem. Water only as necessary. The organic program will reduce the frequency and volume needed. Add a tablespoon of apple cider vinegar per gallon when watering pots. Do as often as time permits. Use 1 oz. of liquid humate in areas with acid soils and water.

Mow Smartly
Frequency of mowing varies with grass varieties. Leave the clippings on the lawn to return nutrients and organic matter to the soil. Mulching mowers are the best but are not essential. Put occasional excess clippings in the compost pile. *Do not ever let clippings leave the site.* Do not use, or allow maintenance people to use, line trimmers around shrubs and trees. They can do serious damage to plants.

Prune Carefully
Remove dead, diseased, and conflicting limbs. Do not overprune. Do not make flush cuts. Leave the branch collars intact. Do not paint cuts except on red oaks and live oaks in oak-wilt areas when spring pruning can't be avoided. Remember that pruning cuts hurt trees. For the most part, pruning is done for your benefit, not for the benefit of the trees.

Make and Use Compost
Compost, Nature's own living fertilizer, can be made at home or purchased ready-to-use. Compost can be started any time of the year in sun or shade. Anything once living can go in the compost—grass clippings, tree trimmings, food scraps, bark, sawdust, rice hulls, weeds, nut hulls, animal manure, and the carcasses of animals. Mix the ingredients together and simply pile the material on the ground. The ideal mixture is 80 percent vegetative matter and 20 percent animal waste, although any mix will compost. Oxygen is a critical component. Ingredients should be a mix of coarse- and fine-textured materials to promote air circulation through the pile. Turn the pile as time allows to speed up the process. Another critical component is water. A compost pile should contain

Fire ant mounds in a chemically maintained pasture. Heavy infestations like this are not present in biodiverse pastures, turf areas, and landscapes.

roughly the moisture of a squeezed-out sponge to help the living organisms thrive and work their magic. Compost is ready to use as a soil amendment when the ingredients are no longer identifiable. Compost will be dark brown, soft, and crumbly and it will smell like the forest floor. Rough, unfinished compost can be used as a topdressing mulch around all plantings.

Make and Use Compost Tea

Manure compost tea is an effective foliar spray because of its many mineral nutrients and naturally occurring microorganisms. Fill any container half full of compost and finish filling with water. Let the mix sit a few days and then dilute and spray on the foliage of any and all plants. Pumping air into the tea with a simple aquarium pump increases its power. How to dilute the dark compost tea before using depends on the compost used. A rule of thumb is to dilute the leachate down to one part compost liquid to four to ten parts water. The ready-to-use spray should look like iced tea. Be sure to strain the solids out with old pantyhose, cheesecloth, or floating row-cover material. Full-strength tea makes an excellent fire ant mound drench when mixed with 2 oz. molasses and 2 oz. orange oil per gallon. Add vinegar, molasses, and seaweed to compost tea to make Garrett Juice.

Control Pests Naturally

Adapted plants growing in healthy soil have a powerful built-in immunity to insect pests and diseases. For the limited pest problems that pop up, here are the basics.

Aphids, spider mites, whiteflies, and lacebugs: Release ladybugs and green lacewings regularly until natural populations exist. Spray Garrett Juice or garlic-pepper tea. Use strong water blasts and neem sprays for heavy infestations. For spider mites and whiteflies, make sure seaweed is in the spray mix. *Caterpillars and bagworms:* Release trichogramma wasps. Spray Garrett Juice plus 2 oz. of orange oil per gallon. Spray *Bacillus thuringiensis* with 1 oz. of molasses per gallon of spray as a last resort.

Left: Corn gluten meal—the natural "weed and feed"
Right: mechanical weeder for nontoxic weed control

Fire ants: Drench mounds with Garrett Juice plus orange oil or one of the commercial compost tea, molasses, orange oil products; release beneficial nematodes; and go totally organic. *Grasshoppers:* Eliminate bare soil, apply beneficial nematodes, broadcast Nolo Bait for the young nymphs, and spray kaolin clay particle film on foliage if adults attack. Encourage biodiversity and, most importantly, feed the birds regularly. *Grubworms:* Apply beneficial nematodes and promote general soil health as the primary controls. *Mosquitoes:* Broadcast cedar flakes and use cedar mulch. Use *Bacillus thuringiensis* 'Israelensis' for larvae in standing water that can't be drained. Spray orange-oil-based products or garlic-pepper tea for adult insects. Do not use toxic chemicals such as pyrethrins, pyrethroids, or DEET. For skin repellents use lavender, vanilla, citronella, catnip, or eucalyptus. *Slugs, snails, fleas, ticks, chinch bugs, roaches, crickets:* Spray or dust natural diatomaceous earth products and broadcast cedar flakes and crushed red pepper. Orange-oil-based products also kill these pests. Research now shows that instant coffee at 1 oz. per gallon of spray is also effective. For more details on pest control, check out the *Texas Bug Book*.

Toxic pesticides should not be used because they don't work. They always kill more beneficial organisms than the targeted pests. My recommended pest control for specific insects and diseases is covered at each plant entry if necessary and in Chapter 9 (Pest Management).

Control Weeds Naturally

Most weeds are controlled by having healthy soil and by mulching all plants and bare soil properly with shredded materials. Native cedar is my favorite mulch.

Avoid synthetic herbicides, such as pre-emergents, broadleaf treatments, soil sterilants, and especially the SU (sulfonylurea) herbicides such as Manage and Oust, as well as pichloram and clopyralid products. Spray broadleaf weeds as a last resort with full-strength vinegar mixed with 2 oz. orange oil and 1 teaspoon of liquid soap or remove weeds by hand. Several commercial organic herbicides are now available including

Garden-Ville Organic Weed Control, Weed Eraser, Burn Out, and others. Here are some specific solutions to specific weed problems.

Pre-emergent (before the seeds germinate)—Apply corn gluten meal at 20 lbs. per 1,000 sq. ft. March 1 and October 1.

Post-emergent (after the plants are growing)—Spot-treat annuals and perennial grasses and forbs with Garden-Ville Organic Weed Control, Scythe, Burn Out, Weed Eraser, or other approved organic herbicide.

Control of poison ivy is physical removal followed by spot-spraying the returning young growth with Garden-Ville Organic Weed Control, Scythe, Burn Out, or other approved product.

Post-emergent control of weeds in expansion joints, cracks of parking areas, sidewalks, decomposed granite pathways, and rocked areas can be achieved with Garden-Ville Organic Weed Control, Scythe, Burn Out, or other approved product.

Control Diseases Organically

For black spot, brown patch, powdery mildew, and other fungal problems, the best control is prevention through soil improvement, avoidance of high-nitrogen fertilizers, and proper watering. Spray Garrett Juice plus garlic, potassium bicarbonate, milk, or neem. Treat soil with horticultural cornmeal at about 20 lbs. per 1,000 sq. ft. Organic gardens have few disease problems, but these natural techniques work well for occasional problems. The commonly recommended synthetic neurotoxins like Terrachlor, Daconil, Bayleton, Fung-Away, and Funginex have no place in today's new mainstream in horticulture and agriculture.

SYNTHETIC VERSUS NATURAL FERTILIZERS

A 15-5-10 synthetic fertilizer is the classic 3-1-2 ratio high-nitrogen fertilizer—the kind that the other guys recommend. These numbers mean that the bag contains 15 percent nitrogen, 5 percent phosphorus, and 10 percent potassium. The remaining 70 percent of the material in the bag is "other material," which can even be toxic industrial waste.

There are all kinds of problems with synthetic nitrogen fertilizers. The primary one is that there's too much nitrogen. It creates an unbalanced situation as far as nutrients in the soil and in plants. High nitrogen and low levels of trace minerals force fast growth that results in very weak, watery cell growth in plants. People see that the plants are growing and flowering, so they think everything is fine. But the imbalance and the watery cells bring on insects and diseases. Nature's job is to take out sick plants and to encourage the survival of the fittest. In addition, the form of nitrogen is wrong. It works too fast. Plus, it's soluble. If it rains after you put it out, the nitrogen washes away and leaches through the soil into the water stream.

The second problem is the phosphorous source. The phosphorous in synthetic fertilizer is triple superphosphate 0-46-0. Years ago, the phosphorous source was 0-20-0 superphosphate. It was pretty darn good even though it was created by a synthetic process. Rock phosphate was treated with sulfuric acid. It was a more balanced phosphate and did not tie up

Liriope 'Big Blue,' right, grown with Peter's 20-20-20; left, with Garden-Ville 6-2-2. This is typical of the root growth difference between synthetic and organic fertilizers. The health of the plants comes from the health of the root systems (Malcolm Beck).

trace minerals. Later, somebody came up with the notion to use phosphoric acid to create more phosphorous for less money. So now, all the synthetic-fertilizer manufacturers use triple superphosphate. Big problem—the new material is so raw and so bare that when it's put on the soil, it grabs and locks onto magnesium, manganese, and all sorts of other trace minerals. It ties up these nutrients, making them unavailable to plants.

The third problem is the potassium. The source of potassium in most synthetic fertilizers is muriate of potash, or potassium chloride. Potassium chloride is bad on specific types of crops—especially fruit crops. It's also harsh on the soil. What we like as a potassium source is potassium sulfate, which is made from the salt of Great Salt Lake in Utah. Another excellent potassium source is sul-po-mag, which is a natural product that contains sulfur, potassium, and magnesium.

Types of Organic Fertilizers

My definition of a fertilizer is anything that improves the soil and helps to stimulate plant growth. For example, dead leaves that fall off a tree are fertilizers. As they break down, they turn into organic matter, or humus, and feed the soil microbes. Microbes such as the beneficial fungi on the roots protect and feed the root hairs of the plants. This feeding process releases the nutrients to feed plants. That's how it works on the prairie and in the forest. We're just speeding up the process.

All the basic soil amendments meet that definition, but they are intended for building beds more than for routine fertilizing. They are more gentle and work more slowly over time. The basic soil amendments are manure-based organic compost, cornmeal, lava sand, Texas greensand, zeolite, and dry molasses. These should be applied up to three times a year for the first few years of an organic program.

There are many quality bagged organic fertilizers to choose from. Some people alternate between them on the perfectly logical supposition that since each contains a slightly different combination of nutrients, by rotating them over time, you provide your soil with a more balanced diet.

Some brands that are widely distributed are Alliance, GreenSense, Garden-Ville, Hu-More, Bradfield, Bluebonnet, Sustane, Bioform, and Texas Tee. Several stores carry their own brand, including Redenta's and North Haven Gardens. Other products of which I approve are bagged biosolids products. In general, it is better to select one of these that is produced closer to home—Austin, Denton, and Houston all produce a sludge product. Milorganite is an acceptable product, but be aware that it is shipped all the way from Milwaukee, Wisconsin.

Similarly, there are a lot of great choices in liquid fertilizers. I strongly recommend a regular foliar spray program. You can make your own Garrett Juice—the recipe is at the beginning of the Appendix—or you can buy it commercially. Other good liquid choices include fish and seaweed products like Bioform, Maxicrop, Medina HastaGro, or GreenSense Foliar Juice. These function as fertilizers in the soil as well as a foliar-feeding material when sprayed on plant foliage.

You get indirect pest control from all liquid organic products because they stimulate biological activity. And that's the best way to control pests. Try not to kill, but rather to stimulate, the good guys. Beneficial insects and microbes feed on the pathogens, and balance is the result.

Some of these products do contain some synthetic materials. I don't have a big problem with that. You just have to understand and be honest about it. HastaGro and Bioform 8-8-8 have a little urea in the product. Bioform 4-2-4, however, is a pure organic product. The amount of urea that you're putting on the plants when you use those products is very small. Urea used at a low level really kicks microbes in the rear and gets them going. It probably works almost as well as the molasses. Those are the products I recommend when people ask, "What's an organic equivalent to Miracle Gro?" They perform just like the fast-acting soluble products like Miracle Gro, Peters 20-20-20, or other liquids that are not acceptable in an organic program.

The generalized recommended organic fertilization program is as follows:

First fertilization—As early as January on into March
Second fertilization—Sometime in June
Third fertilization—Between September and October

Microbe Products and Biological Stimulants
Microbe products are those that contain living organisms. Some contain mycorrhizal and other fungi, others contain bacteria. Some products contain a blend of living organisms, others contain ingredients that simply stimulate the dormant microbes in the soil. These products work best when first converting to organic programs, before the soil is healthy.

DIFFERENCES BETWEEN TOXIC CHEMICAL AND ORGANIC APPROACHES

Chemical Approach	Organic Approach
Mow low and often.	Mow higher and less often.
Catch grass clippings.	Leave clippings on the ground.
High-analysis fertilizers 4–5 times per year.	Low-analysis fertilizer 2–3 times per year.
High-nitrogen fertilizers.	Low-nitrogen fertilizers.
Synthetic fertilizer— no organic matter, fillers.	100% organic fertilizer—no fillers.
Fertilizer based on plant needs.	Fertilizer based on soil needs.
Fertilizers with few or no trace minerals.	Fertilizers loaded with trace minerals.
Attempt to control nature.	Attempt to work within nature's systems.
Treat symptoms (insects, diseases).	Treat soil and cultural problems.
Use chemical pesticides at first sign of pests.	Use natural pesticides, but only as last resort.
Poisons used on a calendar basis as preventatives.	Prevention through soil improvements and foliar fertilizers.
Discourage the use of beneficial insects.	Use beneficial insects as a major tool.
Use only university-tested products.	Use food products, teas, and homemade mixtures where appropriate.

This chapter gives a simplified version of the overall basic organic plan, but it should be helpful in giving you a good starting point. More details on each point are found further in the book. Formulas for the homemade brews are in the Appendix.

Welcome aboard. I'm sure you will enjoy learning the Natural Way.

CHAPTER 2

Trees

Trees are by far the most important landscape element. They create the garden space and are the skeleton or framework for all else that happens. They are also the only landscape element that greatly increases the value of your property through the years.

There's only one catch. If the trees aren't healthy and don't grow properly, they won't do you any good at all. They will be a maintenance problem, a headache, and an expense rather than a benefit. To grow properly, trees must be planted properly. Many tree-planting procedures are not only horticulturally incorrect but also substantial wastes of money. My recommendations for tree planting have developed over years of carefully studying many planting techniques and trying to understand what works and what doesn't. Slowly but surely, most of my recommendations have become adapted by the landscape industry. I was delighted to see that the ISA (International Society of Arboriculture) now endorses the Natural Way techniques. Their statement in the *Arborist's Certification Study Guide* that removing one-third of the top growth to compensate for root loss is without basis was welcomed.

The first time I saw trees planted correctly was in 1976. I had been commissioned to design the landscaping for the Harris Corporation on Dallas North Parkway in Addison, Texas. The budget was tight and the site was large and uninteresting. Utilizing the excess soil from the building excavation, we created free-flowing berms to add interest and provide sites for trees to be planted, not realizing at the time the importance of the built-in drainage system the berms provided. An old friend, Cody Carter, planted all the trees on that job. Since that time, I've watched those trees, and I've watched trees on other projects planted using all kinds of techniques. What I learned and now recommend is how to plant trees the Natural Way.

TREE PLANTING—
THE NATURAL WAY

1. Dig an Ugly Hole

Tree holes should be dug about 2" shallower than the height of the ball. Don't guess—actually measure the height of the ball. Never plant trees in slick-sided or glazed holes such as those caused by a tree spade or auger. Holes with glazed sides greatly restrict root penetration into the surrounding soil and consequently limit proper root development. Roughen the sides of the hole with a shovel. Holes should be saucer shaped or square. Both will provide aerated soil and prevent roots from circling in the hole.

2. Establish the Top of the Root Ball

Remove all the excess soil on top of the actual root ball. This can be a problem with container-grown plants or balled and burlapped plants. Set the tree so that the actual root ball top is 2" above the ground grade.

3. Run a Perk Test

After digging the hole, fill with water and wait until the next day. If the water level doesn't drain away overnight, a drainage problem is indicated. At this point, trees need to be moved to another location or have drainage added in the form of a gravel drain line running from the hole to a lower point on the site. Another draining method that sometimes works is to dig a pier hole down from the bottom of the hole into a different soil type and fill it with gravel. A sump from the top of the ball down to the bottom of the ball does little if any good. Positive drainage is critical, so don't shortcut this step unless you are sure the area has good drainage.

4. Backfill with Existing Soil

Place new trees or transplants in the center of the holes, making sure that the top of the ball is about 2" higher than the surrounding grade. Backfill with the soil that came from the hole. This is a critical point. Do not add

Left: tree protected from livestock and deer
Right: improperly planted red oaks

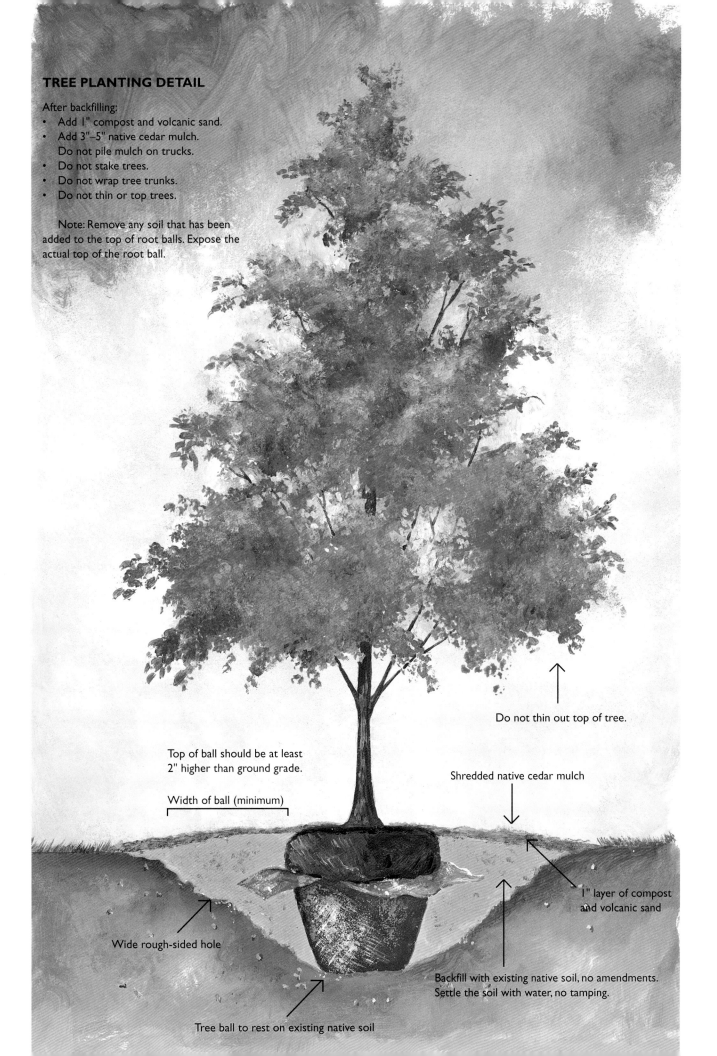

TREE PLANTING DETAIL

After backfilling:
- Add 1" compost and volcanic sand.
- Add 3"–5" native cedar mulch.
  Do not pile mulch on trucks.
- Do not stake trees.
- Do not wrap tree trunks.
- Do not thin or top trees.

Note: Remove any soil that has been added to the top of root balls. Expose the actual top of the root ball.

Do not thin out top of tree.

Top of ball should be at least 2" higher than ground grade.

Width of ball (minimum)

Shredded native cedar mulch

1" layer of compost and volcanic sand

Wide rough-sided hole

Backfill with existing native soil, no amendments. Settle the soil with water, no tamping.

Tree ball to rest on existing native soil

GRAVEL SUMP

sand, foreign soil, organic matter, or fertilizer to the backfill. Adding such amendments to the backfill not only wastes money but is detrimental to the tree. The roots need to start growing in the native soil from the beginning. When holes are dug in solid rock, topsoil from the same area should be used. Some native rock mixed into the backfill is beneficial. Putting gravel in the bottom of tree holes, however, is a total waste of money.

Water the backfill very carefully, making sure to get rid of all air pockets. Do not tamp the soil, as this will cause both compacted soil and air pockets.

When planting balled and burlapped plants, leave the burlap on the sides of the root balls after planting but loosen the burlap at the trunks and remove it from the top of the balls. Remove any nylon or plastic

TREE PLANTING

Rough sides

Mulch

Dig a hole and fill with water (perk test).　　Set tree ball slightly higher than existing grade.　　Backfill with native soil only.

SUBSURFACE DRAINAGE

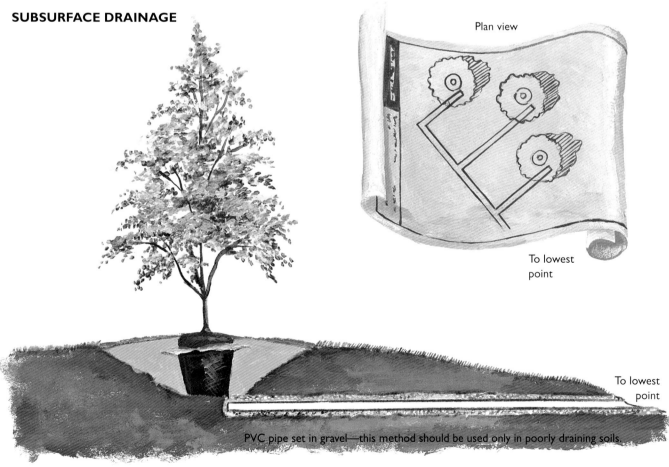

Plan view

To lowest point

To lowest point

PVC pipe set in gravel—this method should be used only in poorly draining soils.

string, since these materials do not decompose and can girdle the trunk and roots as the plant grows. Studies have shown that even wire mesh should be removed to avoid root girdling because wire does not break down very fast in our alkaline soils.

When planting from plastic containers, carefully remove plants and cut or tear the outside roots if they have grown solidly against the container. Never leave plants in containers.

Bare-rooted, balled and burlapped, and container plant materials should all be planted the same way. When planting bare-rooted plants, it is critical to keep the roots moist during the transportation and planting process.

5. Do Not Wrap or Stake

Trunks of newly planted trees should not be wrapped. Yes, that includes red oaks. It's a waste of money, looks unattractive, harbors insects, and leaves the bark weak when removed. Tree wrapping is similar to leaving a bandage on your finger too long. If you are worried about the unlikely possibility of sunburn, it's much better to paint the trunk with a diluted white latex paint. This is what the ISA has to say about wrapping:

Many early references recommend wrapping the trunks of newly planted trees to protect against temperature extremes, sunscald, boring insects and drying. More recent research indicates that temperature differentials at the bark are greater with

Improperly staked and wrapped tree. It also is planted too deep because of the added bed.

Improperly wrapped tree, although any trunk wrapping is improper.

tree wrap than without. Further, tree wrap tends to hold moisture on the bark and can lead to fungal problems. Also, insects tend to burrow between the bark and the wrap and can be worse with wrap than without it.

If nurseries would mark the north side of the trees as oriented in the nursery, the trees could be planted with exactly the same orientation and never experience any burn.

Staking and guying is usually unnecessary if the tree has been planted properly, with the proper earth ball size of at least 9" of ball for each inch of trunk diameter. Staking is often a waste of money and always detrimental to the proper trunk development of the plant. Staked trees consistently produce less trunk taper, develop a smaller root system, and are subject to leaning when stakes are removed. In rare circumstances (sandy soil, tall evergreen trees, etc.) where the tree needs to be staked for a while, connect the guy wires as low on the trunk as possible and remove the stakes as soon as possible. Never leave staking on more than one growing season. Temporary staking should be done with strong wire and metal eyebolts screwed into the trunk. Staking should only be done as a last resort—it is unsightly, expensive, adds to mowing and trimming costs, and restricts the tree's ability to develop tensile strength in the trunk. It can also cause damage to the cambium layer even when soft materials are used. Remove all identification tags at planting. Keep records on labels not connected to the tree.

6. Do Not Overprune

Only those not up with current industry standards of proper horticulture recommend that limb pruning should be done to compensate for the loss of roots during transplanting or planting. Most trees fare much better if all the limbs and foliage are left intact. The more foliage, the more food can be produced to build the root system. The health of the root system is the key to the overall health of the tree.

The only trees that seem to respond positively to thinning at the time of transplanting are field-collected live oak, yaupon holly, and other evergreens. Plants purchased in containers definitely need no pruning, and deciduous trees don't need to be thinned. Pruning in general should be limited to dead, damaged, or otherwise unsightly or rubbing limbs and branches.

7. Mulch the Top of the Ball

Mulch the top of balls after planting with 1" of a 50 percent mix of compost/lava and then 3" of shredded native mulch such as shredded cedar. This step is important in lawn areas or in beds. Don't ever plant grass over tree balls until the trees are established. Do not build water-ring dikes. They are unnecessary and get in the way, especially for long-term maintenance.

8. Enjoy Watching Your Trees Grow

MANAGEMENT OF TREES

Trees are not grown by people. Trees grow in spite of people. If you simply put the proper conditions in place, your trees will do just fine.

Fertilizing and Watering

Trees need very little fertilizer and not much water except during periods of drought. The use of organic fertilizers on the turf and other plantings under the trees is usually enough. Most trees have a great ability to access nutrients from the soil, even unbalanced, unhealthy soils.

Watering properly starts at planting time. When a tree is planted properly—backfilled with native soil and watered thoroughly, letting the weight of the water settle the soil, and then mulched with shredded material—it rarely needs additional watering above that used to keep the surrounding plants alive. Extremely hot, dry summers are of course the exception to that advice. Without question, many more trees die of overwatering and poor drainage than of underwatering.

Parasitic Growths on Trees

Mistletoe—This plant parasite primarily attaches to limbs and trunks of low-quality or stressed trees, such as Arizona ash, hackberry, bois d'arc, locust, box elder, and weak elms and ashes. Remove by cutting infected limbs off the tree. If that can't be done, notch into the limb to remove the rooting structure of the mistletoe and paint with Lac Balsam to prevent resprout. There are no magic chemical or organic sprays. Keeping the soil and trees healthy is the best preventative.

Ball Moss—This parasite can be killed with an organic spray. Use ½ cup of baking soda per gallon of water. Potassium bicarbonate will usually work as well, and it is much more beneficial to the soil and the tree roots as it drifts to the ground.

Other Tree Problems

Galls—There are many different kinds of galls. They are primarily caused by wasp, fly, and aphid insects and are usually more cosmetic than damaging. Wasp, fly, or aphid gall insects "sting" a plant, which causes a growth that the insect uses as a home for its young. The gall serves as a shelter and food supply. Although unsightly, most are not considered very damaging. Tannic acid from galls has been used for centuries to tan skins of animals. Many galls contain materials that make the finest inks and dyes. Some galls contain products that have been used in medicine since the fifth century B.C. No control is needed, although healthy plants seem to have fewer galls. Scientists do not yet know what makes the plants, in the absence of the gall insect, grow the curious, elaborate, and at times even beautiful structures that are absolutely foreign to the plant. The same species of gall insects on different species of plants causes galls that are similar, and different gall insects attacking the same plant cause galls that are different. Galls also become homes for other insects besides the initial ones.

Sapsuckers—If your tree looks as if it has been shot with a machine gun (holes drilled through the bark arranged in nice tidy rows), your tree is

Ball moss

Spanish moss, another parasite

Left: improper flush cut. Right: proper cut leaving the branch collar. It is always better to leave too long a stub rather than cut too close to the trunk.

Cut healing improperly

unhappy. The stress leading to this unhappiness can be caused by several factors. The tree may be planted too low in the soil. Scrape the excess soil off the root ball if that's the case. Or it may be an ill-adapted tree. Change to a good one. The tree may be getting too much or too little water or have poor drainage. The cause of stress can also be too much fertilizer—of any kind, but the synthetic stuff, especially if it contains herbicides, is the worst. Treat the sapsucker holes with Tree Trunk Goop and apply the Sick Tree Treatment to the soil. Most tree problems can be solved by removing the conditions that put the tree under stress and invited pests.

Pruning

1. Pruning should only be done to remove broken or diseased limbs or those causing a specific problem. Tree pruning shall never change or alter the natural shape of the tree unless otherwise instructed.
2. Suckers on the trunks of trees, dead wood, broken or unsightly branches, and diseased or insect-damaged growth can be removed from trees; however, it is perfectly natural to allow some dead branches to remain for the use of birds, beneficial insects, and other wildlife. Absolutely **do not** use line trimmers around the trunk of any trees.
3. Proper pruning cuts use a three-step process on limbs larger than 2".
   (1) Make the first cut under the limb about a foot from the trunk.
   (2) Make the second cut on top of the limb outside the first cut to remove the bulk of the limb. (3) Make the final cut just outside the branch collar to protect the tree's healing zone. Do not paint the cuts with wound dressing. Small pruning cuts should not be done in a sloppy manner. It's easy to cut too closely to the trunk and cause long-term injury.

PLANTING DEPTHS

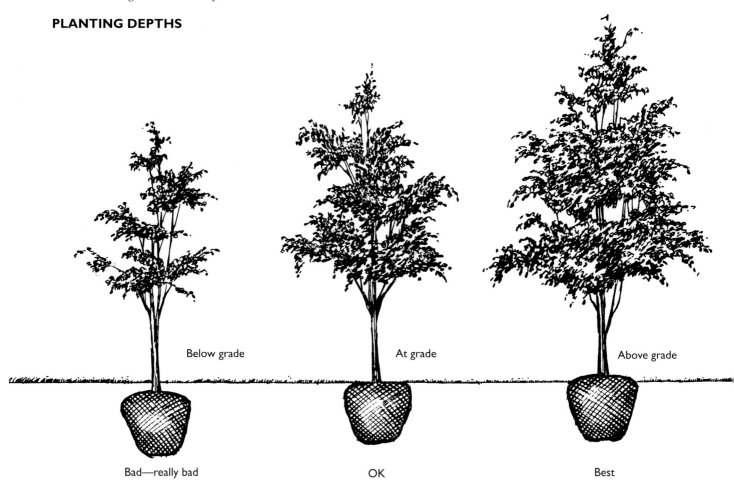

Below grade

At grade

Above grade

Bad—really bad

OK

Best

Incorrect cuts are those made flush or too close to the trunks. These cuts are too large, violate the trunk tissue, encourage disease, and slow the healing process. Correct pruning cuts leave a small stub, the branch collar, and preserve nature's healing device. It's better to leave too long a stub than to cut too close to the trunk.

When you are uncertain about what, when, and how to prune your trees, it's best to call in a professional arborist. Make sure to hire one that uses only organic techniques.

Planting Trees Too Low

One thing that's really fun about my job is learning new stuff all the time. Sometimes it's not good stuff. I have been stunned to discover what a huge number of trees have been planted too low. There seem to be several reasons for this problem. Many trees have simply been set too low in the planting operation; holes were too deeply dug. Other trees were planted at about the right level, but settled due to the wrong backfill or weak root balls. But one of the most common causes of deep tree-planting problems starts during the growing operations and sometimes in the nurseries. As trees grow, they are stepped up from seedlings to 1-gallon pots and then to increasingly larger containers. Often during this process, more and more soil is added to the top of the root ball. Why, I don't know. By the time the tree is ready to plant, it may be several inches deep in the container. That fact, combined with the planting mistakes, often puts the true top of the root ball several inches underground. This covering of the tree ball with soil can also happen on field-grown trees— caused by the cultivating plows. Trees that are planted too low have several problems. Soil above the root ball shuts off oxygen to the feeder roots and prevents carbon dioxide from escaping from the soil. Roots that do grow often circle and grow primarily in the soft, loose-textured added soil. The coiling roots can girdle trees several years after planting. Then also there is a girdling action from the soil moisture on the bark of the tree. A frustrating part of the problem is that the damage doesn't start to show up until sometimes 10–15 years after planting, when the tree is trying to mature and offer its beauty and shade. The symptoms can also show up during the first few years. Watch for poor top growth, light-colored foliage, and a thinning canopy.

It's easy to tell if a tree has been planted too low. The trunk will go straight into the ground like a telephone pole instead of having a distinctive flair at the soil surface. The solution is relatively easy too. Remove the excess soil down to the true top of the original root ball. This work can be done by homeowners with a hard rake or by professional arborists with a special tool called an air spade, which is basically a sand blaster with a customized nozzle that blows the soil away from roots without injuring them. Girdling roots can also be pruned away at this time if needed. If the excavation down to the top of the ball is not too deep, the area can be left concaved and lightly mulched with shredded tree trimmings. If the soil removal leaves a deep hole, a grate may have to be added that can serve as an arbor for ground cover. The long-term solution to this problem is to plant your trees according to my drawing, leaving the actual root ball 2" higher than grade and backfilling the hole with native soil only. With this technique, not even settling will leave the tree too deep in the ground.

EASY REFERENCE FOR TREES

Evergreen
Camphor
Cedar
Cypress, Italian
Holly
Magnolia
Myrtle, wax
Oak, live
Palm
Pine

Fall/Winter Berries or Other Fruit
Acacia
Buckeye, Mexican
Buckthorn, Carolina
Cherry laurel
Chinaberry
Eve's necklace
Holly, deciduous
Holly, East Palatka
Holly, Savannah
Holly, yaupon
Madrone
Soapberry
Viburnum, rusty blackhaw

Flowering Trees
Ash, fragrant
Catalpa
Cherry
Chitalpa
Crabapple
Crape myrtle
Dogwood
Eve's necklace
Fringe tree
Goldenball leadtree
Goldenrain tree
Hawthorn
Kidneywood, Texas
Linden
Madrone
Magnolia
Mexican elder
Parkinsonia
Peach
Pear
Plum
Redbud
Soapberry
Tulip tree

Viburnum
Vitex
Willow, desert

Yellow Fall Color
Ash
Birch, river
Blackberry
Buckeye, Mexican
Chitalpa
Cottonwood
Crape myrtle—white
Elm
Eve's necklace
Ginkgo
Goldenrain tree
Maple, Caddo
Maple, Japanese 'Coral Bark'
Maple, Shantung
Oak, bur
Pecan
Persimmon
Pistachio, Chinese
Redbud
Soapberry
Sweetgum
Tulip tree
Walnut
Willow
Witch hazel

Orange Fall Color
Ash, Texas
Maple, Japanese
Plum, Mexican

Red Fall Color
Ash, Texas
Black gum
Crape myrtle—red, pink, purple
Cypress
Dogwood
Maple, Japanese
Maple, red
Oak, red
Oak, white
Pear
Pistachio, Chinese
Sassafras
Sumac, flameleaf
Sweetgum
Viburnum, rusty blackhaw

THE TREES

ACACIA (Catclaw)

Acacia greggii var. *wrightii*
ah-KAY-shuh GREG-ee-eye, WRITE-ee-eye

Deciduous—Sun
Ht. 15'–30' Spread 10'–12'
Spacing 10'–15'

HABIT Native to South Texas. Small tree with feathery foliage and fragrant flowers in the spring. It is thorny and thicket-forming, with a spreading, irregular overall form. Flowers are off-white to creamy yellow. Seeds are dark brown and shiny.

CULTURE Extremely drought tolerant and needs little fertilizer. Can grow in rocky soils but adapts to fairly heavy clay soils as well if they are well drained.

USES Small ornamental tree.

PROBLEMS Not widely available.

NOTES Flowers are fragrant and make a superb honey.

ANACUA (Sandpaper Tree)

Ehretia anacua
eh-REE-shah ah-NOK-you-ah or ah-NOK-wha

Semi-evergreen—Sun
Ht. 30'–50' Spread 30'–40'
Spacing 30'–40'

HABIT Anacua is native to southern Texas. It could be introduced fairly successfully as far north as Austin. Dense crown that creates heavy shade. Distinctive, gnarled appearance often multitrunked, mostly evergreen. Blooms late fall through the winter into the early spring. Flowers are pure white and fragrant. Spring-ripening fruits are bright orange drupes about the size of hackberries. Foliage is dark green and has a rough sandpaper texture.

CULTURE Needs plenty of water to become established and then becomes very drought tolerant. Can be killed by overwatering.

USES Shade tree for southern part of the state.

PROBLEMS Few problems other than those caused by poor drainage, improper planting, or environmental damage.

NOTES Anacua is a great honeybee attractant. Terrific specimens grow around the Alamo in San Antonio. One is growing in the Texas Discovery Garden's parking lot at the state fairgrounds.

Acacia

Acacia

Anacua

Anacua fruit

Arizona Ash

ASH, ARIZONA
Fraxinus velutina 'Arizona'
FRAK-suh-nus vel-u-TEA-na

Deciduous—Sun
Ht. 30' Spread 30'
DO NOT PLANT

HABIT   Fast-growing junk tree. Brittle wood, yellow fall color, smooth bark.
CULTURE   Any soil, medium to heavy water, and light fertilization.
USES   Fast-growing temporary shade tree.
PROBLEMS   Borers, brittle wood, short-lived, destructive roots. Subject to freeze damage.
NOTES   This plant was introduced as a drought-tolerant, low-maintenance tree, but it is far from it. I once thought all ash trees were bad because of this one. Native to Arizona and New Mexico.

ASH, FRAGRANT
Fraxinus cuspidata
FRAK-suh-nus cus-pi-DA-tah

Deciduous ornamental—
Sun/Part Shade
Ht. 10'–20' Spread 8'–12'
Spacing 8'–15'

HABIT   It grows naturally in canyons, on mountain slopes, and primarily in rocky soil conditions. White flowers, very fragrant. Only ash with this kind of flower. More shrubby than treelike and has long, thin leaflets on compound leaves.
CULTURE   Fragrant ash will grow equally well in slightly alkaline limestone soils or slightly acidic igneous soils. It even does well in the heavy black clay soils.
USES   Small ornamental tree or specimen.
PROBLEMS   Poor availability in the nursery trade is the biggest problem.
NOTES   Showy as flowering dogwood and should be planted much more in Texas.

Fragrant Ash

ASH, GREEN
Fraxinus pennsylvanica
FRAK-suh-nus pen-cil-VAN-ik-a

Deciduous—Sun
Ht. 50' Spread 40'
Spacing 20'

HABIT   Fast-growing, large compound leaves, dark green foliage, yellow fall color. Smooth, mottled bark when young, rougher with age.
CULTURE   Easy to grow when young in any soil. Needs more water than Texas ash.
USES   Shade tree, fall color, background tree, mass tree planting.
PROBLEMS   Aphids in early summer. Not a long-lived tree.
NOTES   Native to North America. *F. pennsylvanica* 'Marshalli' is a seedless form of green ash and even less adapted than the parent.

Above: Green Ash; Left: Green Ash, showing fall color

Prickly Ash

Texas Ash

Texas Ash

ASH, PRICKLY (Toothache Tree)
Zanthoxylum clava herculis
zanth-OX-ih-lum CLA-va her-CUE-lis

Deciduous—Sun
Ht. 15'–30' Spread 15'–30'
Spacing 10'–15'

HABIT   Normally found along hedgerows, in thickets, and on edges of forests in East Texas but also spreading farther west. Adapted to a wide range of soils and prefers full sun. It likes deep, heavily alkaline clay soils but will also grow in the almost sterile sands.

CULTURE   Easy to grow in most any soil. Not really recommended for planting, it is easy to keep alive if it already exists on-site. Seldom planted.

USES   Interesting small native tree.

PROBLEMS   Foliage gets eaten by caterpillars, but the caterpillar that loves the foliage most is the giant swallowtail, so care should be given to protect these beautiful butterflies.

NOTES   All parts of the tree, including the bark, will numb the gums and tongue when chewed or sucked. Prickly ash provides cover for wildlife, and the blooms help to make a delicious honey. Also called tickletongue tree.

ASH, TEXAS (White Ash)
Fraxinus texensis
FRAK-suh-nus tex-EN-sis

Deciduous—Sun
Ht. 50' Spread 40'
Spacing 20'–30'

HABIT   Small greenish yellow flowers and dry-winged samara containing a single seed. Medium growth, large compound leaves with rounded leaflets, especially on young growth. White splotches on trunk and limbs. Orange to purple fall color.

CULTURE   Easy to grow in any well-drained soil, grows readily in alkaline soil on rock or steep slopes. Low water and fertilizer needs. Needs excellent drainage. Easy to transplant.

USES   Shade tree, fall color.

PROBLEMS   Poor drainage, borers.

NOTES   One of Texas' best-kept secrets. White ash (*F. americana*), kin to the Texas ash, is also a good tree and should be used much more.

Wafer Ash

River Birch

River Birch

ASH, WAFER
Ptelea trifoliata
TEL-ee-ah tri-fole-ee-AH-tah

Deciduous—Sun/Part Shade
Ht. 5'–20' Spread 5'–10'
Spacing 6'–12'

HABIT   Will grow almost throughout the entire state except for the extreme southern tip of Texas. Will grow as a complete (total shade) understory tree. It can take a wide range of soils and grows well in both moist conditions as well as dry, rocky sites. Aromatic foliage. Has slender branches and pale compound leaves with three leaflets that vary in shape. Flowers are greenish white. Fruits (samaras) follow and sport a distinctive single, disc-shaped wing.

CULTURE   Easy to grow and should be used more. It is drought tolerant and can stand soils ranging from sandy to heavy clays and can even grow in rocky soil. It is adapted to full sun but does better with light shade as an understory tree. It needs very little, if any, fertilizer to survive and thrive.

USES   Interesting small tree.

PROBLEMS   Relatively few.

NOTES   Wafer ash is a good tree to provide food and shelter for wildlife.

BIRCH, RIVER
Betula nigra
BET-ew-la NI-gra

Deciduous—Sun
Ht. 30'–50' Spread 15'–20'
Spacing 20'–25'

HABIT   Usually has multiple trunks. Young bark is smooth and pinkish, bark on older trees is brown, flaky, and curling. Diamond-shaped leaves. Yellow fall color.

CULTURE   Needs plenty of moisture. Very fast-growing but not long-lived.

USES   Shade tree or specimen tree.

PROBLEMS   Does not do well in heavy alkaline clay soils and hot climates.

NOTES   Interesting tree but not usually highly recommended in Texas. Does well in an organic program.

BIRD OF PARADISE
Caesalpinia spp.
kie-sal-PEEN-ee-ah

Deciduous—Sun
Ht. 8'–15' Spread 10'–15'
Spacing 8'–10'

HABIT   Small decorative tree or large shrub, dramatic yellow flowers spring and summer. Finely textured foliage.

CULTURE   Easy, any soil, drought tolerant.

USES   Ornamental tree, yellow summer flowers.

PROBLEMS   Few if any. Freeze damage in northern part of the state.

NOTES   Native from central United States to Texas, Argentina, and Uruguay. *C. mexicana* is a yellow-flowering Texas native that grows wild in the far southern tip of the state. *C. gilliesii* (also called Pride of Barbados) has tiny leaflets and yellow flowers with distinctive long, red stamens. In Dallas, mine have frozen to the ground in harsh winters but returned in spring.

Bird of Paradise

Black Cherry

Black Cherry

Black Cherry

Black Gum in fall

BLACK CHERRY (Wild Cherry)
Prunus serotina
PROO-nus ser-oh-TEEN-ah

Deciduous—Sun
Ht. 25'-50' Spread 25'-30'
Spacing 25'-30'

HABIT Graceful medium-sized tree with a narrow crown and slender trunk, open branching, white drooping flowers when the leaves have just emerged, and beautiful shiny foliage. Clusters of green, red, and black fruit that can all be on the tree at the same time. Most of the fruit ripens at the same time. Grows wild primarily in fencerows, thickets, and on the edges of woods in sandy to acid soils.

CULTURE Minimum of maintenance in a wide range of soils from sand to well-drained heavy clays. Best in moist, well-drained soils.

USES Specimen landscape tree or fence line tree. Food for birds and other wildlife.

PROBLEMS Thin bark that is easily damaged in planting, also in fires. Tent caterpillars sometimes as well as black not fungal galls. Twigs and leaves can be toxic to animals and humans.

NOTES Escarpment black cherry, *Prunus serotina* var. *eximia*, is found in the Hill Country area of Central Texas. Southwestern black cherry, *Prunus serotina* var. *rufula*, is found in the Trans-Pecos and far West Texas. Can grow to even greater heights in deep acid soils of East Texas.

BLACK GUM (Black Tupelo)
Nyssa sylvatica var. *sylvatica*
NI-sa sil-VA-ti-ka

Deciduous—Sun
Ht. 50'–100' Spread 30'
Spacing 30'

HABIT Clusters of shiny blue-black fruit enjoyed by many wild animals. Foliage is shiny green in the summer and scarlet in the fall. A few leaves will sometimes turn red in the late summer. One of the best Texas trees for fall color. Relatively slow-growing.

CULTURE Unfortunately, it won't grow in alkaline soils. Prefers East Texas acid sand or Houston-area clays. Likes moist to wet soils best.

USES Shade tree, fall color.

PROBLEMS Needs acid soil.

NOTES *Nyssa* also includes the East Texas tupelo tree. *N. aquatica* is water tupelo. *N. sylvatica* var. *biflora* is the swamp tupelo. All these trees can grow well over 100' tall in the right conditions.

Black Locust

Bois d'Arc

Box Elder Maple

BLACK LOCUST
Robinia pseudoacacia
row-BIN-ee-ah sue-dough-ah-KAY-shuh

Deciduous—Sun
Ht. 40' Spread 40'
Spacing 20'–30'

HABIT Upright and spreading, with small oval leaflets on large compound leaves. Very fragrant white flowers in spring. Yellow fall color. Fast-growing.
CULTURE Grows well in most soils. Drought tolerant.
USES Shade tree.
PROBLEMS Few if any other than short-lived.
NOTES Beautiful tree that should be used in more small gardens and courtyards. Native to Oklahoma, Arkansas, and east to New York. Has naturalized in Texas.

BOIS D'ARC (Osage Orange)
Maclura pomifera
ma-CLUE-ra puh-MIFF-er-ah

Deciduous—Sun
Ht. 40' Spread 40'
DO NOT PLANT

HABIT Fast-growing, spreading, dense foliage, thorny branches, "horse apples" on female trees, wood like iron. Yellow fall color.
CULTURE Full sun, any soil, drought tolerant, low fertilization, and good drainage.
USES Shade, background.
PROBLEMS Messy, hard to grow anything beneath, weak root system. Trees tend to fall over.
NOTES Also called Horse Apple, Hedge Apple, and Yellow Wood. Bois d'arc trees should be removed to favor more desirable plants. Native from Texas to Arkansas.

BOX ELDER (Box Elder Maple)
Acer negundo
A-sir nay-GOON-do

Deciduous—Sun
Ht. 40'–50' Spread 40'–50'
DO NOT PLANT

HABIT Differs from other maples by having 3–9 leaflets. New growth is olive green; mature foliage is bright pea green. Native to the eastern half of the state.
CULTURE Very fast-growing. Needs lots of water.
USES Wild areas.
PROBLEMS Dry conditions, insects, heart rot.
NOTES The red-and-black boxelder bug loves this tree—you probably won't.

Mexican Buckeye

BUCKEYE, MEXICAN
Ungnadia speciosa
oong-NAD-ee-ah spee-see-OH-sa

Deciduous—Sun/Shade
Ht. 20' Spread 20'
Spacing 10'–20'

HABIT Moderate growth, fragrant purple flowers in spring. Brilliant yellow fall color. Decorative 3-pod seeds on bare branches in winter.
CULTURE Easy, any soil, little fertilization. Although drought tolerant, can stand moist soils. Likes limestone alkaline soils, but will grow in any soil.
USES Spring and fall color, understory tree, specimen courtyard tree.
PROBLEMS Few if any.
NOTES Can be easily grown from seed. The sweet seeds are poisonous to humans. Great tree—should be used more. Native to Texas and Mexico.

BUCKEYE, TEXAS
Aesculus glabra
ESS-kah-lus GLA-bra

Deciduous—Sun/Part Shade
Ht. 20'–40' Spread 10'–20'
Spacing 10'–15'

HABIT Creamy white to yellow flowers in spring. Leathery capsule has 1–3 large shiny seeds that are poisonous. Compound leaves with 7–9 leaflets. Very upright growth.
CULTURE Drought tolerant, easy to grow.
USES Ornamental tree.
PROBLEMS Summer defoliation.
NOTES *A. glabra* var. *glabra*, the Ohio buckeye, is not as well adapted in Texas but will grow here. *A. pavia* var. *pavia*, the red buckeye or scarlet buckeye, reaches heights of 15'–25' and has red flower spikes in spring. Most buckeyes lose their foliage in the heat of summer. Don't worry—that's normal.

Mexican Buckeye

Texas Buckeye

Scarlet Buckeye

43

Camphor Tree

Carolina Buckthorn

Catalpa

Deodar Cedar

CAMPHOR TREE
Cinnamomum camphora
sin-ah-MO-mum cam-FOE-rah

Evergreen—Full Sun
Ht. 40'–50' Spread 30'
Spacing 20'–30'

HABIT   Clusters of very small, fragrant white flowers in late spring, followed by small black fruits. Beautiful shiny fragrant leaves that smell like camphor.
CULTURE   Needs protection in winter and excellent drainage.
USES   Potpourri, specimen tree.
PROBLEMS   Roots are very competitive. May freeze at 20° and below. Possible root rot.
NOTES   Use from San Antonio south. The official tree of Hiroshima because it survived the atomic bombing.

CAROLINA BUCKTHORN
(Indian Cherry)
Rhamnus caroliniana
RAM-nus care-o-lin-ee-ANE-uh

Deciduous—Sun/Shade
Ht. 15' Spread 15'
Spacing 4'–10'

HABIT   Bushy shrub or small tree. Large glossy leaves, yellow-orange fall color, red berries in late summer, turning black in fall. Can grow to 30'.
CULTURE   Easy to grow in any soil with good drainage. Drought tolerant.
USES   Specimen understory plant, ornamental tree, background plant.
PROBLEMS   Few if any.
NOTES   Beautiful native plant that should certainly be used more.

CATALPA (Cigar Tree)
Catalpa bignonioides
kuh-TALL-puh big-none-ee-OY-dees

Deciduous—Sun
Ht. 60' Spread 40'
Spacing 30'–40'

HABIT   Large, fast-growing, open-branching. Smooth bark, very large light green leaves, white flower clusters in early summer, cigarlike seedpods.
CULTURE   Easy, any soil, rarely needs pruning. Grown in East Texas.
USES   Shade tree for large estates, parks, golf courses. Early summer flowers.
PROBLEMS   Messy flowers and catalpa worms in summer.
NOTES   Native to the southern United States.

CEDAR, DEODAR
Cedrus deodara
SEE-drus dee-o-DAR-a

Evergreen—Sun
Ht. 50' Spread 30'
Spacing 20'–40'

HABIT   Moderate growth rate, large conical shape, pointed to drooping top, foliage to the ground; foliage consists of small, pinelike needles. Rounded form with age.
CULTURE   Any soil, good drainage, plenty of room.
USES   Parks, large estates, evergreen backdrop.
PROBLEMS   Too large at the base for most residential gardens, freeze damage, diseases, bagworms, and spider mites.
NOTES   Sometimes called "California Christmas tree." Graceful when healthy, but I would not invest much money in this plant in the northern part of the state. Native to the Himalayas.

Eastern Red Cedar

Mountain Cedar

Incense Cedar

Cherry Laurel

CEDAR, EASTERN RED (Native Cedar) Evergreen—Sun

Juniperus virginiana   Ht. 40' Spread 20'

joo-NIP-er-us ver-gin-ee-AN-ah   Spacing 20'–30'

HABIT   Very small unimpressive flowers in spring; small blue-purple berries in the fall on female plants. Single trunk, upright and conical when young, spreading with age. Dark green juniper-like foliage, hard fragrant wood.

CULTURE   Easy to grow in any soil (even solid rock) if drainage is positive. Drought tolerant.

USES   Shade tree, screen for bad views, evergreen backdrop.

PROBLEMS   Bagworms, spider mites.

NOTES   Is becoming more available as a nursery-grown tree. Many people are allergic to the pollen, but it's in the air already from the wild trees. Native from the eastern United States to Texas. Mountain cedar (*J. ashei*) is similar but usually has multiple-stem trunk and does not suffer cedar apple rust fungus.

CEDAR, INCENSE   Evergreen—Sun

Calocedrus decurrens   Ht. 70'–90' Spread 20'–30'

cal-oh-SEED-rus day-KER-enz   Spacing 15'–30'

HABIT   Incense cedar is native to Asia, but it has been used extensively in California. The specimens I know of exist in the black soil of Garland and in east Dallas.

CULTURE   Adapted to a wide variety of soils, although very few plants have been attempted to date in Texas.

USES   Specimen or screening tree.

PROBLEMS   Finding the tree in the nursery trade is difficult, and root rot diseases can develop during establishment when the plant is overwatered and overfertilized.

NOTES   An upright evergreen tree with arborvitae-like foliage. It is tall-growing, symmetrical, and straight-trunked. The foliage is very dark green and dense. Gives off a pleasant fragrance in the summer. It makes a beautiful single specimen or can be planted closely together to form a windbreak or tall screen.

CHERRY LAUREL   Evergreen—Sun/Part Shade

Prunus caroliniana   Ht. 25'–40' Spread 15'–20'

PROO-nus ka-ro-lin-ee-AY-nah   Spacing 8'–20'

HABIT   Evergreen tree with shiny, smooth evergreen leaves. Small off-white flowers bloom in the spring, followed by black fruit.

CULTURE   Relatively easy to grow in most soils, although it will tend to become chlorotic in alkaline soils. This problem can usually be eliminated with the use of Texas greensand or the overall Sick Tree Treatment.

USES   Small ornamental tree or screening plant.

PROBLEMS   Highly susceptible to cotton root rot and ice-storm damage. Relatively short-lived tree and not highly recommended.

NOTES   Native from the eastern United States to Texas. The improved hybrids seem to do fairly well here.

CHERRY, WILD   See Black Cherry

Chinaberry

Chitalpa

Chittamwood

CHINABERRY (Umbrella Tree)   Deciduous—Sun
Melia azedarach   Ht. 30'–50' Spread 20'–30'
ME-lee-ah ah-ZED-ah-rack   Spacing 15'–20'

HABIT A fast-growing junk tree to many, but it has delicate dark green foliage and strongly fragrant lilac flowers in spring. Yellow fall color.
CULTURE Grows easily in any soil.
USES Shade tree, spring color, and fragrance.
PROBLEMS Fast growth but short life. Brittle wood and suckers.
NOTES Close kin to the tropical neem tree (*Azadirachta indica*).

CHITALPA   Deciduous—Sun
Chilopsis × Catalpa   Ht. 30' Spread 30'
KY-lop-sis × kuh-TALL-puh   Spacing 20'–30'

HABIT Cross between catalpa and desert willow; lovely, open-branching tree. Leaves are 6"–8" long and 1"–2" wide. Pink catalpa-like flowers bloom all summer.
CULTURE Easy to grow in any soil. Rarely needs pruning.
USES Distinctive garden or small-area tree.
PROBLEMS Root rot if drainage is poor.
NOTES Relatively new to the scene and appears to be more healthy than either of its parent plants. A hybrid cultivar that Dr. Carl Whitcomb says is not a cross with catalpa, just a sport of desert willow.

CHITTAMWOOD (Gum Elastic)   Deciduous—Sun
Bumelia lanuginosa   Ht. 60' Spread 30'
Boo-ME-lee-ah lay-noo-gee-NO-sah   Spacing 20'–40'

HABIT Slow-growing, upright, dark stiff branches, small leaves similar to live oak. Yellow fall color, thorns. Resembles live oak at a distance.
CULTURE Easy to grow in any soil.
USES Shade tree.
PROBLEMS Borers can be a bad problem if the tree gets in stress.
NOTES Not many have been used as landscape plants. I usually try to keep them alive if existing on a site. Native to southern and southwestern United States. Difficult to find in nurseries.

CITRUS See Chapter 7 (Fruits, Nuts, and Vegetables)

Cottonwood

Crabapple

COTTONWOOD
Populus deltoides
POP-ewe-lus dell-TOY-deez

Deciduous—Sun
Ht. 100' Spread 50'
DO NOT PLANT

HABIT   Very fast-growing, upright, light-color bark, brittle wood, yellow fall color.

CULTURE   Very easy to grow. Very easy to transplant.

USES   Shade tree.

PROBLEMS   Short-lived, destructive root system, cotton from females, wind damage, borers, cotton root rot, very dangerous tree because of large limbs or entire tree falling in wind storms.

NOTES   Cotton from female plants is not only ugly but can do severe damage to air conditioners. This is one tree I almost always recommend removing from residential gardens. Native from eastern United States to New Mexico.

CRABAPPLE
Malus spp.
MAY-lus

Deciduous—Sun/Part Shade
Ht. 25' Spread 25'
Spacing 15'–20'

HABIT   Spring flowers (white, red, pink), half-inch fruit matures in fall.

CULTURE   Easy to grow in most soils. Fall color is yellow usually, but red in some varieties.

USES   Ornamental tree, spring flowers.

PROBLEMS   Aphids, scale, spider mites, webworms, rust, apple scab, fire blight, root rot, short life.

NOTES   At least 500 species exist. *M. floribunda* has white flowers with a pink tinge. 'Snowdrift' has white flowers, orange-red fruit. 'Sargent' has white flowers, dark red fruit. 'Callaway' has light pink flowers, large red fruit. 'Radiant' has single red flowers, red fruit. Native to China and Japan.

Crape Myrtle

Crape Myrtle

CRAPE MYRTLE

Lagerstroemia indica
lah-ger-STROH-me-ah IN-dik-kah

Deciduous—Sun
Ht. 25' Spread 15'
Spacing 15'–20'

HABIT   Slow-growing, light smooth bark, small oval leaflets on compound leaves, flowers all summer (red, purple, pink, white). Fall color is red on all except white-flowering varieties (yellow).

CULTURE   Easy to grow in any soil. Responds to regular fertilization.

USES   Ornamental tree, summer color, fall color, beautiful bare branches in winter.

PROBLEMS   Aphids, mildew, suckers at the ground.

NOTES   Do not trim back in winter—old wives' tale that it increases flower production—besides, the seedpods are decorative. Native to China. Dwarf forms are available in a range of sizes. *L. fauriei* is the only other available species. The Indian-named crosses of *L. fauriei* and *L. indica* are beautiful and much more disease resistant. 'Natchez' is one of the most popular, with dramatic rusty brown bark. Others are 'Apalachee,' 'Tonto,' and 'Sioux.' 'Chickasaw' and 'Pocomoke' are true genetic dwarfs with strong mildew resistance. These and dozens more were introduced by Dr. Donald Egolf of the U.S. National Arboretum.

Montezuma and Bald Cypress
in early December

Arizona Cypress

CYPRESS, ARIZONA
Cupressus arizonica
koo-PRESS-us air-ah-ZON-ih-ca

Evergreen—Sun
Ht. 40'–50' Spread 30'–40'
Spacing 20'–30'

HABIT Upright, aromatic blue-green evergreen foliage. Fast-growing for 30–40 years. Colorful flaky bark.

CULTURE Must have extremely well-drained soil.

USES Specimen, windbreak. Grows best in West Texas, only fair in the rest of the state.

PROBLEMS Doesn't like the heat and humidity of typical Texas summers.

NOTES Native to Big Bend's Chisos Mountains, where it grows to 90'. Shouldn't be used east of Dallas because of higher rainfall.

CYPRESS, BALD
Taxodium distichum
tax-OH-dee-um DIS-tick-um

Deciduous—Sun
Ht. 80' Spread 50'
Spacing 20'–40'

HABIT Moderately fast-growing, upright, pyramidal when young but spreading with age. Light green lacy foliage, reddish brown fall color. Branching structure is layered and distinctive. Root "knees" will appear in wet soil.

CULTURE Easily grown in any soil except solid rock. Drought tolerant, although can grow in wet areas. Cannot take any shade—must have full sun to avoid limb dieback.

USES Specimen, shade tree, background tree, fall color, delicate foliage texture.

PROBLEMS Chlorosis and crown gall occasionally, bagworms.

NOTES Likes well-drained soils best. The often seen lake habitation results from a seed germination need and a protection against prairie fires through the years. Native from eastern United States to Texas. Montezuma cypress (*T. mucronatum*) is a faster-growing tree that also has a much longer green-foliage period.

49

Italian Cypress

CYPRESS, ITALIAN
Cupressus sempervirens
koo-PRESS-us sem-per-VYE-rens

Evergreen—Sun
Ht. 40' Spread 12'
Spacing 6'–10'

HABIT   Golf-ball-size cones of shield-shaped scales. Tiny, scalelike leaves. Slow-growing, unusually upright. Very dark green juniper-like foliage.
CULTURE   Relatively easy to grow in any well-drained soil.
USES   Background, tall border, screen, specimen tree for formal gardens, windbreak.
PROBLEMS   Spider mites, bagworms, disease problems, short-lived in this area due to heat and humidity.
NOTES   Looks out of place in Texas. Unless you have formal Italian gardens, I would avoid this plant. Native to southern Europe.

CYPRESS, POND
Taxodium ascendens
tax-OH-dee-um uh-SEND-enz

Deciduous—Sun
Ht. 70' Spread 30'
Spacing 20'–40'

HABIT   Rapid growth, narrower than regular bald cypress, green earlier in spring and longer into fall. Leaves spiral out from the stem and do not open. Long delicate filament-like leaves. Lovely, soft overall appearance. Rust fall color.
CULTURE   Easy to grow in any soil, normal water and nutrient requirements. Can tolerate wet soil. Doesn't like white rock.
USES   Specimen, shade tree, mass planting, background tree.
PROBLEMS   Availability.
NOTES   Also called *T. distichum* 'Nutans.' Best place to see this tree is the grove in Dallas at Central Expressway and McCommas. Native from southeastern United States to Alabama.

Pond Cypress

DOGWOOD, FLOWERING
Cornus florida
KOR-nus FLOR-eh-duh

Deciduous—Shade/Part Shade
Ht. 20' Spread 20'
Spacing 15'–20'

HABIT   Graceful, layered structure. Pink or white flowers in spring. Red fall color.
CULTURE   Needs loose, acid, well-drained soil. Needs plenty of moisture, but drainage is a must. Will do best in beds with heavy percentage of organic material.

Flowering Dogwood

Flowering Dogwood fall color

American Elm

American Elm

USES   Ornamental tree, spring flowers, red fall color. Oriental gardens.

PROBLEMS   Cotton root rot, soil alkalinity, borers.

NOTES   Would not be considered a low-maintenance plant. This tree is native to acid, sandy soils like those in East Texas. Many improved cultivars available.

Rough-Leaf Dogwood

DOGWOOD, ROUGH-LEAF
Cornus drummondii
KOR-nus druh-MUN-dee-eye

Deciduous—Sun/Shade
Ht. 15' Spread 15'
Spacing 6'–12'

HABIT   Small bushy tree, blooms after leaves have formed in late spring with white flower clusters. White seedpods in late summer and purple fall color. Plant spreads easily by seeds and suckers but is not a problem. Stems are reddish and very decorative in winter.

CULTURE   Easy, any soil, drought tolerant. Very easy to grow.

USES   Background mass, understory tree, seeds for birds.

PROBLEMS   Few if any.

NOTES   Many have been cut down by people thinking they are weeds. This plant is graceful, tough, and should be used more. Native from eastern United States to Texas.

Dogwood

ELM, AMERICAN
Ulmus americana
ULL-mus uh-mer-ee-KAH-nah

Deciduous—Sun
Ht. 70' Spread 70'
DO NOT PLANT

HABIT   Fast-growing, gracefully spreading form, large leaves, yellow fall color.

CULTURE   Mostly easy to grow in any soil, normal water and nutrients.

USES   Shade tree, large estate, park, yellow fall color.

PROBLEMS   Dutch elm disease, elm leaf beetle, cotton root rot.

NOTES   Ascending elm is an upright-growing version that was a failure. Neither of these plants is recommended, although I would certainly save any existing ones. Native to the eastern half of the United States. *Zelkova* is being used as an American elm substitute. It is a similar tree but has more upright growth. I don't recommend it either.

Cedar Elm

Cedar Elm fall color

Above and below: Lacebark Elm

ELM, CEDAR
Ulmus crassifolia
ULL-mus krass-ee-FOAL-ee-uh

Deciduous—Sun
Ht. 80' Spread 60'
Spacing 20'–40'

HABIT   Upright, moderate growth, yellow/gold fall color, irregular growth
pattern, rough-textured leaves.

CULTURE   Grows well in any soil, drought tolerant but can stand fairly wet
soil also.

USES   Shade tree, street tree.

PROBLEMS   Aphids, elm leaf beetle, mildew, mistletoe. Seems to be sensitive to
air pollution.

NOTES   Native to Texas. Referred to as "poor man's live oak." Winged elm
(*U. alata*), a close kin, has the same characteristics as cedar elm with the
addition of wings on the stems. Native from the southern United States to
West Texas.

ELM, LACEBARK (Evergreen Elm)
Ulmus parvifolia sempervirens
ULL-mus par-vi-FOAL-ee-uh sem-per-VYE-rens

Deciduous—Sun
Ht. 50' Spread 40'
Spacing 20'–30'

HABIT   Upright and spreading, delicate foliage on limber stems, trunk bark is
distinctively mottled. Fall color is so-so yellow.

CULTURE   Fast-growing in most any soil. Drought tolerant and cannot tolerate
wet soil. Does the best in West Texas.

USES   Shade tree.

PROBLEMS   Easily susceptible to cotton root rot in black soils. Very tender bark
in early spring just at leaf break.

NOTES   Often confused with Siberian elm (*U. pumila*), which is a trash tree.
Lacebark elm is a perfect example of an introduced tree that is better than its
native counterpart. Sold as Drake elm, evergreen elm, or Chinese elm. Native
to China. Not nearly as good as we once thought.

Siberian Elm

Eve's Necklace

Fringe Tree

ELM, SIBERIAN (Chinese Elm)
Ulmus pumila
ULL-mus PEW-mi-lah

Deciduous—Sun
Ht. 50' Spread 50'
DO NOT PLANT

HABIT   Upright to spreading shade tree, leaves just smaller than American elm.
CULTURE   Grows anywhere.
USES   Shade tree.
PROBLEMS   Elm leaf beetle, Dutch elm disease, brittle wood. Often confused with lacebark elm (*U. parvifolia*).
NOTES   Extremely unhealthy plant. I would even recommend removing existing ones. Native to Asia.

EVE'S NECKLACE (Texas Sophora)
Sophora affinis
so-FORE-uh af-FIN-is

Deciduous—Sun/Shade
Ht. 30' Spread 20'
Spacing 10'–15'

HABIT   Moderately fast-growing, upright, usually in the wild as an understory tree. Pink wisteria-like flowers and black beadlike seedpods in fall. Bark, especially new young growth, is greenish.
CULTURE   Easy, any soil, drought tolerant.
USES   Small garden tree, specimen, natural settings.
PROBLEMS   Few if any.
NOTES   Excellent small tree for residential gardens. Native to Texas, Arkansas, Oklahoma, and Louisiana.

FRINGE TREE
Chionanthus virginicus
key-oh-NAN-thus ver-JIN-eh-kus

Deciduous—Part Shade
Ht. 15'–30' Spread 15'–20'
Spacing 10'–25'

HABIT   Lacy, fragrant white flower clusters in spring just before foliage appears and immediately after the dogwoods bloom. Both male and female flowers

Ginkgo

Ginkgo

Goldenball Leadtree

are beautiful. Female plants have dark blue clusters of berries that ripen in late summer to fall. Gorgeous, slow-growing ornamental native tree.

CULTURE   Does best in sandy acid soils but will grow in soil with a neutral pH—in Houston, for example. Yellow fall color. Moderate water requirements. Can grow in wet soil.

USES   Ornamental understory tree, spring color.

PROBLEMS   Not adapted to alkaline soil.

NOTES   Flowers form on year-old growth, so prune only after blooming.

GINKGO (Maidenhair Tree)
Ginkgo biloba
GINK-o bye-LOBE-ah

Deciduous—Sun
Ht. 50' Spread 30'
Spacing 20'–40'

HABIT   Unique, open-branching tree with vibrant yellow fall color. Foliage is medium green, fan shaped, and beautiful. Light-color bark and slow growth. Excellent climbing tree.

CULTURE   Any well-drained soil. Doesn't like solid rock. Moderate water and fertilization needs. Grows the best in deep, moist organic soils.

USES   Shade tree, fall color, distinctive foliage.

PROBLEMS   Fruit on female trees smells bad and can cause a mess if not picked up regularly. Slow grower.

NOTES   One of the oldest trees on earth and can be found on almost every continent in the world. The largest I've seen is in Frank Lloyd Wright's office garden in Chicago. First identified from fossil records in China. Concentrated ginkgo is a powerful medicinal herb that some research shows may improve mental functions.

GOLDENBALL LEADTREE
(Lemonball Tree)
Leucaena retusa
loo-SEE-nah reh-TOO-sah

Deciduous—Sun/Part Shade
Ht. 12'–20' Spread 10'–15'
Spacing 12'–15'

HABIT   Small tree with delicate foliage and distinctive round, golden yellow flowers in the spring and summer. Open-branching with lacy foliage and is naturally multitrunked. Flowers bloom from April to October. They are the most showy in spring but also flower again after every rain throughout the summer. Bright yellow, compact with round heads and bloom at the end of branches. Fruit is a woody legume.

CULTURE   Needs well-drained soils and does well in extremely rocky, infertile soils. It will grow in sand or clay as long as drainage is good. Very low water and fertilizer requirements.

USES   Colorful ornamental native tree.

PROBLEMS   Wind damage, root rot if overwatered, freeze damage in the northern part of the state, and destruction by browsing animals.

NOTES   Highly palatable to grazing animals and can be wiped out of its native habitat easily if the animals have access to the plants. That goes for your landscaping, too, if you live in Central Texas.

Goldenrain Tree

GOLDENRAIN TREE
Koelreuteria paniculata
cole-roo-TEH-ree-ah pan-ik-you-LAH-tah

Deciduous—Sun
Ht. 30' Spread 20'
Spacing 15'–20'

HABIT   Upright and open-branching, yellow flowers in summer, decorative pods following.
CULTURE   Will adapt to most any soil. Moderately drought tolerant. Does not like heavy fertilization.
USES   Medium-sized shade tree, dramatic summer color. Good for hot spots.
PROBLEMS   Few, if any, other than relatively short-lived.
NOTES   Ugly duckling when small but develops into a beautiful tree. Native to Asia. *K. bipinnata,* a close kin, is not as cold hardy.

HACKBERRY
Celtis laevigata
SEL-tis lie-vee-GAH-tah

Deciduous—Sun
Ht. 40'–60' Spread 40'
DO NOT PLANT

HABIT   Scruffy-looking shade tree with medium green foliage and berries in the fall. It has smooth bark when young, adding warts with age. It tends to always have some portion of the tree turning brown, dying, or falling apart.
CULTURE   Fast-growing, short-lived tree. It self-propagates easily from every seed that falls and does not need a lot of water or fertilizer.
USES   Habitat and food for wildlife.
PROBLEMS   Short-lived and prone to twig dieback, root fungal problems, leaf galls, generally untidy appearance, brittle wood, falling limbs, and so on.
NOTES   Native to the southeastern United States, including Texas.

Hackberry

HAWTHORN, DOWNY (Red Haw)
Crataegus mollis
krah-TEEG-us MAH-lis

Deciduous—Sun/Shade
Ht. 25' Spread 25'
Spacing 10'–20'

HABIT   White flowers in spring, delicate foliage, and red berries in fall. Flaky bark and usually multitrunked.
CULTURE   Easy to grow in most any soil, drought tolerant.
USES   Understory tree, specimen garden tree.
PROBLEMS   Cedar apple rust, aphids, and other insects.
NOTES   Found mostly in higher, well-drained rocky soils. Native to Texas and Oklahoma. Texas Hawthorn (*C. texana*) is quite similar. Parsley hawthorn has foliage that looks like parsley. There are several native hawthorns, and they crossbreed freely.

Parsley Hawthorn

Downy Hawthorn

Texas Hawthorn

Washington Hawthorn

Deciduous Yaupon Holly

Hickory

HAWTHORN, WASHINGTON
Crataegus phaenopyrum
krah-TEEG-us fa-no-PIE-rum

Deciduous—Sun/Part Shade
Ht. 25' Spread 15'
Spacing 10'–15'

HABIT   Upright, densely branching, thorns, red berries in winter, yellow fall color. Clusters of white flowers in spring, blooming later than most spring-flowering trees.

CULTURE   Easy to grow. Not susceptible to rust as the natives tend to be.

USES   Specimen garden tree.

PROBLEMS   Some folks don't like the thorns—they don't bother me.

NOTES   Excellent introduced ornamental tree, showier than most of the natives. Should be used more in this area. Native to eastern and northeastern United States.

HICKORY
Carya spp.
CARE-ee-ah

Deciduous—Sun
Ht. 50'–140' Spread 30'–50'
Spacing 20'–30'

HABIT   About eight species in Texas, hard to tell apart. They have very similar characteristics and hybridize freely between species. Foliage looks similar to that of pecan, but the leaflets are bigger.

CULTURE   Generally like moist, acid soils of East Texas. *C. glabra*, pignut hickory, likes well-drained ridges. *C. texana*, black hickory, likes dry, granite-rock hillsides. *C. ovata*, shagbark hickory, has the sweetest nuts.

USES   Shade tree, edible nuts.

PROBLEMS   Won't grow in alkaline soils.

NOTES   Hickan is a grafted cross between pecan rootstock and hickory top.

HOLLY, DECIDUOUS YAUPON
(Possumhaw)
Ilex decidua
EYE-lex dee-SID-you-uh

Deciduous—Sun/Shade
Ht. 20' Spread 15'
Spacing 12'–15'

HABIT   Bushy growth if not trimmed, small leaves, red berries on bare branches all winter long—on female plants only. Male plants don't have berries but grow larger.

CULTURE   Easy, any soil, drought tolerant.

USES   Winter color, understory tree, specimen garden tree.

PROBLEMS   Suckers from base, buying male plants accidentally.

NOTES   Best to purchase when the berries can be seen on the plant. Native to southeastern United States to Texas.

Foster Holly

Savannah Holly

HOLLY, EAST PALATKA
Ilex × attenuata 'East Palatka'
EYE-lex ah-ten-you-AH-tah

Evergreen—Sun/Part Shade
Ht. 15'–30' Spread 10'–15'
Spacing 8'–10'

HABIT Small white flowers in spring, red berries in fall and winter. Large bush or small tree with upright, moderate growth, rather open-branching. Smooth, light bark.
CULTURE Grows in any soil except solid rock, needs good drainage.
USES Specimen ornamental, evergreen border, small garden tree.
PROBLEMS Scale, mealybugs, iron deficiency, although none are serious.
NOTES Distinguished by one spine on end of leaf rather than several, as with 'Savannah' and 'Foster.' All are hybrids of *I. opaca,* American holly.

HOLLY, FOSTER
Ilex × attenuata 'Foster'
EYE-lex ah-ten-you-AH-tah

Evergreen—Sun/Shade
Ht. 20' Spread 10'
Spacing 3'–10'

HABIT Small white flowers in spring, many small red berries in fall and winter. Small, spiny dark green leaves, upright pyramidal growth. Fairly slow grower.
CULTURE Relatively easy to grow in any well-drained soil, prefers slightly acid soil but adapts well to alkaline clays.
USES Specimen evergreen tree, border or background plant. Berry color in winter.
PROBLEMS Leaf miners occasionally.
NOTES Excellent plant for dark green color. Cultivated.

HOLLY, SAVANNAH
Ilex opaca × attenuata 'Savannah'
EYE-lex o-PAY-kuh

Evergreen—Sun/Shade
Ht. 15'–30' Spread 10'–15'
Spacing 8'–12'

HABIT Small white flowers in spring, lots of red berries in fall and winter. Moderate upright, pyramidal growth, with medium green, spiny leaves.
CULTURE Easy to grow in any well-drained soil.
USES Small specimen garden tree, border, or evergreen background.
PROBLEMS Few. Leaf miners occasionally.
NOTES Good small evergreen cultivar.

East Palatka Holly

East Palatka Holly

Yaupon Holly

Weeping Yaupon

Honey Locust

Huisache

HOLLY, YAUPON

Ilex vomitoria
EYE-lex vom-ee-TORE-ee-uh

Evergreen—Sun/Shade
Ht. 20' Spread 20'
Spacing 10'–15'

HABIT   Bushy unless trimmed into tree form. Light-colored bark, interesting branching. Red berries in fall and winter on female plants.

CULTURE   Easy in all soils. Drought tolerant but grows much faster when irrigated regularly. Can stand fairly wet soil.

USES   Ornamental understory or specimen tree. Good for courtyards and small garden spaces.

PROBLEMS   Occasional leaf miners in summer—nothing serious.

NOTES   Native to Central Texas—not North Texas. Weeping yaupon is the same in every way except for the weeping branch structure.

HONEY LOCUST

Gleditsia triacanthos
glah-DIT-see-ah try-ah-CAN-thos

Deciduous—Sun
Ht. 50' Spread 30'
DO NOT PLANT

HABIT   Narrow, upright, open, with lacy foliage, yellow fall color. The native plants have huge thorns on the limbs with clusters on the trunk. Also has large dark brown beans in fall and winter.

CULTURE   Any soil, drought tolerant, tough—in fact, hard to get rid of.

USES   Shade tree.

PROBLEMS   Thorns, borers, dieback.

NOTES   If nice specimens exist on your property, try to use them, but I don't recommend planting new ones. Native from eastern United States to Texas. The thornless hybrids do not seem healthy either.

HUISACHE (Sweet Acacia)

Acacia farnesiana
ah-KAY-shuh far-nes-ee-AN-ah

Semi-evergreen to deciduous
Ht. 20'–30' Spread 15'–20'
Spacing 15'–20'

HABIT   Small, spreading tree with a rounded or flattened crown. It is armed with 1"–3" spines at the base of each leaf. Leaves are compound and feathery-looking, with tiny leaflets and yellow fall color. Spring flowers are round, yellow, and fragrant.

CULTURE   Fast-growing pioneer-type plant. Grows easily in lousy soils and needs almost no care. Likes sandy or silty soil but can also take well-drained clays.

USES   Good tree for xeriscape (or desert) landscaping.

PROBLEMS   Freeze damage in the northern half of the state, poorly drained soil.

NOTES   Sometimes confused with mesquite, but its wood is not good to use for barbecue because of the unpleasant flavor it can give food. It is adapted as far north as Austin and seems to be quite comfortable in landscape gardens.

JUJUBE   See Chapter 7 (Fruits, Nuts, and Vegetables)

Katsura

Kidneywood

Linden, Carolina Basswood

Little-Leaf Linden

Little-Leaf Linden

KATSURA (Japanese Katsura)
Cercidiphyllum japonicum
ker-ki-dee-FILE-um jah-PON-ih-cum

Deciduous—Morning Sun
Afternoon Shade
Ht. 30'–40' Spread 20'
Spacing 10'–15'

HABIT Inconspicuous, slow-growing flowers. Delicate branching and leaf pattern. Lovely blue-green foliage shows tints of red through the growing season. Red or yellow fall color. Slow-growing with nearly round 2"–3" leaves spaced in pairs along arching branches.
CULTURE Plant in deep, healthy soil in filtered light or in morning sun with afternoon shade.
USES Understory ornamental tree.
PROBLEMS Leaves will burn in hot afternoon sun.
NOTES Worth a try. 'Pendula' is a weeping form. Does well in wet soil. I designed one into the black clay soils of Collin County Community College in 1987, and it is still beautiful today.

KIDNEYWOOD (Texas Kidneywood)
Eysenhardtia texana
eye-zen-HAR-dee-ah tex-AN-ah

Deciduous—Sun
Ht. 8'–15' Spread 6'–8'
Spacing 6'–8'

HABIT Wonderfully fragrant white 3"–4" flower spikes; blooms from April to November after rains. Shrubby, multistemmed tree with fine-textured foliage and open growth. Leaves have a citrus smell when crushed.
CULTURE Drought tolerant, but grows better with adequate moisture.
USES Attracts bees and butterflies.
PROBLEMS Freezes in harsh winters in the northern half of the state.
NOTES Beautiful little tree, should be used more.

LINDEN (Basswood)
Tilia spp.
TILL-ee-ah

Deciduous—Sun/Part Shade
Ht. 30'–50' Spread 20'–30'
Spacing 20'

HABIT Small, fragrant off-white flowers in drooping clusters attached to a leaflike bract, heart-shaped leaves. Fruit is a winged hard capsule with one or two seeds. Straight trunk, symmetrical growth, very neat appearance. Moderate growth rate.
CULTURE Grows much taller in deep, moist soils.
USES Shade tree, fragrant flowers, lumber. The flowers make excellent honey.
PROBLEMS Aphids sometimes.
NOTES *T. caroliniana,* Carolina basswood, is native to Central and East Texas. It grows to 90' in deep, rich soils and flowers from April to June. *T. cordata,* little-leaf linden, is adapted for all of Texas. Its leaves are silvery on the underside, and it flowers in summer. Dense symmetrical growth.

59

Madrone

MADRONE (Texas Madrone)   Evergreen—Sun/Light Shade
Arbutus texana   Ht. 20'–30' Spread 20'–30'
ar-BYOO-tus tex-AN-ah   Spacing 15'–25'

HABIT   White to pale pink flowers in spring. Raspberry-like fruit clusters in fall. Spring-blooming ornamental, usually multitrunked, with thin, flaky bark and leathery dark green leaves. Slow growth.

CULTURE   Any well-drained soil.

USES   Ornamental tree. Can be used anywhere in Texas if drainage is good.

PROBLEMS   Wet feet, root fungi, and other problems related to poor drainage. Hard to transplant.

NOTES   Beautiful tree that should be used more. Much more cold hardy than sometimes reported. Although probably not politically correct, it is also called Naked Lady because of the beautiful bark.

'Little Gem' Magnolia

Southern Magnolia

MAGNOLIA
Magnolia grandiflora
mag-NOLE-ee-uh gran-dee-FLORE-uh

Evergreen—Sun
Ht. 60' Spread 30'
Spacing 30'–50'

HABIT   Large white flowers bloom a few at a time in summer. Conelike fruits full of bright red seeds open in fall. Straight central stem, foliage to ground unless trimmed up. Fibrous, shallow root system.

CULTURE   Relatively easy, although they like sandy acid soils best. Do not even try in solid rock areas. Will grow to 100' in deep sandy soils. Needs lots of room.

USES   Specimen tree for large area.

PROBLEMS   Chlorosis. Difficult to grow anything beneath this plant. Messy—almost continuous leaf drop.

NOTES   Native from southeastern United States to East Texas. Saucer magnolia (*M. soulangiana*), or tulip magnolia, is deciduous, with pink flowers in spring, and grows to 20'. Star magnolia (*M. stellata*) has white flowers, is deciduous, and grows to 12'. Both do better with some shade. Many cultivars exist. Excellent small-leafed variety is *M. grandiflora* 'Little Gem'. It is not a dwarf plant. *M. virginiana*, bay magnolia, is deciduous or semi-evergreen and has fragrant creamy white flowers from summer to fall. Leaves are grayish green and almost white underneath. Native to deep East Texas.

Saucer Magnolia

Bay Magnolia

Southern Magnolia

Star Magnolia

Big Tooth Maple

Big Tooth Maple

Caddo Maple

Caddo Maple

Big Tooth Maple

Caddo Maple

Chalk Maple

MAPLE, BIG TOOTH

Acer grandidentatum
A-sir gran-dee-den-TA-tum

Deciduous—Sun
Ht. 40'–50' Spread 20'–30'
Spacing 20'–30'

HABIT   Beautiful upright to spreading tree, growing to 50', with yellow to golden fall color.

CULTURE   Can be easily grown in a variety of well-drained soils from sand to clays and even white limestone rock areas. It is drought tolerant and does not need heavy fertilization.

USES   Native shade tree with great fall color.

PROBLEMS   Slow-growing when young, and the foliage can sometimes burn on the tips in extremely hot summers.

NOTES   Wonderful tree that should be planted more. It is becoming more available in the nursery trade but has been scarce in the past.

MAPLE, CADDO

Acer saccharum 'Caddo'
A-sir sah-KAR-um

Deciduous—Sun
Ht. 60' Spread 30'
Spacing 20'–30'

HABIT   Upright to spreading, yellow to golden fall color.

CULTURE   Easy to grow in most soils, drought tolerant. Grows well in rocky, alkaline soil.

USES   Shade tree, great fall color.

PROBLEMS   Few if any, other than still somewhat hard to find.

NOTES   Excellent large-growing maple tree for this area. *Acer leucoderme,* the chalk maple, is another good choice for Texas soils.

MAPLE, JAPANESE

Acer palmatum
A-sir pal-MAY-tum

Deciduous—Shade/Part Shade
Ht. 6'–20' Spread 10'–20'
Spacing 10'–15'

HABIT   Bloom effect comes from the unfolding of the colorful new growth. Beautiful spreading branches on various-sized varieties; some are tall, others dwarf, some red, others green.

Japanese 'Crimson Queen' Maple

Japanese Maple

Japanese Maple

Paperbark Maple fall color

Paperbark Maple

CULTURE   Easy to grow in any soil with normal water and fertilization. Best in light shade or morning sun with afternoon shade.

USES   Specimen garden tree, understory tree, year-round color. Smaller varieties are good in pots.

PROBLEMS   Delicate foliage will sometimes burn in the heat of summer, especially in western exposure.

NOTES   The green variety of *Acer palmatum* is the largest-growing and toughest. 'Bloodgood,' 'Burgundy Flame,' and several other cultivars have red foliage color. 'Crimson Queen Dissectum' is the dwarf lacy-leaf variety. 'Waterfall,' or 'Viridis,' is a distinctive green dissectum. 'Orangeola' is a vigorous weeping dissectum with long-lasting fall color and the greatest heat tolerance. 'Coral Bark' has bright red stems in winter. 'Beni Kawa' is a newer version. 'Emerald Queen' is my favorite dwarf form. There are hundreds of choices, even variegated forms; over 400 varieties exist worldwide. Native to Japan.

MAPLE, PAPERBARK

Acer griseum
A-sir GRIS-ee-um

Deciduous—Sun
Ht. 20'–30' Spread 15'–20'
Spacing 20'–30'

HABIT   Distinctive small tree with beautiful foliage and bark. Leaves are opposite and compound with three distinct coarse-edged leaflets that are dark green above and pale greenish white beneath. Fall color is a nice red-orange to red. Petioles are hairy and the buds in spring look like pussy willow. Bark is cinnamon brown and exfoliating. Leaf emergence is usually late in the spring.

CULTURE   Slow-growing but easy to maintain. Likes moist but well-drained soil. Is also fairly drought tolerant.

USES   Small to medium ornamental tree that makes a terrific specimen. This excellent tree is perfect for courtyards and other small areas.

PROBLEMS   Availability, but that will change with this book.

NOTES   Foliage is beautiful spring through fall and the river birch–like bark is an additional treat. I love this little tree!

Trident Maple

Red Maple

Red Maple—in trouble with cops?

Above and below: Shantung Maple

MAPLE, RED

Acer rubrum

A-sir ROO-brum

Deciduous—Sun
Ht. 60'–90' Spread 30'–40'
Spacing 20'–40'

HABIT   Rounded to upright growth. Leaves are usually green above and powdery silver white and hairy underneath. Leaf stems are reddish in the spring. Fall color is red-orange to red. Seeds are showy.

CULTURE   Grows in a wide range of soils but not highly drought tolerant. Best in moist to poorly drained locations. Responds very well to the organic program.

USES   Shade tree.

PROBLEMS   Drought conditions and white-rock soils.

NOTES   'Drummondii' maple has dramatic scarlet fruit in the spring that is larger than the seed on the species tree. Trident red maple (*A. rubrum* var. *tridens*) has distinctive three-lobed leaves and yellow fall color.

MAPLE, SHANTUNG

Acer truncatum

A-sir trun-KAH-tum

Deciduous—Sun
Ht. 30'–60' Spread 20'–40'
Spacing 20'–30'

HABIT   Attractive moderate- to fast-growing maple similar in appearance and characteristics to Caddo maple except that it is much faster growing. Leaves are smooth and glossy and exude a milky sap when torn. Smooth bark, flowers not showy. Yellow-orange to orange fall color.

CULTURE   Tolerates most soils, wet and dry weather conditions, high winds, and other environmental stresses. Does best in deep, healthy, well-drained soils.

USES   Fast-growing shade tree with good fall color.

PROBLEMS   Haven't found any so far except for one: it is very sensitive to drift of 2,4-D and other toxic herbicides.

NOTES   A relatively new introduction, but this tree appears to be a real winner. Native to an area of central China where the weather is similar to North Texas. This is a tree that Dr. Carl Whitcomb introduced me to. Currently, the largest specimens are in Oklahoma. There are also some in the Fort Worth Botanical Gardens. I think this tree will become a staple tree in Texas.

Caddo Maple left, Shantung Maples right. These trees are the same age.

Silver Maple

MAPLE, SILVER
Acer saccharinum
A-sir sah-kar-RINE-um

Deciduous—Sun
Ht. 40' Spread 20'–30'
DO NOT PLANT

HABIT   Fast-growing, weak-wooded, short-lived junk tree. Leaves green on top and silver on bottom.
CULTURE   Grows about the same in any soil.
USES   Fast-growing temporary tree, low-quality firewood.
PROBLEMS   Chlorosis, borers, cotton root rot, short-lived, weak wood.
NOTES   Trash tree—do not plant! This is a true junk tree. This, like all fast-growing trees, will live longer under an organic program. Native to eastern United States.

MAPLE, TRIDENT   See Red Maple

Mesquite

MESQUITE
Prosopis glandulosa
pruh-SO-pis glan-due-LOW-suh

Deciduous—Sun
Ht. 25' Spread 30'
Spacing 20'–40'

HABIT   Interesting branching, spreading with age. Delicate foliage, thorns, and subtle yellow flowers in spring.
CULTURE   Grows well in most soils. Drought tolerant. Existing or newly planted mesquites can be killed by overwatering.
USES   Shade tree for low-water gardens.
PROBLEMS   Borers, too much water.
NOTES   Not as hard to transplant as once thought. Nursery-grown plants are easier to keep alive. Ranchers make a big mistake cutting down the large trees. Bushy plants return from the latent buds, creating a maintenance nightmare. Native from Kansas to Mexico.

Mexican Elder

MEXICAN ELDER (Mexican Elderberry)
Sambucus mexicana
sam-BEW-cus mex-ee-KAH-nah

Mostly Evergreen—Sun
Ht. 10'–15' Spread 10'–15'
Spacing 10'–15'

HABIT   Beautiful small tree that is usually evergreen but sometimes drops its leaves during hot summers if not watered regularly. If you don't mind the partial defoliation, the tree is relatively drought tolerant. Flower clusters are white to pale yellow and bloom primarily in the early summer and in the fall. Small fruits look like clusters of dark blue or black berries.
CULTURE   Likes moist soils. Could probably be used in much more of Texas except for the most northern parts. Responds well to soil moisture even though it is a drought-tolerant tree. Few pest problems and needs little fertilizer.
USES   Small specimen tree, winter interest for its unusual form.
PROBLEMS   Few problems other than freeze damage in the northern part of the state and limbs are brittle and subject to breakage.
NOTES   Sometimes flowers in the winter. Dye from the stems can be used to color baskets. Native to warm, arid regions of the South.

Mimosa

White Mulberry

Red Mulberry

Blackjack Oak

MIMOSA

Albizia julibrissin
al-BIZ-ee-ah jul-leh-BRY-sin

Deciduous—Sun
Ht. 20' Spread 30'
DO NOT PLANT

HABIT   Spreading limber branches that droop to the ground. Lacy foliage with small leaflets that close at night. Shallow, destructive root system.
CULTURE   Needs lots of room and lots of water.
USES   Not even good for firewood.
PROBLEMS   Destructive roots, short-lived, crowds out good plants.
NOTES   Dying out from fungal disease. Pretty when in bloom but not a good tree to plant.

MULBERRY, FRUITLESS

Morus alba 'Fruitless'
MORE-us AL-bah

Deciduous—Sun
Ht. 30' Spread 40'
DO NOT PLANT

HABIT   Fast-growing junk tree. Large various-shaped leaves. Very shallow and destructive root system. Smooth bark.
CULTURE   Grows anywhere. Uses huge quantities of water.
USES   None of redeeming value.
PROBLEMS   Webworms, cotton root rot, destructive roots, ugly.
NOTES   Undesirable tree. This is the most overplanted junk tree in the United States. The fruiting varieties are messy when the birds are around, but the trees are better and the fruit is delicious—especially the white-fruited form.

MULBERRY, RED

Morus rubra
MORE-us ROO-bra

Deciduous—Sun
Ht. 30'–50' Spread 40'–50'
Spacing 20'–40'

HABIT   Large, spreading tree with big leaves, edible fruit, and yellow fall color. Flowers are inconspicuous drupes in the early spring, followed by blackberry-like fruit, which ripens and drops from the tree from May through August. Fruit is sweet, edible, and attractive to wildlife, especially birds.
CULTURE   Easy to grow in any soil that is well drained.
PROBLEMS   Mulberries can have several pest problems, even cotton root rot. The most common problem is the mess that is made from birds after they eat the ripe fruit, so be very careful where you plant these trees.
NOTES   Hybrid fruitless mulberry is a fast-growing junk tree. White mulberry (*M. alba*) from China grows leaves used to feed silkworms. Small weeping forms of mulberry are available and are effective in Oriental gardens. White fruit doesn't stain, and trees of that variety are available from www.raintreenursery.com.

OAK, BLACKJACK

Quercus marilandica
KWER-kus mar-ah-LAN-di-cah

Deciduous—Sun
Ht. 50'–60' Spread 30'–40'
Spacing 30'–40'

HABIT   Grows in the eastern half of Texas, especially in the sandy acid soils. Rounded, symmetrical tree has clublike leaves and very dark, heavily textured bark. It is stiff in overall appearance. Fall color is yellow but not a knockout.
CULTURE   Needs sandy acid soil to survive. It does not do well in the black and white soils of North Texas. It is drought tolerant and needs very little fertilization.

Blackjack Oak

Bur Oak

Canby Oak

Canby Oak

Bur Oak—young foliage in spring

USES   Shade tree.

PROBLEMS   It does not do well in alkaline clay soils.

NOTES   Rarely cultivated because it is difficult to transplant.

OAK, BUR

Deciduous—Sun
Ht. 80' Spread 80'
Spacing 20'–50'

Quercus macrocarpa
KWER-kus mack-row-CAR-puh

HABIT   Spreading branching structure, large leaves, golf-ball-size acorns, yellow fall color. Thick, corklike stems, branches, and trunk. Fast-growing oak. Can grow to 150'.

CULTURE   Easy to grow in any well-drained soil, including solid rock. Drought tolerant. Grows almost anywhere in the United States.

USES   Handsome and hardy shade tree.

PROBLEMS   Few if any. Lacebugs are sometimes a nuisance in the summer.

NOTES   Possibly my favorite shade tree. One of the longest-lived oaks. Also called mossy oak or cup oak. Native to Texas, Oklahoma, and eastern United States.

OAK, CANBY

Semi-evergreen—Sun
Ht. 50' Spread 30'–40'
Spacing 20'–30'

Quercus canbyi
KWER-kus CAN-bee-eye

HABIT   Upright red oak–like tree with a very neat appearance. It is mostly evergreen in the San Antonio Botanic Gardens.

CULTURE   Easy to grow in most any soil.

USES   Shade tree.

PROBLEMS   None serious.

NOTES   Beautiful tree that should be used much more. Chisos oak is a similar tree. Simpson's *A Field Guide to Texas Trees* explains the differences between them best by saying that the Chisos oak grows primarily west of the Pecos, the Shumard red oak grows west and north of the Balcones escarpment and the White Rock escarpment just west of Dallas, and the Canby oak grows east of that line.

Chinkapin Oak

Durand Oak

Bigelow Oak

OAK, CHINKAPIN
Quercus muhlenbergii
KWER-kus mew-lin-BERG-ee-eye

Deciduous—Sun
Ht. 80' Spread 80'
Spacing 20'–50'

HABIT   Irregularly spreading, relatively fast growth, dark purple acorns, and yellow-brown fall color.
CULTURE   Any soil, very sensitive to poor drainage, drought tolerant.
USES   Shade tree.
PROBLEMS   Wet feet and transplant difficulties.
NOTES   Easily confused with swamp chestnut oak (*Q. michauxii*), which will not grow here. Chestnut oak leaves have rounded lobes in contrast to the Chinkapin's sharp-pointed edges. Native to Texas, Oklahoma, and eastern United States.

OAK, DURAND
Quercus sinuata var. *sinuata*
KWER-kus sin-you-AH-tah

Deciduous—Sun
Ht. 60' Spread 40'
Spacing 20'–50'

HABIT   Upright, open-branching, dense rounded top, smallish leaves with rounded lobes. Handsome tree with reddish fall color.
CULTURE   Easy in any well-drained soil. Drought tolerant and doesn't mind rocky soil.
USES   Shade tree.
PROBLEMS   Few if any. Not easily available in the nursery trade at this time.
NOTES   Bigelow oak (*Q. sinuata* var. *breviloba)* is a small-growing close kin. Bigelow is native to the North Texas area. Durand is native to Waco and Central Texas.

OAK, GRACEFUL
(Evergreen oak, Chisos oak)
Quercus graciliformis
KWER-kus grace-ih-li-FORM-iss

Semi-evergreen—Sun
Ht. 20'–40' Spread 20'–25'
Spacing 15'–30'

HABIT   Attractive, shiny-leafed oak; a small- to medium-sized tree that will grow in a wide range of soils.

Chisos Oak

Langtry Oak

Lacey Oak

CULTURE Typically is seen growing above 5,000 feet but does seem to adapt to
regular garden settings in most of Texas. Needs excellent drainage.

USES Shade tree.

PROBLEMS Finding it in the nursery trade.

NOTES True evergreen but not as evergreen as the live oak. They should be
used much more in the landscape when they become available in the nursery
trade. Canby oak (*Q. canbyi*) is closely related. Langtry oak is the name given
to the trees from Benny Simpson's collection that are planted in the parking
lot of the Dallas Discovery Gardens. They are so similar to graceful oak, they
may be the same tree. They are almost completely evergreen.

OAK, LACEY

Quercus laceyi (syn. *Q. glaucoides*)
KWER-kus LACE-ee-eye

Deciduous—Sun
Ht. 25'–35' Spread 15'–20'
Spacing 15'–20'

HABIT Beautiful, small- to medium-sized tree with blue-green mature foliage,
peach-colored new growth and fall color.

CULTURE Easy to grow and adapts to many soils, from sand to heavy clays.

USES Small shade tree.

PROBLEMS It lacks availability in the trade. Not able to stand wet soil
continuously.

NOTES The leaves are quite small in comparison to other oaks. Lacey oak is a
trouble-free tree that should be used much more in the landscape. This is one
of the shin oaks, which means small oak.

Live Oak

Escarpment Live Oak in Spring

Coastal Live Oak

OAK, LIVE (Coastal Live Oak)

Quercus virginiana
KWER-kus ver-gin-ee-AN-ah

Evergreen—Sun
Ht. 50' Spread 60'
Spacing 20'–60'

HABIT   Spreading evergreen shade tree. Small glossy leaves vary in shape and size. Single and multiple trunks. Black acorns.

CULTURE   Easy to establish, hard to maintain. Any soil, drought tolerant. Needs thinning at transplant.

USES   Shade tree, evergreen background.

PROBLEMS   Aphids, ice damage, galls, oak wilt. High-maintenance tree requiring regular pruning. Continuous leaf drop, particularly messy in early spring. Declining specimens are subject to ball moss and gall infestation. Expose root balls that have been planted too deep and apply the Sick Tree Treatment.

NOTES   Can freeze during severe winters. Looks its worst in spring when new leaves are kicking off the old leaves. Native to South, Central, and West Texas and southeastern United States. *Q. fusiformis* is the drought-tolerant and cold-hardy native Escarpment Live Oak. It tends to have narrower leaves than Coastal Live Oak.

Mohr Oak

Monterrey Oak

Pin Oak

Pin Oak trying to grow in alkaline black and white soils

OAK, MOHR
Quercus mohriana
KWER-kus more-ee-AN-ah

Almost Evergreen—Sun
Ht. 15'–40' Spread 20' or greater
Spacing 12'–20'

HABIT Beautiful small or shrubby oak (shin oak) that grows to a maximum height of about 40'. The leaves are shiny gray-green on top and fuzzy white underneath.

CULTURE This drought-tolerant plant is easy to grow in a wide range of well-drained soils. It tends to sucker into groves, which can become somewhat of a problem.

USES Unique small native tree.

PROBLEMS Few, although this tree must have good drainage. It cannot stand wet feet.

NOTES Gray oak (*Q. grisea*) is a similar tree that also grows in the dry gravel soils of the West Texas mountains; its leaves are gray-green as well but hairy on both sides. One of the shin oaks.

OAK, MONTERREY
Quercus polymorpha
KWER-kus poly-MORE-fah

Deciduous to Semi-deciduous—Sun
Ht. 40'–60' Spread 30'–40'
Spacing 20'–30'

HABIT Monterrey oak is a deciduous to evergreen, medium-sized shade tree that has thick, rounded dark green leaves. It has little to no fall color.

CULTURE Easy to grow in well-drained soil with one exception—freeze damage is a possibility in the northern part of the state.

USES Unusual shade tree.

PROBLEMS It has few problems other than possible freeze damage in the far northern part of the state.

NOTES Beavers seem to love chewing on this tree—I learned that the hard way. Monterrey oak is said to be a trademarked name owned by Lone Star Growers of San Antonio. Evergreen in the southern tip of Texas and in Mexico.

OAK, PIN (Swamp Oak)
Quercus palustris
KWER-kus pah-LUS-trus

Deciduous—Sun
Ht. 50' to over 100' Spread 40'–50'
Spacing 30'–40'

HABIT Pyramidal shaped, especially when young, spreading with age. It has red oak–type leaves and usually a weeping nature, especially on the lower limbs. It has a stiff overall appearance.

CULTURE Will not grow well in the alkaline, calcareous soils of North and Central Texas.

USES Shade tree for sandy soil areas of the state.

PROBLEMS Pin oak develops chlorosis quickly in alkaline soils. This trace-mineral deficiency leads to attack by other insects and diseases.

NOTES Oaks are quite promiscuous and crossbreed readily, and pin oaks crossing with Texas red oak or Shumard red oak (*Q. shumardii*) continues to be a major problem in Texas. Red oaks that have much pin oak "blood" will not grow in the black and white soils of North Texas.

Post Oak

Red Oak

Red Oak

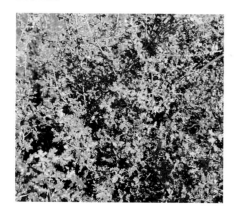

Sandpaper Oak

OAK, POST

Quercus stellata
KWER-kus steh-LAH-tah

Deciduous—Sun
Ht. 30'–80' Spread 20'–30'
Spacing 20'–40'

HABIT   Grows in sandy loam soils that range from neutral to acid, but it can also grow in acidic or neutral clay soils. It does not grow in the black and white alkaline or calcareous soils. Rounded tree with stout, interestingly branched limbs, gnarly growth, and round-lobed leaves. Fall color is less than spectacular—yellow to brown.

CULTURE   Slow-growing native oak that hates human activities. Very difficult to transplant, needs extremely well-drained soil and neutral to acid soil conditioning. Compaction, construction, and application of herbicides and synthetic fertilizers have killed many thousands of post oaks and other native oaks in Texas.

USES   Shade tree.

PROBLEMS   Post oak suffers from wet feet, human impact, and secondary attack by insect pests and diseases. Heat stress brought on an epidemic of hypoxolyn canker that killed thousands of trees in 2001 and 2002.

NOTES   The most common native oak in North Texas. Many thousands of these trees die every year from damage during construction of new developments because contractors scrape away the topsoil and the native understory, compact the soil, and change the environment of the feeder roots.

OAK, RED (Shumard Red Oak)

Quercus shumardii or *texana*
KWER-kus shoe-MAR-dee-eye, tex-AN-ah

Deciduous—Sun
Ht. 80' Spread 80'
Spacing 20'–50'

HABIT   Graceful, upright, and spreading, typically no central stem. Fall color varies from brown to yellow to red. Fast-growing oak.

CULTURE   Hard to establish, must have excellent drainage, any soil, drought tolerant.

USES   Shade tree, fall color.

PROBLEMS   Borers, scale, wet feet, oak wilt.

NOTES   Red oak has always been one of my favorite trees, but it is the subject of a multimillion-dollar tree problem. The problem is buying the right plant. Only two kinds will work in alkaline soils, Texas red oak (*Q. texana*) and Shumard oak (*Q. shumardii*). Pin oak (*Q. palustris*) and crossbreeds of southern red oak (*Q. falcata*) and others are being sold in great quantities and will not survive here.

OAK, SANDPAPER

Quercus pungens var. *pungens*
KWER-kus PUN-gens

Deciduous—Sun
Ht. 15'–20' Spread 10'–15'
Spacing 10'–15'

HABIT   Small tree similar in appearance to the Vasey oak. Gray-green sandpapery leaves that are slightly larger than those of Vasey oak.

CULTURE   Drought-tolerant, easy-to-grow tree that needs little fertilizer.

USES   Small, interesting native tree.

PROBLEMS   Hard to find in the nursery industry.

NOTES   The name comes from the sandpaper-like feel of its leaves. Sandpaper oak closely resembles Vasey oak (*Q. pungens* var. *vaseyana*).

Sawtooth Oak shown struggling in the black and white alkaline soils

Shin Oak

OAK, SAWTOOTH
Quercus acutissima
KWER-kus ah-cue-TISS-eh-mah

Deciduous—Sun
Ht. 50' Spread 40'
Spacing 20'–40'

HABIT   Fast-growing oak, yellow-brown fall color. Golden brown leaves stay on tree all winter. Long, narrow, serrated leaves.
CULTURE   Will not grow in white rock. Doesn't like high-pH soils.
USES   Shade tree.
PROBLEMS   Some chlorosis in highly alkaline areas. Wet feet.
NOTES   Excellent fast-growing shade tree in deep-soil areas. Not a good choice for the black and white soils of North Texas. Native to Asia.

OAK, SHIN—
Generic name for all the small-scale oaks like Lacey, Vasey, Mohr, and sandpaper.

OAK, SHUMARD RED   See Red Oak

Vasey Oak

Southern Red Oak

OAK, SOUTHERN RED
Quercus falcata
KWER-kus fal-KAY-tah

Deciduous—Sun
Ht. 60' to over 100' Spread 50'–60'
Spacing 30'–50'

HABIT   Large-growing, graceful tree with an open top, droopy leaves, and
unimpressive yellow fall color most years. Leaves vary from 4" to 10" in
length, are variable in shape and lobe, and tend to have a wilted look. Moderately fast-growing.

CULTURE   Needs sandy acid soil and moderate moisture. Has few pest problems.

USES   Shade tree.

PROBLEMS   It is relatively pest-free in sandy acid soils. It will not grow in
alkaline soils.

NOTES   Nurseries and homeowners tend to confuse this tree with Shumard red
oak. The photo with Logan shows the tree's ability to adapt to unusual
conditions.

OAK, VASEY
Quercus pungens var. *vaseyana*
KWER-kus PUN-gens, vase-ee-ANN-ah

Deciduous to Evergreen—Sun
Ht. 20'–40' Spread 20'–30'
Spacing 15'–20'

HABIT   Small, compact, native tree with small, gently lobed, wavy-edged leaves
with short tips on the edges. It is almost evergreen and has the smallest leaves
of all the shin oaks. It looks like a small live oak but has a lighter-colored,
almost silvery bark.

CULTURE   Easy-to-grow tree that needs minimum amounts of fertilizer and
water. It can grow in alkaline soils but adapts to deeper, sandier, more acid
soils as well.

USES   Small, interesting native shade tree.

PROBLEMS   The main problem with Vasey oak is finding specimens in the
nursery industry.

NOTES   This excellent small tree should be used for landscaping considerably
more than it currently is. Native to far West Texas.

Water Oak

White Oak

Willow Oak

OAK, WATER

Quercus nigra
KWER-kus NI-gra

Deciduous to Semi-evergreen—Sun
Ht. 50'–80' Spread 30'–50'
Spacing 20'–50'

HABIT Large-growing and wide-spreading shade tree. The leaves are spoon-shaped, persistent, and sometimes evergreen. Some trees will be completely deciduous and others almost totally evergreen. Weak fall color varies from yellow to brown.

CULTURE Likes moist, neutral-to-acid soils and can even be grown in water-logged, oxygen-deficient soils where other trees would have a great problem.

USES Shade tree.

PROBLEMS This tree needs plenty of moisture and neutral-to-acid soils. It will not grow well in the alkaline black and white soils of North and Central Texas.

NOTES Laurel oak (*Q. laurifolia*) is similar in appearance and adaptability and is often found growing near water oak.

OAK, WHITE

Quercus alba
KWER-kus ALL-ba

Deciduous—Sun
Ht. 80' to over 100' Spread 50'–60'
Spacing 30'–50'

HABIT Large gorgeous tree with beautiful summer foliage and excellent red fall color. White oak has my favorite tree foliage. Leaves are deeply cut and rounded on the edges. Summer foliage color is deep green to slightly blue-green. Fall color will range from wine red to orange red.

CULTURE White oak is easy to grow in neutral-to-acid soils. Likes sandy soils best. It is fairly drought tolerant and requires little fertilizer.

USES Shade tree.

PROBLEMS Unfortunately, this tree will not grow adequately in the black and white soils of North and Central Texas. It must have deep, neutral-to-acid sandy loam.

NOTES White oak is without doubt one of our state's most beautiful trees.

OAK, WILLOW

Quercus phellos
KWER-kus FELL-oss

Deciduous—Sun
Ht. 80'–100' Spread 40'–60'
Spacing 30'–50'

HABIT Often seen along stream bottoms and frequently flooded drainage ways. Pyramidal when young but spreads into a rounded crown with age. Narrow, delicate leaves. Yellow fall color.

CULTURE Needs the moist, acid, sandy soils of East Texas and other parts of the state. Can grow in clays and loams, but will not grow in alkaline soils, especially where white limestone is present. Requires plenty of moisture but minimal fertilization.

USES Shade tree.

PROBLEMS Nutrient deficiency and chlorosis can result when it is planted in the improper soil.

NOTES Its acorns are a favorite of several forms of wildlife. Willow oak is easily confused with its close relatives laurel oak and water oak.

Russian Olive

Olive

Wild Olive at the Alamo

OLIVE, RUSSIAN

Elaeagnus angustifolia
eel-ee-AG-nus an-gus-ti-FOAL-ee-ah

Deciduous—Sun
Ht. 30' Spread 20'
Spacing 15'–20'

HABIT   Silvery gray foliage, bushy unless trimmed. Relatively short-lived.
CULTURE   Easy to grow in any well-drained soil, drought tolerant. Moderate fertilizer needs.
USES   Shade tree, gray color.
PROBLEMS   Too much water is the only serious problem. The related stress brings on several insect pests and diseases.
NOTES   Likes the arid parts of the state best. Native to Europe and Asia.

OLIVE, WILD

Cordia boissieri
KOR-dee-ah bois-see-ERR-ee

Evergreen—Sun
Ht. 15'–25' Spread 10'–15'
Spacing 10'–15'

HABIT   Grows in the far southern tip of Texas in the counties along the Rio Grande. Adaptable as far north as San Antonio but will freeze to the ground there in harsh winters. A rounded evergreen tree with dramatic, hibiscus-like white flowers and velvety leaves.
CULTURE   Needs a lot of water to get established but is drought tolerant once established.
USES   Small, dramatic specimen tree.
PROBLEMS   Freeze damage can occur anywhere north of San Antonio.
NOTES   Fruit is reported to be sweet, pulpy, and edible, although warnings exist that it can cause dizziness when eaten in excess. This is the beautiful tree just to the left of the front door of the Alamo in San Antonio.

Orchid Tree

Texas Palm

Needle Palm

ORANGE, TRIFOLIATE
(Hardy Orange)
Poncirus trifoliata
pon-SI-rus tri-fo-lee-AH-ta

Deciduous—Sun/Part Shade
Ht. 15' Spread 15'
Spacing 10'–15'

HABIT   Fragrant spring flowers. Hard, bitter, inedible yellow-orange fruit.
CULTURE   Easy to grow just about anywhere.
USES   Impenetrable hedge, rootstock for other citrus trees.
PROBLEMS   Ugly and thorny.
NOTES   A false orange with nasty thorns. Makes a great barrier plant. Provides the rootstock of most citrus production in Texas.

ORCHID TREE
Bauhinia congesta (syn. *B. lunarioides*)
baw-HIN-ee-ah kun-JESS-tah

Deciduous—Sun/Part Shade
Ht. 6'–10' Spread 6'–10'
Spacing 10'–12'

HABIT   Southern part of the state. Can stand temperatures down to 10°F and does well in the Austin, Houston, and San Antonio climates. Marginal in the Dallas/Fort Worth area. Usually multitrunked and deciduous. Beautiful light green leaves divided at the base into two leaflets. Showy flowers in the spring and yellow fall color.
CULTURE   Will grow in a wide range of well-drained soils, from clay and rocky soils to sandy loams, if protected from harsh winter temperatures. Seems to like limestone conditions. Drought tolerant and needs little fertilizer or pest control.
USES   Best used as an understory tree.
PROBLEMS   Freeze damage is possible in the northern half of the state.
NOTES   Orchid tree is a terrific specimen tree. Even if you live in the northern part of the state, try it in pots and move it to a protected area in the winter.

PALM, TEXAS (Sabal Palm)
Sabal mexicana (syn. *S. texana*)
SAY-ball mex-ee-KAH-nah

Evergreen—Sun/Part Shade
Ht. 20'–50' Spread 5'–8'
Spacing 8'–10'

HABIT   Native to the southern tip of Texas but will adapt to landscape sites as far north as the Dallas/Fort Worth area. Small palm tree with a single trunk and large, fan-shaped leaves forming a rounded crown. For eight to ten years, the tree grows into a large clump before the trunk starts to appear at the base. Slow-growing.
CULTURE   Easy to grow in a wide range of soils and fairly drought tolerant. Has an enormous root system, which makes it rather hard to transplant after the plant is large.
USES   Evergreen specimen tree.
PROBLEMS   Freeze damage occurs in the far northern part of the state.
NOTES   Texas palm is the only tree-sized palm native to Texas. *Sabal minor* is the Texas fan palm, or palmetto. It only grows 4'–6'. Other palms that grow well in most of Texas include Mexican Fan Palm, *Washingtonia robusta*, and Needle Palm, *Rhapidophyllum hystrix.*

Sabal Minor

Parasol Tree

Parkinsonia

Flowering Peach

PARASOL TREE (Chinese Varnish Tree)
Firmiana simplex
fir-me-ANE-ah SIM-plex

Deciduous—Sun
Ht. 30'–50' Spread 50'
Spacing 20'–50'

HABIT   Fast-growing and upright, with smooth green bark when young, huge leaves, thick stems.
CULTURE   Very easy to grow in any soil. Relatively drought tolerant. Average water and fertilizer needs.
USES   Shade tree, conversation piece.
PROBLEMS   Coarse-looking, weak wood.
NOTES   Native to China and Japan.

PARKINSONIA (Jerusalem Thorn)
Parkinsonia aculeata
Par-kin-SOH-nee-ah ak-you-lee-AH-tah

Deciduous—Sun
Ht. 12'–30' Spread 15'–20'
Spacing 12'–15'

HABIT   Fragrant yellow flower clusters from spring to fall. On older blooms, one petal turns orange. Light, lacy foliage, green trunk and limbs.
CULTURE   Grows in any soil. Drought tolerant but tolerates moist soil.
USES   Flowering summer tree.
PROBLEMS   Freeze damage is possible in the northern part of the state.
NOTES   Also called Retama. *P. texana*, paloverde, is more drought tolerant and has a smoother, greener bark. Native to the Rio Grande Valley.

PEACH, FLOWERING
Prunus persica
PROO-nus PURR-si-cah

Deciduous—Sun
Ht. 15' Spread 15'
Spacing 10'–15'

HABIT   Spreading ornamental tree, early spring flowers of all colors.
CULTURE   Relatively easy to grow in most soils. Relatively drought tolerant.
USES   Ornamental spring-flowering tree.
PROBLEMS   Borers, leaf rollers, crown gall.
NOTES   Flowers occur on second year's growth, so prune carefully. Cultivated.

PEAR, BRADFORD (Ornamental Pear)
Pyrus calleryana 'Bradford'
PIE-rus cah-ler-ee-AH-nah

Deciduous—Sun
Ht. 25'–30' Spread 25'
Spacing 10'–20'

HABIT   White flowers in early spring, red fall color. Upright, very symmetrical, with stiff, candelabra-like branching. Short-lived.
CULTURE   Easy to grow in most well-drained soils with normal water and fertilization.
USES   Specimen ornamental tree, spring flower color.
PROBLEMS   Overused, very weak branching structure, short-lived. Highly susceptible to soil-borne fungi and is a favorite hangout for grackles.
NOTES   'Aristocrat' is an excellent cultivar that has a more open branching structure and long drooping leaves. It is much more graceful than 'Bradford.' 'Capital' is a good narrow-growing cultivar. 'Whitehouse' has not had good reviews.

PEAR, CALLERY
Pyrus calleryana
PIE-rus cal-er-ee-AH-nah

Deciduous—Sun
Ht. 25'–30' Spread 25'
Spacing 15'–20'

HABIT   Pure white flower clusters in early spring, followed by small, hard, round inedible fruit. More open than 'Bradford,' limbs almost perpendicular to trunk. Red fall color.
CULTURE   Easy to grow in any soil. Needs average maintenance and water.
USES   Specimen ornamental tree.
PROBLEMS   Fire blight possible but rare. Some think the thorns are a problem— I don't.
NOTES   This is the mother plant of the 'Bradford' pear and other ornamental pears. I like this plant better because it is more treelike and graceful.

Aristocrat Pear

Bradford Pear

Callery Pear

Pecan

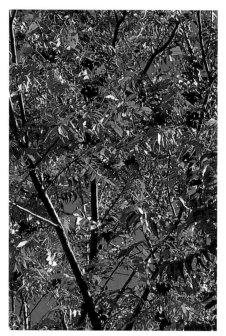

Pecan

PECAN

Deciduous—Sun
Ht. 100' Spread 100'
Spacing 30'–50'

Carya illinoinensis
CARE-ee-uh ill-e-noy-NEN-sis

HABIT Irregularly spreading, extremely graceful, yellow fall color, very long-lived. Deeply rooted.
CULTURE Easy to grow in most soils. Grows pretty much anywhere in Texas.
USES Shade tree, pecan crop.
PROBLEMS Worst is webworms, which are mainly an aesthetic problem. Somewhat messy most of the time.
NOTES Great choice for State Tree. The native varieties make better landscape trees than those grown for pecan crops. Native to the eastern half of Texas.

PERSIMMON, COMMON

Deciduous—Sun
Ht. 60' Spread 30'
Spacing 20'–40'

Diospyros virginiana
dye-OS-pear-us ver-gin-ee-AN-ah

HABIT Yellow fall color; dark, deeply fissured bark. Shiny foliage that gracefully droops. 1" orange fruit matures after first frost. Fruit is tasty unless you eat it before it is ripe.
CULTURE Easy to grow in any well-drained soil. Drought tolerant.
USES Shade tree.
PROBLEMS Webworms, messy fruit.
NOTES This tree's few problems don't keep it from being an excellent shade tree. Japanese varieties are smaller plants but have large fruit the size of apples. Wooden golf clubs are made from persimmon. Native to Texas and the eastern United States.

PERSIMMON, TEXAS

Deciduous—Sun/Shade
Ht. 20'–40' Spread 15'–20'
Spacing 12'–15'

Diospyros texana
dye-OS-pear-us tex-AN-ah

HABIT Trunks and branches resemble crape myrtle. Small leaves, insignificant fall color. Slow-growing. Small leathery leaves. 1" fruit turns black in fall.
CULTURE Easy to grow in any well-drained soil. Drought tolerant. Can grow easily in rocky areas.
USES Ornamental garden tree, decorative bark.
PROBLEMS Few if any. Hard to find in nurseries.
NOTES Native to South and Central Texas.

Above: Common Persimmon;
right: Texas Persimmon

Austrian Pine

Eldarica Pine

Old Italian Stone Pine

Young Italian Stone Pine

PINE, AUSTRIAN
Pinus nigra
PIE-nus NI-gra

Evergreen—Sun
Ht. 30' Spread 30'
Spacing 15'–30'

HABIT   Slow-growing. Has thick foliage to ground.
CULTURE   Easy, any soil except solid rock.
USES   Ornamental evergreen tree, background, evergreen screen.
PROBLEMS   Chlorosis occasionally.
NOTES   This tree is probably the best pine choice for the heavy clay soil areas of the state. Native to Europe and Asia.

PINE, ELDARICA
(Mondell Pine, Afghan Pine)
Pinus eldarica
PIE-nus ell-DAR-eh-kah

Evergreen—Sun
Ht. 40' Spread 20'
Spacing 12'–20'

HABIT   Upright, medium green needles, foliage to the ground.
CULTURE   Any soil, drought tolerant.
USES   Shade tree for the drier parts of the state.
PROBLEMS   Pine tip moth and root fungal problems.
NOTES   Grows well in the alkaline clay soils. Does very well in the drier parts of the state. Has one fatal flaw—the roots will develop diseases in heavy irrigation or high-rainfall areas. It is a desert tree and cannot stand wet feet.

PINE, ITALIAN STONE
Pinus pinea
PIE-nus PEA-nee-ah

Evergreen—Sun
Ht. 40'–60' Spread 15'–20'
Spacing 15'–30'

HABIT   Bushy, soft, medium green foliage, rounded form when young, umbrella-shaped with age. Two needles per bunch. Large-growing with age.
CULTURE   Will grow in most areas of Texas. Cold tolerant; heat and drought tolerant once established. One of the few pines that will grow well in the black and white soils.
USES   Specimen evergreen tree.
PROBLEMS   Few—should be planted more often.
NOTES   Dramatically formed pine that will grow well in a wide range of soils and climates. Should be used a lot more often. Native to Southern Europe and Turkey.

Japanese Black Pine

PINE, JAPANESE BLACK
Pinus thunbergii
PIE-nus thun-BERG-ee-eye

Evergreen—Sun
Ht. 30' Spread 20'
Spacing 15'–20'

HABIT   Irregular form, foliage to ground. Central stem is not well defined.
CULTURE   Any soil but solid rock, likes slightly acid soil best.
USES   Evergreen ornamental, background, Oriental gardens.
PROBLEMS   Chlorosis is a major problem. This tree has really gone downhill in the last decade. That's one of the pitfalls of using introduced plants.
NOTES   Not quite as good as Austrian and cross pine. Native to Japan.

PINE, LOBLOLLY
Pinus taeda
PIE-nus TIE-dah

Evergreen—Sun
Ht. 80'–100' Spread 20'–30'
Spacing 20'–30'

HABIT   Most numerous pine in Texas. Found throughout the Piney Woods and the far eastern side of the state. Grows in low areas primarily but adapts to more well-drained sites quite well. Fastest-growing of all the southern pines. Needles are almost always in groups of three, are 5"–9" long, and are light to medium green.
CULTURE   Fast-growing. Easy to grow in acid, sandy soils. Does not do well at all in alkaline soils, especially white rock. Responds to fertilizer, although overfertilization and use of pesticides is the cause of the typical pine tree pest problems.
USES   Specimen or shade tree.
PROBLEMS   Fusarium gall rust. Southern pine beetle. Ice-storm damage.
NOTES   Loblolly means "mud holes" and refers to its ability to grow in wetter soils. Slash pine (*P. elliottii*) is a native of the southeastern states and is also often planted commercially in Texas. It closely resembles loblolly pine but differs by having glossy brown cones on short stalks. Shortleaf pine or yellow pine is *P. echinata;* longleaf pine is *P. palustris.* Aleppo pine (*P. halepensis*) is one of the most commonly used pines in the Houston area. It will have some freeze damage problems in the northern parts of the state.

Loblolly Pine

PISTACHE, TEXAS
Pistacia texana
pis-TA-see-ah tex-AN-ah

Semi-evergreen to Evergreen
Sun/Part Shade
Ht. 10'–40' Spread 10'–15'
Spacing 15'–20'

HABIT   Canyons and cliffs near the junction of the Rio Grande and the Pecos River in West Texas. Grows in streambeds and likes rocky limestone soils. Texas pistache is a small, bushy evergreen tree that has small leaflets and is often a multitrunked plant. Clusters of white flowers in the spring before the new leaves emerge. Fruit is an inedible, nutlike drupe. New leaves are reddish, later turning dark green and glossy. Foliage is evergreen.
CULTURE   Easy to grow in well-drained soil, drought tolerant, and needs a minimum amount of fertilizer. It needs protection in the winter in the northern part of the state.
USES   Small tree with interesting foliage texture.
PROBLEMS   Will freeze in the northern part of the state in severe winters and does not like heavily irrigated or high-rainfall areas.
NOTES   Native to South Texas.

Texas Pistache

Mexican Plum

Chinese Pistachio

PISTACHIO, CHINESE
(Chinese Pistache)
Pistacia chinensis
pis-TA-see-ah chi-NEN-sis

Deciduous—Sun
Ht. 50'–70' Spread 50'
Spacing 20'–50'

HABIT   Inconspicuous flowers in spring. Clusters of red berries on female trees in late summer. Fast-growing shade tree with open structure and yellow, red, and orange fall color—sometimes all at once. Compound leaves with 10–16 paired leaflets. Light, smooth bark when young. Branching structure is poor when young but quickly fills out.

CULTURE   Easy to grow in any well-drained soil, drought tolerant.

USES   Shade tree, fall color.

PROBLEMS   Tip growth sometimes burns in early summer from too much water.

NOTES   Incorrectly called Chinese pistache. One of the best fast-growing trees. Native to China but acts like a native Texan. The pistachio that produces the delicious nut is *P. vera,* a desert plant that can't take much water at all.

Mexican Plum

PLUM, MEXICAN
Prunus mexicana
PROO-nus mex-ee-KAH-nah

Deciduous—Sun/Shade
Ht. 25' Spread 25'
Spacing 12'–20'

HABIT   Showy white flowers in spring and orange fall color. Exfoliating bark and graceful branching structure. Small edible plums. Has thorns but the coverage is moderate.

CULTURE   Easy to grow in most any soil. Drought tolerant and can do well in sun or as an understory plant.

USES   Specimen garden tree, understory tree, spring and fall color.

PROBLEMS   Insects chew on the leaves occasionally, but no major problems.

NOTES   Wonderful tree, being used more and more. Smaller-growing hog plum (*P. rivularis*) is less desirable. Native from Oklahoma to Mexico.

Purple Plum

Lombardy Poplar

PLUM, PURPLE
Prunus cerasifera
PROO-nus ser-as-SIFF-eh-ruh

Deciduous—Sun/Shade
Ht. 20' Spread 15'
Spacing 12'–15'

HABIT   Small ornamental tree with bronze or purple foliage after pink spring flowers.
CULTURE   Does okay in any soil, moderate maintenance. Needs good drainage, as most trees do.
USES   Ornamental garden tree, summer color.
PROBLEMS   Borers, freeze damage, and root disease. Short-lived tree.
NOTES   'Krauter Vesuvius' is the most colorful and my favorite. Native to Asia. Don't invest a lot in this tree.

POPLAR, LOMBARDY
Populus nigra 'Italica'
POP-pew-lus NI-gra eh-TAL-eh-kuh

Deciduous—Sun
Ht. 70' Spread 10'
DO NOT PLANT

HABIT   Slender and extremely fast-growing junk tree. Very short-lived.
CULTURE   Grows anywhere for a while.
USES   A good way to waste your money.
PROBLEMS   Borers, root rot, short life, trunk canker, scale.
NOTES   Usually not healthy and never desirable—do not plant! Native to Europe and Asia.

REDBUD
Cercis canadensis
SER-sis kan-ah-DEN-sis

Deciduous—Sun/Shade
Ht. 30' Spread 30'
Spacing 15'–20'

HABIT   Wide-spreading ornamental, purple or white spring color, yellow fall color.
CULTURE   Easy to grow in any soil, drought tolerant.
USES   Ornamental garden tree, understory. Flowers are edible.
PROBLEMS   Borers, leaf rollers.
NOTES   White variety seems healthier than the purple native. Crinkled-leaf Mexican variety is the most drought tolerant, 'Oklahoma' has dark green glossy foliage, and 'Forest Pansy' has red-purple foliage in summer. Native to the eastern half of Texas.

Oklahoma Redbud

Mexican Redbud

Dawn Redwood

Royal Paulownia

Sassafras

REDWOOD, DAWN
Metasequoia glyptostroboides
met-ah-see-QUOI-ah glip-toe-stro-BOY-deez

Deciduous—Sun
Ht. 80' Spread 30'
Spacing 20'–40'

HABIT   Narrow and pyramidal, branches angle up rather than grow perpendicular like those of bald cypress. Fine, lacy foliage, reddish brown fall color.
CULTURE   Likes deep, slightly acid soils best, but adapts to our alkaline soils quite well. Several large specimens are doing well in Dallas.
USES   Specimen garden tree, backdrop.
PROBLEMS   Chlorosis and foliage burn in shallow soils.
NOTES   An ancient tree native to China and Japan. Distinctive and worth trying.

ROYAL PAULOWNIA
(Princess or Empress Tree)
Paulownia tomentosa
pa-LONE-ee-ah toe-men-TOSE-ah

Deciduous—Sun
Ht. 50' Spread 50'
Spacing 30'–50'

HABIT   Very large, simple, heart-shaped leaf, 5"–12" long. Typically quite velvety to the touch. Green above and paler below. Large, showy, upright clusters of purple flowers from late spring to early summer. Very fragrant fruit 1"–1½" long filled with thousands of small seeds that are initially sticky and green, and later turn brown and dry.
CULTURE   Best in full sun. Grows well in wet, deep, well-drained soil. Drought tolerant. Aggressive ornamental tree that grows rapidly in disturbed natural areas, including forests, stream banks, and steep rocky slopes.
USES   Highly prized lumber, shade tree, open spaces, specimen tree.
PROBLEMS   Aggressive and considered weedy. Bark is easily damaged. Mildew, leaf spot, and twig canker.
NOTES   Environmentalists are concerned about it escaping into the wild. Native to China.

SASSAFRAS (White Sassafras)
Sassafras albidum
SASS-ah-frass al-BEE-dum

Deciduous—Sun
Ht. 20'–50' Spread 25'–30'
Spacing 15'–30'

HABIT   Lives in East Texas sandy acid soils. Often grows as an understory tree. Does not adapt to any other soil. Frequently found along fence lines where the seeds have been planted by birds. Beautiful red fall color and spicy, aromatic bark and leaves. All three leaf shapes can be found on the tree at the same time. Leaves are dark green on top, paler beneath. Fall color can range from orange to pinks, salmons, and dark reds.
CULTURE   Easy to grow as long as you have nice sandy acid soil. In that situation it grows quickly, especially when young. It spreads by rhizomes to create mottes or groves. It is very sensitive to physical disturbance in the root system.
USES   Shade tree for sandy acid soils. Medium-sized shade tree.
PROBLEMS   Some insect attacks and root rot in heavy clay soil.
NOTES   Dried sassafras leaves are used to make filé, a Creole ingredient used in gumbos and other dishes. Aromatic roots were once used to make teas, but are now considered toxic.

Soapberry

Sweetgum

SOAPBERRY (Indian Lilac)
Sapindus drummondii
sap-IN-dus druh-MUN-dee-eye

Deciduous—Sun/Part Shade
Ht. 40' Spread 30'
Spacing 20'–40'

HABIT   Foliage similar to Chinese Pistachio. White flower clusters in spring, golden fall color, and winter berries; light gray bark and brittle wood.

CULTURE   Easy to grow anywhere. Drought tolerant. Low fertilization requirements.

USES   Shade tree.

PROBLEMS   Hard to transplant. Not a good tree to invest much in.

NOTES   Berries are used as a soap in Mexico. Native to western, central, and southwestern United States.

SWEETGUM
Liquidambar styraciflua
lick-wid-AM-bur sty-rah-SIFF-flu-ah

Deciduous—Sun/Part Shade
Ht. 70' Spread 30'
Spacing 20'–30'

HABIT   Vertical, cone-shaped, spreading with age. Red, salmon, orange, and yellow fall color. Stiff branching. Round spiny seedpods.

CULTURE   Needs deep, moist soil and prefers sandy acid conditions—hates solid rock. Quite easy to transplant if given ample water.

USES   Shade tree, great fall color.

PROBLEMS   Chlorosis and dry, rocky soil. Seedpods are considered a nuisance by many people, but they don't bother me.

NOTES   Native to East Texas and other sandy soil areas. Will grow much larger in sandy acid soils. Cultivars such as 'Palo Alto' and 'Burgundy' have excellent fall color but are much more problematic and not recommended.

Above and below: Sycamore   Chinese Tallow

SYCAMORE (Plane Tree)
Platanus occidentalis
PLAH-ta-nus ok-si-den-TALL-is

Deciduous—Sun
Ht. 90' Spread 70'
DO NOT PLANT

HABIT   Fast-growing, with large fuzzy leaves, white and gray flaky bark, yellow-brown fall color.

CULTURE   Anywhere, easy at first.

USES   Shade. The white trunks and limbs are lovely.

PROBLEMS   Messy leaves that take a long time to break down. Anthracnose, leaf spot, aphids, scale, bagworms, borers, and other problems. Destructive root system.

NOTES   Poor choice. The London plane tree (*P.* × *acerifolia*) is supposed to be healthier, but I still don't recommend it.

TALLOW, CHINESE
Sapium sebiferum
SAY-pee-um seb-eh-FARE-um

Deciduous—Sun
Ht. 30' Spread 30'
DO NOT PLANT

HABIT   Fast-growing, short-lived, poor-quality shade tree. Yellow to red fall color and white berries in winter.

CULTURE   Grows easily but not for a long time.

USES   Temporary tree. Excellent fall and winter color.

PROBLEMS   Freeze damage, borers, cotton root rot, and short life. Wildly self-propagating in moist soil environments.

NOTES   I used to mistakenly recommend this tree, but there are lots of better choices. Native to China and Japan.

Tree of Heaven

Texas Mountain Laurel

TEXAS MOUNTAIN LAUREL
(Mescal Bean)
Sophora secundiflora
so-FORE-uh se-kune-di-FLOOR-uh

Evergreen—Sun/Part Shade
Ht. 20' Spread 10'
Spacing 8'–15'

HABIT   Slow-growing, dense foliage, bushy unless trimmed into tree form. Fragrant, purple, wisteria-like flowers in spring. They actually smell like grape soda.
CULTURE   Any well-drained soil. Moderate to low water and feeding requirements.
USES   Specimen ornamental tree or large shrub. Drought-tolerant gardens. Can be grown in containers.
PROBLEMS   Winter damage in the northern parts of the state.
NOTES   Great in Central Texas but needs some protection in North Texas. Native to southwestern United States, Texas, and Mexico.

TREE OF HEAVEN
Ailanthus altissima
eye-LAN-thus all-TISS-eh-mah

Deciduous—Sun
Ht. 50' Spread 20'–40'
Spacing 20'–30'

HABIT   Inconspicuous green flowers, followed by large clusters of reddish brown winged seeds from September to October. Upright, extremely tolerant of the harshest conditions, including drought, heat, wind, and lousy soil.
CULTURE   Easiest tree in the world to grow.
USES   Grows where nothing else will grow.
PROBLEMS   Can become an obnoxious weed. Also listed as *Ailanthus glandulosa*.
NOTES   Often grows in urban areas from cracks in concrete.

Tulip Tree

Tulip Tree fall color

Tulip Tree

TULIP TREE (Tulip Poplar)

Liriodendron tulipifera

lir-ee-ah-DEN-dron too-li-PIF-err-ah

Deciduous—Sun
Ht. 70' Spread 40'
Spacing 30'–40'

HABIT   Straight trunk, smooth bark, leaves shaped like tulips, yellow fall color. Interesting yellow and orange flowers in late spring but sometimes hard to see. Flowers will sometimes cover the entire tree.

CULTURE   Grows well in any deep, well-drained soil. Does not like rock. High water requirement in heat of summer.

USES   Shade tree.

PROBLEMS   Leaf drop in mid to late summer.

NOTES   Also called yellow poplar and whitewood. Native to midwestern, northeastern, and southeastern United States.

Tulip Tree

Rusty Blackhaw Viburnum

Rusty Blackhaw Viburnum

Vitex

VIBURNUM, RUSTY BLACKHAW
(Black Haw)
Viburnum rufidulum
vi-BUR-num rue-FID-you-lum

Deciduous—Sun/Shade
Ht. 20' Spread 20'
Spacing 10'–20'

HABIT Beautiful shrubby tree, with glossy leaves, white flower clusters in
spring, reddish fall color, and blue-black berries late summer. Can grow to 40'
in deep soil.

CULTURE Easy to grow but not always easy to transplant. Extremely drought
tolerant.

USES Specimen garden tree, understory tree, background mass planting.
Excellent small tree for sun or shade. Will have the best color in full sun.

PROBLEMS Few if any—practically maintenance free.

NOTES Great shrub or little tree. Native to Texas and Oklahoma. This is one of
my favorite trees.

VITEX (Lilac Chaste Tree)
Vitex agnus-castus
VI-teks AG-nus CAST-us

Deciduous—Sun
Ht. 20' Spread 25'
Spacing 15'–20'

HABIT Spreading, usually multistemmed, brittle wood, not long-lived. Purple
or white flowers in early summer. Nicely textured foliage.

CULTURE Easy to grow in most any soil, drought tolerant.

USES Summer flowers, foliage texture.

PROBLEMS Short life, freeze damage, and partial dieback.

NOTES Native to Europe and Asia. Should not be used as a primary tree but
rather as a secondary tree for special interest. Some people mistake the foliage
for marijuana.

Black Walnut

Black Walnut

WALNUT, BLACK
Juglans nigra
JEW-gluns NI-gra

Deciduous—Sun
Ht. 50' Spread 50'
Spacing 20'–50'

HABIT   Open-branching character, large distinctive leaves with evenly sized and arranged leaflets on each side of stem. Yellow fall color. Dark bark. Moderate to slow growth.

CULTURE   Likes deep soil, good drainage. Although tolerates alkaline soil, likes a more neutral soil.

USES   Shade tree. Delicious nuts.

PROBLEMS   Roots give off a toxin harmful to some other plants, especially tomatoes and others in nightshade family.

NOTES   Nut is almost all structure and little meat—but delicious. Native to the southern United States.

WAX MYRTLE
Myrica cerifera
MY-ruh-kuh sir-RIFF-eh-ruh

Evergreen—Sun/Part Shade
Ht. 15' Spread 10'
Spacing 8'–12'

HABIT   Golden yellow and green male and female flowers on different plants. Flowers from March through April. Fruit of the female plants are small blue drupes clustered along the stems. Moderately fast-growing and spreading, with many small medium green leaves, blue-gray berries in fall. Aromatic foliage dotted above and below.

CULTURE   Easy to grow in any soil, drought tolerant.

USES   Specimen garden tree, evergreen background. Good alternative to yaupon holly.

PROBLEMS   Brittle wood, suckers.

NOTES   Birds like the berries. *M. pusilla*, dwarf wax myrtle, is a good dwarf form that works as a shrub, although not as tough as the larger plant. Native to the southern states and the eastern half of the United States.

Wax Myrtle

Desert Willow

Weeping Willow

Black Willow

WILLOW, DESERT
Chilopsis linearis
KY-lop-sis lin-ee-ERR-is

Deciduous—Sun
Ht. 30' Spread 25'
Spacing 15'–20'

HABIT   Open branching; delicate foliage; lavender, pink, or white orchidlike blossoms in summer. No fall color to speak of.
CULTURE   Easy to grow in any soil, drought tolerant. Does better with more water.
USES   Specimen garden tree, summer color.
PROBLEMS   Brittle wood and a little wild-looking for some gardens.
NOTES   Good small ornamental tree, should be used more. Native to southwestern United States.

WILLOW, WEEPING
Salix babylonica
SAY-lix bab-eh-LON-eh-kah

Deciduous—Sun
Ht. 40' Spread 30'
Spacing 20'–40'

HABIT   Graceful, fast-growing. First tree with leaves in spring, last to lose them in fall—almost evergreen. Dense, fibrous root system.
CULTURE   Easy to grow in any deep soil, high water needs.
USES   Softening effect, edges of lakes and streams, temporary tree.
PROBLEMS   Brittle wood, borers, cotton root rot, short life.
NOTES   Corkscrew willows (*S. matsudana* 'Tortuosa') are more upright, with twisted limbs and branches. Root problems are actually worse on other trees such as mulberry and sycamore. The native black willow (*S. nigra*) is not a very good landscape tree. White weeping willow (*S. alba*) has yellow stems. Blue weeping willow (*S. blanda*) is supposed to be a healthier variety. People are tempted to stake young trees, but it's a bad idea.

Witch Hazel

Witch Hazel

Witch Hazel

WITCH HAZEL
Hamamelis virginiana
ham-ma-MAY-liss ver-gin-ee-AN-ah

Deciduous—Sun/Part Shade
Ht. 10'–20' Spread 8'–10'
Spacing 8'–10'

HABIT   Shrubby plant or small, open-growing tree. It grows to a maximum
height of about 20', with single or multiple trunks and an irregularly shaped
top. Foliage and flowers are distinctive, and the yellow fall color is usually
quite good. Golden yellow flowers bloom in the fall and winter after the
leaves have fallen. Flowers of some species have a red or purple cast at the
base. Fruit and flowers form simultaneously. Fruit ripens in the second season.

CULTURE   Easy to grow in various well-drained soils. It works very well as an
understory plant, but can take full sun as well.

USES   Interesting small tree with herbal uses.

PROBLEMS   Few exist, other than scarce availability in the nursery trade.

NOTES   Wonderful little tree that should be planted more often. The name
comes from the fact that dousers, or diviners, like to use this plant for finding
water. The seeds are edible, and the leaves are used in herb teas. The seeds are
also excellent bird food.

WORST TREES FOR TEXAS

In addition to the good tree choices for Texas, it's important to identify
the bad choices. Here they are.

Arizona ash
is a short-lived high water user, has destructive roots, is subject to several insect
and disease problems, and will suffer freeze damage.

Chinese tallow
freezes back every hard winter in the northern part of the state and has lots of
insect and disease problems.

Cottonwood

trees are stately and beautiful when healthy, but they are a bad investment. They are short-lived, have brittle wood, and are subject to wind damage and insects, especially borers. The female plants produce messy cotton that clogs air conditioners.

Fruitless mulberry

is the most overused junk tree. It shades the ground too heavily, uses too much water, and is the target for several insects and diseases. Its root system is highly destructive to lawns, walks, driveways, and pipes. It is also short-lived.

Hackberry

is just a big weed.

Honey locust

continues to be used by some people, but borers love it, and it just never seems to be healthy here.

Italian cypress

trees are prone to freeze damage, insect problems, and diseases.

Mimosa

is another real dog. Although beautiful when healthy, it never is. The root system is ravenous and destructive, and the tree is highly vulnerable to insects and diseases.

Pin oak

grows well in sandy acid soil but is a disaster in alkaline clay soils. Red oaks accidentally crossed with pin oak will always be yellow and sick in alkaline soils.

Poplars

in general are fast-growing, unhealthy trees and should be avoided.

Siberian elm

is the worst choice of all. It is incorrectly called Chinese elm. It has severe elm leaf beetle infestation every year and is susceptible to Dutch elm disease. Wind damage due to weak wood is also a problem.

Silver maple

is a lousy tree. It is usually chlorotic (yellow from iron deficiency), subject to insects and diseases, and has weak, brittle wood.

Sycamore

trees are gorgeous when healthy, but disease problems are wiping them out. Bacterial leaf scorch is the culprit.

Working with nature is what organics is all about. Trying to use problem trees is fighting nature because these plants just don't like it here in Texas. Some of them don't like it anywhere. Stick with recommended varieties and enjoy your trees and the birds in them.

Shrubs and Specialty Plants

BED PREP

Proper soil preparation is necessary for all shrubs and other small plants. The heavy black soils of Texas have two basic problems: (1) lack of organic matter (humus) and related biological activity, and (2) density of the soil particles, causing drainage problems and lack of oxygen in the root zone. Sandy soils, on the other hand, are deficient in everything except sand. In order to help overcome these problems, the following soil preparations are recommended:

Excavate beds to the depth necessary to remove all weeds and grass, including rhizomes (underground stems). No excavation should be done in bare soil areas.

If needed, add topsoil to all beds to within 2" of the adjacent finished grade. Use native topsoil similar to that which is on the site. I do not recommend using herbicides to kill grass and weeds prior to excavation.

Cover areas to be planted with a 4"–6" depth of compost and apply a 100 percent organic fertilizer at the rate of 20 lbs./1,000 sq. ft.

Add dry molasses at 5–10 lbs./1,000 sq. ft.

Add lava sand or volcanic sand blend at 80 lbs./1,000 sq. ft.

Add Texas greensand to alkaline soils and high-calcium lime to acid soils.

Add horticultural cornmeal at 20 lbs./1,000 sq. ft. A mixture of wheat bran, cornmeal, and dry molasses can be used instead for dramatic results.

Till the amendments and the existing topsoil together to a depth of 6"–8".

After thoroughly tilling all beds, rake smooth all areas to eliminate undulations.

The top of the beds should be flat and higher than surrounding grade with sloped edges and a slight ditch at the edge of the bed for drainage.

HOW TO INSTALL A PLANT PROPERLY

1) Cut or tear pot-bound roots from the outside edge of the ball. 2) Dig a dish-shaped hole and set the plant so that the bottom is on firm existing soil and the top of the plant ball is slightly higher than the existing grade. 3) Backfill with the prepared bed soil. Settle the soil around the plant by watering slowly to remove all air pockets. Mulch bare soil, but do not allow mulch to pile up against the trunk of the plant.

PLANT SIZES

Balled & burlapped   B & B   7–15 gal.   5 gal.   2–3 gal.   1 gal.   2¼–4" pots

Planting holes should be dug slightly less deep than the height of the earth ball. The top of the ball after watering should be slightly higher than the ground scale.

Planting beds should be moistened before planting begins. Do not plant in dry soil! Shrubs and vines should be planted from 1-, 2-, 3-, 5-, or 7-gallon containers in well-prepared beds and backfilled with the improved bed-preparation soil. Plants should be watered by sticking the hose down beside the ball and soaking thoroughly. Do not tamp the soil around plants.

BED EDGE TREATMENTS

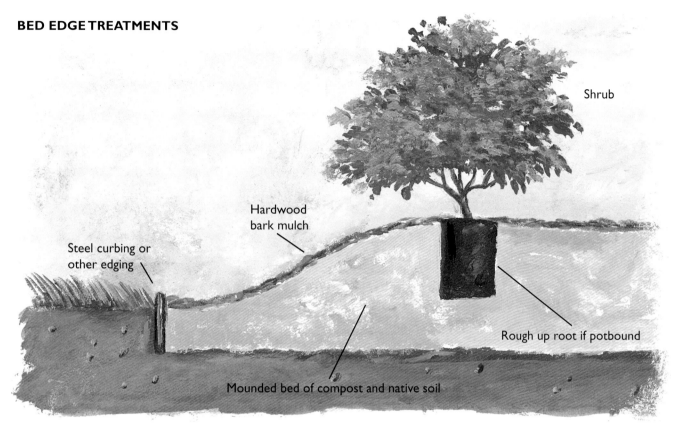

Shrub

Hardwood
bark mulch

Steel curbing or
other edging

Rough up root if potbound

Mounded bed of compost and native soil

The top of the finished raised bed
should be flat and higher than
surrounding grade with sloped
edges for drainage.

Azaleas, Camellias, Gardenias, and Rhododendrons

These acid-loving plants require specially prepared beds. Here's what is
needed if you want go grow these introduced plants:

Excavate and remove existing soil to a depth of 4" or place all of the new bed
   material on top of the native soil with no excavation. Allow for the width
   of the bed to be at least 24" for each row of plants.

Backfill with a mixture of 50 percent compost; 50 percent fine-textured
   native cedar flakes; Texas greensand and horticultural cornmeal, both at
   1 gallon per cubic yard of mix; and lava sand at 5 gallons per cubic yard of
   mix. Place in the bed area to a depth of 16". Be sure to thoroughly
   moisten this mixture in a tub or wheelbarrow or on a paved surface prior
   to placing it in the bed. This mixture is much easier to moisten than the
   peat moss mixes that I no longer recommend.

Mound the beds so that the finished grade is about 12" above the adjacent
   grade. Putting all of the new material on top of the existing grade works
   well.

Tear or cut pot-bound roots before planting. This is very important, for
   without this step, the roots will never break away from the ball and the
   plant often dies. Soak the root balls in water before planting in moist
   beds. Garrett Juice can be used as a natural root stimulator on all newly
   planted plants.

Note: If you live in an acid soil area, simply add 8" of quality compost and
   correct the mineral deficiencies that show up on the soil test.

EASY REFERENCE
FOR SHRUBS

For Sun

Abelia
Agarita
Agave
Althea
Barberry
Buttonbush
Cleyera
Cotoneaster
Crape myrtle, dwarf
Cyperus
Elaeagnus
Euonymus, flameleaf
Forsythia
Hawthorn, Indian
Holly
Honeysuckle
Hypericum
Jasmine, Italian
Juniper
Ligustrum
Loquat
Nandina
Oleander
Ornamental grasses
Photinia
Pittosporum
Pomegranate
Pyracantha
Smoketree
Spirea
Sumac
Texas sage
Viburnum
Yucca

For Shade

American beautyberry
Aralia
Aspidistra
Aucuba
Azalea
Camellia
Chinese fringe flower
Coralberry
Elaeagnus
Fern
Forsythia
Gardenia

Holly
Hosta
Hydrangea
Mahonia
Nandina
Podocarpus
Viburnum

Spring Flowering

Agarita
Azalea
Camellia
Forsythia
Hawthorn, Indian
Jasmine, Italian
Ligustrum
Mahonia
Photinia
Pyracantha
Quince, flowering
Rhododendron
Spirea

Summer Flowering

Abelia
Althea
Bottlebrush
Crape myrtle, dwarf
Gardenia
Hydrangea
Hypericum
Jasmine, Italian
Oleander
Pampas grass
Pomegranate
Sage, Texas
Smoketree
Thryallis
Yucca

Treeform Shrubs

Althea
Holly
Laurel, cherry
Laurel, Texas mountain
Ligustrum
Photinia
Viburnum

THE PLANTS

Abelia

Agarita

Agave

Althea

ABELIA

Abelia grandiflora
ah-BEE-li-ah gran-dee-FLORE-ah

Evergreen—Sun/Part Shade
Ht. 6'–8' Spread 6'–8'
Spacing 3'–6'

HABIT   Summer-flowering shrub, with tiny white or pink flowers. New growth in long shoots, bronze foliage color.
CULTURE   Easy to grow in any soil, drought tolerant.
USES   Boundary hedge, screen, barrier. Dwarf varieties are good for mass plantings.
PROBLEMS   Few; plant looks bad when sheared into a hedge.
NOTES   Dwarf varieties (3'–5' ht.) suited to smaller gardens are available: 'Sherwood,' 'Prostrata,' and 'Edward Goucher.' Abelia is native to Asia.

AGARITA (Desert Holly)

Berberis trifoliolata
BER-ber-is try-fole-ee-o-LAH-tah

Evergreen—Sun/Shade
Ht. 3'–6' Spread 3'–6'
Spacing 3'

HABIT   Spiny leaves always in threes. Yellow flowers in spring. Red berries in May. Irregular branching pattern that is more open in shade, tighter in full sun.
CULTURE   Easy to grow in any well-drained soil, drought tolerant.
USES   Evergreen border, boundary, or background plant.
PROBLEMS   None.
NOTES   Native from Central and West Texas to Mexico.

AGAVE (Century Plant)

Agave spp.
ah-GAH-vee

Evergreen—Sun
Ht. 6'–13' Spread 6'
Spacing: One as a specimen

HABIT   Yellowish green flowers on tall stalks after ten years or so. Some species have pinkish white flowers. Most agaves form a rosette of thick, leathery, yellow-green leaves.
CULTURE   Dry, well-drained soil is the best situation.
USES   Specimen for dramatic accent and texture change.
PROBLEMS   Coarse texture, sharp spines, hard to work around, dangerous.
NOTES   *Agave americana,* the century plant, has blue-green leaves up to 6' long with hooked spines along the edges and a wicked spine at the tip. Several varieties have yellow- or white-striped leaves. More than 300 species exist.

ALTHEA (Rose of Sharon)

Hibiscus syriacus
hi-BIS-kus si-ri-AH-kus

Deciduous—Sun/Shade
Ht. 10'–15' Spread 8'–10'
Spacing 8'–10'

HABIT   Summer-flowering shrub, upright growth. Bare branches in winter. Yellow fall color.
CULTURE   Easy to grow in any soil, fairly drought tolerant.
USES   Summer flowers. Should always be used with evergreens, since it is so homely in the winter.
PROBLEMS   Cotton root rot, aphids.
NOTES   Native to Asia.

White American Beautyberry

American Beautyberry

Aralia

Arborvitae

AMERICAN BEAUTYBERRY
Callicarpa americana
cal-eh-CAR-pah uh-mer-ee-KAH-nah

Deciduous—Part Shade/Shade
Ht. 4'–8' Spread 5'–8'
Spacing 3'–5'

HABIT Sprawling native shrub with insignificant pink flowers in spring and extremely showy purple berries in fall that last into the winter. Versatile, carefree plant.

CULTURE Well-drained soil is important, but adapts to any soil type. Very easy to grow. Does not work well for cutting, as the berries fall off.

USES Free-form shrub or mass planting. Fall berry color.

PROBLEMS Needs more water than most native plants.

NOTES White-berried plants are available. Native from eastern United States to Texas.

ARALIA (Japanese Aralia)
Fatsia japonica
FAT-si-ah jah-PON-ih-kah

Evergreen—Shade
Ht. 4'–6' Spread 4'–6'
Spacing 30"–36"

HABIT Single stem, large tropical-looking leaves, rounded overall shape.

CULTURE Needs well-prepared bed, good drainage, and protection from freezing weather.

USES Shade gardens, Oriental gardens, tropical effects, and coarse texture.

PROBLEMS Aphids on new growth and freeze damage. Severe winter can kill this plant.

NOTES Native to Japan.

ARBORVITAE (Cemetery Plant)
Thuja occidentalis
THU-ya ok-si-den-TALL-is

Evergreen—Sun
Ht. 25' Spread 15'
DO NOT PLANT

HABIT Upright, multitrunked evergreen shrub or small tree. Plated or juniper-like foliage. Tight, pearlike shape when young, opening with age.

CULTURE Grows anywhere.

USES Cemeteries are the primary habitat of this plant.

PROBLEMS Every insect known to man either eats or lives in this plant.

NOTES Native to northeastern United States.

Arborvitae

ASPIDISTRA (Cast Iron Plant)
Aspidistra elliator
as-pi-DIS-tra ee-LAY-she-or

Evergreen—Shade
Ht. 24" Spread 24"
Spacing 18"

HABIT   Dark green, large-leafed foliage plant. Leaves sprout from the ground. Spreads by rhizomes.
CULTURE   Easy to grow in any well-drained soil. Likes shade and plenty of water.
USES   Tall ground cover, coarse texture, low-light area. Container plant.
PROBLEMS   Edges of foliage get ragged, especially in windy areas. Grasshoppers occasionally.
NOTES   Called cast iron plant because of its toughness. Native to Japan.

AUCUBA
Aucuba japonica
ah-CUBE-ah jah-PON-ih-kah

Evergreen—Shade
Ht. 5'–6' Spread 5'–6'
Spacing 3'

HABIT   Upright on thick green stems. Yellow spots on long oval leaves.
CULTURE   Shade, moist soil, and good drainage.
USES   Background, coarse texture, screen or accent plant.
PROBLEMS   Scale, nematodes, mealybugs, spider mites—although none of these are serious.
NOTES   Also available in green and dwarf forms. Judy still does not like the spotty ones, but I do. Native to Japan.

Aspidistra

Aucuba

101

BED PREPARATION FOR AZALEAS, RHODODENDRONS, AND CAMELLIAS

Use a mixture of 50% quality compost, 50% fine-textured native cedar flakes with 5 gallons of lava sand, 1 gallon of Texas greensand, and 1 gallon of horticultural cornmeal per cubic yard of mix. Moisten the mix thoroughly before adding to the bed. Cut or tear the bound roots and soak the root ball before planting in the moist bed.

← Drain line in Gravel (optional for use in poorly drained soils)

Deciduous Azalea

'Fielder's White' Azalea

Deciduous Azalea

AZALEA
Rhododendron spp.
row-doe-DEN-dron

Evergreen—Shade/Part Shade
Ht. 3'–6' Spread 3'–6'
Spacing 3'–6'

HABIT Fibrous-rooted shrubs with spectacular spring colors of red, white, pink, lavender, and all sorts of combinations. Some varieties have attractive evergreen foliage; others are deciduous.

CULTURE Must be grown in special beds of mostly organic material—half shredded pine bark or cotton gin trash and half peat moss is a good mixture.

USES Evergreen hedge or mass, spring color.

PROBLEMS Summer heat, chlorosis, poor drainage, scale, and spider mites.

NOTES Indica azaleas such as 'Fielder's White' and 'Pride of Mobile' can take more sun and are more open growing. Kurume azaleas such as 'Hino Crimson,' 'Snow,' and 'Coral Bells' are tighter growing and need more shade. Satsuki azaleas are relatively low-growing varieties from Japan that have large, showy flowers that are often striped. Gumpos are dwarf and bloom later than all other azaleas. Huge numbers of species, varieties, and cultivars are native to various parts of the world. See page 97 and above for azalea bed preparation instructions.

Bamboo

BAMBOO
Bambusa spp.
bam-BEW-sa

Evergreen—Sun/Part Shade
Ht. 2'–30' Spread unlimited
Spacing 2'–4'

HABIT   Giant varieties and low-growing ground covers, all bamboos spread like
grasses. New sprouts come up once per year in the spring.
CULTURE   Best in partial shade, any soil, no special needs. Bamboo dies after
flowering, which usually happens every 50–60 years. It comes back slowly from
the secondary rhizome system.
USES   Evergreen background, container plant.
PROBLEMS   Spreads and invades other plants. Some varieties will freeze in winter.
NOTES   Spreading can be controlled by kicking over the shoots just as they
emerge in the spring. Native to Asia.

BARBERRY
Berberis thunbergii
BER-ber-is thun-BERG-ee-eye

Semi-deciduous—Sun/Shade
Ht. 3'–6' Spread 3'–6'
Spacing 2'–3'

HABIT   Thorny, dense, yellow flowers in spring, red foliage in summer. Regular
and dwarf forms are available.
CULTURE   Easy, any soil, drought tolerant.
USES   Colorful barrier or low hedge.
PROBLEMS   None serious other than the thorns.
NOTES   Thorns create a good barrier. The dwarf pygmy variety is an ugly little thing
at first. Mentor barberry (*B.* × *mentorensis*) is a larger-growing plant with green
foliage in summer and red fall and winter color. 'Rose Glow' is a pink-tinged
cultivar. Wintergreen barberry (*B. julianae*) is one of the best. Can withstand
drought and very low temperatures. Native to Japan.

BOTTLEBRUSH
Callistemon citrinus
kal-LIS-ta-mon ki-TREE-nus

Evergreen—Sun
8'–12' Spread 4'–8'
Spacing 4'–5'

HABIT   Showy red bushlike flowers in spring, sporadic through summer.
CULTURE   Large upright-growing shrub with red flowers throughout the
growing season. Long, slender, medium green leaves.
USES   Colorful hedge or screen plant for the South.
PROBLEMS   Freeze damage in most of Texas. Not reliably hardy above Houston.
NOTES   Native to Australia.

Wintergreen Barberry

Bottlebrush

Buffalo Currant

Boxwood

BOXWOOD
Buxus microphylla
BUX-us mike-ro-FILL-ah

Evergreen—Sun/Part Shade
Ht. 3'–5' Spread 3'
Spacing 2'–3'

HABIT   Compact shrub with rounded leaves. Medium to light green color and soft texture. Shallow roots.
CULTURE   Any well-drained soil, moderate water and fertilizer needs.
USES   Border, low hedge, foundation planting. Not recommended unless a short, clipped hedge is needed. Can be kept trimmed to 12" height.
PROBLEMS   Nematodes, leaf miners, scale, soil fungus, and freeze damage.
NOTES   *B. koreana* 'Green Mountain' is a great-looking compact form. Native to Asia, Europe, and North Africa.

BUFFALO CURRANT
Ribes aureum
RYE-beez AH-re-um

Deciduous—Sun
Ht. 6'–9' Spread 8'–10'
Spacing 3'–4'

HABIT   Spreading bush with light green glossy leaves and fragrant yellow flowers in the spring.
CULTURE   Easy to grow in most well-drained soils, including rocky slopes and ravines. Drought tolerant. Easily transplanted or grown from seed.
USES   Yellow spring flowers and fragrance. Edible berries mature in June to August and are primarily used for jellies and jams.
PROBLEMS   Spreads aggressively, but the new shoots can be removed to grow new plants.
NOTES   Fruit is eaten by wildlife and birds. Native to Oklahoma, Arkansas, and Texas.

Prickly Pear Cactus

Buttonbush

BUTTONBUSH
Cephalanthus occidentalis
sef-ah-LAN-thus ox-eh-DEN-tal-is

Deciduous—Sun/Part Shade
Ht. 10'–12' Spread 10'–12'
Spacing 6'–8'

HABIT   Fragrant white or pale pink summer flowers in 1"–2" globes. Fruit in heavy brown clusters. Trunks of older plants become twisted and gnarled.

CULTURE   Bush or small tree with round, fragrant pale pink to white flowers that bloom all summer in the sun, off and on in the shade. Will grow in wet soil and even in shallow water.

USES   Attracts bees, butterflies, and waterfowl.

PROBLEMS   Few other than hard to find in the nursery trade.

NOTES   Native Texas plant that will bloom in sun or shade but more consistently in full sun.

CACTUS
Opuntia spp.
o-PUN-tee-ah

Evergreen—Sun
Ht. 2'–6' Spread 4'–6'
Spacing 2'–4'

HABIT   Yellow to red flowers in spring, red to purple edible fruit in fall.

CULTURE   Flat pads covered with tufts of spines.

USES   Maintenance-free spring flowers.

PROBLEMS   Spines can be a nuisance. Control by scraping the whole plant into piles. Add dry molasses and it turns into beautiful compost.

NOTES   Texas prickly pear is *O. lindheimeri. O. imbricata* is the native cholla or walking stick.

Camellia

Cane in winter

'White Dove' Camellia

Chinese Fringe Flower

CAMELLIA
Camellia spp.
cah-ME-li-ah

Evergreen—Part Shade
Ht. 6'–8' Spread 3'–6'
Spacing 3'–5'

HABIT   Dark glossy foliage with flowers from fall to early spring. Slow-growing.

CULTURE   Needs loose, well-drained acid soil and protection from winter winds for best performance. Filtered light is best sun exposure. Full sun in the afternoon will burn foliage. Fertilize with special camellia food starting just after blooms fade in spring. Osmacote is good, and so is a mixture of fish emulsion, cottonseed meal, and copperas.

USES   Evergreen accent plant, border, container plant.

PROBLEMS   Scale, aphids, winter damage, iron deficiency.

NOTES   Over 5,000 varieties. *C. sasanqua* 'White Dove' is a good choice. *C. japonica* has larger leaves and flowers. Sasanquas are easier to grow than Japonicas. Japonicas have the largest, most showy blooms. Native to China and Japan.

CANE
Arundo donax
a-RUN-doe DOE-nax

Perennial—Sun
Ht. 8'–10' Spread: Wide-spreading
Spacing 3'–5'

HABIT   Many-flowered panicles with off-white flowers. Tall grass that spreads by thick, knotty rhizomes. Has large summer flowers like those of pampas grass.

CULTURE   Extremely easy to grow, especially in moist soil.

USES   Tall screening plant, erosion protection, and texture contrast.

PROBLEMS   Very aggressive.

NOTES   The plumes in full bloom make beautiful cut flowers.

CHINESE FRINGE FLOWER
Loropetalum chinense 'Plum Delight'
lore-ah-PED-ah-lum chi-NEN-se

Evergreen—Sun/Part Shade
Ht. 4'–6' Spread 4'–5'
Spacing 3'

HABIT   Evergreen or semi-evergreen rounded shrub with bronzy foliage and dramatic shocking pink flowers in late spring.

CULTURE   Prefers moist, well-drained soils. Gets chlorotic under a chemical program. Really likes compost, organic fertilizers, and a total organic program. Can be sheared.

USES   Colorful shrub.

PROBLEMS   Chlorosis unless in healthy, organic soils.

Cleyera

CLEYERA
Ternstroemia gymnanthera
tern-STROH-me-ah gym-NAN-tha-rah

Evergreen—Sun/Part Shade
Ht. 4'–10' Spread 4'–6'
Spacing 3'

HABIT   Soft, glossy foliage, reddish color especially in the spring and fall. Insignificant flowers. Berries ripen in late summer.
CULTURE   Good drainage critical to avoid root rot. Do not box or shear this plant.
USES   Background, border, or accent plant. Can be trimmed into small ornamental tree and does well in containers.
PROBLEMS   Aphids on new growth, root rot in wet soil. Healthy if planted properly.
NOTES   Native from Japan to India.

CORALBERRY (Indian Currant)
Symphoricarpos orbiculatus
sim-for-eh-CAR-pus or-bih-cue-LAH-tus

Deciduous—Sun/Shade
Ht. 2'–3' Spread 5'
Spacing 2'–3'

HABIT   Blue-green foliage, low-growing, spreads by root suckers to form a shrubby thicket. Small pink or white flowers in spring. Berries form in summer along the stem and remain with their red-purple color after the leaves drop in fall. Can grow as tall as 6'.
CULTURE   Easy, any soil, drought tolerant. Cut to the ground in late winter.
USES   Naturalizing shrub, winter berry color. Tall ground cover.
PROBLEMS   Mildew sometimes.
NOTES   Too many people mow the plant down. If it exists on a site, try to save it. Also called snowberry. Native from the eastern United States to Texas and Mexico.

Coralberry

Rock Cotoneaster

Gray Cotoneaster

Cyperus

COTONEASTER, GRAY	Evergreen—Sun
Cotoneaster glaucophyllus	Ht. 2'–3' Spread 3'–4'
co-ton-ee-AS-ter glau-co-FILE-us	Spacing 2'–3'

HABIT   Low, very compact and dense, small gray leaves.
CULTURE   Any soil with excellent drainage. Can stand extreme heat and reflected light. Needs to be in full sun.
USES   Low mass, color contrast.
PROBLEMS   Fire blight, too much water.
NOTES   Not as foolproof as rock cotoneaster. Native to China.

COTONEASTER, ROCK	Deciduous—Sun
Cotoneaster horizontalis	Ht. 2'–3' Spread 5'–6'
co-ton-ee-AS-ter hor-eh-zon-TALL-us	Spacing 2'–3'

HABIT   Low, horizontal, spreading; branches are layered and arch downward. Very graceful. Reddish purple fall color and bare branches in winter. Small pink flowers in late spring.
CULTURE   Must have good drainage. Well-prepared beds are best, and it likes being on the dry side.
USES   Mass planting, accent, distinctive texture.
PROBLEMS   Several insects and fire blight can attack this plant if in stress.
NOTES   *C. dameri* is similar to rock cotoneaster but smaller and has larger flowers in the spring. Native to China.

CYPERUS (Umbrella Plant)	Perennial—Sun/Part Shade
Cyperus alternifolius	Ht. 4'–8' Spread 4'–8'
cy-PEAR-us all-ter-ni-FOAL-ee-us	Spacing 2'–3'

HABIT   Light and graceful plant with thin upright shoots. Dies to ground each winter but returns in the spring. Plant early in the season so root system will develop fully before freeze. More like a shrub than a flower.
CULTURE   Likes good planting soil best. Grows well in wet areas and even under water.

Leyland Cypress

Elaeagnus showing its colorful fruit

Leyland Cypress

USES   Accent plant, distinctive foliage, bog or aquatic plant.

PROBLEMS   Grasshoppers; severe winter might kill the plant. No problem—buy another one. It is worth it.

NOTES   Fun for kids to cut stems in late winter, remove foliage, and put in water upside down—will sprout and root for planting outside the following spring. Native to Madagascar.

CYPRESS, LEYLAND

Cupressocyparis leylandii
koo-press-oh-SY-pear-us lay-LAN-dee-eye

Evergreen—Sun
Ht. 30'–40' Spread 20'–30'
Spacing 10'–15'

HABIT   Evergreen with pyramidal overall shape, moderate to fast growth. Looks the same year-round. Soft foliage.

CULTURE   Adapts to most well-drained soils.

USES   Background plants, evergreen screen, specimen.

PROBLEMS   Root rot in poorly drained soils. Not a foolproof plant in Texas.

NOTES   Makes a decent living Christmas tree.

ELAEAGNUS (Silverberry)

Elaeagnus macrophylla
eel-ee-AG-nus mac-crow-FILE-ah

Evergreen—Sun/Part Shade
Ht. 6'–8' Spread 6'–8'
Spacing 3'–4'

HABIT   Tough, gray-green plant. New growth in long shoots that arch out and down. Fragrant fall blooms hidden within the foliage. Fruit in spring is tasty and good for jellies.

CULTURE   Any soil, anywhere, fairly drought tolerant. Responds well to shearing if necessary.

USES   Border, background, screen.

PROBLEMS   None except its pruning requirements.

NOTES   'Ebbenji' is my favorite, since it seems to be the most compact form. *E. pungens* is the larger-growing and less desirable variety and has hidden thorns. Native to Europe, Asia, and North America.

Elbow Bush

Elbow Bush, spring flowers

Evergreen Euonymus

ELBOW BUSH
Forestiera pubescens
for-est-tea-ERE-ah pew-BESS-enz

Deciduous—Sun/Part Shade
Ht. 8'–10' Spread 8'–10'
Spacing 4'–6'

HABIT Small yellowish flowers in clusters. Dark purple berries. One of the first plants to flower and leaf out in the spring. Leaves are opposite and alternate, giving a very angular but interesting appearance. Forms thickets by self-layering. Looks similar to yaupon holly.
CULTURE Grows well in any soil with little care.
USES Natural shrub, wildlife food, screen.
PROBLEMS Caterpillars. Not much color or excitement.
NOTES Effective for attracting wildlife.

EUONYMUS, EVERGREEN
Euonymus japonicus
ewe-ON-eh-mus jah-PON-ih-cus

Evergreen—Sun/Shade
Ht. 5'–8' Spread 4'–6'
DO NOT PLANT

HABIT Upright thick stems, thick waxy leaves.
CULTURE Any soil, anywhere.
USES None—do not plant!
PROBLEMS You name it! Scale, powdery mildew, aphids, leaf spots, crown gall, anthracnose, nematodes, heat, and so on.
NOTES Probably the worst shrub you can buy. The yellow variegated varieties are disgusting even when healthy, which is not often. Native to Japan.

EUONYMUS, FLAMELEAF
(Burning Bush)
Euonymus alatus
ewe-ON-eh-mus ah-LAH-tus

Deciduous—Sun/Part Shade
Ht. 8'–15' Spread 8'–15'
Spacing 4'–8'

HABIT Thick, winged stems. Excellent red fall color.
CULTURE Any soil, sun or shade. Best fall color in sun. Moderate water and fertilization requirements.
USES Specimen, accent, fall color. Can be trimmed into small tree. Should be used more often.
PROBLEMS None serious.
NOTES 'Compacta' is the dwarf version and better for small gardens. 'Rudy Haag' is even smaller—4'–5' height. They can be planted 3'–4' apart. Native to northeast Asia.

False Indigo

FALSE INDIGO

Amorpha fruticosa
a-MOR-fah froo-teh-COE-sah

Deciduous—Full Sun/Part Shade
Ht. 10' Spread 10'–12'
Spacing 7'–12'

HABIT   Dark purple 6"–8" vertical spikes with bright orange anthers in late spring. Usually has many stems from the ground but can be trimmed into a small tree.

CULTURE   Grows well in wet soils but can adapt to normal garden soil.

USES   Excellent for creek banks and poorly drained soils. Can be used in the landscape as a specimen plant for wet-soil areas and for erosion control. Extracts from the leaves and seeds can be used to control aphids, grain moths, cotton bollworms, and other pests. Crush 1 part leaves with 25 parts water, filter, and spray on food and ornamental crops. It is harmless to beneficial insects and animals. It also repels pests when interplanted with other food crops or garden plants.

PROBLEMS   Few if any because it contains natural insect repellents. Caterpillars will sometimes attack, but they can easily be removed by hand.

NOTES   'Dark Lance' is a good-looking cultivar. The herb known as wild false indigo is *Baptisia australis* and is a dye plant.

Flameleaf Euonymus, or Burning Bush

Holly Fern

Wood Fern

Forsythia

Gardenia

FERN, HOLLY (Japanese Holly Fern)
Cyrtomium falcatum
sir-TOE-me-um foul-KAH-tum

Evergreen—Shade/Part Shade
Ht. 2' Spread 2'–3'
Spacing 1'–2'

HABIT   Low-growing, compact, evergreen clumps. Dark green fronds.
CULTURE   Likes moist, well-drained, highly organic soil in partial or full shade.
USES   Mass planting, softening element, and good in containers.
PROBLEMS   Sunburn and freeze damage are the main dangers, caterpillars
   occasionally.
NOTES   The dark spots under the leaves (fronds) are spores, not insects, so do
   not spray them. Native to Asia, South Africa, and Polynesia.

FERN, WOOD
Dryopteris normalis
dry-OP-ter-is nor-MAL-is

Perennial—Sun/Part Shade
Ht. 18"–24" Spread 2'–3'
Spacing 12"–18"

HABIT   Low, spreading fern. Delicate, deeply cut fronds, light green color
   giving good contrast with darker plants.
CULTURE   Needs shade or filtered light. Can grow in any soil but likes loose,
   well-drained beds best. Plant from 4" pots.
USES   Great for a softening effect in almost any garden.
PROBLEMS   Occasional insect munchings.
NOTES   Mysterious dark spots under leaves are spores, not insects. There are
   several other species of hardy ferns that are becoming more available in the
   garden centers.

FORSYTHIA
Forsythia intermedia
for-SITH-ee-ah in-ter-ME-dee-ah

Deciduous—Sun/Part Shade
Ht. 6'–7' Spread 5'–6'
Spacing 3'–4'

HABIT   Fountainlike growth, bare branches covered with bright yellow bell-
   shaped flowers in early spring. Flowers last about two weeks.
CULTURE   Any soil, sun or shade. Better flower production in full sun. Good
   drainage is important. Prune after blooms fade.
USES   Specimen, background plant, yellow spring color, and cut flowers. Best to
   use with evergreen plants, since winter look is bare and uninteresting.
PROBLEMS   None that are too serious.
NOTES   'Linwood Gold' and 'Spring Glory' are two excellent choices of the
   many available cultivars. There are also dwarf forms available. Native to
   China.

GARDENIA
Gardenia jasminoides
gar-DEN-ee-ah jas-mi-NOY-deez

Evergreen—Shade/Part Shade
Ht. 4'–6' Spread 3'–5'
Spacing 3'

HABIT   Glossy foliage, large white flowers in early summer.
CULTURE   Needs highly organic soil with good drainage. Even moisture is
   important. Milorganite or manure in winter is a good idea. Chelated iron and
   soil acidifiers are often needed.
USES   Screen, specimen, accent, flower fragrance, container plant.
PROBLEMS   Aphids, scale, whiteflies, chlorosis.
NOTES   A good dwarf variety exists, but it has the same problems as the full-
   size plant. Native to China.

Indian Hawthorn

Fountain Grass

Zebra Grass

Indian Hawthorn

GRASS, ORNAMENTAL

Pennisetum spp.; *Miscanthus* spp.
pen-eh-SEE-tum; miss-CAN-thus

Perennial—Sun
Ht. 3'–4' Spread 3'–4'
Spacing 3'–4'

HABIT   Showy ornamental grasses with slender leaves and flower plumes from July to October. Several similar varieties available with different heights and flower colors.

CULTURE   Easy to grow in most any soil in sun to light shade. Moderate water and fertilizer requirements. Some are very tender and must be used as annuals.

USES   Specimen, medium-height border, summer flowers. Flowers are great for indoor arrangements.

PROBLEMS   Few other than freeze damage on the tender varieties.

NOTES   The ornamental grasses are wonderful and should be used more often. *M. sinensis* 'Gracillimus,' maidengrass, has slender weeping leaves and feathery beige flowers. 'Variegatus' is variegated Japanese silvergrass. 'Zebrinus' is zebragrass. *P. alopecuroides* is the fountain grass shown, and *M. sinensis* is the zebragrass. Native to Central America.

HAWTHORN, INDIAN

Rhapiolepsis indica
rah-pee-oh-LEP-sis IN-dee-kah

Evergreen—Sun/Light Shade
Ht. 2'–5' Spread 3'–5'
Spacing 2'–3'

HABIT   Sizes of the varieties vary, but it is generally a small evergreen shrub. Blue-black berries in fall. White or pink spring flowers.

CULTURE   New varieties seem to be healthier, but all like well-prepared, well-drained beds. Use lots of quality compost, rock powders, and cornmeal in the bed preparation.

USES   Mass, foundation planting, low border, spring color.

PROBLEMS   Leaf fungus, fire blight, and root fungal diseases.

NOTES   Roundleaf hawthorn (*R. ovata*) is a large-growing white-flowering variety. 'Clara' and 'Snow' are white-flowering compact varieties. 'Spring Rapture' is a dark pink. 'Jack Evans' and 'Enchantress' are pink. Native to Korea and Japan.

113

Burford Holly

Luster Leaf Holly

Dwarf Burford Holly

'Carissa' Holly

'Willowleaf' Holly

HOLLY, BURFORD
Ilex cornuta 'Burfordii'
EYE-lex cor-NUTE-ah

Evergreen—Sun/Shade
Ht. 15' Spread 15'
Spacing 4'–8'

HABIT   Upright, hard, single-spined leaves and red berries in winter.
CULTURE   Any soil, any exposure, good drainage. Should not be sheared into hedge.
USES   Specimen shrub or small tree, background, screen, or tall border.
PROBLEMS   Scale, chlorosis.
NOTES   Always buy full, bushy plants. Leggy bargains never fill in well. An interesting large-leafed holly is luster leaf holly (*I. latifolia*). Other large-growing hollies that do well in Texas are 'Emily Brunner' and 'Mary Nell.' Native to China and Korea.

HOLLY, DWARF BURFORD
Ilex cornuta 'Burfordii Nana'
EYE-lex cor-NUTE-ah

Evergreen—Sun/Shade
Ht. 3'–5' Spread 3'–5'
Spacing 2'–3'

HABIT   Same characteristics as Burford holly but smaller, more compact, and lower-growing.
CULTURE   Sun or shade, any soil with good drainage. Moderate water and fertilization.
USES   Medium-height border, mass, screen, or background.
PROBLEMS   Scale occasionally, chlorosis.
NOTES   'Willowleaf' is a close kin with the same characteristics but narrow leaves—an excellent plant. 'Dazzler' is a good heavy-berried holly. 'Berries Jubilee' is a coarse plant and a poor choice. 'Carissa' is a compact, single-pointed, wavy-leaf holly.

Dwarf Chinese Holly

HOLLY, DWARF CHINESE

Ilex cornuta 'Rotunda'
EYE-lex cor-NUTE-ah

Evergreen—Sun/Shade
Ht. 18"–36" Spread 24"–36"
Spacing 18"–24"

HABIT   Low-growing, rounded, compact, very dense spiny foliage. No berries.

CULTURE   Any well-drained soil, but good organic bed preparation is best. Moderate water and fertilizer needs. Best to prune in late February or early March just before the new growth.

USES   Low border, mass, or barrier. People and pets won't walk through this plant but once. One of the best low-growing evergreens for commercial use.

PROBLEMS   Scale, but not serious.

NOTES   Avoid using at home if you like to work in your garden barefooted. The large Chinese holly that the dwarf was bred from is a coarse, undesirable plant. After removal, it will try to grow back for years. 'Carissa' is a crinkly-leafed, single-spined close kin. Originally from China—the dwarf forms are cultivated.

HOLLY, DWARF YAUPON

Ilex vomitoria 'Nana'
EYE-lex vom-ee-TORE-ee-ah

Evergreen—Sun/Shade
Ht. 18"–36" Spread 24"–36"
Spacing 18"–24"

HABIT   Rounded, compact, dense foliage; small shiny oval leaves. A very tidy plant. Flowers insignificant, no berries.

CULTURE   Any soil, likes well-prepared beds best. Seems to tolerate fairly wet soils but prefers good drainage.

USES   Low border or mass planting.

PROBLEMS   Leaf rollers occasionally.

NOTES   This is the dwarf form of the Texas native yaupon holly tree. New version called soft yaupon is, in my opinion, still unproven as to hardiness here.

Dwarf Yaupon Holly

Dwarf Yaupon Holly

'Nellie R. Stevens' Holly

'Mary Nell' Holly

'Nellie R. Stevens' Holly

Winter Honeysuckle

HOLLY, 'NELLIE R. STEVENS'
Ilex × 'Nellie R. Stevens'
EYE-lex

Evergreen—Sun/Shade
Ht. 10'–20' Spread 10'–20'
Spacing 4'–14'

HABIT   Insignificant white flowers in spring, large, showy red berries in fall and
winter. Large, dark green leaves. Extremely durable. Functions like a native plant.
CULTURE   More compact and healthy in full sun, but can tolerate fairly heavy
shade. Tolerates severe weather conditions.
USES   Screen or specimen plant. Can be trimmed into ornamental tree. Good in
containers.
PROBLEMS   One of the most durable plants available.
NOTES   'Nellie R. Stevens' is a cross between English holly (*I. aquifolium*) and
Chinese holly (*I. cornuta*). 'Mary Nell' holly is a similar large-growing holly
with serrated leaves.

HONEYSUCKLE, WINTER
(Bush Honeysuckle)
Lonicera albiflora
lon-ISS-er-ah al-bi-FLOOR-ah

Deciduous—Sun/Part Shade
Ht. 8'–10' Spread 8'–10'
Spacing 6'–8'

HABIT   Many stems grow up from ground and arch over to form a loosely shaped
shrub. Fragrant white flowers in late winter. Bare branches most of winter.
CULTURE   Easy to grow in any soil, drought tolerant.
USES   Shrub mass for soft, natural effect. Garden fragrance.
PROBLEMS   A little wild-looking for formal gardens. Otherwise few problems
other than dieback of entire branches.
NOTES   *L. fragrantissima* has sharp-pointed leaves and flowers in spring. It is an
import that has naturalized in Texas—not a good plant.

HORSETAIL REED
Equisetum hyemale or *arvense*
eh-kwee-SEAT-um HIM-ah-lee or AR-vens

Evergreen—Sun/Part Shade
Ht. 2'–4' Spread unlimited
Spacing 18"

HABIT   Slender, hollow, vertical stems. Green with black rings at each joint.
Nonflowering spores in conelike spikes at the end of the stems.

Hydrangea

Oak Leaf Hydrangea

Horsetail Reed

CULTURE   Grows in soil or water. This is a bog or aquatic plant, so it does not need good drainage.

USES   Marshy or wet areas, bog gardens, aquatic gardens. Distinctive accent. Can be grown in containers. Florists use this plant in fresh and dried arrangements.

PROBLEMS   Will spread.

NOTES   Prehistoric plant, very interesting and easy to use. Native to Eurasia and the Pacific Northwest.

HYDRANGEA (Florist's Hydrangea)
Hydrangea macrophylla
hi-DRAN-ja mac-crow-FILE-ah

Deciduous—Sun/Part Shade
Ht. 3'–5' Spread 3'–5'
Spacing 3'–4'

HABIT   Big, bold-textured foliage and long-lasting blue or pink flowers through the summer. Completely bare in winter.

CULTURE   Although shade-loving, will produce more and larger flowers in bright places. Likes moist, richly organic soil best. Prune immediately after blooms fade away. Add acidifiers for blue flowers.

USES   Summer leaf texture and flower color.

PROBLEMS   None serious. Likes a lot of water.

NOTES   Should be used in association with evergreen plants. Native to Japan and China.

HYDRANGEA, OAK LEAF
Hydrangea quercifolia
hi-DRAN-ja kwer-si-FOAL-ee-ah

Deciduous—Sun/Part Shade
Ht. 6'–7' Spread 6'–8'
Spacing 3'–4'

HABIT   Good-looking, coarse-textured foliage that has excellent orange to reddish purple fall color. Showy white flowers in late spring to early summer. The bare stems are even attractive in winter.

CULTURE   Easy to grow but likes well-prepared, well-drained beds best.

USES   Great understory plants. Interesting texture, spring and fall color. Accent plant.

PROBLEMS   Leaf burn in afternoon full sun.

NOTES   More deciduous shrubs should be used in general, but this is one of the best. Native to Georgia, Mississippi, and Florida. Don't cut back in winter.

Hypericum

Italian Jasmine

Tam Juniper and Shore Juniper

Pfitzer Juniper

HYPERICUM (St. John's Wort)   Evergreen—Sun/Part Shade
Hypericum spp.   Ht. 2'–3' Spread 3'–4'
hi-PEAR-ih-cum   Spacing 18"–24"

HABIT   Low-growing, attractive foliage and showy yellow flowers in summer. Foliage is sometimes reddish in fall.
CULTURE   Any soil, sun or part shade. Prepared beds, moderate water and food requirements.
USES   Mass, accent, summer color.
PROBLEMS   Gets a little ratty-looking after severe winters.
NOTES   Several good varieties available. *H. patulum henryi* is the most commonly used here. *H. beanii* is apparently the correct name. Native to Europe.

JASMINE, ITALIAN   Semi-evergreen—Sun
Jasminum humile   Ht. 5'–6' Spread 5'–6'
JAS-mih-num HUME-eh-lee   Spacing 3'–4'

HABIT   Gracefully arching shrub with green stems and small yellow flowers in early summer. Loses one-half to two-thirds of its foliage in winter.
CULTURE   Well-prepared, well-drained soil. Moderate water and fertilization needs. Little pruning needed. In fact, heavy clipping or shearing will ruin this plant.
USES   Border, hedge.
PROBLEMS   Freeze damage in harsh winters.
NOTES   *J. nudiflorum,* a close kin, is completely deciduous. Native to China.

JUNIPER, CREEPING   Evergreen—Sun
Juniperus horizontalis   Ht. 1'–2' Spread 3'–6'
Joo-NIP-er-us hor-eh-zon-TALL-us   Spacing 18"–24"

HABIT   Low, spreading juniper that acts like a ground cover.
CULTURE   Well-prepared, well-drained soil. Drought tolerant, although responds well to even moisture and regular fertilization.
USES   Ground cover for hot areas, raised planters.
PROBLEMS   Spider mites, juniper blight.
NOTES   Shore juniper (*J. conferta*), also a low-growing juniper, has soft, light green foliage. 'Bar Harbour' is blue-green in summer with a nice purple color in the winter. 'Wiltoni' (blue rug) is silver-blue in summer with a light purple cast in winter. Dozens of other varieties. Native to Nova Scotia, Canada, and the northern United States. These northern junipers are not recommended.

JUNIPER, TAM   Evergreen—Sun
Juniperus sabina 'Tamariscifolia'   Ht. 5' Spread 6'
joo-NIP-er-us sa-BEAN-ah   Spacing 3'

HABIT   Medium height, dark green foliage, dense to the ground.
CULTURE   Needs open, well-drained area, any soil, average water and fertilization.
USES   Evergreen mass, tall ground cover. Good cold tolerance.
PROBLEMS   Spider mites, bagworms, and several diseases. None of the introduced junipers are very good except in the far western and northern part of the state.
NOTES   I prefer leafy shrubs that are more insect resistant. Pfitzer juniper (*J. chinensis* 'Pfitzeriana') is a larger-growing introduced juniper with gray-green foliage.

Variegated Ligustrum

Wax Ligustrum

Japanese Ligustrum

LIGUSTRUM, JAPANESE
Ligustrum lucidum
li-GUS-trum loo-SEE-dum

Evergreen—Sun/Part Shade
Ht. 15'–20' Spread 8'–10'
Spacing 4'–8'

HABIT   Very large, vigorous shrub with larger, duller leaves than wax ligustrum. Fragrant white flowers in late spring. Clusters of blue berries in winter.
CULTURE   Any soil, sun or part shade. Low water and fertilizer requirements.
USES   Tall screen, ornamental tree.
PROBLEMS   Cotton root rot, whiteflies, and ice-storm damage. Invasive.
NOTES   The 1983 freeze killed or severely damaged many of these plants. I try to keep this plant if existing on a site, but I seldom plant new ones. Native to Asia.

LIGUSTRUM, VARIEGATED (Privet)
Ligustrum lucidum 'Variegata'
li-GUS-trum loo-SEE-dum

Evergreen—Sun/Part Shade
Ht. 6'–10' Spread 6'–8'
Spacing 3'–4'

HABIT   Small rounded leaves, dense branching. Light, variegated foliage.
CULTURE   Easy to grow in any soil, drought tolerant.
USES   Color contrast, hedge or screen.
PROBLEMS   Relatively pest free except for occasional whiteflies. Invasive.
NOTES   Often called variegated privet. This version of the plant is so plentiful now, it has become a pest. Naturalizes readily from seed. Native to China and Korea.

LIGUSTRUM, WAX (Wax Leaf)
Ligustrum japonicum
li-GUS-trum jah-PON-ih-cum

Evergreen—Sun/Part Shade
Ht. 10'–15' Spread 8'–10'
Spacing 3'–4'

HABIT   Glossy leaves, blue berries in winter. Very fragrant white flowers in late spring. Usually multitrunked, but single-stem plants available at nurseries.
CULTURE   Any soil and condition as long as drainage is good. Light shearing or pick-pruning in March and July is helpful to keep the plant compact.
USES   Ornamental tree, screen, tall border, background plant.
PROBLEMS   Whiteflies, cotton root rot. Freeze damage in severe winters.
NOTES   Wax leaf has been grossly misused as a foundation planting or low hedge. I also think pyramid-, poodle-, and globe-shaped pruning is a silly thing to do with this plant. Native to Asia.

Lilac

Loquat

Leather Leaf Mahonia

LILAC
Syringa spp.
si-RING-ga

Deciduous—Sun/Light Shade
Ht. 8'–10' Spread 8'–10'
Spacing 4'–6'

HABIT   Very fragrant lavender flower spikes in April and May. Light green foliage, purple as it emerges in the spring. Best adapted to the cooler parts of Texas. Needs winter chilling to set strong blooms.

CULTURE   Not that easy to grow in most of Texas. Does the best in the western and northern parts of the state.

USES   Summer color.

PROBLEMS   Leaf miners, scale insects, borers, several diseases. Does not like the hot weather in most of the state.

NOTES   There are about 30 species of lilac from Asia and southern Europe, but none of them do very well in the southern two-thirds of Texas. *S. persica,* Persian lilac, is the best species for Texas. Under an organic program, it does better than most people would think.

LOQUAT
Eriobotrya japonica
err-ee-o-BOT-tree-ah jah-PON-ih-kah

Evergreen—Sun/Part Shade
Ht. 10'–15' Spread 10'–15'
Spacing 8'–12'

HABIT   Large shrub or small tree. Large, leathery, gray-green leaves. Fragrant off-white flowers in fall and edible fruit in the spring.

CULTURE   Any soil with moderate water and fertilizer. Does best in well-prepared beds in areas protected from winter winds.

USES   Screen, specimen, or background plant. Lower foliage can be trimmed off to form small ornamental tree.

PROBLEMS   Fire blight (spray with streptomycin in fall when plant is in bloom). Freeze damage in northern part of the state.

NOTES   Many loquats died in the 1983 freeze. Native to China and Japan.

MAHONIA, LEATHER LEAF
Mahonia bealei
mah-HONE-ee-ah BEAL-ee-eye

Evergreen—Shade
Ht. 5'–7' Spread 3'–5'
Spacing 3'

HABIT   Unique shrub with vertical stems, thick spiny leaves, yellow early spring flowers, and blue berries following. Tends to get leggy, but that gives it the dramatic character.

CULTURE   Easy to grow. Best in prepared beds in shade. Moderate water and food requirements. Remove one-third of the canes per year if a bushier effect is desired.

USES   Accent, distinctive foliage and character, good for Oriental gardens.

PROBLEMS   Relatively few.

NOTES   Native to China. The closely kin Oregon grape (*M. aquifolium*) is unsuccessful here, despite what you may have heard. It needs a cooler climate such as its own native home, the Pacific Northwest.

Compact Nandina

'Gulfstream' Nandina

'Harbour Dwarf' Nandina

'Nana' Nandina

Nandina

NANDINA (Heavenly Bamboo)
Nandina domestica
nan-DEE-nah doe-MESS-ti-ka

Evergreen—Sun/Shade
Ht. 1'–8' Spread 2'–6'
Spacing 2'–4'

HABIT Pinkish or purplish white flowers in clusters at branch ends in early spring. Red berries in winter. Vertical unbranching shoots, leggy but distinctive. Soft, delicate red-orange foliage. Regular nandina is 5'–8' tall, compact nandina 3'–4', 'Gulfstream' 3'–4', 'Harbour Dwarf' 1'–2', and 'Nana' 1'–2'.

CULTURE Any soil, anywhere. Drought tolerant. Do not shear or box—ever! Can take an unbelievable amount of neglect. To lower height, cut the tallest shoots off at ground level.

USES Specimen, container, accent, screen, hedge, Oriental gardens, mass, or border plant.

PROBLEMS Relatively few. Can be invasive.

NOTES Native to China. Nandinas have a curious negative connotation with many people—probably because they are often seen growing wild around abandoned properties. This just shows how tough they really are. All varieties are good except 'Nana,' which looks like a chlorotic basketball all summer. Nandina 'San Gabriel' has distinctively thin foliage.

Oleander

Natal Plum

NATAL PLUM
Carissa macrocarpa
ka-RISS-ah mac-row-CAR-pa

Evergreen—Sun/Part Shade
Ht. 4'–6' Spread 4'–6'
Spacing 2'–3'

HABIT   Very fragrant white flowers throughout the summer, followed by red
   plume-shaped edible fruit.
CULTURE   Easy-to-grow, salt-tolerant plant for the lower third of the state.
   Thick dark green leaves, spines on branches and at the end of each twig.
   Thick and bushy. Needs loose healthy soil and moderate water and fertilizer.
USES   Screen or hedge, fragrance.
PROBLEMS   Will freeze except in the far southern part of Texas.
NOTES   Also referred to as *C. grandiflora.* 'Boxwood Beauty' has no thorns.
   Dwarf variety 'Minima' grows only to 24" or so. Native to South Africa.

OLEANDER
Nerium oleander
NEAR-ee-um oh-lee-AN-der

Evergreen—Sun
Ht. 8'–12' Spread 8'–12'
Spacing 5'–8'

HABIT   Upright shrub with many ascending stems that are bare below. Long
   thin leaves and red, white, or pink flowers all summer long.
CULTURE   Plant in well-prepared beds with protection from the winter winds.
USES   Screen, background, summer color.
PROBLEMS   Very poisonous plant parts, freeze damage. Xylella is a serious
   bacterial disease that can be controlled with the Sick Tree Treatment.
NOTES   Red and pink selections are the most cold hardy here. 'Mrs. Roeding' is
   a gorgeous salmon-color cultivar. It needs protection in harsh winters. Native
   to the Mediterranean.

Variegated Osmanthus

OSMANTHUS
Osmanthus spp.
oss-MAN-thus

Evergreen—Sun/Shade
Ht. 4'–10' Spread 5'–8'
Spacing 3'–4'

HABIT   Small fragrant flowers that bloom mostly in spring but sporadically all summer. Spiny, hollylike leaves.

CULTURE   Needs moist, well-drained soil and more care than hollies. Careful bed preparation is imperative.

USES   Hedge, specimen, garden fragrance.

PROBLEMS   Possible freeze damage.

NOTES   Not used much, probably should be. *O.* 'Variegatus' is variegated, with white edges on spiny leaves. *O. fragrans,* sweet olive, has larger leaves and grows into a bigger plant than other varieties.

Pampas Grass

PAMPAS GRASS
Cortaderia selloana
core-ta-DER-ee-ah sell-oh-AN-ah

Perennial—Sun
Ht. 8' Spread 8'
Spacing 8'–10'

HABIT   Fountainlike grass clump with long, slender, sharp-edged blades of foliage. White flower plumes in late summer last quite long into the winter. Foliage turns brown in harsh winter and should be cut back.

CULTURE   Easy in any soil. Low water and food requirements. Needs good drainage, like most plants.

USES   Accent plant, border for roads, drives, or parks. Good for distant viewing.

PROBLEMS   Few if any.

NOTES   White plumes are good for interior arrangements. Female plants have the showiest plumes. Native to South America. Muhlygrass (*Muhlenbergia lindheimeri*) is similar but more natural-looking and native to Texas.

Philadelphus

Chinese Photinia in spring

Chinese Photinia in fall

Chinese Photinia

Fraser's Red Tip Photinia

PHILADELPHUS (Mock Orange)
Philadelphus spp.
fil-ah-DEL-fus

Deciduous—Sun/Shade
Ht. 8'–15' Spread 8'–10'
Spacing 4'–6'

HABIT Fragrant white flowers in late spring or early summer. Large-growing fountainlike shrubs, medium green foliage.

CULTURE Normal soil and maintenance requirements. Prune immediately after blooms fade; cut oldest shoots all the way back to the ground.

USES Background shrub, late-spring color, garden fragrance, specimen.

PROBLEMS Cotton root rot and other fungal diseases. Messy and bare in the winter.

NOTES Should be used more. Native to the northwestern United States.

PHOTINIA, CHINESE
Photinia serrulata
foe-TIN-ee-ah sir-roo-LAH-tah

Evergreen—Sun/Part Shade
Ht. 15'–20' Spread 15'–20'
Spacing 5'–10'

HABIT Massive, spreading evergreen shrub. Can be trimmed into small tree. Clusters of white flowers in spring and red berries in winter.

CULTURE Any soil, low water and food requirements.

USES Background, screen, small garden tree.

PROBLEMS Poisonous, powdery mildew, aphids, borers, leaf spot, and fire blight.

NOTES Native to China. Larger-growing than Fraser's photinia.

PHOTINIA, FRASER'S (Red Tip)
Photinia × 'Fraseri'
foe-TIN-ee-ah FRAY-ser-eye

Evergreen—Sun/Part Shade
Ht. 10'–15' Spread 8'–10'
Spacing 4'–6'

HABIT Very colorful, multistemmed, upright oval in shape. New growth in spring is red. No flowers or berries.

CULTURE Likes well-drained, prepared beds. Avoid wet soils. Drainage is critical.

USES Screen, background, spring color. Foliage makes good cut-flower material.

PROBLEMS Poisonous, grossly overused. When the wax ligustrum froze in 1983, everyone replaced it with photinia. Root fungus problem and nitrogen deficiency.

NOTES Also called red tip photinia, a cross between Chinese photinia (*P. serrulata*) and Japanese photinia (*P. glabra*), which is a smaller plant. Cultivated. Root fungus problems are quite significant and sometimes strike after the plant has been healthy for seven or eight years. It can be saved by the Sick Tree Treatment. Native to Asia.

124

Variegated Pittosporum

Korean Pittosporum

"Wheeler's Dwarf" Pittosporum

PITTOSPORUM, VARIEGATED
Pittosporum tobira 'Variegata'
pit-tos-SPOR-um toe-BY-rah

Evergreen—Sun/Part Shade
Ht. 6'–7' Spread 5'–6'
Spacing 3'

HABIT Soft, billowy-shaped shrub. Gray-green foliage edged in white. Although will grow much taller, can be kept trimmed to a 3' height.

CULTURE Plant in well-prepared, well-drained beds with protection against the winter winds. Moderate water and food needs.

USES Foundation, mass, tall border, cut-flower foliage.

PROBLEMS Severe freeze damage.

NOTES Although the 1983 freeze killed almost every pittosporum in North Texas, people are still planting them. I do not advise using them. Solid green form exists and has the same characteristics. Korean pittosporum was discovered by J. C. Raulston of the North Carolina State University arboretum. It is better-looking and much more cold tolerant. Native to China and Japan.

PITTOSPORUM, 'WHEELER'S DWARF'
Pittosporum tobira 'Wheeler's Dwarf'
pit-tos-SPOR-um toe-BY-rah

Evergreen—Sun/Part Shade
Ht. 3'–4' Spread 3'–4'
Spacing 2'

HABIT Very low, dense, and compact. Available in green or variegated form. Same soft foliage as the full-size variety.

CULTURE Plant in well-prepared, well-drained beds with good protection from north winds.

USES Low border, mass, or foundation plant.

PROBLEMS With the exception of Korean pittosporum, pittosporums can freeze easily.

NOTES Limbs are easily broken by pets and kids. Native to China and Japan.

Podocarpus

Pomegranate

PODOCARPUS (False Japanese Yew)
Podocarpus macrophyllus
po-doe-CAR-pus mac-crow-FILE-us

Evergreen—Shade/Part Shade
Ht. 10'–15' Spread 4'–6'
Spacing 3'–4'

HABIT   Vertical-growing shrub with dark green foliage and blue berries in winter.
CULTURE   Plant in well-prepared bed. Needs excellent drainage, moderate food.
USES   Specimen, background plant, screen.
PROBLEMS   Root rot, nematodes.
NOTES   *P. sinensis* is short and bushy and very cold hardy.

POMEGRANATE
Punica granatum
PEW-ni-kah grah-NAY-tum

Deciduous—Sun/Part Shade
Ht. 10'–15' Spread 8'–10'
Spacing 6'–8'

HABIT   Upright growth, many stems. Showy red-orange flowers in summer and yellow fall color. Narrow glossy leaves, bronze new growth.
CULTURE   Any soil, anywhere. Quite tolerant of our soil and heat. Full sun for best blooms. Drought tolerant.
USES   Specimen, barrier, summer color.
PROBLEMS   Few if any.
NOTES   Like other deciduous flowering shrubs, the pomegranate has not been used enough. Several improved cultivars exist—'Albescens' is a white-flowering selection. Native to Europe and Asia.

PYRACANTHA (Firethorn)
Pyracantha spp.
pie-ra-CAN-tha

Evergreen—Sun
Ht. 3'–15' Spread 3'–15'
Spacing 4'–8'

HABIT   Large, sprawling, vinelike, thorny shrub. White flowers in spring, red or orange berries in fall and winter. Can grow free-form as a shrub or be trained to wall or fence.

Pomegranate flowers in early summer

Pomegranate

Pyracantha

Pyracantha fall color

Flowering Quince

Rice Paper Plant

CULTURE   Likes well-prepared, well-drained beds. Good positive drainage is critical. Needs careful pruning to control growth. Consistent fertilization is important.

USES   Barrier, screen, or mass planting.

PROBLEMS   Aphids, scale, lacebugs, mealybugs, spider mites, root rot.

NOTES   Dwarf forms are available and are better for mass planting. I don't really recommend any of them. Many have died out around the state. Native to Europe and Asia.

QUINCE, FLOWERING (Japonica)
Chaenomeles japonica
key-NO-me-lees jah-PON-ih-kah

Deciduous—Sun/Shade
Ht. 4'–6' Spread 4'–6'
Spacing 3'–4'

HABIT   First shrub to bloom each year in late winter. Flowers are various shades of red, pink, and white.

CULTURE   Grows best in prepared beds but tolerates a wide range of soils. Will grow in sun or shade but blooms better in sun. Relatively drought tolerant.

USES   Spring flower display.

PROBLEMS   Leaf spot, chlorosis, heat.

NOTES   I use this plant more as a source of cut flowers than as a shrub, since it looks so bad in the summer months. Native to China. Common flowering quince (*C. speciosa*) is the larger-growing variety.

RICE PAPER PLANT
Tetrapanax papyriferus
teh-tra-PAN-nax pah-pa-RIF-er-us

Perennial to Evergreen—Shade
Ht. 8'–10' Spread unlimited
Spacing 3'–5'

HABIT   Clusters of creamy white flowers in fall. Shrubby but striking, with large, 1'–2' leaves, dark green on top and whitish beneath, tan trunk. Spreads underground and can become invasive.

CULTURE   Easy to grow in any soil.

USES   Dramatic texture.

PROBLEMS   Fuzz on the leaves is irritating to eyes and tender skin. Can become invasive.

Texas Sage

Santolina

SAGE, TEXAS (Cenizo, Purple Sage)
Leucophyllum frutescens
lew-co-FI-lum FRU-tes-sens

Evergreen—Sun
Ht. 5'–7' Spread 5'–7'
Spacing 3'

HABIT   Compact, soft, and slow-growing. Silver gray foliage. Purple or white flowers in summer. Tends to flower after it rains.

CULTURE   Any soil with good drainage. Drought and heat tolerant. Will grow better if not overwatered.

USES   Specimen, mass, summer color, gray foliage.

PROBLEMS   Too much water can kill it quickly.

NOTES   'Compactum' is the dwarf form, 'Green Cloud' has darker foliage, and 'White Cloud' has white flowers. Native to Texas and Mexico.

SANTOLINA (Lavender Cotton)
Santolina chamaecyparissus
san-toe-LEAN-ah kam-ah-sip-eh-RIS-us

Evergreen—Sun
Ht. 12'–18' Spread 24'
Spacing 18'–24'

HABIT   Low, compact, and spreading. Herblike foliage that is fragrant when crushed.

CULTURE   Drought tolerant and undemanding except for needing excellent drainage.

USES   Low border, mass, rock gardens, extremely hot, dry places.

PROBLEMS   Poor drainage, too much water, spider mites.

NOTES   There is also a dark green variety (*S. virens*) with the same characteristics. Native to Europe.

Smoketree

Bridal Wreath Spirea

'Anthony Waterer' Spirea

Aromatic Sumac or Skunkbush

SMOKETREE
Cotinus spp.
co-TIN-us

Deciduous—Sun/Part Shade
Ht. 10'–15' Spread 10'–15'
Spacing 6'–8'

HABIT   Upright and open, beautiful round leaves. Several cultivars are available with a wide range of yellow, red, and purple spring, summer, and fall colors. Smokelike false flowers in midsummer.

CULTURE   Tough plant, any soil, drought tolerant. Needs excellent drainage.

USES   Specimen, foliage color, unique flowers.

PROBLEMS   Few if any in well-drained soil.

NOTES   *C. coggyria* is the introduction from Europe and Asia. Two good purple-leaf cultivars are 'Royal Purple' and 'Velvet Cloak.' *C. obovatus* is the native with fall color that changes from yellow to apricot to scarlet. Its foliage is green in the summer.

SPIREA (Bridal Wreath)
Spirea spp.
spy-REE-ah

Deciduous—Sun/Part Shade
Ht. 5'–7' Spread 6'–8'
Spacing 3'–5'

HABIT   Rounded overall form, many stems from the ground, showy white or coral flowers in spring. Bare in the winter. Minimal fall color. Many good species and cultivars.

CULTURE   Extremely tough plant that will grow anywhere.

USES   Specimen, accent, screen, white or coral spring flowers. Should be used with evergreens.

PROBLEMS   Relatively few.

NOTES   Landscape snobs think spirea is old fashioned—I think they are missing out on a great plant. 'Vanhouttei' spirea is a cross between two spireas from China. Double Reeves spirea (*S. cantoniensis* 'Lanceata') is another excellent choice. *S. bumalda* 'Anthony Waterer' has beautiful coral-color flowers that bloom later in the spring. Native to Asia.

SUMAC, AROMATIC (Skunkbush)
Rhus aromatica
RUSE err-oh-MAT-eh-kuh

Deciduous—Sun/Part Shade
Ht. 4'–6' Spread 5'–7'
Spacing 3'–4'

HABIT   Leaves have three leaflets that are fragrant when crushed. Plant will sucker and spread but usually not a problem. Yellow flowers in early spring, followed by red berries. Red-orange fall color. Can grow as high as 12'.

CULTURE   Grows in any soil that has good drainage, even in rock. Fibrous roots, easy to transplant.

USES   Naturalizing an area, attracting birds.

PROBLEMS   None.

NOTES   Also called fragrant sumac. A good place to see this and other natives is the nature trail at Mountain View College in Dallas. 'Gro-Low' is a compact form. 'Green Glove' is a larger cultivar. Native from the eastern United States to Texas.

Flameleaf Sumac

Evergreen Sumac

SUMAC, EVERGREEN
Rhus virens
RUSE VIE-rens

Evergreen—Sun
Ht. 7' Spread 7'
Spacing 3'–4'

HABIT Bushy growth. Rounded leaves do not look like other sumacs. Red berries in summer. Reddish-purple fall color.

CULTURE Drought tolerant and carefree. May need some protection from winter winds in North Texas. Overwatering is sure to kill.

USES Specimen, mass planting, natural areas.

PROBLEMS Possible freeze damage in the northern part of the state.

NOTES Native to Central Texas. Deer love this plant.

SUMAC, FLAMELEAF
Rhus copallina
RUSE ko-pal-LINE-ah

Deciduous—Sun/Shade
Ht. 15' Spread 15'
Spacing 5'–10'

HABIT Small, open-growing tree. Leafy wings along stems. Brilliant red fall color. Seed clusters in winter. Spreads by suckers.

CULTURE Easy, any soil. Can be bare-rooted and likes little water.

USES Specimen garden tree or background mass.

PROBLEMS None except overwatering, which is sure to kill it.

NOTES Also called shining sumac because the top of the leaf is dark green and shiny above and hairy below. Prairie flameleaf sumac is *R. lanceolata*.

Smooth Sumac

SUMAC, SMOOTH
Rhus glabra
RUSE GLA-bra

Deciduous—Sun/Part Shade
Ht. 10' Spread 10'
Spacing 4'–8'

HABIT Thick stems with foliage at ends, spreads by suckers out from the mother plant. Excellent orange to red fall color. Vertical flowers and fruit that matures by fall and remains on bare stems through the winter.
CULTURE Unbelievably durable and widely adaptable. Can be transplanted easily—even bare root. Can take more water than the other sumacs.
USES Background, mass, natural areas, fall color.
PROBLEMS Spreads.
NOTES 'Lancinata' is a cut-leaf cultivar that is almost fernlike.

THRYALLIS (Shower of Gold)
Galphimia gracilis
Gal-FEE-mee-ah GRASS-il-is

Evergreen—Sun
Ht. 5'–8' Spread 4'–5'
Spacing 3'

HABIT Rounded compact shrub with small yellow flowers all summer. Fast grower, medium texture. Fruit is in small three-part seed capsules.
CULTURE Flowers appear on new wood so prune in the early spring. Needs little care after establishment. Moderate watering and fertilizing needs. Likes sandy soil or well-prepared beds. Dies to the ground in temperatures below 30°.
USES Natural hedge, backdrop, summer color. Attracts butterflies and birds.
PROBLEMS Finding it in the nurseries is currently the biggest problem.
NOTES Native from Mexico to Guatemala. Also sold as *Thryallis glauca*. This plant was introduced to me and has been growing at Hickory Hill Herbs in Lampasas, Texas, for many years without freeze damage.

Thryallis

Snowball Bush Viburnum

'Doublefile' Viburnum

Burkwoodii Viburnum

'Blanco' Viburnum

Evergreen Viburnum

Spanish DaggerYucca

VIBURNUM (Snowball Bush)
Viburnum spp.
vi-BUR-num

Deciduous or Evergreen—
Sun/Fairly Heavy Shade
Ht. 6'–15' Spread 5'–8'
Spacing 4'–8'

HABIT   Beautiful white or pink-tinged flowers in spring, sizes vary from small to huge and showy. Full, rounded shrubs with a variety of leaf and flower sizes. Some are open-growing. Deciduous viburnums are the most cold hardy; evergreens are the most sensitive and are best used in the southern half of the state.
CULTURE   Grows best in well-prepared, healthy soil.
USES   Background, screen, spring color, cut flowers.
PROBLEMS   Very few, should be used more.
NOTES   *V. macrocephalum* is the more showy-blooming Chinese snowball. *V. burkwoodii* is an excellent semi-evergreen with gorgeous spring flowers. *V. caricephalum* is the fragrant viburnum. 'Spring Bouquet' is a smaller evergreen cultivar. *Viburnum plicatum* var. *tomentosum* 'Doublefile' is a gorgeous dogwoodlike small tree. *V.* 'Blanco' is a small-leafed cultivar.

VIBURNUM, EVERGREEN
(Japanese Viburnum)
Viburnum odoratissimum
vi-BUR-num oh-doe-ra-TISS-eh-mum

Evergreen—Sun/Shade
Ht. 10' Spread 5'–7'
Spacing 4'–6'

HABIT   Clusters of fragrant flowers, followed by clusters of colorful fruit. Upright growth on thick stems. Large glossy leaves turn a slight bronze color in fall. Bushy but can be trimmed into a tree form.
CULTURE   Needs well-prepared and well-drained beds, moderate water and food.
USES   Specimen, screen, background. Foliage is wonderful, long-lasting cut-flower material. In fact, it will easily root in water.
PROBLEMS   Freeze damage in severe winters.
NOTES   The flowers are more subtle on this variety than on other viburnums. Often sold as *V. macrophyllum*. 'Doublefile' viburnum is *V. plicatum* var. *tomentosum* 'Mariesii.' There are beautiful specimens at the Dallas Arboretum. Best suited to the southern half of the state.

YUCCA, HARD (Spanish Dagger)
Yucca aloifolia
YUCK-ah al-oh-eh-FOE-lee-ah

Evergreen—Sun
Ht. 8'–10' Spread 8'–10'
Spacing 6'–8'

HABIT   Dangerously stiff leaves. Attractive white flower cluster in early summer.
CULTURE   Sun, any soil, and very little water. Needs excellent drainage.
USES   Desert-type gardens, specimen, accent.
PROBLEMS   Sharp, spiny leaves are very dangerous.
NOTES   Handle with care and do not use where children might be playing. Native to the southern United States.

Red Yucca

Soft Yucca

YUCCA, RED (Red Hesperaloe)   Evergreen—Sun
Hesperaloe parviflora   Ht. 3' Spread 3'–5'
hess-per-RAY-low par-vi-FLOOR-ah   Spacing 3'–4'

HABIT   Slender, fountainlike blue-green foliage that is fairly slow-growing.
   Reddish pink flowers bloom almost all summer.
CULTURE   Extremely drought tolerant, any soil as long as it is well drained.
   Low food needs.
USES   Specimen, accent, summer color.
PROBLEMS   None.
NOTES   Native to West Texas. Not a true yucca.

YUCCA, SOFT (Adam's Needle)   Evergreen—Sun
Yucca filamentosa   Ht. 3'–8' Spread 3'–4'
YUCK-ah fill-uh-men-TOE-suh   Spacing 3'–4'

HABIT   Almost trunkless. Spreads by offshoots to make new plants. Fragrant
   white flower stalk (4'–8' tall) in summer. Has soft, flexible gray-green leaves.
CULTURE   Any soil as long as it is well drained. Drought tolerant.
USES   Accent or dramatic mass.
PROBLEMS   Not easily transplanted. Best to buy container-grown plants.
NOTES   Native to the southern United States.

CHAPTER 4

Ground Covers and Vines

BED PREP

Bed preparation for this group of plants should include the same amendments as described for shrubs, but less material will be needed because of the smaller root systems.

Ground covers should be planted from 2¼"–4" pots or 1-gallon containers. It is extremely important to dampen the soil prior to planting. Soak root balls in water prior to planting. In the hot months, this will greatly reduce plant losses. Consistent watering and mulching are also critical during the establishment period (first growing season). These small plants should be planted only in well-prepared beds.

Small ground-cover plants often have overgrown root systems. Roots coming out of the holes in the bottom of containers should be removed by hand.

EASY REFERENCE FOR GROUND COVERS AND VINES

Ground Covers for Sun
Clover fern
Dalea, silver
Honeysuckle
Houttuynia
Jasmine, Asian
Juniper, creeping
Liriope
Ophiopogon
Potentilla
Sedum
Thyme, creeping
Vetch
Vinca minor
Wintercreeper

Ground Covers for Shade
Ardesia
Gill ivy
Horseherb
Houttuynia
Inland seaoats
Ivy, English
Jasmine, Asian
Lamium
Liriope

Moneywort
Ophiopogon
Pachysandra
Pigeonberry
Snakeroot
Vinca major

Vines for Sun
Allamanda
Bougainvillea
Clematis
Coral vine
Crossvine
Cypress vine
Gourd
Grape
Honeysuckle
Hyacinth bean
Ivy, Boston
Ivy, fig

Jasmine, Confederate
Jessamine, Carolina
Lacevine, silver
Mandevilla
Morning glory
Passion vine
Rose, Lady Banks
Sweet peas
Trumpet vine
Virginia creeper
Wisteria

Vines for Shade
Clematis
Fatshedera
Ivy, Boston
Ivy, English
Ivy, fig
Jasmine, Confederate
Virginia creeper

THE PLANTS

Ajuga

Ardisia

Allamanda

AJUGA
Ajuga reptans 'Atropurpurea'
ah-JOO-ga REP-tans

Evergreen Ground Cover—Sun/Part Shade
Ht. 3"–6"
Spacing 6"–9"

HABIT   Low-growing, spreads by runners. Bronzy purple leaves and purple flowers on short stalks.
CULTURE   Well-prepared beds with good drainage. Fairly high water and fertilizer requirements.
USES   Ground cover for small areas.
PROBLEMS   Nematodes are a real problem. Do not invest much money in this plant.
NOTES   Native to Europe. It's pretty when healthy, but it rarely is.

ALLAMANDA
Allamanda spp.
al-ah-MAN-da

Tropical Vine—Sun/Part Shade
Climbing and wide-spreading
Spacing 3'–5'

HABIT   Fragrant yellow trumpet-shaped 3" flowers. Slow-vining and sprawling.
CULTURE   Requires moderate water and fertility. Nonclinging.
USES   Summer color.
PROBLEMS   All parts are poisonous.
NOTES   Best in coastal regions.

ARDISIA (Japanese Ardisia)
Ardisia japonica
ar-DIS-ee-ah jah-PON-ih-kah

Evergreen Ground Cover—Morning Sun/
Partial Shade
Ht. 12"–15" Spread 36" or more
Spacing 12"

HABIT   Small white flowers in clusters in fall, followed by red berries from fall through winter.
CULTURE   Slow-growing, moisture-loving, clumping ground cover. Spreads by underground stems.
USES   Ground cover for shaded areas in the warmer parts of Texas.
PROBLEMS   Temperatures below 15° may damage plants.
NOTES   Risky to use in the northern part of Texas. Dies to the ground but usually returns in the spring. Does well in Dallas in my garden.

Carolina Jessamine

Carolina Snailseed

Bougainvillea

BOUGAINVILLEA
Bougainvillea spp.
boo-gan-VIL-lee-ah

Tropical Vine—Full Sun
Ht. 15' Spread 10'–15'
Spacing 5'–6'

HABIT   Purple, red, gold, pink, orange, and white flowers called bracts.
Climbing and sprawling vine with thorny stems.
CULTURE   Permanent only in the extreme southern part of Texas. Fertile soil
not important, but good drainage is.
USES   Summer color and tropical effect. Good in pots and hanging baskets.
PROBLEMS   Will freeze in most of the state.

CAROLINA JESSAMINE
Gelsemium sempervirens
jel-SEE-mee-um sem-per-VYE-rens

Evergreen Vine—Full Sun/Part Shade
High-climbing and wide-spreading
Spacing 4'–8'

HABIT   Climbing vine that needs support to start. Profuse yellow flowers in the
early spring. Will sometimes bloom during warm spells in winter—no
problem.
CULTURE   Well-prepared soil, good drainage, moderate water and fertilizer. Top
of plant sometimes needs thinning to prevent a large mass from forming.
Will grow in shade but will not bloom well.
USES   Climbing vine in full sun for arbors, fences, walls, screens. Early spring
color. Should not be used as a ground cover.
PROBLEMS   Is not a jasmine. All parts of plant are poisonous, but not to the
touch. Children have died from chewing leaves and sucking on flowers.
Native to East Texas, Florida, and Virginia.

CAROLINA SNAILSEED
Cocculus carolinus
COKE-cue-lus kar-oh-LINN-us

Perennial Vine—Sun/Part Shade
Ht. 10'–15' Spread 10'–15'
Spacing 8'–10'

HABIT   Small off-white flowers from July to October, clusters of red berries in
the fall. Twining native vine with heart-shaped leaves and unspectacular
flowers, followed by showy clusters of bright, shiny red berries. Vine looks
like greenbriar but has no lobes.

'Jackman' Clematis

Texas Clematis

Scarlet Clematis

Sweet Autumn Clematis

Evergreen Clematis

CULTURE   Grows easily in most soils. Birds spread the seeds, and they sprout easily.

USES   Native vine, food for wildlife.

PROBLEMS   Can spread to become quite a pest.

NOTES   Considered a weed by many but actually a pretty nice-looking vine.

CLEMATIS, FALL
(Sweet Autumn Clematis)
Clematis maximowicziana
KLEM-ah-tis max-eh-mow-WITCH-ee-ah-nah

Perennial Vine—Sun/Shade
High-climbing
Spacing 3'–6'

HABIT   Vigorous semi-evergreen climbing vine with profusion of fragrant 1" white flowers in the late summer.

CULTURE   Easy to grow in any well-drained soil. Low to moderate water and light fertilizer needs. Don't prune the first year.

USES   Climbing vine for fences, arbors, and decorative screens. Late-summer flower color.

PROBLEMS   Somewhat aggressive.

NOTES   Also sold as *C. paniculata*, sweet autumn clematis. Native to Japan. *C. × jackmanii* also does pretty well here in filtered light. Scarlet clematis (*C. texensis*) is native and has small unusual red flowers. *C. pitcheri* is the purple-flowering native. *C. armandii*, evergreen clematis, has star-shaped white flowers in late summer.

Clover Fern

Coral Vine

CLOVER FERN (Water Clover) Evergreen Ground Cover—Sun/Part Shade
Marsilea macropoda Ht. 8"–12" Spreads rapidly
mar-SILL-ee-ah mac-crow-PO-dah Spacing 12"–18"

HABIT Easy-to-grow native ground cover for full sun to light shade. Grows naturally around lakes, streams, and ponds in muddy areas but is also drought tolerant.

CULTURE Easy to grow, adapts to a range of soils and moisture levels. Cut back once a year in February for a neater appearance.

USES Low-maintenance ground cover.

PROBLEMS Can be invasive.

NOTES Very interesting texture. Native Texas plant.

CORAL VINE (Queen's Wreath) Deciduous Vine—Sun/Light Shade
Antigonon leptopus Ht. 20'–30' Spread 10'–20'
an-TIG-oh-nom LEP-to-pus Spacing 5'–10'

HABIT Large-growing vine with dark green foliage and bright pink flowers from late summer through fall. Evergreen in frost-free areas. Freezes to the ground in most of Texas but returns in the spring.

CULTURE Easy to grow in most soils.

USES Colorful fast-growing vine.

PROBLEMS Can have permanent freeze damage in far North Texas.

Crossvine

Crown Vetch

Cypress Vine

CROSSVINE (Iron Cross Vine) Evergreen Vine—Sun/Part Shade
Bignonia capreolata High-climbing
big-NONE-ee-ah kap-ree-o-LAH-tah Spacing 4'–8'

HABIT Climbs by tendrils and has unusual yellow and red flower in the spring.
CULTURE Any soil, sun or shade. Moderate water and fertilization. Easy to control.
USES Vine for fences, overhead structures, and decorative screens.
PROBLEMS Few if any.
NOTES Interesting vine to use because it hasn't been used much. Native to Texas and the southern United States.

CROWN VETCH Perennial Ground Cover—Sun/Part Shade
Coronilla varia Ht. 24" Spread: Wide-spreading
ko-row-NIL-ah VAR-ee-ah DO NOT PLANT

HABIT Lavender-pink flowers in 1" clusters, followed by brown seedpods. Legume that spreads aggressively by creeping roots and rhizomes.
CULTURE Very easy to grow in any part of the state.
USES Ground cover for cut banks and erosion control on slopes.
PROBLEMS Rank growth habit, invasive. Once established, it's difficult to eliminate.
NOTES Is now considered an invasive weed dangerous to native species and should not be planted.

CYPRESS VINE Annual Vine—Full Sun
Ipomoea quamoclit High-climbing and wide-spreading
Eye-po-MAY-ah KWAII-mo-klit Spacing 2'–6'

HABIT Small red flowers and delicate fernlike foliage. Fast-growing summer-flowering vine. Returns from seed readily.
CULTURE Does well in fertile, well-prepared, healthy soil. Plant seed or transplants in spring when soil has warmed.
USES Excellent vine for attracting hummingbirds. Good choice for arbors and fences.
PROBLEMS Caterpillars, can become invasive.
NOTES Cardinal climber or red morning glory has similar flowers but less lacy foliage. There is also a white selection.

141

Black Dalea

Silver Dalea

Fatshedera

DALEA   Evergreen Ground Cover—Full Sun
Dalea spp.   Ht. 2'–3' Spread 2'
DAL-ee-ah   Spacing 18"

HABIT   Low-growing shrubby ground cover with tiny fragrant leaves. Pink summer flowers.

CULTURE   Drought-tolerant native plant. Needs excellent drainage.

USES   Low shrub or ground cover for low-maintenance sunny garden spots.

PROBLEMS   Wet feet and related fungal diseases.

NOTES   *D. bicolor*, silver dalea, has fuzzy gray-green foliage. *D. frutescens*, black dalea, is widespread throughout Texas and has dark green foliage.

FATSHEDERA   Evergreen Vine—Shade/Filtered Light
Fatshedera lizei   Ht. 10' Spread 8'–10'
fats-HEAD-ra LEE-zay-ee   Spacing 3'–5'

HABIT   Foliage looks like large English ivy. Climbing, sprawling vine, usually bare at the base.

CULTURE   Likes plenty of water in well-prepared, well-drained beds. Grows well in heavy shade, even indoors. Needs to be tied to a structure or it will fall over.

USES   Evergreen vine, coarse texture.

PROBLEMS   Freeze damage in the northern part of the state. Aphids on new growth.

NOTES   This is a cross between *Fatsia japonica* and *Hedera helix*. 'Variegata' has white-bordered leaves.

142

Ground Ivy

Greenbriar

FROGFRUIT   Perennial Ground Cover—Sun/Shade
Phyla nodiflora   Ht. 3"–4" Spread 18"–24"
FYE-lah no-deh-FLOR-ah   Spacing 12"

HABIT   Tiny white verbena-like flowers from spring until fall. Low-growing, spreading native ground cover for sun or shade.
CULTURE   Spreads by stolons. Very low maintenance.
USES   Ground cover for low-maintenance areas.
PROBLEMS   Dies out if mowed or overwatered.
NOTES   Delicate flowering plant that many would consider a weed.

GRAPE   See Chapter 7 (Fruits, Nuts, and Vegetables)

GREENBRIAR (Smilax)   Perennial Vine—Sun/Shade
Smilax spp.   Ht.: High-climbing Spread 25' or more
SMY-laks   Spacing: No need to plant

HABIT   Flowers from February to June. Black berries in September and October. Woody vine with strong, thorny stems from large underground tubers. Leaves are tardily deciduous and sometimes white-blotched.
CULTURE   Grows without your help.
USES   Deer like it. The new tender growth is delicious in salads or grazed fresh off the vine.
PROBLEMS   A weedy pest for most folks. Control by digging out the woody underground tubers.

GROUND IVY (Gill Ivy)   Perennial Ground Cover—Shade
Glechoma hederacea   Ht. 3"–6" Spread unlimited
glay-KO-ma he-de-RAH-kee-a   Spacing 6"–18"

HABIT   Small trumpet-shaped blue flowers from spring to fall. Low-growing, aggressive ground cover, evergreen in the southern half of the state. Round leaves resembling dichondra, but larger and with scalloped edges. Fragrant when crushed.
CULTURE   Needs little to no bed preparation. Very easy to transplant and grow. Spreads freely and roots at joints.
USES   Ground cover in shade.
PROBLEMS   Spreads easily and can be very invasive.
NOTES   Be careful where you plant it—you'll have it forever.

Frogfruit

Japanese Honeysuckle

Coral Honeysuckle

HONEYSUCKLE	Evergreen Vine/Ground Cover—
(Japanese Honeysuckle)	Sun/Part Shade
Lonicera japonica	Ht. 12"–20"
loh-NISS-er-ah jah-PON-ih-kah	Spacing 12" (G.C.), 6' (Vine)

HABIT   Aggressive climbing vine or ground cover. Needs support at first to
     climb. Fragrant white and yellow blooms. Tends to get leggy.
CULTURE   Any soil, anywhere. Very drought tolerant.
USES   None—should be banned. Very invasive.
PROBLEMS   Too aggressive and invasive. Chokes out more desirable plants.
NOTES   There are several choices better than honeysuckle, but it exists in many
     places, so we have to deal with it. Native to Asia. Should be banned from use
     in this country. Has been a serious weed.

HONEYSUCKLE, CORAL	Semi-evergreen Vine—Sun
Lonicera sempervirens	High-climbing and wide-spreading
lon-ISS-er-ah sem-per-VYE-rens	Spacing 3'–8'

HABIT   Climbing vine that needs support to start. Coral-red flowers all summer.
CULTURE   Any soil; drought tolerant but does better with irrigation.
USES   Climbing vine for fences, walls, arbors, and decorative screens. Good
     plant for attracting hummingbirds.
PROBLEMS   Few if any.
NOTES   *L. sempervirens* 'Sulphurea' is a beautiful yellow-flowering variety.
     Native from eastern United States to Texas.

Horseherb

HORSEHERB
Calyptocarpus vialis
ka-lip-toe-CAR-pus vi-AL-iss

Deciduous to Semi-evergreen Ground Cover—Shade/Part Shade
Ht. 8"–10" Spread 18"–36"
Spacing 12"–15"

HABIT Everblooming tiny yellow flowers. Evergreen in the southern half of the state. Freezes to the ground in the northern areas but returns each spring.
CULTURE Very easy to grow in any soil. Drought tolerant and pest free.
USES Natural ground cover.
PROBLEMS Some people still consider it a weed—that's too bad.
NOTES Should be used more. Looks terrific when planted with wild violets.

HOUTTUYNIA
(Hootenanny Plant)
Houttuynia cordata 'Variegata'
who-TEEN-yah core-DAH-tah

Perennial Ground Cover—Sun/Shade
Ht. 1' Extremely wide-spreading
Spacing 1'–2'

HABIT Colorful ground cover that spreads aggressively and has yellow, rosy, and red foliage color in full sun.
CULTURE Can take any soil condition but does best in wet or boggy soil.
USES Ground cover for poorly drained areas.
PROBLEMS Needs to be contained, as it's very invasive. One of the most invasive plants I have ever grown.
NOTES Bruised foliage smells like citrus. Dies completely away in winter. Native to Japan.

Houttuynia

HYACINTH BEAN
Dolichos lablab
DOE-lee-chos LAB-lab

Annual Vine—Sun
High-climbing and wide-spreading
Spacing 4'–8'

HABIT Purple flowers in late summer, followed by short, deep purple seedpods. Tall-climbing annual vine planted from pretty black-and-white seeds in the spring. Fast-growing and beautiful.
CULTURE Very easy to grow in most soils.
USES Late-summer color, shade for arbor or trellis.
PROBLEMS Black fuzzy caterpillars. Good news is that they grow up to be beautiful butterflies.
NOTES Name is now *Lablab purpureus*. Beans are edible but not very good. They should be cooked when very young and tender.

Above and right: Hyacinth Bean

Inland Seaoats

Boston Ivy

English Ivy

Persian Ivy

INLAND SEAOATS (Wild Oats)
Chasmanthium latifolium
chas-MAN-thee-um lah-teh-FOLE-ee-um

Perennial Grass—Shade/Part Shade
Ht. 2'–4' Spread unlimited
Spacing 2'–3'

HABIT Insignificant flowers, followed by very decorative pale tan seedpods. Looks like dwarf bamboo.
CULTURE Easy to grow in any soil in shady areas. Can tolerate morning sun. In large areas, sow ½–2 lbs. seed per 1,000 sq. ft.
USES Great plant for erosion control in the shade. Can also adapt to sunny spots.
PROBLEMS Spreads aggressively by seed and rhizomes, so be careful where you plant it.
NOTES Stems with dry seed heads can be cut for long-lasting dry-flower arrangements. Cutting the seed heads off before they mature helps to prevent spreading.

IVY, BOSTON
Parthenocissus tricuspidata 'Lowii'
par-then-oh-SIS-us try-cus-pi-DA-tah

Deciduous Vine—Sun/Shade
High-climbing and wide-spreading
Spacing 6'–8'

HABIT Fast-growing, clinging vine. No showy flowers, but its fall color ranges from weak reddish brown to bright scarlet.
CULTURE Easy to grow most anywhere. Likes good bed preparation and partial shade best.
USES Vine for brick, wood, or other slick surfaces.
PROBLEMS Black caterpillars in spring.
NOTES Native to China and Japan. 'Beverly Brooks' is the large-leafed plant, and 'Lowii' is the small-leafed plant that I prefer.

IVY, ENGLISH
Hedera helix
HEAD-eh-rah HE-lix

Evergreen Vine/Ground Cover—
Shade/Part Shade
Ht. 1'–50'
Spacing 12" (G.C.) 4' (Vine)

HABIT Relatively fast-growing vine for northern exposure or other shady spot. Excellent ground cover for shade or partial shade. Will climb any surface.
CULTURE Needs good bed preparation, good drainage, and mulch for establishment. Keep trimmed from windows, eaves, and trees.
USES Ground cover for shade and part shade, vine for shade.
PROBLEMS Aphids, cotton root rot, leaf spot, root and stem fungus.
NOTES Plant should be cut back from the limbs and trunks of trees to prevent rot. 'Needlepoint' and 'Hahns' are smaller-leafed cultivars. 'Wilsoni' is a crinkled-leaf choice. Persian ivy (*Hedera colchica*) is an excellent ground cover with large leaves. It's hard to find currently but should be used more often. Native to Europe, Asia, and Africa.

IVY, FIG
Ficus pumila
FIE-cus PEW-mi-lah

Evergreen Vine—Sun/Shade
High-climbing and wide-spreading
Spacing 3'–5'

HABIT Small-leafed climbing vine that needs no support. Climbs by aerial roots.
CULTURE Prefers a moist, well-drained soil and high humidity. Needs protection from winter winds. Sunny southern exposure is best.

Fig Ivy

Asian Jasmine

Confederate Jasmine

Persian Ivy

USES   Climbing vine for protected courtyards, conservatories, and garden rooms.
PROBLEMS   Freeze damage in severe winters.
NOTES   Also called climbing or creeping fig. Native to Southeast Asia and Japan.

JASMINE, ASIAN
Trachelospermum asiaticum
tray-kell-oh-SPER-mum ah-she-AT-ti-cum

Evergreen Ground Cover—Sun/Shade
Ht. 6"–12"
Spacing 12"

HABIT   Dense, low-growing ground cover that will climb, but not readily. Small oval leaves, no flowers.
CULTURE   Needs moist, well-drained, well-prepared soil for establishment. Once established, fairly drought tolerant. Cut down by mowing at highest setting in late winter—again in July if wanted.
USES   Ground cover for large areas.
PROBLEMS   Extreme winters can severely damage or kill this plant. Average winters will often burn the foliage brown, but it will recover in spring.
NOTES   A variegated form and a dwarf called 'Elegans' now exist. Also called Japanese Star Jasmine and Asiatic Jasmine. Native to Japan and Korea.
   If any of your Asian Jasmine has flowers, it's the wrong plant—either Confederate or Yellow Star Jasmine.

JASMINE, CONFEDERATE
Trachelospermum jasminoides
tray-kell-oh-SPER-mum jazz-min-OY-deez

Evergreen Vine—Sun/Shade
High-climbing and wide-spreading
Spacing 3'–5'

HABIT   Fast, open-growing, climbing vine with dark green leaves, white flowers in summer. Will bloom in sun or shade. Requires support to climb.
CULTURE   Well-prepared and well-drained beds. Moderate water and fertilizer needs. Freezes fairly often—best to treat as an annual. Does best in full sun.
USES   Climbing vine for fence, trellis, pole, or decorative screen.
PROBLEMS   Freeze damage in northern part of the state. I usually treat this plant like an annual and just plant another if it freezes. Yellow Jasmine (*T. mandaianum*) is lemon scented and more cold tolerant.

147

Silver Lacevine

Lamium

Liriope

KUDZU Deciduous Vine—Full Sun/Part Shade
Pueraria lobata Height/Spread unlimited
pew-RARE-ee-ah lo-BA-ta Plant only in controlled plots.

HABIT Purple pea-shaped flowers. Extremely fast-growing, aggressive vine that spreads quickly by underground runners. Leaves 3"–6" long on hard, slender, hairy stems. Each leaf has three dark leaflets.
CULTURE Very easy to grow in any soil.
USES Nitrogen-fixing, protein source for livestock, and compost pile.
PROBLEMS Spreads too aggressively; however, livestock will keep it under control. See Chapter 8 (Herbs) for more information.
NOTES Japanese farmers are growing kudzu as a high-protein food crop.

LACEVINE, SILVER Deciduous Vine—Sun/Part Shade
Polygonum aubertii High-climbing and wide-spreading
poe-LIG-eh-num awe-BERT-ee-eye Spacing 4'–8'

HABIT Fast-growing, climbing vine that spreads by rhizomes. Twining character. Masses of small white flowers in summer.
CULTURE Easy to grow, drought tolerant, low fertilizer requirements. Also grows well in partial shade.
USES Climbing vine for hot, dry areas, summer flower color.
PROBLEMS Can be aggressive and weedlike.
NOTES Native to China.

LAMIUM (Spotted Dead Nettle) Perennial Ground Cover—Shade/Part Shade
Lamium maculatum 'Variegatum' Ht. 9"–12"
LAM-ee-um mac-you-LAH-tum Spacing 9"–12"

HABIT Low-growing, silvery-leafed ground cover that spreads easily. Purple, red, or white flowers in summer.
CULTURE Easy to grow in any well-drained soil. Moderate water and fertilizer. Needs afternoon shade. Does best in moist soil.
USES Ground cover, containers.
PROBLEMS Fairly carefree.
NOTES 'White Nancy' is a nice white-flowering cultivar. Several other improved cultivars exist.

LIRIOPE (Monkey Grass) Evergreen Ground Cover—Sun/Shade
Liriope muscari Ht. 9"–15" Spread: Wide-spreading
li-RYE-oh-pee mus-KAH-ree Spacing 12"

HABIT Grasslike clumps that spread by underground stems to form a solid mass planting. Has primarily one flush of growth in the spring. Blue flowers on stalks in early summer.
CULTURE Easy to grow in well-prepared beds that drain well. Does best in shade or partial shade. Mow or clip down to 3" in late winter just before the new spring growth. Easy to divide and transplant anytime.
USES Low border or ground cover. Good for texture change.
PROBLEMS Snails and slugs sometimes, though usually not a big problem.
NOTES Also called monkey grass and lilyturf. Variegated form is called 'Silvery Sunproof.' My favorites are two of the green forms, 'Big Blue' and 'Majestic.' The giant form, *L. gigantea*, is also good. Native to China and Japan.

Mandevilla

Moneywort

Morning Glory

MANDEVILLA
Mandevilla × 'Alice du Pont'
man-da-VEE-yah

Tropical Vine—Full Sun
High-climbing
Spacing 3'–7'

HABIT   Fast-growing climbing vine with large oval leaves and pink trumpetlike
    flowers that bloom from early summer until the first hard freeze. Needs wire or
    structure to get started.
CULTURE   Treat this tropical vine as an annual—when it freezes, throw it away.
    Likes well-prepared soil, moisture, and regular fertilization.
USES   Climbing vine for summer color. Good in pots set by post or arbor.
PROBLEMS   Few if any. Spider mites if in stress.
NOTES   Tough and dramatic annual color. A lovely white-flowering variety also
    exists. Native to Central and South America.

MONEYWORT
(Creeping Jenny)
Lysimachia nummularia
liz-se-MACH-ee-ah
num-mew-LARR-ee-ah

Evergreen Ground Cover—
Shade/Part Shade
Ht. 3" Spread unlimited
Spacing 9"–12"

HABIT   Very low-growing, soft round leaves, spreads by runners. Roots easily where
    stem touches ground.
CULTURE   Grows best in shade or part shade in moist, well-prepared beds.
USES   Ground cover for small shady places.
PROBLEMS   Starts easily from broken pieces in areas where it may not be wanted.
NOTES   Native to Europe.

MORNING GLORY
Ipomoea spp.
eye-po-MAY-ah

Annual and Perennial Vine—Sun/Part Shade
High-climbing and wide-spreading
Spacing 4'–8'

HABIT   Summer flowers in many colors. Fast-growing annuals.
CULTURE   Grows easily in any soil with very little maintenance.
USES   Summer color.
PROBLEMS   Various caterpillars.
NOTES   *I. leptophylla* is the native bush morning glory. It is a big, durable, and
    beautiful plant that should be used much more. See Chapter 5 (Annuals and
    Perennials). *I. alba* is the night-blooming moonflower. *I. tricolor* is the common
    morning glory. *I. quamoclit* is the cypress vine or cardinal climber. Morning glory
    is a kissing cousin to field bindweed and can grow to 16', depending on the
    species. Control by increasing organic matter in the soil.

149

Ophiopogon

Pachysandra

Passion Flower

OPHIOPOGON
(Mondo Grass)
Ophiopogon japonicus
oh-fee-oh-POE-gon jah-PON-ih-cus

Evergreen Ground Cover—
Shade/Part Shade
Ht. 8"–10" Spread unlimited
Spacing 9"

HABIT Low-growing, grasslike ground cover. Grows in clumps but spreads by rhizomes to form a solid mass.
CULTURE Best in shade or partial shade but will grow in sun. Needs even moisture and regular fertilization. Mow down once a year in late winter just before the new growth breaks.
USES Low ground cover for small- to medium-sized areas.
PROBLEMS Nematodes, rabbits.
NOTES A dwarf form, *O. japonicus* 'Nana,' is very compact, dark green, and slow-growing. It should be planted at least 6" on center. It is not as easy to grow. A black form exists that is expensive and extremely slow-growing. Native to Japan and Korea.

PACHYSANDRA
Pachysandra terminalis
pack-eh-SAN-drah term-eh-NAH-lus

Evergreen Ground Cover—Shade
Ht. 6"–8" Spread 18"–36"
Spacing 9"–12"

HABIT White fragrant flowers in summer, followed by white fruit. Low-growing ground cover that spreads by underground rhizomes.
CULTURE Does best in highly organic soils in deep shade. Plant in well-prepared, shaded areas. Needs lots of organic material, good drainage, ample water, and fertilizer.
USES Ground cover for small areas in heavy shade, interesting foliage texture.
PROBLEMS Summer heat, alkaline soils, leaf blight, scale, nematodes.
NOTES Native to Japan.

PASSION FLOWER
(Passion Vine)
Passiflora incarnata
pass-sih-FLO-ruh in-kar-NAY-tuh

Perennial Vine—Full Sun
High-climbing and wide-spreading
Spacing 3'–6'

HABIT Large, deeply cut leaves. Climbs quickly by tendrils. Blooms almost all summer with spectacular purple and white flowers.
CULTURE Easy, any soil, drought tolerant. Dies to the ground each winter but returns in spring.
USES Summer climbing vine, flower display.
PROBLEMS Can spread and be seriously invasive.
NOTES Native from East Texas to Florida. The introduced varieties have dramatic flowers, but most are not winter hardy.

PENNYROYAL
Mentha pulegium
MEN-tha poo-LEG-ee-um

Tender Perennial Ground Cover—
Part Shade/Full Shade
Ht. 2"–6" Spread 3'–4'
Spacing 12"–18"

HABIT Small lavender flowers in tight whorls. Low-growing, creeping, matted, small-leafed mint with very strong fragrance. One of the smaller mints, it creeps along the ground rarely more than a few inches high and forms a fragrant mat of green.

Pigeonberry

Purple Heart

Purple Heart

CULTURE   Likes moist soil and moderate fertilization.

USES   Some people recommend using pennyroyal as a tea, but I strongly advise against it. It especially shouldn't be used by children, pregnant women, or pregnant animals. Flea, fly, and tick repellent. A strong infusion (tea) of its leaves has been used as an insect spray.

PROBLEMS   Spider mites occasionally, rust. Adjust the watering schedule and these problems usually go away.

HARVEST   Dry and store in a cool dry place.

NOTES   Known abortifacient (causes miscarriages).

PIGEONBERRY
Rivina humilis
rah-VYE-nah HEW-muh-liss

Perennial Ground Cover—Shade
Ht. 1'–2' Spread 3'
Spacing 12"

HABIT   Pink and white 2" spikes during warm weather. Red berries from spring through fall. Pink and white flowers and red berries are on the plant at the same time throughout the summer.

CULTURE   Easy to grow in shade in well-drained soil. Excellent tall ground cover for otherwise hard-to-grow spots.

USES   Birds love the fruit. Colorful ground cover in shade.

PROBLEMS   Few if any.

NOTES   Looks like miniature poke salad.

PURPLE HEART
(Purple Wandering Jew)
Setcreasea pallida
set-KRESS-ee-ah PA-li-da

Perennial Ground Cover—Sun/Part Shade
Ht. 12"–18" Spread 24" and more
Spacing 12"–18"

HABIT   White, pink, or light purple flower in spring and summer.

CULTURE   Easy to grow in well-drained soil.

USES   Pots, hanging baskets, colorful ground cover, effective annual color. Looks great when used with pink verbena.

PROBLEMS   Few if any.

NOTES   An excellent plant for dependably returning perennial color.

Climbing Rose

Sedum

Snakeroot

ROSE, CLIMBING Semi-evergreen Vine—Full Sun
Rosa banksiae High-climbing and wide-spreading
ROW-sa BANK-see-eye Spacing 4'–8'

HABIT Massive, free-flowing, bushy vine. Shoots grow up and arch over. Small yellow or white flowers.
CULTURE Likes even moisture but is fairly drought tolerant. Tough, grows in any soil; well-prepared soil is better. Low maintenance other than pruning to control aggressive growth.
USES Vining rose for walls, fences, and overhead structures.
PROBLEMS Fast-growing, needs regular pruning.
NOTES This plant needs plenty of room—not good for small garden spaces. 'Alba Plena' is the white-flowering cultivar. Native to China.

SEDUM Evergreen Ground Cover—Sun/Part Shade
Sedum spp. Ht. 2"–6" Spread 8"–24"
SEE-dum Spacing 6"–9"

HABIT White, pink, rose, yellow, or red flowers. Finely textured, succulent ground cover. Easily damaged by foot traffic or pets when the succulent leaves and stems are crushed.
CULTURE Easy, any soil, prefers well-prepared and well-drained beds. Best exposure is partial shade.
USES Ground cover for small areas, Oriental gardens, rock gardens, stone walls, and small accent areas.
PROBLEMS Damage from foot traffic.
NOTES Native to Europe and Asia. *Sedum* 'Autumn Joy' is a tall-growing perennial with dramatic flowers that are white as they start developing in the summer and end up red in the fall. *S.* 'Ruby Glow' is lower-growing and blooms all summer.

SNAKEROOT
(Sampson's Snakeroot) Evergreen Ground Cover—Shade/Part Shade
Orbexilum pendunculatum Ht. 1'–3'
or-BEX-ee-lum pen-dunk-you-LAH-tum Spacing 1'–2'

HABIT Native ground cover for shady areas. Purple flower spikes in mid June.
CULTURE Easy to grow, low water and fertilizer requirements.
USES Ground cover for areas too shady to grow grass.
PROBLEMS Not easily available at this printing.

SWEET POTATO See Chapter 7 (Fruits, Nuts, and Vegetables)

TRUMPET VINE Deciduous Vine—Sun/Part Shade
Campsis radicans High-climbing
KAMP-sis RAD-ee-kans Spacing 5'–8'

HABIT Large sprawling vine with showy orange and red trumpetlike flowers that bloom all summer. Climbs by aerial roots. Bare in winter.
CULTURE Easy to grow in any soil, drought tolerant. Prune back to the main trunk after leaves fall in the spring. Does best in full sun.
USES Climbing vine for fence, arbor, screens, or poles. Summer flower color.

PROBLEMS   Native plant spreads badly to become a huge pest causing a severe maintenance problem.
NOTES   Native to the East Coast, Florida, and Texas. 'Madame Galen' introduced by French nurseries doesn't spread as much as the native plant. *C. radicans* 'Flava' has pure yellow flowers. *C.* × 'Crimson Trumpet' is pure red.

Trumpet Vine

Vinca

Virginia Creeper and Poison Ivy. Small leaves in the center are also Virginia Creeper.

VETCH
Vicia spp.
vi-KEY-ah

Annual Ground Cover—Full Sun
Ht. 12"–36"
Spacing 20–30 lbs. of seed per acre

HABIT   White or purple flowers. Seeds are round and contained inside hard, elongated pods. Vinelike annuals with long stems, small leaves, and tendrils that attach to other plants.
CULTURE   Plant in October at a rate of 20–30 lbs. per acre. Higher rates can be used on home vegetable gardens and then tilled into the soil in the spring as a green manure. If the soil is healthy, the vetch can simply be mowed in the spring and then tomatoes, peppers, and other plants can be planted through the mulch without any tilling. University tests on this technique show significant increased production, as much as 100 percent.
USES   Green manure, cover crop, forage. I use vetches sometimes as decorative plants.
PROBLEMS   Can become invasive.
NOTES   *Vicia villosa*, hairy vetch, is one of the best choices for Texas and makes an attractive winter cover crop. *Vicia sativa*, common vetch, is less cold hardy but will grow well in Texas. Crown vetch is the perennial *Coronilla varia*.

VINCA
Vinca major (*minor*)
VIN-cah

Evergreen Ground Cover—Shade/Part Shade
Ht. 6"–18"
Spacing 12"

HABIT   Coarse ground cover for large areas in shade. Spreads quickly and has blue flowers in late spring.
CULTURE   Plant in any soil in shade. Relatively drought tolerant once established.
USES   Good plant for a naturally wooded area.
PROBLEMS   Leaf rollers, cutworms.
NOTES   Native to Europe and Asia. Not very good to use on residential property where closely viewed. *V. major* is the large-leafed, more commonly used variety. *V. minor* has smaller, shinier leaves, is more refined in appearance, and can tolerate more sun.

VIRGINIA CREEPER
Parthenocissus quinquefolia
par-thuh-no-SIS-us
kwin-kuh-FOLE-ee-uh

Deciduous Vine—Sun/Shade
High-climbing and wide-spreading
Spacing 3'–8'

HABIT   Vigorous climbing vine. Looser growth and larger leaves than Boston ivy. Red foliage in fall. Climbs to great heights.
CULTURE   Needs pruning to keep under control. Any soil in sun or shade. Responds well to well-prepared beds and moderate water and fertilizer.
USES   Interesting texture and good fall color. Good for arbor, fence, or large building. Makes an effective natural-looking ground cover.
PROBLEMS   None serious.
NOTES   Often confused with poison ivy, but this plant has five leaflets instead of poison ivy's three. Native to Texas and the eastern United States. Photo shows Virginia creeper on the left and poison ivy on the right.

153

Purple Wintercreeper

WINTERCREEPER, PURPLE   Evergreen Ground Cover—Sun/Shade
Euonymus fortunei 'Coloratus'   8"–12"
you-ON-eh-mus for-TUNE-ee-eye   Spacing 12"

HABIT   Evergreen ground cover, spreads by runners; reddish fall color that lasts through winter.
CULTURE   Well-drained, well-prepared beds; moderate water and fertilization requirements. Sun or partial shade is best exposure. Establishes fast if planted properly with mulch applied after planting.
USES   Ground cover for large areas.
PROBLEMS   Scale insects occasionally.
NOTES   Avoid *E. radicans* and other larger-leafed varieties because of their coarseness. Native to China.

Japanese Wisteria

WISTERIA, CHINESE   Deciduous Vine—Sun/Part Shade
Wisteria sinensis   High-climbing and spreading
wiss-TER-ee-ah sigh-NEN-sis   Spacing 8'–10'

HABIT   Fast-growing, twining vine that can grow to great heights. Purple spring flowers.
CULTURE   Easy, any soil.
USES   Climbing vine for arbor, fence, or wall. Spring flowers.
PROBLEMS   Can take over if not pruned to keep in shape; grasshoppers.
NOTES   'Alba' has white flowers. Japanese wisteria (*W. floribunda*) has longer flowers that don't open until the foliage is on the plant. The harder-to-find native Texas wisteria (*W. macrostachya*) grows wild on banks in the moist woods of East and Southeast Texas. Most wisteria are native to China.

WISTERIA, EVERGREEN   Evergreen Vine—Sun/Part Shade
Millettia reticulata
mill-LEE-she-ah re-ti-cue-LAH-tah   Spacing 5'–8'

HABIT   Climbing vine having lighter and more refined growth and texture than regular wisteria. Sparse purple orchidlike flowers in summer.
CULTURE   Loose, well-drained soil; moderate water and fertilizer.
USES   Evergreen climbing vine for fences, arbors, and other structures.
PROBLEMS   Possible freeze damage in the northern part of the state.
NOTES   Native to China.

Evergreen Wisteria

Chinese Wisteria

CHAPTER 5

Annuals and Perennials

BED PREP

Flowerbeds should be built the same as for shrubs, but with the addition of more compost. Fluffy, raised beds are very important. You'll be impressed with the improved growth and bloom production you'll get with healthy beds. These beds should also be mounded or raised more than other plant beds if possible.

PLANTING

Flowers (annuals and perennials) are often planted in the same beds as shrubs and ground covers. Some annuals and perennials can tolerate this, but gardeners would have greater success with their flowers if they would do one simple thing—raise or mound the flowerbeds. Flowerbeds can simply be mounded 6"–9" by adding compost and the other organic amendments. Mixing at least some of the existing soil into the concoction is a good idea.

Bulbs should always be planted in prepared beds. Bulbs will do better with a tablespoon of soft rock phosphate or earthworm castings cultivated into the bottom of the hole. Plants will be larger and showier if the bulbs are soaked in liquid seaweed or Garrett Juice prior to planting.

Transplanting

Established plants should be relocated only during the dormant periods—usually in the fall or winter. The larger the plant, the more difficult a successful transplant will be. Smaller plants that have not developed an extensive root system can be moved during the growing season if watered in immediately. Transplanted plants should be installed with the same techniques used for new plants, as explained in the first chapter. Dig

ANNUAL AND PERENNIAL BED PREPARATION

Underground drainage. PVC pipe surrounded by gravel. Gravel only will often be enough.

Drainage system needed only in poorly drained soils.

Mounded bed

Raised bed with wall: use concrete or natural stone—never wood, especially treated wood that contains toxic chemicals. Railroad ties and CCA-treated wood should never be used.

transplants keeping as much root system intact as possible to minimize shock and increase the chance of success.

Mulching

Mulching should be done after planting is completed. Acceptable mulches include shredded hardwood bark, pine needles, coarse compost, pecan shells, and shredded cypress bark. Shredded native cedar is the best of all. Mulch should be at least 2" deep on top of planting beds, deeper around larger plants. Mulching helps hold moisture in the beds, controls weeds, and buffers soil temperature. It also enriches the soil as it decomposes.

Do not use plastic sheets or weed-blocking material. These artificial materials provide nothing beneficial, and the plant's root system can cook from the heat buildup. Plastic also cuts off the oxygen needed by the soil. I also do not recommend fabrics or gravel as mulches. Nothing compares to a thick layer of shredded organic material. Lava gravel is the only possible exception. It works almost as well and helps to keep the neighborhood cats out of the beds.

MAINTENANCE

Annuals and perennials have a wide range of maintenance requirements. See the specific plant for detailed maintenance instructions.

Fertilize most annuals and perennials with 20 lbs. per 1,000 sq. ft. (2 lbs. per 100 sq. ft.) of organic fertilizer three times a year. Spray Garrett Juice at least monthly and drench plants with it for additional power. Additional dry products can be added to push flower production. See the Appendix for the various choices.

BULB PLANTING DEPTHS

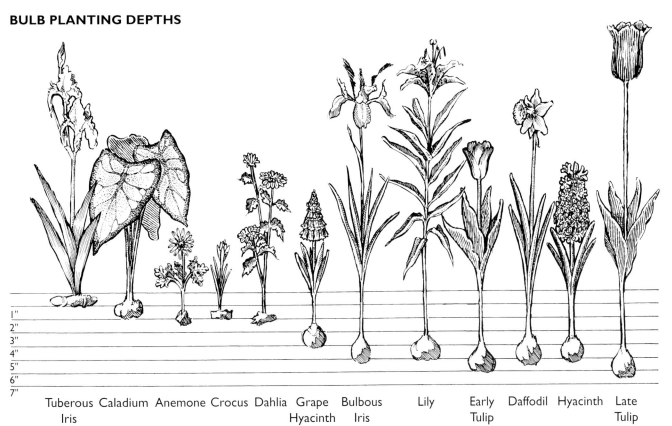

1"
2"
3"
4"
5"
6"
7"

Tuberous Caladium Anemone Crocus Dahlia Grape Bulbous   Lily   Early   Daffodil Hyacinth Late
Iris   Hyacinth Iris   Tulip   Tulip

EASY REFERENCE FOR ANNUALS AND PERENNIALS

Fall Color
Aster
Calendula
Candletree
Chrysanthemum
Crocus
Marigold
Rain lily
Salvia
Sedum 'Autumn Joy'

Winter Color
Calendula
Dianthus
Kale
Lenten rose
Pansy
Snapdragon

Summer Color (Shade)
Astilbe
Begonia
Caladium
Coleus
Columbine
Crocosmia
Four o'clock
Geranium
Impatiens
Lobelia
Nicotiana
Plumeria
Rock rose

Spring Color
Alyssum
Amaryllis
Anemone
Aster, Stokes
Bluebonnet
Candytuft
Coralbells
Coreopsis
Cornflower
Crocus
Daffodil
Daisy
Daylily

Dianthus
Firebush
Foxglove
Geranium
Horsemint
Hummingbird bush
Indian blanket
Indian paintbrush
Iris
Iris, butterfly
Ixora
Jerusalem sage
Lamb's ear
Larkspur
Mexican hat
Mexican heather
Mexican oregano
Mexican petunia
Monarda
Oxalis
Peony
Petunia
Phlox
Poppy
Ranunculus
Rose
Snapdragon
Stock
Thrift
Tulip
Wallflower
Winecup
Yarrow

Summer Color (Sun)
Ageratum
Alyssum
Aster frikartii
Aster, Stokes
Begonia
Black-eyed peas
Blue mist
Bouncing Bet
Butterfly bush
Butterfly weed
Candletree
Canna
Chenille plant

Clammy weed
Cleome
Coneflower, purple
Copperleaf
Coreopsis
Cosmos
Cockscomb
Crinum lily
Dahlberg daisy
Dahlia
Daisy
Datura
Daylily
Dusty miller
Esperanza
Fan flower
Gayfeather
Gazania
Globe amaranth
Hibiscus
Hollyhock
Jatropha
Lantana
Lisianthus
Lythrum
Marigold

Nasturtium
Nierembergia
Obedient plant
Oxalis
Penstemon
Pentas
Periwinkle
Phlox
Plumbago
Portulaca
Primrose
Purslane
Rain lily
Rock rose
Rose
Rosemary
Salvia
Spider lily
Texas betony
Turk's cap
Verbena
Veronica
Wallflower
Yarrow
Zexmenia
Zinnia

THE PLANTS

Above: Alyssum and Purple Heart;
below: Alyssum

Below: Ageratum

AGERATUM
Ageratum houstonianum
ag-er-RAH-tum huse-tone-ee-AN-um

Annual—Morning Sun/Part Shade
Ht. 8"–12" Spread 12"–15"
Spacing 9"–12"

HABIT   Round, fluffy lavender or white flowers all summer. Rounded overall
   shape, heart-shaped leaves.
CULTURE   Does well in properly prepared beds. Avoid overwatering.
USES   Small groupings or borders. Good in pots.
PROBLEMS   Spider mites in the heat of summer.
NOTES   Likes cool weather best.

ALYSSUM
Lobularia maritima
lob-ew-LAR-ee-ah ma-RI-tim-ah

Annual—Sun
Ht. 3"–4" Spread 9"–12"
Spacing 6"

HABIT   Low-growing, small delicate flowers of white and lavender that bloom
   in summer.
CULTURE   Requires little care but is damaged easily by foot traffic and pets. Any
   soil, relatively drought tolerant. Likes cool weather. Can take light frost.
USES   Rock gardens, pockets in stone walls, small accent areas of annual color.
PROBLEMS   Few if any.
NOTES   Native to Turkey. Purple heart is also shown.

Hardy Amaryllis

Anemone

Japanese Anemone

Aster

AMARYLLIS (Hardy Amaryllis) Perennial—Full Sun
Hippeastrum × johnsonii Ht. 2' Spread 2'
hip-ee-AS-trum jon-SOHN-ee-eye Spacing 2'

HABIT Spectacular spring-flowering bulbs. Long straplike foliage that often does not appear until flowers fade away. Red funnel-shaped flowers.
CULTURE Easy to grow in well-prepared soil, but will adapt to most all soils. Clumps can be divided and replanted in the fall or winter. Necks of the bulbs should be left just above ground level.
USES Spring color.
PROBLEMS Finding the plant in nurseries.
NOTES Christmas amaryllis can be brought back into bloom after fading by allowing to dry out after blooming and then starting to water again in the fall.

ANEMONE Annual—Sun/Part Shade
Anemone coronaria Ht. 6"–15" Spread 6"–12"
ah-NEM-oh-nee core-oh-NAIR-ee-ah Spacing 3"–4"

HABIT Multicolored flower on long slender stems. Colors include white, red, pink, purple, and rose. Single and double forms available. Lacy foliage and colorful poppylike flowers in spring. Actually a tuberous root but performs as an annual.
CULTURE Plant in late winter in full sun or partial shade with the claws pointed down. Soak in mixture of 1 tablespoon liquid seaweed per gallon of water before planting just under the soil surface. Must be replanted each year in Texas.
USES Multicolored spring flowers.
PROBLEMS Aphids, cutworms.
NOTES Use a knife or clippers to pick anemones because pulling may tear the crown of the tuber. Japanese anemone (*A. japonica*) is a lovely perennial that blooms primarily in the fall.

ASTER Perennial—Sun
Aster spp. Ht. 1'–3' Spread 2'–4'
AS-ter Spacing 12"–18"

HABIT Daisylike perennial that blooms summer through fall. Light blue flowers.
CULTURE Plant in well-prepared, well-drained beds. Moderate water and fertilization requirements. Divide established plants in spring every three or four years.
USES Fall color, borders, cutting gardens. Considered to be one of the best perennial flowers in the world.
PROBLEMS Cutworms, powdery mildew. Can be overwatered easily.
NOTES Plant in fall or early spring. The hardy blue aster is the common fall-blooming variety. Many other varieties and colors are available, but *A. frikartii* is the showiest and blooms the longest. Others mainly bloom in the fall. Roadside aster is considered a noxious weed by many, a beautiful wildflower by others.

Red Banana

Banana

BANANA
Musa spp.
MEW-sa

Perennial—Sun
Ht. 5'–20' Spread 5'–10'
Spacing 5'–10'

HABIT   All species have thick stems and spread by suckers to form clumps. Large, heavy red or purple flower clusters, followed by edible bananas in the warmer parts of the state where the growing season is longer. Also grows in greenhouses.

CULTURE   In cooler parts of the state, protect in winter by cutting off the top and putting a thick mulch layer over the stump. If the roots don't stay too wet and rot, the plant will return in the spring.

PROBLEMS   Freeze damage in the northern half of the state. Huge leaves are easily torn by the wind.

NOTES   Pieces of banana leaves and stalk are said to repel fleas. The decorative red-leaf *Ensete* varieties are not true bananas.

BEGONIA
Begonia spp.
beh-GON-ee-ah

Annual—Sun/Shade
Ht. 6"–15" Spread 12"–18"
Spacing 9"–12"

HABIT   Erect or trailing; soft shiny foliage that is sometimes red. Blooms throughout the summer.

CULTURE   Needs loose, well-prepared beds, lots of organic material, and good positive drainage. Some varieties need sun, others shade.

USES   Summer color, hanging baskets, pots. Delicious edible flowers.

PROBLEMS   Slugs, cutworms.

NOTES   Plants grown in pots can be moved indoors and saved through winter. Plant after the last freeze. Native to Brazil.

Begonia

162

Bluebonnet

Blue-Eyed Grass

BLUEBONNET (Texas Bluebonnet)
Lupinus texensis
loo-PYE nus tex-IN-sis

Annual—Sun
Ht. 9"–12" Spread 12"–15"
Seed @ 1 lb./1,000 sq. ft.

HABIT   Blue 2"–4" spikes of wonderfully fragrant flowers in spring. Upright to sprawling spring wildflower. Germinates from seed in fall. Leaves and stems are hairy.

CULTURE   Sometimes hard to get going, but once established, is reliable in returning each year. Likes poor soil.

USES   Wildflower.

PROBLEMS   Hard seed to germinate. Poisonous to horses.

NOTES   Do not fertilize wildflowers. Nurseries are now selling 2¼" pots for planting small garden areas in the spring. Many people recommend scarified seed, which germinates the first year, but it's more natural to plant untreated seed and have some sprouting for several years. Native to Texas and is the state flower. Also called buffalo clover and Texas lupine.

BLUE-EYED GRASS
Sisyrinchium spp.
siss-ee-RINK-ee-um

Perennial—Sun
Ht. 6"–12" Spread 12"
Spacing 9"

HABIT   Purple-blue ½" flower with yellow center in spring. Bulb member of the iris family, grasslike foliage, beautiful light blue flowers in spring.

CULTURE   Grows easily in all types of soils.

USES   Beautiful wildflower that should be used more.

PROBLEMS   Looks rough in the summer.

NOTES   Goes dormant and looks pretty ratty in the summer. Don't mow it down until it has gone dormant.

163

Blue Mist

BLUE MIST (Bluebeard)
Caryopteris spp.
ka-ree-OP-te-ris

Perennial—Sun/Part Shade
Ht. 2'–4' Spread 2'–3'
Spacing 2'–3'

HABIT   Deep blue to lavender flowers in summer. *Caryopteris clandonensis* is low-growing, usually about 2' high and 2' wide. 'Azure' and 'Heavenly Blue' are available cultivars. *Caryopteris incana* is taller-growing, usually up to 4'. Dies to the ground in winter and usually returns in spring in the northern half of the state. Makes a bushy evergreen in the southern part of the state.

CULTURE   Grows well in prepared beds with good drainage.

USES   Summer color. Excellent for use with white-flowering plants.

PROBLEMS   May freeze out in harsh winters. Should be treated as an annual.

NOTES   Hasn't been used much in the past. Should be planted more often.

Bouncing Bet

BOUNCING BET
Saponaria officinalis
sap-oh-NAR-ee-ah oh-fih-sih-NAY-lis

Perennial—Sun/Part Shade
Ht. 1'–2' Spread 2'–3'
Spacing 12"–18"

HABIT   Fragrant double pink and white phloxlike flowers from late spring until fall. 3"–4" leaves, prefers morning sun and afternoon shade.

CULTURE   Easy-to-grow, drought-tolerant perennial. Cut back to encourage a second round of flowers.

USES   Perennial garden. Roots contain a cleansing agent that substitutes for soap.

PROBLEMS   Few if any.

Butterfly Bush

BUTTERFLY BUSH (Summer Lilac)
Buddleia spp.
BUD-lee-ah

Deciduous—Sun/Part Shade
Ht. 3'–8' Spread 4'–6'
Spacing 3'–4'

HABIT   Long clusters of fragrant flowers in many colors, from white to dark purple, mostly in July and August. Arching, open-branching woody growth, unusually thinly foliated. Blooms on new growth from early summer till fall.

CULTURE   Drought tolerant. Easy to grow in well-prepared beds. Prune after flowers have faded.

USES   Summer color attracts butterflies, bees, and hummingbirds. Borders, perennial garden.

PROBLEMS   Can suffer freeze damage.

NOTES   *B. alternifolia* and *B. davidii* have lilac flowers. The native *B. marrubiifolia* has orange flowers. Cultivars available in several colors.

BUTTERFLY WEED
Asclepias tuberosa
az-KLEP-ee-us too-ber-OH-sah

Perennial—Sun
Ht. 1½'–2' Spread 2'
Spacing 2'

HABIT   2"–4" clusters of yellow or orange blooms from April to September.

CULTURE   Relatively easy to grow in any soil. Slow-growing. Does not grow well in pots.

USES   Summer color to attract butterflies.

PROBLEMS   Aphids on new growth. Can die out from too much water. Hard to transplant.

NOTES   Plant a few, but don't invest a lot of money in this plant.

Butterfly Weed

Calendula

Caladium

Caladium and Hoja Santa

CALADIUM
Caladium × hortulanum
ca-LAY-dee-um hor-too-LAN-um

Annual—Shade/Part Shade
Ht. 2' Spread 12"–18"
Spacing 8"–12"

HABIT   Brightly colored leaves on tall stems from tubers. White varieties seem
   to be more sun tolerant.
CULTURE   Plant tubers in well-prepared beds after the soil temperatures have
   warmed in the later spring (April 15–30). Dies at frost. Not worth trying to
   save the tubers through the winter. Keep the flowers cut off.
USES   Color in ground cover areas, containers.
PROBLEMS   Wind damage.
NOTES   The whites are my favorites, such as 'Candidum,' 'Aaron,' 'White
   Wing,' and 'Jackie Suthers.' Plant a second round of tubers in late summer for
   a fall color display that's impressive. Mother plants are native to the
   riverbanks of the Amazon.

CALENDULA
Calendula officinalis
ka-LEN-dew-la oh-fih-sih-NAY-lis

Annual—Sun/Light Shade
Ht. 12"–15" Spread 15"
Spacing 12"

HABIT   Composite orange or yellow daisylike flowers. Cool-season annual
   flower and herb. Set out transplants in the fall or early spring in the northern
   part of the state. Sow seed in mid to late summer in flats.
CULTURE   Plant in healthy, well-drained soils.
USES   Annual flower color for the cooler months, good in pots. Used as a
   pot herb.
PROBLEMS   Can't stand hot weather.

Calylophus and Bluebonnets

Candletree

CALYLOPHUS
Calylophus spp.
kal-ee-LOH-fuss

Perennial—Sun
Ht. 1'–1½' Spread 1½'
Spacing 1'

HABIT Similar look to the evening primrose but more upright. Narrow leaves and brilliant yellow flowers that open around sunset and stay open all the next day. Blooms from March to November but heaviest in the spring.

CULTURE Easy to grow, very low water needs, evergreen in the southern part of the state. Cut back to 8" in the fall.

USES Rock garden or other low-water garden. Perennial garden.

PROBLEMS Poor drainage or too much water will kill it quickly.

CANDLETREE
Cassia alata
CASS-ee-ah ah-LAH-tah

Annual—Sun
Ht. 6'–8' Spread 6'–8'
Spacing 3'–4'

HABIT Open, spreading growth in summer. Yellow flowers in spiked clusters. Large compound leaves. Gets large in one season.

CULTURE Needs sun, loose organic soil, and moderate water and fertilization. Prune back after flowering.

USES Dramatic accent plant, late-summer color, background and annual color for large open areas.

PROBLEMS Too large for small residential gardens.

NOTES Parks departments use it together with cannas for a carefree colorful show. Native to the tropics.

Candytuft

Canna

Cashmere Bouquet

Castor Bean

CANDYTUFT

Iberis sempervirens
eye-BER-is sem-per-VYE-rens

Perennial—Sun/Part Shade
Ht. 8"–12" Spread 12"–15"
Spacing 9"–12"

HABIT Low, compact, neat perennial that produces pure white flowers that
bloom in spring. Will usually return for a few years.
CULTURE Plant in sun or partial shade in well-prepared soil that drains easily.
Moderate water and fertilizer requirements.
USES Small gardens, rock walls, small containers.
PROBLEMS Very short-lived perennial.
NOTES Also called evergreen or perennial candytuft.

CANNA

Canna generalis
CAN-ah jen-er-ALL-is

Perennial—Sun
Ht. 2'–6' Spread 3'–6'
Spacing 18"–24"

HABIT Coarse perennial that spreads from underground stems. Large leaves and
flowers. Most popular is dwarf red. Dies to ground at frost, returns the next spring.
CULTURE Full sun, loose soil, plenty of water, and healthy amounts of fertilizer
for good blooms.
USES Use as a background flower or in large open areas.
PROBLEMS Wind damage, coarseness.
NOTES Native to the tropics. Easy to grow but too coarse for most residential
gardens. The red-foliage selections tend to have smaller flowers but are better-
looking plants.

CASHMERE BOUQUET

Clerodendrum bungei
kle-ro-DEN-drum BUNG-gee-eye

Perennial—Sun/Shade
Ht. 3'–6' Spread 6' and more
Spacing 3'

HABIT Fragrant pink to red ½" flowers in 6"–8" clusters. Large dark green leaves
with fuzzy undersides. Showy summer flowers. Spreads aggressively by
underground suckers. Cut back severely in the spring and pick-prune through
the growing season to maintain interesting summer color and texture.
CULTURE Very easy to grow—maybe a little too easy. Drought tolerant and
needs little care.
USES Attracts hummingbirds. Good with other aggressive plants like perilla,
houttuynia, and hoja santa where spreading is not a worry.
PROBLEMS Is very invasive.
NOTES *C. paniculatum* is the pagoda flower. *C. speciosissimum* is the dramatic
java plant.

CASTOR BEAN

Ricinus communis
RI-ki-nus kom-EW-nis

Annual—Sun
Ht. 6'–15' Spread 3'–4'
Spacing 6'–8'

HABIT Clusters of small white flowers, followed by prickly husks with shiny
black seeds. Very large, tropical-looking foliage.
CULTURE Easy to grow in any soil, likes hot weather. Pinch off burlike seed
capsules to prevent seed from maturing.
USES Bold texture, tall and quick-growing, inexpensive screen.
PROBLEMS Seeds are highly poisonous. Foliage and stems are also toxic and can
cause severe skin irritation.

Chenille Plant

Chrysanthemum

Clammy Weed

Cleome

CHENILLE PLANT   Annual—Sun
Acalypha hispida   Ht. 18"–36" Spread 15"–18"
ah-ka-LEE-fa HIS-pid-a   Spacing 12"–15"

HABIT   Long, fuzzy red tassels all summer. Annual foliage and flower plant; kin
   to copperleaf but has long, showy flowers and green foliage.
CULTURE   Very cold tender.
USES   Annual beds, pots, hanging baskets.
PROBLEMS   Freeze damage.

CHRYSANTHEMUM (Mum)   Perennial—Sun
Chrysanthemum spp.   Ht. 12"–36" Spread 18"–36"
kris-AN-tha-mum   Spacing 12"–18"

HABIT   Fall-blooming perennials with lots of colors and combinations. Attractive foliage that looks good most of the year. Some bloom in spring and fall.
CULTURE   Loose soil, good drainage, ample water, and regular fertilization. For
   best blooms, pinch new growth off until August 1. Stop fertilization when
   the buds show color. Avoid light at night, for it retards blooms.
USES   Perennial gardens, border, pots, cutting gardens.
PROBLEMS   Aphids.
NOTES   There are 13 different categories established by the National Chrysan-
   themum Society: Spoon, Reflexing Incurve, Semidouble, Decorative,
   Anemone, Spider, Single, Reflex, Pompom, Thistle, Laciniated, Quile, and
   Incurve. They are all beautiful. Native to Europe, Asia, and South Africa.

CLAMMY WEED   Annual—Sun
Polanisia dodecandra   Ht. 1'–3' Spread 2'–3'
po-lan-ESS-ee-ah do-dec-CAN-dra   Spacing 18"–24"

HABIT   Sticky, hairy, tall-growing annual with a strong, rank odor. Grows wild
   in sandy soil but adapts to heavy soils. Blooms are white to pink from May to
   October.
CULTURE   Easy to grow with low fertilizer and water requirements. Self-sowing
   but not invasive.
USES   Summer color. Terrific plant for attracting beneficial insects and butterflies.
PROBLEMS   Unpleasant smell when rubbed against.

CLEOME (Spider Flower)   Annual—Sun/Part Shade
Cleome spinosa   Ht. 3'–5' Spread 3'–4'
CLAY-oh-mee spin-OH-sa   Spacing 2'–3'

HABIT   White, pink, and purple flowers primarily early to midsummer.
CULTURE   Plant in morning sun for best results. Needs healthy, well-drained
   soil. Plant transplants or sow seed directly into garden soil after soil has
   warmed in the spring. Will reseed readily.
USES   Dramatic background summer color. Interesting texture.
PROBLEMS   Wet soil will do it in.

Cockscomb

Coleus 'Inky Fingers'

COCKSCOMB
Celosia spp.
sey-LOW-see-ah

Annual—Sun
Ht. 12"–24" Spread 12"–18"
Spacing 10"–12"

HABIT Bright red, pink, orange, or yellow flowers in summer. Bold-textured summer color. Red is the most common flower. Some varieties also have red foliage. Plant in spring from transplants after last frost. Plant in midsummer for fall color. Cutting back to stimulate more flowers is not recommended.
CULTURE Easy summer color plant in well-prepared beds.
USES Low border, dramatic color splashes.
PROBLEMS Slugs and snails.
NOTES Dry by hanging upside down in a paper bag. Color will last all winter.

COLEUS
Coleus hybrids
COLE-ee-uhs

Annual—Shade
Ht. 18"–24" Spread 18"–24"
Spacing 12"–18"

HABIT Colorful leaves of red, yellow, orange, green, and all combinations. Dies at frost, very cold tender.
CULTURE Needs shade, drainage, moisture, and protection from wind. Keep flowers pinched off.
USES Summer color, border or mass plantings. Containers or hanging baskets.
PROBLEMS Slugs, snails, mealybugs, and aphids.
NOTES Roots easily in water and can be grown indoors. Native to the tropics.

Sun Coleus

Columbine

Purple Coneflower

Columbine

Autumn Sun Coneflower (*Rudbeckia*)

Copperleaf

COLUMBINE

Aquilegia spp.
ah-kwi-LEE-ji-ah

Perennial—Shade/Part Shade
Ht. 12"–24" Spread 12"–18"
Spacing 12"–18"

HABIT Delicate, woodsy-type flowers that bloom in late spring and summer on long stems from lacy foliage. Dies to ground at frost, returns the following spring.

CULTURE Loose, well-drained soil. Light water and fertilizer requirements. It goes dormant in the heat of summer if not irrigated.

USES Color in shady area. Excellent in natural gardens.

PROBLEMS Few if any once established.

NOTES *A. canadensis* is the red-and-yellow-flowered native and is very carefree. *A. longissima* is the pure yellow native. *A. hinckleyana*, native to far West Texas, has been renamed 'Texas Gold.'

CONEFLOWER, PURPLE

Echinacea angustifolia
ek-uh-NAY-see-uh an-gus-ti-FOAL-ee-ah

Perennial—Sun
Ht. 2'–3' Spread 3'–4'
Spacing 1'–2'

HABIT Brightly flowered perennial that blooms early to midsummer. Flowers are dark pink with a yellow center.

CULTURE Carefree and drought tolerant.

USES Perennial beds, natural areas, and most anywhere—it's a great plant.

PROBLEMS Few if any.

NOTES *E. purpurea* is a lower-blooming variety with larger flowers. *E.* 'White Swan' is a white-flowering cultivar. Yellow coneflower (*Rudbeckia nitida*) is a much taller-growing and tougher perennial.

COPPERLEAF (Copperplant)

Acalypha wilkesiana
ah-ca-LEE-fa wilk-see-AN-ah

Annual—Sun
Ht. 24"–36" Spread 24"–36"
Spacing 18"

HABIT Fast-growing tropical shrub that works like an annual for us. Flowers are insignificant. Colorful foliage all summer. Dies at frost.

CULTURE Best in full sun in prepared beds with good drainage and ample water and fertilizer.

USES Background for other bedding plants.

PROBLEMS Extensive root system often competes with other bedding plants.

NOTES Native to the Pacific Islands.

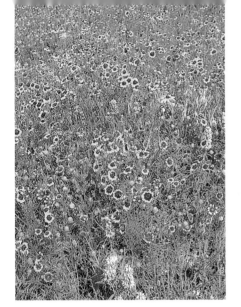

Coreopsis tinctoria

'Moonbeam' Coreopsis

Cosmos

Crinum Lily

COREOPSIS
Coreopsis spp.
ko-ree-OP-sis

Perennial—Sun/Light Shade
Ht. 12"–24" Spread 24"
Spacing 12"–24"

HABIT Perennial that looks good most of the year and great while in bloom May to August. Will reseed and spread—which is okay. Primarily yellow flowers.
CULTURE Easy in any soil, sun to light shade, low water and food needs. Can be planted from seed.
USES Summer color, perennial beds, and cut flowers.
PROBLEMS Few serious ones.
NOTES *C. lanceolata* is a pure yellow native. Several excellent hybrids such as 'Sun Ray' and 'Baby Sun' are on the market. *C. tinctoria* is an annual with a red center. *C. verticillata* 'Moonbeam' is an excellent fern-leafed perennial. There are many other choices, and almost all of them are good.

COSMOS
Cosmos sulphureus
KOS-mos sul-FEW-ree-us

Annual—Sun
Ht. 12"–18" Spread 18"–24"
Spacing 12"

HABIT Lacy foliage and flowers on long stems. Multicolored flowers in summer.
CULTURE Any soil, drought tolerant. Can be easily grown from seed. Plant in late spring or early summer. Plant from seed directly in beds after last frost and beyond.
USES Summer flowers.
PROBLEMS Few if any. Fungus if planted too early in the season.
NOTES White varieties are also available. Native to Mexico.

CRINUM LILY
Crinum spp.
CRY-num

Perennial—Sun/Part Shade
Ht. 2'–4' Spread 24"–40"
Spacing 24"–40"

HABIT Some bloom in early summer, others in late summer. Lily-shaped flowers in white, pink, and rose. Clumping perennial with long stalks, 4"–6" fragrant flowers. Thick fleshy roots from large bulbs.
CULTURE Plant in spring or fall in rich, healthy soil.
USES Wildflower, perennial garden, bold foliage texture.
PROBLEMS Slugs and snails.
NOTES Flowering is more prolific if clumps are left undisturbed for several years.

Crocosmia

Crocus

Saffron

CROCOSMIA (Montbretia)
Crocosmia pottsii
crow-KOS-me-ah POTS-ee-eye

Perennial—Sun/Part Shade
Ht. 18"–24" Spread 24"–36"
Spacing 12"–18"

HABIT   Red-orange flowers in early summer. Spreading perennial with sword-shaped gladiola-like leaves.
CULTURE   Easy to grow from corms that send out stolons to form new plants.
USES   Perennial garden color, cut flowers.
PROBLEMS   Tends to sprawl. Too much water and fertilizer can cause weak growth. Can become invasive in healthy soils.
NOTES   There is also a yellow-flowered variety. Native to South Africa.

CROCUS
Crocus spp.
CROW-kus

Perennial—Sun/Part Shade
Ht. 4"–8" Spread 4"–8"
Spacing 3"–6"

HABIT   Blooms in many colors, mostly from late winter through early spring. Some bloom in the fall. Leaves are basal and grasslike, often with a silver midrib. Purple, blue, yellow, and white flowers are available.
CULTURE   Plant in well-prepared soil and use the basic watering and fertilizing program. Plant corms in the fall.
USES   Low-growing perennial color.
PROBLEMS   Squirrels, rabbits, gophers.
NOTES   *C. sativus,* saffron, should be planted in the summer, as it blooms in fall with gorgeous purple flowers and bright red stigmas, the source of the delicious and valuable spice. This crocus perennializes better than others. *Sternbergia lutea,* a yellow fall-blooming bulb often called autumn crocus, naturalizes better and lasts longer than most true crocuses.

CROTON
Codiaeum variegatum
ko-dee-EYE-um var-ee-uh-GAH-tum

Evergreen Shrub—Sun/Part Shade
Ht. 3'–6' Spread 3'
Spacing 2'

HABIT   Tender evergreen shrub used as an annual for foliage color. Large colorful leaves with yellow and red variegations.

Croton

Paperwhite Daffodil

Daffodil

CULTURE Plant in well-prepared beds. Color is better in full sun than in shade.
USES Summer color.
PROBLEMS Spider mites on stressed plants, root rot in poorly drained soils.
NOTES Very sensitive to cold weather; use in pots and move indoors in winter or treat as an annual.

African Bush Daisy

DAFFODIL (Jonquil)
Narcissus spp.
narr-SIS-us

Perennial—Sun
Ht. 9"–18" Spread 12"–18"
Spacing 6"–12"

HABIT Lovely bell-shaped flowers in early spring. Colors are white, yellow, orange, and combinations. Foliage of vertical blades from the ground. Flowers last about two weeks, usually less. The smaller white narcissus has same characteristics.
CULTURE Plant bulbs in loose organic beds with good drainage. Add 1 tablespoon bone meal per bulb and work into the soil before planting. Foliage must be left to turn brown on the plant before removing, to form the bulbs for next year.
USES Spring flowers, naturalized area, cutting garden.
PROBLEMS Snails, slugs.

DAISY, AFRICAN BUSH
Euryops spp.
YEW-ree-ops

Tender Perennial or Annual—Sun
Ht. 3'–4' Spread 2'–3'
Spacing 18"–24"

HABIT Bright yellow daisylike flowers. Lacy foliage and bushy growth.
CULTURE Easy to grow in any well-drained soil. Needs minimal water and fertilizer. Shrubby tender perennial used as an annual except in the extreme southern part of the state. Cut back after heavy flush of flowers to prolong blooming.
USES Pots, summer color.
PROBLEMS Mostly pest free.

Blackfoot Daisy

Dahlberg Daisy

Engelmann Daisy

Four-Nerve Daisy

DAISY, BLACKFOOT   Perennial—Sun/Part Shade
Melampodium leucanthum   Ht. 12" Spread 12"–15"
meh-lam-PODE-ee-um loo-KAN-thum   Spacing 9"–12"

HABIT   Low-growing, compact daisy. White blossoms throughout the growing
season. Dies to the ground in winter, but returns faithfully each year.
CULTURE   Easy in any soil. Easy to transplant or plant any time of the year.
USES   Perennial garden, border, white spring, summer, and fall flowers.
PROBLEMS   Fungus caused by overwatering.
NOTES   This is one of my favorites. A taller-growing, yellow-flowering annual
variety (*M. cinereum*) is also quite good.

DAISY, DAHLBERG   Annual—Sun
Dyssodia tenuiloba   Ht. 12" Spread 12"
die-SO-de-ah ten-you-ee-LOW-ba   Spacing 9"–12"

HABIT   Nickel-size golden yellow-orange flowers that bloom most of the
summer. Delicate bright green, fragrant foliage.
CULTURE   Likes well-drained soil.
USES   Summer color.
PROBLEMS   Few if any.
NOTES   Looks great when planted with copperleaf, firebush, Mexican petunia,
and other bronze- or purple-leaf plants.

DAISY, ENGELMANN   Perennial—Full Sun
Engelmannia pinnatifida   Ht. 1'–3' Spread 3'
eng-gull-MAHN-ee-ah pin-ah-TIFF-ih-dah Spacing 2'–3'

HABIT   Yellow 1" flowers from spring to fall, mostly in May. Forms rosette of
lobed foliage in winter, strong taproot, blooms well with low to medium
moisture. Flower petals curl under on the ends during extremely hot weather.
Carefree after established.
CULTURE   Easy to grow in almost any soil.
USES   Perennial color, wildflower, livestock forage.
PROBLEMS   Sometimes hard to establish.

DAISY, FOUR-NERVE   Perennial—Sun/Part Shade
Hymenoxys scaposa   Ht. 12" Spread 6"–9"
hye-men-OX-iss skay-POH-sah   Spacing 9"

HABIT   Solitary yellow 1"–2" daisylike flowers from March to October. Small,
easy-to-grow native perennial with pale gray-green leaves, furry or shiny bare
stems. Foliage has strong, bitter fragrance when crushed.
CULTURE   Drought tolerant and carefree.
USES   Rock gardens, xeriscapes.
PROBLEMS   Too much water will rot the plant.
NOTES   Name comes from the four veins on each flower petal. This is a plant
growing in a trial planting. A thin layer of mulch should have been used.

Gerber Daisy

Oxeye Daisy

Gloriosa Daisy

DAISY, GERBERA
Gerbera jamesonii
GER-ba-ra jaym-SON-ee-eye

Annual—Morning Sun
Ht. 12"–18" Spread 12"–15"
Spacing 12"

HABIT Large lettuce-looking foliage and very showy daisylike flowers in various shades of reds, pinks, and yellows on long stems.

CULTURE Plant in moist but well-drained soil and fertilize every two weeks. Mulch heavily.

USES Color for cooler parts of the growing season. Container plant.

PROBLEMS Whiteflies, slugs, and snails. Doesn't like hot weather.

NOTES Use a few in the early spring for a splash of color, but don't invest a lot of money in these plants. They don't last very well.

DAISY, GLORIOSA (Black-eyed Susan)
Rudbeckia hirta
rude-BECK-ee-ah HIR-ta

Perennial—Sun
Ht. 18"–36" Spread 18"–24"
Spacing 12"–18"

HABIT Fuzzy foliage and yellow flowers with dark brown centers that bloom from June into August.

CULTURE Grows okay in dry soil but responds favorably to moist, well-prepared beds. Needs good drainage. Can be planted from seed or pots.

USES Summer flowers, low-water areas.

PROBLEMS None.

NOTES Also called coneflower. Native to Texas. *Rudbeckia* 'Goldstrum' is an improved variety.

DAISY, OXEYE
Chrysanthemum leucanthemum
kruh-SAN-thuh-mum loo-KAN-thuh-mum

Perennial—Sun
Ht. 12"–36" Spread 18"–36"
Spacing 12"–18"

HABIT Large, showy flowers that are great for cutting from early June to August. Returns very well each year.

CULTURE Easy, any well-drained soil. Low water and fertilizer requirements. Established plants should be divided every few years.

USES Summer flowers, perennial gardens.

PROBLEMS None serious.

NOTES Cut flowers have a bad odor. This plant is similar to Shasta daisy but tougher and more drought tolerant. Dwarf Shasta daisy is also a good choice, and 'Silver Princess' is a particularly good one. Tahoka daisy (*Machaeranthera tanacetifolia*) is a Texas native that blooms all summer with blue flowers. Lazy daisy (*Aphanostephus skirrhobasis*) is a low-growing annual.

Datura

Brugmansia

Daylily

DATURA (Jimsonweed)
Datura wrightii
day-TOO-rah RITE-ee-eye

Perennial—Sun
Ht. 3'–5' Spread 5'–6'
Spacing 4'–6'

HABIT Fragrant white or purple night-opening flowers 4"–6" wide. Blooms all summer the first season. Large, fuzzy, dark green foliage, thick succulent stems that stink when crushed or broken. Dies to ground in winter but returns each spring. Spreads easily by seed.

CULTURE Very easy to grow in any soil. Doesn't always return as a true perennial.

USES Dramatic color and fragrance.

PROBLEMS Coarse, weedy, and poisonous. Tender skin can easily get a rash from contact with stems or foliage.

NOTES Mistakenly called moonflower, which is a nonpoisonous member of the morning glory family. *D. metel* has double purple flowers and is naturalized here in Texas. A closely related plant, *Brugmansia* spp., has larger flowers in several colors that hang down. Native to Texas.

DAYLILY
Hemerocallis spp.
him-er-oh-CALL-us

Perennial—Sun/Part Shade
Ht. 8"–36" Spread 24"–36"
Spacing 18"–24"

HABIT Foliage resembles large-leafed grass. Many colors, shapes of blooms, and heights of plants available. Blooms from late May until September. Each bloom lasts only one day, but others follow. Blooms range in size from 2" to 8" across.

CULTURE Easy to grow in any well-prepared, well-drained soil. Average water and heavy fertilizer needs. Divide in October or November every few years. Plant from containers year-round.

USES Summer flowers, background or accent plant, cut flowers.

PROBLEMS Few serious other than aphids in the spring. Ladybugs usually take care of them. The solution to rust is cornmeal and the overall organic program.

NOTES Called poor man's orchid. Native to Europe, China, and Japan. Daylily flowers are a gourmet vegetable.

Dianthus

Elderberry

Above: Elephant Ear; below: Esperanza

DIANTHUS

Dianthus spp.
dye-AN-thus

Perennial—Sun
Ht. 8"–12" Spread 12"–18"
Spacing 9"–12"

HABIT Delicate-looking cool-weather flowers that come in a variety of colors ranging from reds and purples to pinks and whites. Some are annual, others perennial. Some varieties will bloom all winter if weather is not severe.

CULTURE Prepared and well-drained beds in full sun. Moderate water and fertilizer. Plant in the fall or late winter.

USES Cool-season color.

PROBLEMS None serious.

NOTES A good perennial variety is *D. allwoodii.* Carnations, pinks, and sweet Williams are all variations of this genus.

ELDERBERRY

Sambucus canadensis
sam-BEW-cus can-ah-DEN-sis

Perennial—Sun/Part Shade
Ht. 10'–12' Spread 8'–10'
Spacing 6'–8'

HABIT White flower clusters in spring. Edible purple-black berries ripen in August. Shrubby, tall, and multitrunked.

CULTURE Grows easily to 12'. Plant in most any soil and stay out of the way. Likes to have plenty of moisture.

USES Excellent for attracting birds. Diuretic. Flower heads and berries are used for wines, jellies, pies, and excellent fritters. Good landscape plant. Delicious berries if you can get them before the birds do.

PROBLEMS Can be invasive.

NOTES Known for its ability to produce humus quickly.

ELEPHANT EAR

Alocasia spp.
al-oh-KAY-see-ah

Perennial—Sun/Filtered Light
Ht. 3'–5' Spread 3'–4'
Spacing 2'–3'

HABIT Flowers similar to the calla lilies but unimpressive. Huge caladium-like leaves on three to five stalks.

CULTURE Needs loose, moist, highly organic soil for best results.

USES Large foliage texture, tropical effect.

PROBLEMS Few; freeze damage in the northern part of the state.

NOTES *Colocasia* is very similar but doesn't have raised veins as does *Alocasia.* *Colocasia* is the mass planting that grows on the edge of Turtle Creek in Dallas.

ESPERANZA (Gold Star Esperanza)

Tecoma stans 'Gold Star'
tea-COE-ma STANS

Annual—Sun
Ht. 4' Spread 3'
Spacing 3'–4'

HABIT Showy selection of a bushy native. Blooms all summer with dramatic yellow flowers.

CULTURE Although technically a shrub, it is normally treated as a summer annual. Will perennialize in the southern half of the state, especially in an organic program.

USES Large color plant for summer.

PROBLEMS Not very winter hardy.

NOTES Also called yellow bells. Texas A&M has recently made this plant a Texas Superstar, but it's a native that has been around a long time.

Evening Primrose

Firebush

Fan Flower

EVENING PRIMROSE
Oenothera spp.
ee-NOTH-er-ah

Perennial—Sun
Ht. 12"–18" Spread 24"–36"
Spacing 12"–18"

HABIT   Sprawling perennial with showy, long-lasting flower display in the spring. Pink or white 2" blooms in spring.

CULTURE   Plant from containers in the spring or seeds in the fall.

USES   Wildflowers in grassy areas, carefree perennial garden. Attracts beneficial ground beetles.

PROBLEMS   Ragged-looking when not in bloom; not for the well-groomed garden. Can take over an area.

NOTES   Native from Missouri to Texas.

FAN FLOWER
Scaevola 'Mauve Clusters'
ska-VO-la

Tender Perennial—Full Sun
Ht. 4"–6" Spread 24"–36"
Spacing 12"–18"

HABIT   Bluish or lilac flowers in 1½" clusters. Flowers are fan-shaped, with petals all on one side. Everblooming bedding plant that forms a mat; evergreen in South Texas. Moderately drought tolerant.

CULTURE   Needs well-prepared soil. Be sure to add Texas greensand and cornmeal.

USES   Summer-color bedding plant, excellent for hanging baskets.

PROBLEMS   Chlorosis unless iron and magnesium amendments are used.

FIREBUSH (Mexican Firebush)
Hamelia spp.
ha-MEEL-yah

Annual—Sun
Ht. 24" Spread 24"
Spacing 18"

HABIT   Coral red flowers. Perennializes in the southern half of the state.

CULTURE   Drought tolerant, easy to grow in loose, well-drained soils. Dies from a hard freeze.

USES   Summer color, hummingbird attractant, pot plant.

PROBLEMS   Few if any.

Gayfeather

FOUR O'CLOCK
Mirabilis jalapa
mee-RAH-bi-lis ha-LAH-pa

Perennial—Shade/Part Shade
Ht. 24"–48" Spread 24"–36"
Spacing 18"–24"

HABIT Fragrant trumpet-shaped red, pink, yellow, and white flowers that open
in mid-afternoon. Upright-growing, summer-flowering perennial. Sow seed
in full sun in early spring for color from midsummer to fall. Reseeds readily.
As name implies, flowers open in late afternoon and last into the evening.

CULTURE Easy to grow in any soil but responds to healthy beds. Drought
tolerant.

USES Summer color.

PROBLEMS Can develop into a weedy pest.

NOTES Very tough perennial, can survive lots of abuse.

FOXGLOVE
Digitalis spp.
di-gi-TAH-lis

Annual/Biennial—Sun/Shade
Ht. 2'–6' Spread 2'
Spacing 2'

HABIT Vertical stalks with white, pink, red, and yellow flowers from May
through June. Prolific biennial or wildflower with tubular flowers shaped like
fingers of a glove. Hairy gray-green leaves from base clumps.

CULTURE Likes fertile, moist soil. Will grow in full sun or partial shade. In
warm weather, water frequently. Sow seeds in the spring or set out plants in
the fall for blooms the following spring and summer. After the first flowering,
cut the main spike so side shoots will develop and bloom.

USES Background flower, source of a powerful heart medicine that should be
administered only by a doctor.

PROBLEMS Snails and slugs. Entire plant is toxic. Don't plant in garden where
small children play. Teach children to look but not touch.

GAYFEATHER
Liatris spp.
lee-AT-tris

Perennial—Sun
Ht. 1'–2' Spread 1'–2'
Spacing 1'–2'

HABIT Tufts of narrow stems topped by narrow plumes of fluffy purple flowers.

CULTURE Tough, drought-tolerant wildflowers that respond fairly well to
maintained gardens. Cut to the ground in winter. Can be planted from pots
or seed.

USES Perennial gardens, borders, summer flowers. Makes a wonderful cut
flower because the purple color lasts indefinitely in a dry arrangement.

PROBLEMS Too much water.

NOTES Several good varieties exist. Native to Texas and Oklahoma.

Below, left: Four O'Clock;
below, right: Foxglove

Gazania

Geranium

Gladiola

Globe Amaranth

GAZANIA

Gazania hybrids
ga-ZANE-ee-ah

Perennial—Sun
Ht. 6"–12" Spread 12"–18"
Spacing 9"–12"

HABIT   Clump-forming summer flower, mostly yellows and oranges.
CULTURE   Plant in full sun, any soil with good drainage. Drought tolerant and has low fertilization requirements. Plant from containers in spring.
USES   Summer color, drought-tolerant gardens.
PROBLEMS   Relatively few.
NOTES   Native to South Africa.

GERANIUM

Pelargonium hortorum
pell-ar-GONE-ee-um hor-TORE-um

Annual—Sun/Part Shade
Ht. 18"–24" Spread 18"–24"
Spacing 12"

HABIT   Upright or trailing; clusters of red, orange, pink, or white flowers.
CULTURE   Sun or part shade, well-prepared beds with good drainage. Cool weather is its favorite time of the year. Plant in late winter from containers.
USES   Annual gardens, pots, hanging baskets.
PROBLEMS   Cutworms, caterpillars, summer heat.
NOTES   Native to South Africa. Scented geraniums bloom only once a year and are grown mostly for their wonderfully varied fragrances. The genus *Geranium* is the true geranium. It is a smaller plant, but perennial.

GLADIOLA (Glads)

Gladiolus hortulanus
glad-ee-OH-lus hor-tew-LAH-nus

Perennial—Morning Sun/
Afternoon Shade
Ht. 24"–48" Spread 12"–15"
Spacing 6"–12"

HABIT   Thin vertical spikes with flowers of many colors from late spring through summer. Various shades of red, pink, salmon, orange, lavender, yellow, and white. *G. byzantinus,* or hardy gladiola, grows 18"–24" and blooms in the spring in a rich purple-maroon color. It is more compact than standard glads and perennializes to return every year.
CULTURE   Plant the bulblike corms in the spring in well-prepared, highly organic soil. Tall types need to be staked.
USES   Summer color, cut flowers.
PROBLEMS   Chewing insects and thrips.
NOTES   Miniature types are available. Corms can be dug, dried, dusted with diatomaceous earth and sulfur, and stored for replanting in the spring. Best to plant new ones each year. Some will return if left in the ground.

GLOBE AMARANTH

Gomphrena globosa
gom-FREE-na glo-BO-sa

Annual—Sun
Ht. 12"–24" Spread 18"–24"
Spacing 12"

HABIT   Long-lasting summer flowers in several colors, including purple, orange, and off-white.
CULTURE   Easy summer annual to grow, but responds well to healthy beds. Likes hot weather and well-drained soil. Plant after risk of frost. Can be planted as late as midsummer for color through fall.
USES   Annual color. Cut flowers can be dried and will last all winter.
PROBLEMS   Poor drainage.

Goldenrod

Hibiscus

GOLDENROD
Solidago virgaurea
sal-eh-DAY-go ver-GAR-ee-ah

Perennial—Sun/Part Shade
Ht. 2'–7' Spread: Wide-spreading
Spacing: One or two is usually
enough

HABIT   Upright perennial with beautiful fall color.

CULTURE   Very easy to grow in any soil. Treat as a wildflower.

USES   Late summer flowers.

PROBLEMS   Very aggressive, sometimes gets out of control. Remove the faded
flowers to prevent spreading.

NOTES   Goldenrod pollen has the undeserved reputation of causing hay fever.
Some people are allergic to the plant, but the pollen is too heavy to cause
common allergies. Dwarf goldenrod only grows 24"–36" high. All goldenrod
species are useful, but *S. odora* is the most fragrant and flavorful.

HIBISCUS
Hibiscus spp.
hi-BIS-cus

Perennial—Sun/Part Shade
Ht. 5'–6' Spread 3'–6'
Spacing 2'–3'

HABIT   Hibiscus are available as annuals or perennials and in many colors.
Blooms all summer.

CULTURE   Easy to grow in any well-drained soil. Moderate water and fertilizer
requirements. Flowers form on new growth so fertilize regularly. Native to
the southern United States.

USES   Summer flower color for beds and pots.

PROBLEMS   Caterpillars occasionally on the foliage.

NOTES   The tropicals, which act as annuals here, are the most colorful, but the
hardy perennial rose mallow (*H. moscheutos*) is beautiful and will usually
overwinter. The perennial Texas Star is *H. coccineus*. 'Frisbee,' 'Southern Bell,'
and 'Marsh' are excellent perennial cultivars. 'Flare' is a large-flowered
perennial with brilliant red color. Confederate rose is *H. mutabilis.*

Hollyhock

HOLLYHOCK

Alcea rosea
AL-see-ah RO-see-ah

Biennial/Short-lived Perennial—
Part Shade
Ht. 2'–8' Spread 2'–3'
Spacing 2'

HABIT   Early to midsummer flowers on coarse-textured vertical stems.
CULTURE   Plant in well-prepared healthy beds. Grows best in morning sun and afternoon shade.
USES   Background perennial garden color
PROBLEMS   Rust, aphids.
NOTES   I wouldn't plant in large numbers. French hollyhock (*Malva sylvestris* or *Alcea zebrina*) is a shorter plant with purple-striped flowers.

HOSTA

Hosta spp.
HOSS-tah

Perennial—Shade/Part Shade
Ht. 1'–3' Spread 2'–3'
Spacing 1'–3'

HABIT   Tufted, leafy plants with fragrant white, lilac, or lavender blue spiked flowers in late summer. Many varieties and cultivars available.
CULTURE   Relatively easy. Moist, well-drained soil. Can be divided in fall. Moderate fertilizer needs. Ample organic material in the soil is best.
USES   Mass or border for shade gardens. Used more for foliage than flowers.
PROBLEMS   Slugs, snails, heat of summer.
NOTES   Also called plantain lily or shade lily. Native to Korea, China, and Japan. Those varieties with blue foliage like shade best, the variegated varieties like a little more sun, but all do best with some shade. 'Royal Standard,' a large white-flowered cultivar, and 'Sieboldii' with lavender flowers are both excellent and immune to sunburn. No transplanting or division necessary.

Hosta

Dutch Hyacinth

Grape Hyacinth

Hummingbird Bush

Impatiens

HUMMINGBIRD BUSH
(Flame Acanthus)   Deciduous—Sun/Part Shade
Anisacanthus quadrifidus   Ht. 3'–4' Spread 3'–4'
ah-nee-sah-CAN-thus kwah-DRIF-eh-dus   Spacing 2'–3'

HABIT   1½"–2" red, orange, or yellow flowers from midsummer to frost.
CULTURE   Easy to grow in well-drained soil in sun or dappled shade. Cut back in late winter to promote full growth and heavy flowering.
USES   Summer color to attract hummingbirds and butterflies.
PROBLEMS   Possible freeze problems in far northern part of the state.

HYACINTH, DUTCH   Perennial—Sun
Hyacinth spp.   Ht. 3"–12" Spread 3"–12"
HI-ah-sinth   Spacing 6"–9"

HABIT   Vertical foliage in spring followed by dramatic flower spike of most any color. Extremely fragrant.
CULTURE   Well-prepared, well-drained soil; moderate water and fertilizer requirements. Add bone meal to soil when planting.
USES   Spring color, fragrance.
PROBLEMS   Expensive for the show.
NOTES   Plant bulbs in December for early spring flowers. Plants will return but will be quite weak. Better to plant new ones again. *Muscari* spp. is the small grape hyacinth. It is much better at returning each year.

IMPATIENS   Annual—Shade
Impatiens spp.   Ht. 10"–24" Spread 18"–24"
im-PAY-shenz   Spacing 9"–12"

HABIT   Colorful low-spreading annual with tender stems, foliage, and flowers. Summer blooms of orange, white, pink, red, and purple.
CULTURE   Plant in well-prepared beds in shade after the last frost. Must have excellent drainage.
USES   Annual beds, pots, hanging baskets. One of the best flowers for shady areas.
PROBLEMS   Cutworms, spider mites, and slugs.
NOTES   Native to India and China. 'New Guinea' hybrids have showy foliage and can take much more sun. All varieties are very susceptible to freezing.

Indian Blanket

Indian Paintbrush

White Perennial Indian Paintbrush

Purple Perennial Indian Paintbrush

INDIAN BLANKET (Mexican Blanket) Annual—Sun
Gaillardia pulchella   Ht. 6"–12" Spread 12"–18"
ga-LAR-dee-ah pul-KELL-ah   Spacing 12"–18"

HABIT Showy Texas wildflower with 2" red-and-yellow flowers.
CULTURE Easy to grow from seed in any soil. *G. amblyodon* grows only in sandy soil and is pure red.
USES Wildflower for meadows, low-maintenance bedding plant.
PROBLEMS Few if any.
NOTES State wildflower of Oklahoma.

INDIAN PAINTBRUSH   Annual/Perennial—Sun
Castilleja spp.   Ht. 6"–12" Spread 9"–12"
kass-teh-LAY-ah   Spacing ¼ lb. of seed per acre

HABIT Vertical spikes bloom from March to May.
CULTURE Very small seed, usually hard to establish. Biologically active soil seems to be important.
USES Wildflower.
PROBLEMS Harder to establish than other wildflowers.
NOTES *C. indivisa* is the annual red-orange Indian paintbrush. *C. purpurea* is the perennial that blooms in red, yellow, white, pink, and orange. All paintbrushes are said to be parasitic on grass roots.

Dutch Iris

IRIS
Iris spp.
EYE-ris

Perennial—Sun
Ht. 10"–40" Spread 36"–48"
Spacing 6"–24"

HABIT   Vertical leaves; most types spread by underground rhizomes; flowers in any color. Beardless and bearded are the major groups. A few types, including Dutch irises, grow from bulbs rather than rhizomes.

CULTURE   Iris culture varies greatly—some of the beardless irises (Japanese and Louisiana) can grow in or on the edge of water. Others, like Siberian, need to be continually moist. Some, like tall bearded, need good drainage. When clumps get too thick, dig with turning fork, cut leaves to 6"–8", and replant, placing bearded iris rhizomes even with the soil surface and beardless ones 1"–2" below the surface.

USES   Spring flowers, perennial gardens, cut flowers.

PROBLEMS   None serious.

NOTES   Iris means "rainbow" in Greek, so I like to plant mixed color masses. Louisianas and spurias grow the tallest. Intermediates are a good choice for landscape irises.

Ixora

IXORA
Ixora coccinea
icks-OH-rah kok-SIN-ee-uh

Tropical used as an Annual—Sun
Ht. 24"–36" Spread 24"–36"
Spacing 18"–24"

HABIT   Clusters of red, yellow, orange, or white flowers all summer.

CULTURE   Tropical, tender plant. Cross-shaped flowers and glossy green crossed foliage; grows into a mounded form covered with long-lasting flowers. Best in healthy, well-drained soil. Blooms best with regular fertilizer applications.

USES   Summer color, potted plant, and hummingbird attractant.

PROBLEMS   Freezes easily. Use as an annual.

NOTES   Add vinegar, seaweed, and fish emulsion to the watering can at every watering for best results. This is an excellent summer-color container plant.

Above: Jatropha; below: Jerusalem Sage

JATROPHA
Jatropha integerima
ja-TRO-fa in-teg-eh-REE-mah

Tender Perennial—Sun
Ht. 3'–8' Spread 3'–4'
Spacing 2'–4'

HABIT   Showy red flowers from spring through fall.

CULTURE   Easy to grow in most any soil.

USES   Summer annual color.

PROBLEMS   Very poisonous. Used for poisonous darts in South America.

NOTES   Available in dwarf forms. Freezes easily in Texas. Best used as an annual.

JERUSALEM SAGE
Phlomis fruticosa
FLO-mis froo-ti-KO-sa

Perennial—Full Sun
Ht. 24"–48" Spread 36"–48"
Spacing 18"–24"

HABIT   Gray, woolly-leafed perennial with tiers of bright yellow flowers in late spring through early summer. Candelabra appearance.

CULTURE   Both forms are drought tolerant and easy to grow in well-drained soil.

USES   Late spring, early summer color for perennial gardens and borders.

PROBLEMS   None serious.

NOTES   *P. russelliana*, also called Jerusalem sage, looks similar but is bigger in every way—flowers are larger, dull green leaves are considerably larger, and plant reaches 3'–4' in height.

185

Joseph's Coat

JOSEPH'S COAT
Amaranthus tricolor
am-ah-RAN-thus TRI-color

Perennial—Sun
Ht. 12"–24" Spread 12"–36"
Spacing 12"–18"

HABIT   Tiny unimportant flowers. Decorative leaves, usually blotched with a variety of colors from yellow to deep maroons.
CULTURE   Responds best to well-prepared beds.
USES   Summer color for borders or masses.
PROBLEMS   Slugs, cutworms.
NOTES   Grown in Asia as a green vegetable. 'Splendens' has deep red foliage with brilliant light red upper leaves. *A. cruentus* is one of the many amaranths that are extremely delicious and healthy to eat.

LAMB'S EAR
Stachys byzantina
STACK-is biz-an-TEEN-ah

Evergreen Herb/Ground Cover—
Sun/Light Shade
Ht. 6"–12" Spread 36" and more
Spacing 12"–18"

HABIT   Purple summer blooms.
CULTURE   Needs loose, well-drained, organic soil. Light-colored, low-growing ground spreader. Drought tolerant.
USES   Ground cover, antiseptic and styptic, teas.
PROBLEMS   Too much water, poorly drained soil. Develops crown rot if kept too wet.
NOTES   Propagates and spreads easily by seeds and rhizomes. Cut back the flower spikes to maintain compact appearance. Flowers are good in dried arrangements. This is a hardy plant with feltlike white leaves as soft as a lamb's ear. It must be grown in dry, sunny conditions. Hard rains beat it down and turn it mushy.

Red Lantana

LANTANA
Lantana spp.
lan-TAN-ah

Perennial—Sun
Ht. 12"–36" Spread 24"–48"
Spacing 12"–18"

HABIT   Bushy growth all summer with flowers of yellow, white, orange, pink, blue, and purple. Trailing varieties are available. Some of the tough varieties will return each year.
CULTURE   Easy, any well-drained soil, likes good bed preparation. Drought tolerant. Regular fertilization will create more blooms.
USES   Summer color, pots, hanging baskets, attracts hummingbirds.
PROBLEMS   Whiteflies, but no big deal. Gets woody with age.
NOTES   Berries are poisonous. Plant in spring. Native Texas lantana is *L. horrida.* Use as an annual in the northern part of the state.

Below, left: Lamb's Ear;
below, right: Lantana

Larkspur

Lythrum

Marigold

LARKSPUR (Delphinium)
Consolida ambigua
kon-SO-li-da am-BIG-you-ah

Annual—Sun/Part Shade
Ht. 18"–36" Spread 18"–24"
Spacing 12"

HABIT Pink, salmon, blue, white, rose, or purple blooms in spring or early summer. Lacy foliage and dense vertical flowers. Blooms best in the cooler part of the growing season.
CULTURE Upright annual that reseeds easily to return year after year.
USES Good annual in perennial beds.
PROBLEMS Poisonous.
NOTES Seed should be planted in fall for best results but can be planted through February.

LYTHRUM (Loosestrife)
Lythrum salicaria
LITH-rum sal-eh-CARE-ee-ah

Perennial—Sun/Light Shade
Ht. 2'–4' Spread 3'–4'
Spacing 3'

HABIT Pink or lavender flowers on terminal spikes. Plant is fairly woody and upright. Species plants are invasive—cultivars are not as bad.
CULTURE Tough and very adaptable. Can grow easily in damp, normal, or dry soils of various pH.
USES Perennial garden, color accent, cutting garden.
PROBLEMS Not a long-lasting perennial in many cases.
NOTES Also called loosestrife. 'Happy,' 'Morden's Gleam,' 'Firecandle,' and 'Morden's Pink' are good cultivars. Some gardeners are reporting that even the cultivars can be invasive, especially in wet soil.

MARIGOLD
Tagetes spp.
ta-GET-tes

Annual—Sun
Ht. 12"–24" Spread 12"–24"
Spacing 9"–12"

HABIT Fast-growing, lacy foliage, yellow or orange flowers. Would last from spring to frost if it weren't for spider mites.
CULTURE Any soil, best in well-drained full-sun location. Will reseed and come up the following year but will be weaker than original plants. Can be planted midsummer for fall flowers.
USES Summer color, cut flowers, border, mass planting.
PROBLEMS Spider mites, short life.
NOTES Native to Central America. The herb Mexican mint marigold or sweet marigold has yellow flowers in late summer. Available in many container sizes.

MAY APPLE
Podophyllum peltatum
po-DOF-eh-lum pell-TAY-tum

Perennial—Shade
Ht. 1'–2' Spread 2'–3'
Spacing 2'

HABIT White flowers in April, pale yellow fruit (May apples) in May. Vigorous spreader that can become invasive. Very large umbrella-looking leaves.
CULTURE Needs sandy acid soil for best results.
USES Woodsy, forest-floor effect.
PROBLEMS Hard to find and somewhat difficult to establish.

May Apple

187

Mexican Hat

Mexican Heather

Mexican Oregano

Mexican Petunia

MEXICAN HAT

Ratibida columnaris
rah-TIB-eh-dah kah-lum-NARE-us

Perennial—Sun/Part Shade
Ht. 18"–36" Spread 18"–24"
Spacing 12"–18"

HABIT   Tough, taprooted perennial wildflower, evergreen in mild winters. Summer flowers in red, yellow, and orange emerge from rosettes of fernlike foliage.

CULTURE   Easy to grow in most soil. Likes rocky slopes as well as moist, low areas. Usually blooms the second season.

USES   Wildflower for large areas.

PROBLEMS   Can become a pest, especially for ranchers on grazing land. Hard to get rid of once established.

MEXICAN HEATHER (False Heather)   Tender tropical—Sun/Part Shade

Cuphea hyssopifolia
KOO-fee-a hi-sop-ih-FO-lee-ah

12"–24" Spread 24"–36"
Spacing 18"

HABIT   Small pink, purple, or white flowers all summer. Lacy foliage, tiny dark green leaves, and very small flowers from spring to frost.

CULTURE   Not picky about soil, likes loose, well-drained, healthy soil best.

USES   Pots, borders, summer color, delicate texture.

PROBLEMS   Freezes easily in the northern half of the state.

NOTES   Performs as an annual in all but the southern half of Texas. Perennializes in mild winters if protected and mulched. *C. micropetala* is the red-flowered cigar plant.

MEXICAN OREGANO

Poliomintha longiflora
Pol-ee-oh-MEN-tuh lon-gi-FLOR-ah

Tender Evergreen—Sun/Part Shade
Ht. 24"–48" Spread 24"–36"
Spacing 18"–24"

HABIT   Beautiful small ornamental herb with aromatic leaves. Clusters of purple flowers in summer. Flowers turn to white as they age.

CULTURE   Does best in healthy, well-drained soils with a modest amount of fertilizer.

USES   Leaves and flowers are edible and can be used like regular oregano. Historically used to flavor *cabrito*.

PROBLEMS   Freeze damage in the northern half of the state.

NOTES   Native to the mountains south of Monterrey, Mexico.

MEXICAN PETUNIA

Ruellia spp.
roo-ELL-ee-a

Perennial—Sun/Part Shade
Ht. 18"–30" Spread 36" and more
Spacing 12"–18"

HABIT   Lavender petunia-like summer flowers. Invasive, easy-to-grow perennial.

CULTURE   Needs moisture, but will grow in almost any soil.

USES   Large informal settings, perennial color.

PROBLEMS   Invasive.

NOTES   Wilts easily without ample moisture. *R. nudiflora* is the Texas native. *R. brittoniana* 'Katie' is a low-growing strap-leafed variety. It freezes more frequently in the northern part of the state.

Left and right: Monarda

Bush Morning Glory

MONARDA
Monarda citriodora
mo-NAR-da sit-ree-oh-DOR-ah

Annual/Biennial—Full Sun
Ht. 12"–18" Spread 36"
Spacing 6"–12" or 3 lbs. of seed
per acre

HABIT   Purple flowers in late summer. Upright and slow-spreading, sturdy
and tough.

CULTURE   Easy to grow in most soils, but performs best in well-prepared beds.

USES   Teas for colds, fevers, and respiratory problems. Similar to mints. Excellent bee plant; repels fleas and chiggers.

PROBLEMS   None serious.

NOTES   Nothing browses any of the monardas—not even deer. The *Monarda*
genus comprises a number of fragrant herbs with especially beautiful flowers.
Most are native plants, such as *M. fistulosa*, wild bergamot; *M. punctata*,
spotted bee balm; and *M. citriodora*, lemon mint. *M. didyma* is the red-
flowering variety. Seeds are increasingly available in mail-order catalogs, and
small plants are being seen more often in retail nurseries.

MORNING GLORY, BUSH
Ipomoea fistulosa
Eye-po-MAY-ah fist-you-LOW-sah

Perennial—Sun
Ht. 8' Spread 5'–8'
Spacing 4'–5'

HABIT   This is a terrific shrublike perennial with pink flowers that dies to the
ground in winter but puts on a show most of the summer. Drought tolerant
and heat tolerant, but can also grow in wet soil.

CULTURE   Plant in dry or moist beds; adapts well to either. Cut top growth off
when it browns in the fall. Cut back in July for a spectacular fall display.
Propagates easily from cuttings.

USES   Summer color, background plant for the border, part of a living fence, and
in wet-soil areas.

PROBLEMS   Relatively few other than availability in garden centers.

NOTES   It is not eaten by ducks, goats, cattle, buffalo, and probably deer. There
is also a white variety that wilts a little quicker in the summer heat.

Nasturtium

Nicotiana

Nierembergia

NASTURTIUM
Tropaeolum majus
tro-PIE-oh-lum MAY-yus

Annual Herb—Sun/Part Shade
High-climbing and wide-spreading
Spacing 1'–3'

HABIT   Fragrant flowers of red, brown, maroon, yellow, gold, and orange. Available in both single and double forms. Fast-growing annual flowering herb. Climbing and dwarf bush types are available.

CULTURE   Easy to grow during the cooler months.

USES   Annual beds, pots, hanging baskets. Leaves, flowers, and unripe seedpods have a delicious peppery flavor and are excellent in salads and other dishes. Source of vitamin C. All parts of the plant are edible.

PROBLEMS   Hot weather, aphids.

NICOTIANA
Nicotiana spp.
nee-ko-she-AH-na

Annual—Morning Sun/
Afternoon Shade
Ht. 12"–24" Spread 12"–18"
Spacing 10"–12"

HABIT   Fragrant star-shaped flowers in red, rose, pink, purple, white, yellow, or green in late spring and summer.

CULTURE   Grows best in healthy, well-drained soil in dappled shade or morning sun with afternoon shade. Flowering tobacco is fairly difficult to grow from seed; transplants are better.

USES   Summer color, fragrance.

PROBLEMS   Slugs and snails.

NIEREMBERGIA (Cup Flower)
Nierembergia spp.
near-im-BERG-ee-ah

Perennial—Sun/Part Shade
Ht. 6"–12" Spread 12"–18"
Spacing 9"–12"

HABIT   Low, bunching growth with blue-purple or white flowers in summer.

CULTURE   Well-drained organic soil is best, moderate water and fertilization. Plant from containers in spring or fall.

USES   Colorful border, rock gardens, perennial gardens, stone walls.

PROBLEMS   Few if any.

NOTES   Native to Argentina.

OBEDIENT PLANT
Physostegia virginiana
fi-so-STEEG-ee-ah ver-gin-ee-AN-ah

Perennial—Sun/Part Shade
Ht. 24"–48" Spread 12"
Spacing 9"–12"

HABIT   Pink, white, and lavender blooms from late summer to frost. When flowers are twisted on the stem, they remain in that position. Slender, upright square stems with long pointed leaves.

CULTURE   Drought tolerant, can grow in most any soil.

USES   Perennial fall color, background flowers.

PROBLEMS   Invasive, spreads by roots.

NOTES   *P. angustifolia* is the spring-blooming obedient plant.

Obedient Plant

Oxalis

Oxblood Lily

Johnny-jump-up

Above: Yellow viola; right: Pansy

OXALIS (Wood Sorrel)
Oxalis spp.
ox-AL-iss

Perennial—Part Shade
Ht. 6"–12" Spread 12"–15"
Spacing 9"–12"

HABIT Tough, low-growing perennial. Available in several colors. Foliage looks like clover.
CULTURE Easy to grow in light to fairly heavy shade. Can grow in full sun but prefers afternoon shade. Normal bed preparation, water, and fertilizer.
USES Low border, perennial gardens.
PROBLEMS Spider mites.
NOTES *O. bowiei* has pink blooms in spring and fall. *O. stricta,* yellow wood sorrel or sheep sorrel, has yellow flowers and small seed capsules that resemble okra pods. Considered a weed by some, it can be removed by hand.

OXBLOOD LILY (Schoolhouse Lily)
Rhodophiala bifida
roe-doe-FEE-ah-luh BIF-ih-duh

Perennial—Full Sun
Ht. 10"–12" Spread 24"–36"
Spacing 6"–8"

HABIT Red fall flowers on bare stems. Blooms in late summer or fall about the same time as the red spider lily, *Lycoris.* Flowers look like small amaryllis. Foliage emerges after flowering.
CULTURE Grows well in sandy or heavy clay soils. Best to dig, divide, and transplant in summer as the foliage turns yellow and dies. Flowering is triggered by late-summer/early-fall rain.
USES Fall color highlights in large drifts or borders.
PROBLEMS Finding any to buy.
NOTES Sometimes called schoolhouse lily because it blooms in the fall about the time school is recommencing. Not a long bloomer.

PANSY
Viola hybrids
vie-OH-la

Annual—Sun
Ht. 6"–8" Spread 8"–12"
Spacing 6"–9"

HABIT Low-growing winter- and spring-flowering annual. Yellow, white, blue, and bronze color combinations.
CULTURE Well-prepared, well-drained beds, ample water and fertilizer.
USES Winter and cool-season flowers. Flowers are edible.
PROBLEMS Extreme freezes, aphids, cutworms.
NOTES Plant in October or late winter. In mild winter, pansies will bloom from fall to spring. Giant flower varieties are available. Native to Europe. *Viola tricolor,* Johnny-jump-up, is a smaller species with purple, yellow, and white flowers.

Penstemon

Pentas

PENSTEMON
Penstemon spp.
PEN-sta-men

Perennial—Sun/Part Shade
Ht. 12"–48" Spread 12"–36"
Spacing 9"–18"

HABIT Several species with many colors and blooming periods, mostly spring
through fall. Most species are very upright and light in appearance.
CULTURE All need good drainage. Most species grow to about 2', some will reach
6'. Cut back brown or unattractive flower stalks for additional flower display.
USES Perennial garden color.
PROBLEMS Root rot, aphids.
NOTES *P. triflorus,* Hill Country penstemon, has dark pink to red blooms and is
one of the best choices, but there are many other good choices. *P. cobaea,* prairie
or wild foxglove, is an excellent wildflower. Penstemon hybridizes readily.

PENTAS
Pentas lanceolata
PEN-tas lan-see-oh-LAH-tah

Annual—Sun/Part Shade
Ht. 24" Spread 18"–24"
Spacing 12"–18"

HABIT Blooms all summer in red, white, lavender, pink, or candy stripe.
CULTURE Easy-to-grow annual. Plant after frost danger in well-drained soil.
Moderate water and fertilizer needs. Best to allow for afternoon shade.
USES Excellent summer annual. Great for true red color, but available in several
colors.
PROBLEMS None serious.
NOTES Not widely used, but should be. Also called Egyptian star cluster.

PEONY
Paeonia hybrids
pie-ON-ee-ah

Perennial—Sun/Part Shade
Ht. 24"–36" Spread 20"–30"
Spacing 18"–24"

HABIT Large, showy, bowl-shaped flowers in midspring, single and double
blooms in white, pink, rose, salmon, and red.
CULTURE Needs morning sun, afternoon shade. Likes deep, rich organic soil and
areas with cold winters best. Plant the roots 2" deep in fall. Cut foliage to the
ground in fall and cover with mulch. Do not overfertilize.

Peony

Tree Peony

USES   Cut flowers, perennial beds, borders.
PROBLEMS   Peonies like cooler weather than most of Texas has to offer. Leaf diseases can be a problem. Peonies have to be considered high-maintenance plants. Tree peonies are easier to grow. Ants crawling on buds are feeding on a sweet exudate and helping the flowers to grow.

PERIWINKLE
Catharanthus roseus
ca-tha-RAN-thus ro-SAY-us

Annual—Full Sun
Ht. 9"–12" Spread 12"–15"
Spacing 9"–12"

HABIT   Low, compact annual for dry, extremely well-drained areas.
CULTURE   Plant in any well-drained bed in full sun after the weather turns permanently warmer. Beds need to be well prepared, with cornmeal as a prime ingredient.
USES   Summer color.
PROBLEMS   Too much water or planting too early in the spring is sure death for this plant.
NOTES   Always plant the dwarf varieties so they won't droop over. Photo shows the most popular variety, 'Bright Eye.' Native to Madagascar. Many gardeners have stopped planting periwinkles because of the fungus *Phytophthora*, but it can be avoided with the organic program.

White Periwinkle

PETUNIA
Petunia × hybrida
pe-TUNE-ee-ah HI-brid-ah

Annual—Sun
Ht. 12"–24" Spread 18"–24"
Spacing 9"–12"

HABIT   Tender summer-flowering annual. Available in many colors.
CULTURE   Plant before last frost in well-prepared beds with good drainage. Needs high fertilization for best blooms.
USES   Summer flowers, pots, hanging baskets.
PROBLEMS   Cutworms, caterpillars, and summer heat.
NOTES   Do not plant as a summer annual. It likes the cool parts of the growing seasons but hates the hot parts. 'Wave' and 'V.I.P.' are new heat-tolerant choices.

Petunia

Blue Phlox

'Mt. Fuji' Phlox and Purple Coneflower

Plumbago larpentae

PHLOX

Phlox paniculata
FLOCKS pa-nik-ew-LAH-tah

Perennial—Sun/Part Shade
Ht. 15"–30" Spread 15"–30"
Spacing 12"–15"

HABIT Early summer flowers on long stalks. Colors include pink, rose, red, white, lavender. Hot pink is the easiest to grow in Texas. 'Mt. Fuji' is a lovely white selection.

CULTURE Needs healthy, well-drained organic soil. Plant transplants in spring.

USES Summer color, perennial beds, background color.

PROBLEMS Powdery mildew.

NOTES *P. divaricata* is the spring-blooming blue phlox, which grows 12" high and likes shady areas best. The best location is one with morning sun and afternoon shade.

PLUMBAGO

Plumbago spp.
plum-BAY-go

Tender Perennial—Sun/Part Shade
Ht. 12"–36" Spread 24"–60"
Spacing 12"–18"

HABIT Sprawling, fast-growing perennial. Blue or white summer blooms. Dies to ground in fall, returns in spring in the southern part of the state. Should be treated as an annual in the northern half.

CULTURE Likes good beds but is drought tolerant.

USES Summer flowers, stone walls, and natural settings.

PROBLEMS Few if any.

NOTES Native to South Africa. *Ceratostigma plumbaginoides* has dark blue flowers. *P. capensis* has baby blue flowers and is larger. *P. auriculata* 'Alba' has white flowers.

Plumeria

Plumbago

Poke Salad

PLUMERIA
Plumeria spp.
ploo-ME-ree-ah

Tropical Shrub or Small Tree—
Sun/Part Shade
Ht. 6'–8' Spread 4'–6'
Spacing: Best in pots

HABIT Fragrant summer flowers in red, pink, purple, rose, salmon, yellow, and white. Open growth habit, thick succulent stems. Clusters of long, pointed, leathery leaves, clusters of very showy and very fragrant flowers.

CULTURE Easy to grow in warm to hot weather. Keep fairly dry in winter, moist during the growing season. Needs rich potting soil.

USES Great plant for pots outdoors in summer.

PROBLEMS Hates cold, wet soil.

POKE SALAD (Poke Salet, Pokeweed)
Phytolacca americana
fye-toe-LAC-ah uh-mer-ee-KAH-nah

Perennial Herb—Sun/Part Shade
Ht. 4'–8' Spread 4'–8'
Spacing: Grows wild

HABIT White flowers on a large raceme from summer to fall. Drooping berry clusters from late summer through fall. Several stalks, with smooth bright red to purple bark. Large smooth green leaves. Small red berries turn purple when ripe; their juice leaves a red stain.

CULTURE Likes rich moist soil, but will grow anywhere in Texas except the far west.

USES Bird attractant. Pot herb that tastes like spinach.

PROBLEMS Deadly poisonous if not carefully prepared.

NOTES The berries, bark, and older leaves contain a very toxic alkaloid. The berries are particularly poisonous to children. Although cooking apparently inactivates the toxins in young leaves, they can enter the body through the skin during harvesting. The young leaves, cooked properly, taste great and are good for you, but they shouldn't be eaten unless the first boil water is poured off. None of the plant should ever be eaten raw.

Oriental Poppy

Iceland Poppies

Purslane

POPPY
Papaver spp.
pa-PAY-ver

Annual—Sun
Ht. 12"–48" Spread 12"–36"
Spacing 9"–15"

HABIT   Annual flower (many colors) but reseeds to return each spring. Lovely flowers on long, slender stems. Lacy and hairy foliage. Blooms usually late April to early May. Some varieties will perennialize.

CULTURE   Plant seeds directly in beds in September. Likes cool weather.

USES   Spring flowers.

PROBLEMS   Heat.

NOTES   Oriental poppy (*P. orientale*), Iceland poppy (*P. nudicaule*), corn poppy (*P. rhoeas*), and opium poppy (*P. somniferum*) are some of the varieties. Native to Greece and Asia.

Native or Wild Purslane

PORTULACA (Purslane)
Portulaca grandiflora
por-chew-LAC-ah gran-dee-FLORE-uh

Annual—Sun
Ht. 6" Spread 12"–18"
Spacing 9"–12"

HABIT   Low-growing annual with succulent stems and roselike flowers in summer. Flowers are open in the morning and close during the heat of the day. New flowers every day.

CULTURE   Easy, any well-drained soil. Low water and food requirements.

USES   Colorful ground cover, summer flowers, pots, hanging baskets.

PROBLEMS   Afternoon heat closes flowers; snails, slugs, and cutworms.

NOTES   Purslane, a close kin, is probably better, since the flowers stay open longer during the day. Native to South America. Native purslane (*Portulaca oleracea*) has small yellow flowers. They and the leaves are delicious cooked or raw and are good for you.

Rain Lily

Rock Rose

Ranunculus

RAIN LILY
Zephyranthes spp.
ze-fi-RAN-theez

Perennial—Sun/Part Shade
Ht. 12" Spread 12"
Spacing 9"–12"

HABIT Various colors of flowers on hollow stems in summer and fall, usually after rain or a climate change. White is the most common; also available in yellow, pink, and rose. Bright green rushlike leaves. Plant in fall in masses for best results.

CULTURE Need some water but are fairly drought tolerant. Foliage looks like chives or thin liriope.

USES Wildflowers, summer color, interesting texture.

PROBLEMS Few if any.

NOTES If plants are kept alternately wet and dry, they will bloom after rain or irrigation.

RANUNCULUS
Ranunculus asiaticus
rah-NUN-kew-lus a-she-AT-ti-kus

Perennial Tuber—Sun
Ht. 12"–15" Spread 6"–8"
Spacing 5"–6"

HABIT White, pink, red, and yellow flowers. Strong upright stems, with extremely colorful flowers in early spring.

CULTURE Tubers should be planted 2" deep in the fall in South Texas, in the late winter in North Texas. Doesn't return well; best planted each year and treated as an annual.

USES Early spring color.

PROBLEMS Aphids.

NOTES Plant the pointed end of the tuber down.

ROCK ROSE
Pavonia lasiopetala
pa-VOH-nee-ah lass-ee-oh-PET-ah-lah

Perennial—Sun/Part Shade
Ht. 3'–4' Spread 3'–4'
Spacing 2'–3'

HABIT Pink, five-petaled 2" blooms from late spring until frost. Hibiscus-like flowers open in the morning and close in the afternoon. Evergreen to almost evergreen in the southern part of the state. Freezes easily north of Waco if not protected. Usually lives three to four years but reseeds freely. Velvety leaves. Shrubby. Occasional shearing keeps plant compact and blooming.

CULTURE Plant as an annual in the spring or in a well-protected place. Best location is morning sun and afternoon shade. Not too fussy about soil preparation.

USES Summer color, perennial gardens, borders, and masses.

PROBLEMS Freeze damage.

NOTES Best to treat as an annual in most of the state.

'Climbing Pinkie' Rose

'Katy Road Pink' Rose

ROSE
Rosa spp.
ROW-sa

Perennial—Sun
Ht. 1'–12' Spread 2'–8'
Spacing 3'–8'

HABIT   Old roses vary from big bushes to low ground covers to large climbing vines. They are better for landscape use than the hybrids because they are prettier plants, more fragrant, and much easier to maintain.

CULTURE   Use lots of organic material and sulfur in the bed preparation. Use the same water and fertilizer program as for your other plantings.

USES   Vines, perennial color, mass, fragrance, nostalgia.

PROBLEMS   Black spot, aphids.

NOTES   Some of the easiest roses to grow include the following: 'Mutabilis,' 'Lamarque,' 'Lady Banks,' 'Climbing Pinkie,' 'Easy Going,' "Livin' Easy,' 'Caldwell Pink,' 'The Fairy,' 'Marie Daly,' 'Belinda's Dream,' 'Katy Road Pink,' 'Knock Out.'

Butterfly Rose ('Mutabilis')

'Livin' Easy' Rose

'Easy Going' Rose

'Knock Out' Rose

198

Gregg Salvia

Mexican Bush Salvia

Pineapple Sage

Russian Sage

Salvia

RUSSIAN SAGE
Perovskia atriplicifolia
per-OVS-key-ah at-tre-plick-ih-FOLE-ee-ah

Perennial—Sun
Ht. 3'–4' Spread 3'–4'
Spacing 2'–3'

HABIT   Small light blue to lavender flowers in whorls along stem. Colorful flower spikes from July through October. Silver-gray foliage.
CULTURE   Likes sunny, dry locations. Very heat tolerant and drought resistant. Needs well-drained soil.
USES   Accent plant, summer color, perennial gardens. Good cut flower.
PROBLEMS   Few if any.
NOTES   Foliage smells like sage when crushed. Several cultivars are available: 'Blue Mist,' 'Blue Haze,' 'Blue Spire,' and 'Longin.'

SALVIA, GREGG
Salvia greggii
SAL-vee-ah GREG-ee-eye

Perennial—Sun
Ht. 2'–3' Spread 3'–4'
Spacing 2'

HABIT   Showy spring to fall flowers in colors of red, pink, orange, salmon, and white. Shrubby perennial with long-lasting summer color.
CULTURE   Grows in any well-drained soil, extremely drought tolerant.
USES   Spring, summer, and fall color, perennial gardens.
PROBLEMS   None.
NOTES   Native to Texas. *S. splendens,* annual salvia (also called scarlet sage), likes plenty of water and fertilizer. *S. coccinea,* scarlet sage, is a native perennial that grows 1'–2' high and looks like the annual salvia. *S. regla,* mountain sage, blooms in the fall. *S. guaranitica,* anise sage, which has intense blue flowers and grows 3'–4' tall, is not quite as winter hearty as *S. greggii.*
S. leucantha, Mexican bush salvia, is a large-growing perennial with beautiful foliage and purple flowers in late summer. *S. elegans,* pineapple sage, has bright red flowers in late summer. *S. officinalis* is common garden sage; see Chapter 8 (Herbs). *S. greggii* is also called autumn sage. The flowers of all sages are edible if you are using an organic program.

199

'Indigo Spires'

Skullcap

Mealy Blue Salvia

SALVIA, MEALY BLUE
Salvia farinacea
SAL-vee-ah far-eh-NAY-ṣee-ah

Perennial—Sun/Part Shade
Ht. 2'–3' Spread 2'–3'
Spacing 1'–2'

HABIT   Gray-green foliage and long blue flowers on vertical stems.
CULTURE   Easy, any well-drained soil, drought tolerant, low fertilizer requirements.
USES   Summer flowers, perennial garden, blue color.
PROBLEMS   None.
NOTES   Native to Central and West Texas and New Mexico. Plant in fall or spring. A compact cultivar is now available. Also called blue sage. 'Indigo Spires' is another tough blue-flowering salvia. The flowers are edible if you are using an organic program.

SKULLCAP
Scutellaria drummondii
sku-te-LAH-ree-ah druh-MUN-dee-eye

Annual—Sun
Ht. 8"–12" Spread 12"
Spacing 6"–9"

HABIT   Bluish purple spring flowers with two white marks in leaf axils of upper leaves.
CULTURE   Soft, hairy stems, grows in clumps opposite hairy leaves. Easy to grow in various soils.
USES   Wildflower.
PROBLEMS   Few of any serious nature.

Snapdragon

Spider Lily, white (*Hymenocallis*)

SNAPDRAGON
Antirrhinum spp.
an-tee-REE-num

Annual—Sun/Part Shade
Ht. 12"–24" Spread 9"–12"
Spacing 9"–12"

HABIT   Upright flower spikes available in many colors.
CULTURE   Plant in sun or semi-shade. Likes alkaline soil, moderate water, and regular fertilization. Likes cool weather.
USES   Cool-season color, cut flowers.
PROBLEMS   Rust, cutworms.
NOTES   Plant in fall or late winter/early spring. Native to the Mediterranean.

SPIDER LILY
Hymenocallis spp.
high-men-oh-KAH-lis

Perennial—Sun/Part Shade
Ht. 3'–5' Spread 4'–6'
Spacing 2'–3'

HABIT   Large, dramatic, spiderlike white flowers in summer. Large, dark green foliage.
CULTURE   Plant in well-prepared beds.
USES   Accent, summer color.
PROBLEMS   Needs plenty of space.
NOTES   'Tropical Giant' is used mostly in the Gulf Coast region but it's adapted to much of Texas.

Spider Lily (*Lycoris*)

Spiderwort

Standing Cypress

SPIDER LILY

Lycoris spp.
li-KO-ris

Perennial—Sun/Part Shade
Ht. 15"–24" Spread 6"–12"
Spacing 6"–12"

HABIT   Clusters of purple, red, pink, white, or yellow summer flowers.

CULTURE   Plant bulbs from spring through late summer. May not bloom the first fall. Narrow leaves appear in spring but die down before the plant blooms.

USES   Perennial summer color.

PROBLEMS   Cutworms, loopers, and other caterpillars.

NOTES   *L. radiata* is the red spider lily. *L. squamigera* is the trumpet-shaped pink belladonna lily that blooms in late summer to early fall. *L. africana* is bright yellow. *L.* × *albiflora* is the white fall spider lily.

SPIDERWORT

Tradescantia spp.
tray-dess-KAN-shah

Perennial—Shade/Dappled Sun
Ht. 6"–24" Spread 12"–18"
Spacing 12"–18"

HABIT   White to deep purple ½"–1" flowers from spring until fall. Drought tolerant, easy to grow in shady perennial gardens. Kin to wandering jew. Slow-growing.

CULTURE   Grows best in well-prepared, well-drained soil.

USES   Summer color; informal, natural settings.

PROBLEMS   Few, mostly a carefree plant. Burns in full sun.

STANDING CYPRESS

Ipomopsis rubra
eye-po-MOP-sis ROO-bra

Biennial—Sun
Ht. 2'–6' Spread 6"–12"
Spacing 6"–9"

HABIT   Red or yellow spires of 1" flowers in May and June.

CULTURE   Requires sandy or gravelly soil with excellent drainage, prefers fertile soil. Plant seed for at least two years, as the blooms come the second season.

USES   Wildflower.

PROBLEMS   Few if any.

NOTES   Let plants go to seed before cutting back. Rosettes can be transplanted in the fall.

STOCK
Matthiola incana
matt-ee-OH-la in-KAH-na

Annual—Morning Sun/
Afternoon Shade
Ht. 12"–18" Spread 18"
Spacing 12"

HABIT   Upright spikes of fragrant white, rose, pink, or lavender flowers in late spring or early summer.

CULTURE   Set out transplants in late winter or early spring, fall okay in South Texas. Needs healthy, well-drained soil and even moisture. Cutting back to stimulate additional flowers is not recommended.

USES   Cut flowers, cool-season flower display, fragrance.

PROBLEMS   Hot weather.

NOTES   Likes cooler weather best.

Stock

SUMMER SNOWFLAKE
Leucojum aestivum
loo-KO-jum EES-ti-vum

Perennial Bulb—Sun/Part Shade
Ht. 14"–16" Spread 18"–24"
Spacing 12"–18"

HABIT   Tiny white bell-shaped flowers from spring to early summer. Attractive upright foliage.

CULTURE   Easy to establish and maintain. Divide in the fall if planting becomes crowded.

USES   Borders, spring and early-summer color.

PROBLEMS   Few of a serious nature.

Summer Snowflake

Mexican Sunflower

Maximilian Sunflower

SUNFLOWER

Helianthus spp.
hee-lee-AN-thus

Annual/Perennial—Sun
Ht. 3'–12' Spread: Single to
spreading
Spacing: Varies with type

HABIT Yellow or red flowers.

CULTURE Plant the seed of annuals or tubers of perennials in any well-drained soil in full sun. Fertilize monthly for the largest flower heads. I recommend it for the lazy gardener's garden. Dig the tubers in the fall after the tops have died.

USES Food, summer color, bird attractant.

PROBLEMS Too large and coarse-textured for many small gardens.

NOTES *H. annuus* is the annual common sunflower. *H. multiflorus* is a perennial. *H. angustifolius*, swamp sunflower, likes wet soil. *H. maximiliani* is Maximilian sunflower, a beautiful clumping perennial that blooms from August to October. *H. tuberosus*, Jerusalem artichoke or sunchoke, is a 6'–8' perennial grown for its edible underground tubers that taste like water chestnuts and are used as a potato substitute. Make sure you want it before you plant it—it spreads easily.

SUNFLOWER, MEXICAN

Tithonia rotundifolia
tee-THO-nee-a ro-tun-di-FO-lee-a

Annual—Sun
Ht. 5'–8' Spread 3'–4'
Spacing 2'–3'

HABIT Red-orange sunflower-like flowers in summer. Habit very similar to that of sunflowers.

CULTURE Grows quickly and easily from seed planted in spring after there is no danger of frost.

USES Butterfly attractant, background summer color, cut flowers.

PROBLEMS Few if any.

Sweet Pea

Tapioca Plant

Texas Betony

Texas Bluebells

SWEET PEA

Lathyrus odoratus

LA-thi-rus o-do-RAH-tus

Annual Vine—Sun/
Afternoon Shade
Ht. 6' or more Spread 3'–6'
Spacing 3'–4'

HABIT   Fragrant pink, red, purple, and white flowers.

CULTURE   Plant seeds in late fall or winter 2" deep in rich, healthy, well-drained soil. Mulch heavily as the plant grows. Needs to be trained on a support.

USES   Vining plant for color in early spring.

PROBLEMS   Heat stress.

TAPIOCA PLANT, VARIEGATED

(Cassava)

Manihot esculenta

MAN-ih-hot es-cue-LEN-tah

Tropical—Sun
Ht. 5'–6' Spread 4'–5'
Spacing 3'

HABIT   Tropical foliage plant with deeply lobed leaves accented by yellow central stripes. Stems are bright red.

CULTURE   Very easy to grow from stem cuttings or transplants. Heat tolerant and has few problems. Treat as a fast-growing, large summer annual.

USES   Accent plant for borders and big pots in the summer.

PROBLEMS   Few other than overwatering.

NOTES   There is also a solid green variety. Indians of South America use the fresh and dried roots as a food for people and livestock, but the safety of regular eating is in question.

TEXAS BETONY

Stachys coccinea

STACK-iss cock-SEAN-ee-ah

Perennial—Sun/Part Shade
Ht. 15"–18" Spread 24"–30"
Spacing 15"–18"

HABIT   Tough, good-looking Texas native perennial for shady areas. Red to red-orange tubular flowers from March to October.

CULTURE   Very drought tolerant once established.

USES   Great for attracting hummingbirds. Deer resistant.

PROBLEMS   Somewhat hard to find in garden centers.

TEXAS BLUEBELLS (Lisianthus)

Eustoma grandiflorum

you-STO-mah gran-dee-FLORE-rum

Annual/Perennial—Sun
Ht. 1'–2' Spread 1'–3'
Spacing 1'–2'

HABIT   Upright plant, bell-shaped spring and summer flowers in white, pink, and blue.

CULTURE   Easy to grow in most soils. Tolerates fairly dry, well-drained soil but likes even moisture better. Does quite well in our heat.

USES   Annual flowers, wildflower.

PROBLEMS   Relatively few. Sometimes gets floppy.

NOTES   Grows wild in Texas but has been picked almost clean. The Japanese genetically altered forms, *Lisianthus,* are annuals. The Texas native *E. exaltatum* lives three to seven years, flowering best in the second and third years.

Thrift

Tulip

Turk's Cap

THRIFT
Phlox subulata
FLOCKS sub-you-LAH-tah

Perennial—Sun
Ht. 6"–8" Spread 10"–12"
Spacing 10"–12"

HABIT   Low-growing and spreading perennial that acts like an evergreen in
mild winters. Blooms in spring in pink, blue, or white. Hot pink is the most
common color.
CULTURE   Easy, any well-drained soil, moderate water and fertilizer needs.
USES   Dwarf border, spring color, stone walls.
PROBLEMS   Pretty much carefree.
NOTES   Reliable to bloom year after year. Plant in fall or spring. Native to
North America. Also called moss phlox. 'Blue Emerald' is the best; its foliage
is lush and dark green all summer.

TULIP
Tulipa spp.
TOO-lip-ah

Annual—Sun
Ht. 9"–12" Spread 6"–9"
Spacing 6"–9"

HABIT   Flowers on long stems in spring. Dwarf and tall-growing varieties
available. Single, double, and parrot-type flowers available. All colors available
except blue.
CULTURE   Bulbs should be chilled at 40°–45° for 40–45 days. *Warning:* Most
refrigerators are colder than that and can injure the bulbs. Plant after the
weather is good and cold in well-prepared and well-drained beds. Pull out
and throw away after blooming.
USES   Spring color.
PROBLEMS   Expensive, will usually not return in this area—should be replanted
each year.
NOTES   Plant in pansy beds for dramatic display in the spring. Can be planted
farther apart (12"–18") if planted in this fashion. Native to Asia. Many quality
garden centers sell pre-chilled bulbs.

TURK'S CAP
Malvaviscus arboreus
mal-vah-VISS-kus ar-BOR-ee-us

Deciduous Perennial Shrub—
Shade/Full Sun
Ht. 5'–8' Spread 5'–8'
Spacing 3'–5'

HABIT   Red, fezlike flowers in summer. Red fruit resembling rose hips in the
late summer. Bushy, shrublike growth with many stems from the ground.
Considered a perennial, but it looks more like a shrub.
CULTURE   Can be grown easily from seed, which can be started indoors in the
winter or outdoors after the last frost. No treatment is needed.
USES   Flowers are excellent for attracting hummingbirds and butterflies.
Flowers and fruit make a good herb tea. The fruit is full of pulp and seed;
cooked down, it produces a good jelly or syrup. The flavor of the raw fruit
resembles that of watermelon or apple. Attracts pollinators like bumblebees
and hummingbirds.
PROBLEMS   Various leaf-chewing insects like caterpillars and grasshoppers, but
none serious if the plant is in healthy soil.
NOTES   One of the best flowering plants for shady areas.

Prairie Verbena   *Verbena bonariensis*

Veronica

Wallflower

VERBENA
Verbena spp.
ver-BEAN-ah

Perennial—Sun
Ht. 9"–12" Spread 12"–18"
Spacing 9"–12"

HABIT   Low, spreading perennial with red, white, salmon, purple blooms all
   summer.
CULTURE   Easy, well-drained beds, low water and fertilization requirements.
USES   Summer color.
PROBLEMS   Spider mites occasionally.
NOTES   The natives are prairie verbena (*V. bipinnatifida*) and moss verbena
   (*V. tenuisecta*). *V. bonariensis* from South America grows 3'–6' tall. The
   cultivated varieties are good as well. 'Pink Parfait' is a beautiful, large-
   flowered evergreen.

VERONICA
Veronica spp.
ve-RON-ee-ka

Perennial—Sun/Part Shade
Ht. 6"–24" Spread 12"–18"
Spacing 9"–12"

HABIT   Vertical flower stalks of white, rose, pink, blue, and purple in summer.
CULTURE   Long-lasting colorful perennial blooms when planted in loose,
   well-drained beds. Gray-green leaves.
USES   Borders, perennial gardens.
PROBLEMS   Slugs and snails.
NOTES   Cut back after heavy flush of bloom for more bloom.

WALLFLOWER
Cheiranthus cheiri
ki-RAN-thus KAY-ree

Perennial—Sun/Part Shade
Ht. 24" Spread 24"
Spacing 18"

HABIT   Yellow, red, orange, or purple flowers in spring. Purple is most common.
CULTURE   Gray-green foliage, fairly drought tolerant. Likes well-drained soils
   and plenty of mulch for best results.
USES   Masses or borders.
PROBLEMS   Doesn't like high humidity and heat.
NOTES   'Bowles Mauve,' the best choice for Texas, has lavender flowers and a
   compact rounded shape.

Yarrow

Zexmenia

WINECUP

Callirhoe involucrata
kal-ih-ROH-ee in-voh-loo-KRAY-tah

Perennial—Sun/Part Shade
Ht. 6"–12" Spread 2"–4"
Spacing 18"–24"

HABIT   Wildflower with 2" wine-red, late-spring blooms. Grows from turniplike tubers. In irrigated gardens, the plant will bloom all summer.
CULTURE   Grows wild in Texas in open woods, on prairies, and along roadsides. Likes dry conditions.
USES   Wildflower.
PROBLEMS   Few if any.

YARROW

Achillea spp.
ah-KILL-ee-ah

Perennial—Sun
Ht. 2' Spread 2'
Spacing 1'–2'

HABIT   Upright, lacy foliage, flat-topped clusters of flowers in white, rose, pink, yellow, and red. Foliage is mostly evergreen.
CULTURE   Easy to grow in any well-drained soil. Plant in spring or fall.
USES   Perennial border, cut flowers.
PROBLEMS   Some varieties grow tall and need to be staked.
NOTES   Native to Europe. *A. millefolium* is a white-blooming, very tough species.

ZEXMENIA

Wedelia hispida
weh-DEEL-ee-ah HISS-peh-dah

Evergreen/Perennial—
Sun/Dappled Shade
Ht. 24"–36"
Spacing 18"–24"

HABIT   Yellow 1" flowers from early summer to fall.
CULTURE   Texas native with sticky foliage. Woody stems, rounded shape, yellow daisylike flowers all summer. Tends to sprawl in shaded locations. Evergreen in the southern half of the state.
USES   Summer color, native perennial garden.
PROBLEMS   Few if any.
NOTES   *W. triloba* is a 12"–15" ground cover that is native to far South Texas and Mexico. Good in sun or part shade in natural settings. *W. texana* is orange zexmenia.

Winecup

Zinnia (also Waymond and Bo)

Zinnea linearis

ZINNIA
Zinnia spp.
ZEN-ee-ah

Annual—Sun
Ht. 8"–36" Spread 12"–24"
Spacing 12"

HABIT   Open, upright growth. Flowers of all colors and sizes on long stems in
summer.
CULTURE   Any loose soil, fairly drought tolerant. Add superphosphate for more
blooms. Plant from seeds or pots in spring.
USES   Summer flowers, cut flowers.
PROBLEMS   Mildew, cutworms, spider mites. Gets ragged toward the end of
summer.
NOTES   Native to Mexico and Central America. *Zinnia linearis* is a low-
growing, sprawling annual with small white or tangerine-colored flowers.

SEEDING RATES FOR WILDFLOWERS

Common Name	Botanical Name	Flower Color	Rate per 1,000 sq. ft.	Rate per acre
Black-eyed Susan	*Rudbeckia hirta*	yellow	5–10 oz.	3 lbs.
Bluebonnet	*Lupinus texensis*	blue	1–2 lbs.	30 lbs.
Butterfly weed	*Asclepias tuberosa*	orange	½ lb.	10 lbs.
Coreopsis	*Coreopsis lanceolata*	yellow	6–12 oz.	10 lbs.
Coreopsis	*Coreopsis tinctoria*	red and yellow	5–10 oz.	2 lbs.
Cosmos	*Cosmos* spp.	multicolors	½ lb.	15 lbs.
Crimson clover	*Trifolium incarnatum*	crimson	½–1 lb.	15–25 lbs.
White clover	*Trifolium repens*	white	¼–½ lb.	5–10 lbs.
Engelmann daisy	*Engelmannia pinnatifida*	yellow	¼–½ lb.	5 lbs.
Evening primrose	*Oenothera* spp.	multicolors	¾–2 oz.	½ lb.
Gaillardia	*Gaillardia* spp.	red/yellow	½ lb.	10 lbs.
Gayfeather	*Liatris* spp.	purple	½ lb.	10 lbs.
Horsemint	*Monarda citriodora*	lavender	5–10 oz.	3 lbs.
Indian blanket	*Gaillardia pulchella*	red and yellow	½ lb.	10 lbs.
Indian paintbrush	*Castilleja indivisa*	orange	½–1 oz.	¼ lb.
Indian paintbrush	*Castilleja purpurea*	purple	½–1 oz.	¼ lb.
Maximilian sunflower	*Helianthus maximiliani*	yellow	5–10 oz.	2 lbs.
Mexican hat	*Ratibida columnaris*	red and yellow	5–10 oz.	2 lbs.
Oxeye daisy	*Chrysanthemum leucanthemum*	white	¼–½ lb.	5 lbs.
Purple coneflower	*Echinacea purpurea*	purple	½ lb.	12 lbs.
Snow-on-the-mountain	*Euphorbia marginata*	white	5–10 oz.	3 lbs.
Tahoka daisy	*Machaeranthera tanacetifolia*	purple	¼–½ lb.	5 lbs.
Verbena	*Verbena* spp.	purple	¼–½ lb.	6 lbs.
White yarrow	*Achillea millefolium*	white	2½–5 lbs.	1½ lbs.
Gold yarrow	*Achillea filipendulina*	yellow	¾–2 lbs.	½ lb.

CHAPTER 6

Texas Lawns

Texas Bluegrass

BED PREP AND PLANTING TECHNIQUES FOR GRASSES

Texans love their lawns—probably a little too much. As a result, turf is subject to lots of synthetic fertilizers, weed-and-feeds, and pesticides. The organic approach is much better, and your yard won't glow in the dark. The Natural Way to lawn care takes less time, saves water, and is less costly. One of the most important parts of the program is to stop catching the clippings. Leave them on the lawn to recycle organic matter to feed the microbes and thus the soil.

Grass-planting techniques can be quite simple or very complicated and a huge waste of money. If you follow these simple tips, your lawn establishment will be enjoyable and affordable.

Soil preparation should include the removal of weed tops, debris, and rocks over 2" in diameter from the surface of the soil. Rocks within the soil are no problem because they help drainage. Till to a depth of 1" and rake topsoil into a smooth grade. Deep rototilling is unnecessary and a waste of money unless the soil is heavily compacted. When planting grass seed, the addition of organic material is beneficial, but strong fertilizer is unnecessary and can even hurt germination. Only on solid-rock areas is the addition of native topsoil needed. Native soil is soil that is naturally present in your area. Imported foreign topsoil is a waste of money and can cause a perched (trapped) water table, the introduction of weeds, and other lawn problems. Mild organic fertilizers and amendments such as earthworm castings (at 10 lbs. per 1,000 sq. ft.) or humate (at 10 lbs. per 1,000 sq. ft. or 1 lb. per 100 sq. ft.) can be helpful at planting time. Some people recommend and use herbicides to kill weeds prior to planting. I don't. These chemicals can be hazardous and can damage the soil biology.

Planting grass by hydromulching (a water, paper, seed, and fertilizer mix) should be done so that the seed is placed in direct contact with the soil. The seed should be broadcast on the bare soil first and then the

211

hydromulch, if used, blown on top of the seed. One of the worst mistakes I see in grass planting is mixing the seed in the hydromulch slurry. This causes the seed to germinate in the mulch, which is suspended above the soil, so many of the seeds are lost from dehydration.

Night temperatures must be 65°–70° for Bermudagrass or buffalograss to germinate and no lower than 40° in the fall and winter for fescue, rye, and other cool-season grasses. After spreading the seed, thoroughly soak the ground and lightly water the seeded area enough to keep it moist until germination is complete. Fertilize with a 100 percent organic fertilizer sometime before the first mowing. As the seed germinates, watch for bare spots. Reseed these bare areas immediately. Continue the light watering until the grass has solidly covered the area. At this time, begin the regular watering and maintenance program.

Spot-sodding is done by countersinking 4-by-4-inch squares into the ground flush with the existing grade 12"–14" apart after grading, then smoothing and leveling the soil. Organic fertilizer should be applied after planting at a rate of 20 lbs. per 1,000 sq. ft. Regular maintenance and watering should be started at this time. Spot-sodding is not a planting procedure I highly recommend because it is slow to cover and often results in an uneven, weedy lawn. It also leaves bare areas that are vulnerable to erosion and soil loss.

Solid-sodding is the best means of grass planting. The squares of sod should be laid joint to joint after first fertilizing the ground with a 100 percent organic fertilizer at a rate of 20 lbs. per 1,000 sq. ft. Grading, leveling, and smoothing prior to planting is very important. The joints between the blocks of sod can be filled with compost to give an even more finished look. The soil-amendment blend of wheat bran, horticultural cornmeal, and dry molasses is the best starter fertilizer. Alliance is the commercial product. The formula is 55 percent wheat bran, 45 percent horticultural cornmeal, and 10 percent dry molasses.

Tifgrasses (TexTurf 10, Tifway 419, Tifgreen 328, and Tifdwarf) are dwarf forms of common Bermudagrass. They should be planted by solid-sodding or hydromulching sprigs with the same procedures as used for planting Bermudagrass seed. Tifgrasses are sterile hybrids and expensive to maintain. They are okay for golf courses, but I don't recommend these grasses for homeowners.

Cool-season grasses such as fescue, ryegrass, bentgrass, and bluegrass should be planted for best results in late September or October, although they can be planted anytime during the winter when the temperature is above 40°. In all cases, the newly applied lawn seed should be watered regularly until the grass has grown to the point of covering the ground.

MAINTENANCE OF GRASSES

Fertilize turf grasses three times a year for the first few years of your organic program. Use an organic product at 20 lbs. per 1,000 sq. ft. in early spring (February–March), early summer (June), and fall (September–October). The rate and times of application can be reduced once healthy soil has been achieved.

Mowing

The most important cultural practice associated with maintaining any turf grass is mowing. When part of the grass plant's leaf system is removed by mowing, the plant reacts by using high amounts of carbohydrates to replace the leaves that were cut off. Only when the leaves are replaced does root and stem growth renew. The greater amount of leaf surface that is cut off at each mowing, the longer root and stem growth is reduced. Research found that when no more than one-third of the leaf system is removed at one cutting, the negative effect on root and stem growth is minimal. There is a direct relationship between cutting height and the total volume of the root system.

Grass clippings should be left on the turf. They do not contribute to thatch, so there is no need to "bag" them if a reasonable mowing program is followed. Clippings should only be caught and moved to the compost pile when scalping prior to overseeding.

Edging and Trimming

Edge along walks and curbs as needed. Monofilament trimmers can be used along steel edging, curbs, and other hard surfaces, but never around trees or shrubs.

Scalping

Scalping involves the removal of the dead upper parts of the plant. The reason scalped lawns "turn" green earlier is that the physical removal of all the brown leaf material allows more of the green leaves to be visible. Scalping a turf in the spring is not a part of any professional turf management program and should not be done on your turf, except prior to overseeding with winter grasses.

Weed Control

Weed-control products are divided into two groups: those that kill weed seed as it germinates (pre-emergent herbicides) and those that control weeds after they are growing (post-emergent herbicides). The organic pre-emergent is corn gluten meal. The organic post-emergent is vinegar.

Pre-emergent Weed Control. Pre-emergent herbicides must be in place before the weed seed begins to grow. Annuals, like henbit and annual bluegrass, germinate in the fall as soon as the weather cools. There could be as much as a month or so difference in the arrival of the first significant cold front. For a pre-emergent to be effective for winter weed control in North Texas, it should be applied around September 15, and a month or so later in the southern part of the state.

The same holds for the spring. Many annual weeds, such as grassburs and crabgrass, germinate in the early spring, again depending on temperatures. In northern Texas, corn gluten meal should be applied by early March, and even earlier farther south. Some years these dates may be too late. Success depends on changes in the weather. Early or late falls and early or late springs make pre-emergent programs difficult. Once in a while the program may fail. Corn gluten meal will fail as a pre-emergent if the soil and weed seed stay moist for a long period after treatment is applied. The constant moisture will override the herbicidal effect, the small roots will start to grow, and the fertilizer value of the corn gluten meal will give you very large weeds. In that case, just mow them.

Post-emergent Weed Control. Post-emergent control of weeds is done in the organic program primarily with vinegar and vinegar-based products. Spray during warm or hot weather. Straight vinegar (10% or 20%) can be used or vinegar-based products such as Garden-Ville. See the Appendix for additional formulas.

SUGGESTED MOWING HEIGHTS

Turf Grass	Best Mowing Height	Mow When Lawn Is
Common Bermudagrass	1½ inches	2¼ inches
Hybrid Bermudagrass	1 inch	1½ inches
Kentucky Bluegrass	2 inches	3 inches
Texas Bluegrass	2 inches	3½ inches
Buffalograss	3 inches	4½ inches
Centipedegrass	2 inches	3 inches
Perennial Ryegrass	2 inches	3 inches
St. Augustine	2 inches	3 inches
Tall Fescue	2 inches	3 inches
Zoysiagrass	1½ inches	2¼ inches

EASY REFERENCE FOR GRASSES

Grasses for Sun	Grasses for Shade
Bermudagrass	Fescue
Bluegrass, hybrid	Reveille Bluegrass
Buffalograss	St. Augustinegrass
Reveille Bluegrass	
St. Augustinegrass	
Tifgrass	
Zoysiagrass	

TURF GRASSES, WEEDS, AND SO-CALLED WEEDS

Reveille Bluegrass

BERMUDAGRASS, COMMON
Cynodon dactylon
SIN-no-don DAC-ti-lon

Warm Season—Sun
Mowing Ht. 1½"–4"
Seed @ 2 lbs./1,000 sq. ft.

HABIT   Narrow leaf blade, spread by stolons and rhizomes. Brown in winter. Low-maintenance, aggressive grass.
CULTURE   Grows in any soil. Does much better with ample water and fertilizer but is quite drought tolerant. Does not develop thatch.
USES   Lawn grass, playing fields.
PROBLEMS   Some insects and diseases but none serious. One of the most serious weeds when growing where it is not wanted.
NOTES   Mixing with St. Augustine and some weeds looks okay. Native to warm regions around the world. Grass planting around new shrubs and trees will retard their growth. TexTurf 10 is a dark green variety, relatively free of seed stems, and a good choice for athletic fields.

BERMUDAGRASS, TIF (Tifgrass)
Cynodon dactylon cultivars
SIN-no-don DAC-ti-lon

Warm Season—Sun
Mowing Ht. ½"–¾"
Stolons @ 10–15 bushels/1,000 sq. ft.

HABIT   Hybrid forms of common Bermudagrass. Narrower leaf blade and finer overall texture. Tifdwarf is the finest-textured. Tifgreen 328 is slightly larger, and Tifway 419 is the largest and the best of the hybrids for residential use.
CULTURE   Higher maintenance than common Bermudagrass, since weeds and imperfections are much more visible.
USES   Refined lawns and putting greens. Also golf course tees and fairways. These grasses are sterile (no seeds) and must be planted solid or from stolons.
PROBLEMS   Some insects and diseases but none serious. Bad thatch buildup.
NOTES   Too much work for home lawns.

BLUEGRASS, HYBRID (Reveille)
Poa arachnifera × *Poa pratensis*
PO-ah a-rak-NIF-er-a pray-TEN-sis

Cool Season—Sun/Part Shade
Mowing Ht. 1½"–2½"
Seed or sod

HABIT   Texas bluegrass/Kentucky bluegrass cross developed by James Read, Phillip Colbaugh, and Bill Knoop at the Texas A&M research station at Dallas. Great-looking insect- and disease-resistant grass.
CULTURE   Cool-season cross that can take heat and cold. Especially suited to Central Texas and southern Oklahoma. Plant sod year-round except during the coldest parts of the winter.
USES   Evergreen grass for sun or part shade.
PROBLEMS   Hates wet feet. Do not overwater. Susceptible to brown patch, but cornmeal and the organic program will solve that. The urine of female dogs like our Tully will also kill spots in this turf. Durability is questionable.

Below, left: Common Bermudagrass; below, right: Dwarf Bermudagrass

Common Buffalograss showing male flowers

'609' Buffalograss

White Clover in bloom

BUFFALOGRASS
Buchloe dactyloides
BUCK-low dac-ti-LOY-deez

Warm Season—Sun
Mowing Ht. 2"–6"
Seed @ 5 lbs./1,000 sq. ft.

HABIT   Low-growing, blue-green foliage, decorative flaglike flower heads—that most people think are the seeds—on the male plants. The seeds are in burs that grow close to the ground, making them hard to harvest.

CULTURE   Easy, any soil except wet areas. Plant from seed in spring (through September if irrigated). Do not water or fertilize often. At most, fertilize once with initial seeding and once a year thereafter.

USES   Lawn grass, large natural areas, low maintenance.

PROBLEMS   Slow to establish, but this is more an adjustment than a problem. It is said to be a problem because it invades Bermudagrass, but that's not true if it is managed properly.

NOTES   Our only native lawn grass and the most drought-tolerant and low-maintenance grass of all. Native from Texas to Minnesota and Montana. Hybrid selections include 'Prairie,' '609,' and 'Stampede.' Hulled choices are available but considerably more expensive.

CLOVER, WHITE
Trifolium repens
tri-FO-lee-um RAY-pens

Perennial—Sun/Heavy Shade
Ht. 6"–8" Spread 12"–15"
Seed @ 1 lb./1,000 sq. ft. or 30–40 lbs./acre

HABIT   Round flower heads consisting of 20–40 white to pinkish white florets on long stems. Creeping stems up to 15' long with dark green three-part leaves. Roots at the joints of the stems. Deeply rooted.

CULTURE   Likes cool weather and clay soils. Evergreen when irrigated in the summer. Plant in September or October for best results.

USES   Ground cover, cover crop, turf plant. One of the nation's most important pasture legumes. Great for soil-building because of its deep roots and nitrogen-fixing ability.

PROBLEMS   Usually considered a weed, but it shouldn't be. I encourage it on my lawn.

NOTES   For a cover crop, plant a clover mixture at a total rate of 30 lbs. seed per acre. White, crimson, and red are good choices. White clover is the best for landscape use because it is the shortest. Native to Europe and Asia Minor. Has naturalized across North America. Source of four-leaf clovers. *T. incarnatum* is crimson clover.

Crabgrass

Dandelion

Dichondra

CRABGRASS

Digitaria spp.
dij-ih-TAYR-ee-ah

Annual—Sun
Ht. 12"–24" Spread 24" and more

HABIT Seed heads like fingers. Propagation by seed or by roots where each nodule touches the ground. Branches grow out along the ground, then turn up after rooting at nodes. Warm-season, shallow-rooted, low-growing annual grass from Europe.

CULTURE Likes moist soil.

USES Foliage crop for cattle.

PROBLEMS Considered a noxious lawn weed.

NOTES Let the soil dry out to get rid of it if unwanted. It indicates poor aeration and limited availability of calcium. It looks much like our normal lawn grasses; don't worry about it. In lawns, just mow it. In beds, smother it with mulch.

DANDELION

Taraxacum officinale
ta-RAX-ah-cum oh-fih-sih-NAY-lee

Perennial—Sun
Ht. 8"–12" Spread 8"–12"

HABIT Yellow flowers and powder-puff seed heads. Lettucelike foliage, deep tap root.

CULTURE About the easiest plant to grow. Control by applying corn gluten meal in the fall at about 20 lbs. per 1,000 sq. ft.

USES Flowers are used in cookies and wine, young foliage in salads, the root in tea. The aggressive root system brings minerals from the subsoil up to the surface.

PROBLEMS Considered a lawn weed.

NOTES Aeration and proper use of organic fertilizers will greatly reduce the population. Easy to kill if necessary by spraying with full-strength vinegar or removing manually.

DICHONDRA

Dichondra micrantha
die-CON-dra my-CRAN-tha

Perennial—Part Shade
Ht. 2"–4" Spread: Runners
Spacing 6"–12" for plugs; or seed @ 1 lb./1,000 sq. ft. in April or May

HABIT Perennial lawn plant or ground cover. Very low-growing, spreads by runners. Tiny lily-pad-looking leaves.

CULTURE Likes partial to heavy shade and moist soil.

USES Excellent between stepping stones. Sometimes used as turf.

PROBLEMS Dichondra flea beetle.

NOTES Many people don't understand that *Dichondra* is a beautiful ground cover instead of a noxious weed to be sprayed with toxic herbicides. Can be killed with broadleaf herbicides, but why? If you don't like it, let the soil dry out more between waterings. Sometimes sold as *D. carolinensis* or *D. repens.*

Fairy Ring

Fescue

FAIRY RING (Toadstool, Mushroom) Temporary—Sun or Shade
Chlorophyllum spp. Ht. 4"–6" Spread 3'–12'
chlo-roe-PHI-lum

HABIT Fruiting bodies of fungi growing on decaying organic matter. White
    caps that look like golf balls when young expand to 4"–8" in diameter at
    maturity. Usually appear in lawns in summer after rainy periods. Caps are
    white at first, then turn gray-green and have distinctive green spores, reddish
    brown "scales" on the cap, and a ring on the smooth stalk.
CULTURE Fairy rings usually grow in soil where wood is decaying, such as roots
    or an old stump.
USES None.
PROBLEMS Visual only, no problem for the turf.
NOTES Very toxic! Known for their tendency to collect heavy metals from the
    air and soil.

FESCUE, TALL Cool Season—Sun/Shade
Festuca spp. Mowing Ht. 3"–4"
fess-TOO-cah Seed @ 8–10 lbs./1,000 sq. ft.

HABIT Bunch-type grass that is planted as a winter overseeding or used in
    shady lawn areas. A permanent grass, especially in the cooler parts of the state.
CULTURE Needs fertile, well-drained soil and should be planted in the fall
    (Sept.–Nov.) for best results.
USES Lawn grass in shade, overseeding.
PROBLEMS Have to mow all winter, looks somewhat artificial in North Texas.
NOTES Best of the cool-season grasses for home use. Native to Europe.
    Ryegrass and roughstalk bluegrass are often used as an overseed grass, but they
    are competitive in the spring with the permanent grasses. Fescue will live year-
    round but needs additional seed planted each fall for best results.

GLAUCA GRASS
Festuca ovina 'Glauca'
fess-TOO-cah oh-VEEN-uh

Evergreen—Sun
Ht. 4"–10"
Spacing 9"–12"

HABIT   Slender, bristly, powdery blue-gray, hairlike leaves forming distinct clumps. Light-colored flowers on thin stalks in early spring.
CULTURE   Easy to grow in any soil, is drought tolerant, and has low fertilization needs. Clip away flowers after the blooms have faded.
USES   Ground cover or low border.
PROBLEMS   Never grows in real solid, so mulching is important to prevent weeds.
NOTES   Also called blue fescue grass. Native to Southeast Asia and Japan.

JOHNSONGRASS
Sorghum halepense
SOR-gum HAL-a-pence

Perennial—Sun
Ht. 3'–6'

HABIT   Wide leaves up to ¾", with light-colored midvein. Tall flower plumes and millions of tiny black seeds.
CULTURE   Grows well in any soil, but this is one of the weeds that likes healthy soil.
USES   Cattle forage, erosion control.
PROBLEMS   Hard-to-control weed in cultivated crops. Prussic acid in the plant can be poisonous to cattle during dry summers, after an application of excess nitrogen fertilizer, or just after the first frost.
NOTES   Native to Africa and India. Introduced to the United States in 1830 as a high-quality pasture and hay grass, but it has become a noxious weed. Control in lawns by mowing or heavy grazing.

RYEGRASS
Lolium spp.
LOW-lee-um

Annual/Perennial—Sun/Part Shade
Ht. 2"–4"
Seed @ 10 lbs./1,000 sq. ft.

HABIT   Cool-season clumping grass.
CULTURE   Plant in the late summer/early fall. Give plenty of water.
USES   Fall overseeding of warm-season grasses.
PROBLEMS   Competition with permanent lawn grasses. Can become a pest, especially in the springs that are cool and wet.
NOTES   The annual *L. multiflorum* is less expensive and very aggressive. *L. perenne*, the perennial choice, is a better-quality grass, although more expensive.

Below, left: Johnsongrass; below, right: Perennial Rye

St. Augustinegrass

'Meyer' Zoysia

'Emerald' Zoysia

ST. AUGUSTINEGRASS

Stenotaphrum secundatum
sten-no-TAY-frum seh-coon-DAY-tum

Warm Season—Sun/Shade
Mowing Ht. 2"
Solid Sod

HABIT Wide-bladed grass, spreads by stolons, most shade tolerant of our warm-season grasses. 'Raleigh' is a hybrid resistant to St. Augustine decline (SAD), and is more cold tolerant than hybrids 'Seville' and 'Floratum.'
CULTURE Any well-drained soil that is fairly fertile. Not as tough as Bermudagrass.
USES Lawn grass, shade.
PROBLEMS Chinch bugs, grubworms, diseases such as brown patch and take-all patch.
NOTES Native to Africa and the Gulf Coast. Treat with horticultural cornmeal.

ZOYSIAGRASS

Zoysia japonica 'Meyer'
ZOY-sha jah-PON-ih-kah

Warm Season—Sun/Part Shade
Mowing Ht. 2"–4"
Solid Sod

HABIT Thick, succulent-looking grass. Very slow to spread.
CULTURE Plant solid sod only, too slow-growing for any other planting techniques.
USES Lawn grass, small areas, Oriental gardens, low-use areas.
PROBLEMS Slow, but that gives it its maintenance advantages. Thatch buildup.
NOTES Avoid using in high-traffic areas. 'Meyer' is wider-leafed and better than 'Emerald,' which has a narrow leaf. Zoysia can be mowed less often than Bermuda and St. Augustine, and it requires far less edging. Native to Japan.

TEXAS COVER CROPS

Cover crops are used, usually in winter months, to add nutrients and organic matter to the soil. Turning cover crops into the soil is called green-manuring.

Sideoats Grama

WINTER

Clover
Plant one or a mix of clovers September–October at a total rate of 30 lbs./acre. White, crimson, and red are good choices.

Elbon rye
Plant September–October at 25–50 lbs./acre as a winter cover crop and deterrent of harmful nematodes.

Hairy vetch
Plant September–October at 20–30 lbs./acre as an attractive winter cover crop. Higher rates can be used on home vegetable gardens.

Oats
Plant September–October at 30–40 lbs./acre. Works well as a winter crop, especially when used along with hairy vetch.

Wheat
Plant September–October at 2 lbs./1,000 sq. ft.

SUMMER

Black-eyed peas
Plant at 20 lbs./acre after the last killing-frost date in spring.

Buckwheat
Plant at 30 lbs./acre after the last killing-frost date in spring.

Hyacinth bean
Plant at 50 lbs./acre after the last killing-frost date in spring.

SO-CALLED WEEDS

Annual bluegrass   *Poa annua*
Annual low-growing, cool-season weed. Apply corn gluten meal late September to early October at 20 lbs. per 1,000 sq. ft.

Aster, roadside   *Aster exilis*
Annual broad-leafed wildflower with white or light blue flowers in fall. Control by improving the moisture level and fertility of the soil. Humates, compost, and cornmeal are all effective.

Bermudagrass   *Cynodon dactylon*
Although this is a widely used turf grass, I consider it to be one of the most troublesome weeds of all. You will, too, if it gets in your beds. Control by physical removal or repeated vinegar sprayings.

Dallisgrass

Bindweed   *Convolvulus arvensis*

Introduced from Eurasia. Ranked among the dozen worst perennial weeds in the world. Roots go 6' deep and can lie in the soil for 30 years and still germinate. Also called wild morning glory. Control by increasing organic matter in the soil and covering with mulch.

Brambles   *Rubus* spp.

Various berry plants with sharp thorns that spread to form dense masses. Control by pulling up. Spray regrowth with vinegar-based herbicide.

Bull nettle   *Cnidoscolus texanus*

Perennial problem weed in deep, sandy soils with low fertility. Leaves and stems are covered with stinging hairs. Huge underground storage tubers. Control by increasing organic matter in the soil. Spray existing plants with vinegar.

Bur clover   *Medicago hispida*

Very low-growing annual cool-weather legume. Small, yellow pealike flowers. Seeds contained in a soft-spined bur. Control by increasing soil health.

Canada thistle   *Circium arvense*

Perennial weed, 1½'–4' in height. Very difficult to control because of its deep root system. Control by mowing when plant is in full bloom. Root system is exhausted when it is the prettiest.

Chickweed   *Stellaria media*

Annual cool-season broadleaf weed with small, bright green leaves. Low-growing benign weed. Just mow it. Control in the fall with corn gluten meal.

Cocklebur   *Xanthium strumarium*

Tall, bushy annual weed with prickly seeds and sandpaper-like leaves. Grows where excess phosphorous is available. Control by building the organic matter in the soil and spraying young plants with vinegar.

Dallisgrass   *Paspalum dilatatum*

Long-lived, warm-season, deep-rooted perennial bunch grass. Forms low, flat clumps with dead-looking centers and tall, fast-growing seed heads. Spray with vinegar and physically remove. Fill holes with compost.

Dodder   *Cuscuta* spp.

Annual weed that reproduces by seed. It starts as an independent plant but establishes a parasitic relationship with the host crop. At that stage it has no chlorophyll and looks like yellow string. Control by balancing the minerals in the soil.

Field bindweed   See Bindweed

Goathead (Puncture Vine)   *Tribulus terrestris*

Hairy, low-growing annual with a taproot and several stems forming a rosette. Has yellow flowers and burs that will puncture tires. Same control as grassburs.

Goosegrass (Silver Crabgrass)   *Eleusine indica*

Annual that reproduces by seed in unhealthy soil. Very similar to crabgrass. Control by improving soil health and removing or spraying young plants with vinegar.

Grassbur   See Sandbur

Nutgrass

Henbit
A species of *Lamium* that I consider a wildflower. Control, if you must, by mowing or spot-spraying with vinegar-based herbicides. Apply corn gluten meal in the fall.

Honeysuckle   See *Lonicera japonica* 'Atropurpurea' in Chapter 4
(Ground Covers and Vines)

Mistletoe   *Phoradendron flavescens*
Plant parasite that primarily attaches to limbs and trunks of low-quality or stressed trees, such as Arizona ash, hackberry, bois d'arc, locust, box elder, and weak elms and ashes. Remove by cutting infected limbs off the tree. If that can't be done, notch into the limb to remove the rooting structure of the mistletoe and paint with black pruning paint to prevent resprout. There are no magic chemical or organic sprays. Keeping the soil and trees healthy is the best preventative.

Nutgrass   *Cyperus rotundus*
Perennial sedge introduced from Eurasia. Spreads by seed, nutlets, and creeping tendrils. Likes wet soil. Remove with mechanical devices. Control in turf by planting ryegrass in the fall. There's only one guaranteed way to control nutgrass: Remove all the plants and nutlets by sifting the soil through wire mesh. Put this material on the driveway, soak with kerosene, and burn to ash. Put the ash in a sealed concrete container, take to the coast, ship 200 miles offshore, and dump in the ocean. No other techniques I know will work. Image, the often recommended chemical, doesn't work, and Manage, the other recommended chemical, does work to a degree, but it will kill your trees. I've received more than one report that heavy applications of sugar work to rot the weed, but the final formula and solution is elusive.

Poison ivy   *Rhus radicans*
Deciduous vine that grows in sun or shade and spreads easily underground. Has red berries and red fall color. Do not allow to flower and produce seed. Remove, compost, and spray new growth with vinegar-based organic herbicides. See photo on page 153.

Purple nutsedge   See Nutgrass

Ragweed   *Ambrosia* spp.
Annual broad-leafed plant that indicates droughty soil. Releases a potent pollen that causes hay fever. Control by cultivation, mowing, building the soil, and spraying with vinegar-based organic herbicides.

Rescuegrass   *Bromus catharticus*
Cool-season annual bromegrass. Control by broadcasting corn gluten meal in early October or before seed germinates.

Sandbur   *Cenchrus pauciflorus*
Annual grass plant that produces a bur with strong, sharp spines. Seeds in the bur can lie dormant in the soil for years before germinating. Control by increasing the carbon in the soil with humates, dry molasses, or corn gluten meal.

Smilax   See Greenbriar in Chapter 4 (Ground Covers and Vines)

Spurge   *Euphorbia* spp.
Sappy, succulent annuals or perennials that like hot, dry weather. Control by spot-spraying vinegar-based organic herbicides.

Pre-emergent control of all weeds growing from seed is done by the application of corn gluten meal at 20 lbs. per 1,000 sq. ft. before the germination of the targeted seed. In general, the timing is February 15–March 15 in the spring for summer weeds and September 15–October 15 in the fall for the winter weeds. It can also be used after tilling or otherwise working soil to prevent the growth of disturbed seed.

TEXAS NATIVE GRASSES

Texas' only native lawn grass, buffalograss, is my favorite choice for full sun, and it should be used more often. Here are some other native grasses that should be preserved and introduced more often.

Common Name	Scientific Name
Bluegrass, Texas	*Poa arachnifera*
Bluestem, big	*Andropogon gerardii*
Bluestem, bushy	*A. glomeratus*
Bluestem, little	*Schizachyrium scoparium*
Bluestem, longspike silver	*Bothriochioa saccharoides* var. *longipaniculata*
Gamagrass, eastern	*Tripsacum dactyloides*
Grama, blue	*Bouteloua gracilis*
Grama, sideoats	*Bouteloua curtipendula*
Indiangrass	*Sorghastrum nutans*
Lovegrass, sand	*Eragrostis trichodes*
Muhly, coastal	*Muhlenbergia filipes*
Muhly, Lindheimer's	*Muhlenbergia lindheimeri*
Seaoats	*Uniola paniculata*
Seaoats, inland	*Chasmanthium latifolium*
Switchgrass	*Panicum virgatum*
Wildrye, Canada	*Elymus canadensis*

SEEDING RATES FOR GRASSES

Common Name	Botanical Name	Lbs./1,000 sq. ft.	Lbs./acre
Barley	*Hordeum vulgare*	4–7	80–100
Bentgrass	*Agrostis* spp.	1½–2	25–30
Bermudagrass, common	*Cynodon dactylon*	2	20–40
Bermudagrass, tif	*Cynodon dactylon* cultivars	5 sprigs per sq. ft. or solid sod	
Bluegrass, Texas	*Poa arachnifera*	½–2	15–20
Bluestem, big	*Andropogon gerardii*	½–2	15–20
Bluestem, little	*Schizachyrium scoparium*	½–2	15–20
Bluestem, bushy	*Andropogon glomeratus*	½–3	15–20
Bluestem, silver	*Andropogon saccharoides*	½–2	15–20
Buffalograss	*Buchloe dactyloides*	2–4	15–40
Centipedegrass	*Eromochloa ophiuroides*	2–4	40–50
Common reed	*Phragmites australis*	Division only	Division only
Fescue, tall	*Festuca* spp.	4–7	80–100
Gamagrass, eastern	*Tripsacum dactyloides*	½–2	15–20
Grama, blue	*Bouteloua gracilis*	½–2	15–20
Grama, sideoats	*Bouteloua curtipendula*	½–2	15–20
Indiangrass	*Sorghastrum nutans*	½–3	15–20
Lovegrass, sand	*Eragrostis trichodes*	½–2	15–20
Lovegrass, weeping	*Eragrostis curvula*	½–2	15–20
Muhly, Gulf	*Muhlenbergia capillaris*	½–2	15–20
Muhly, Lindheimer's	*Muhlenbergia lindheimeri*	½–2	15–20
Oats	*Avena sativa*	4–7	80–100
Rye, cereal (elbon)	*Secale cereale*	4	80–100
Ryegrass, annual	*Lolium multiflorum*	3–5	50
Ryegrass, perennial	*Lolium perenne*	3–5	50
Seaoats, inland	*Chasmanthium latifolium*	½–2	15–20
St. Augustine	*Stenotaphrum secundatum*	Plant solid sod or spot-sod	
Switchgrass, lowland	*Panicum virgatum*	½–2	15–20
Switchgrass, upland	*Panicum virgatum*	½–2	15–20
Wheat	*Triticum* spp.	4–7	80–100
Wildrye, Canada	*Elymus canadensis*	½–2	15–20
Zoysia	*Zoysia japonica*	Plant solid sod only	

Fruits, Nuts, and Vegetables

For the most part, fruit, nut, and vegetable crops need tender loving care. Some are much more carefree than others, but all respond well to healthy, balanced soil. See the end of this chapter for the complete fruit and pecan tree program. For vegetables, excellent bed preparation is very important. As for ornamental plants, use lots of compost, volcanic rock sand, cornmeal, and organic fertilizer.

Remember that a large percentage of these plants are not natives nor even well adapted. We're going to grow them anyway, but they will need special care for good production. There are exceptions. The easiest plants in this category to grow are pecans, asparagus, blackberries, figs, garlic, jujube, greens, native peppers, and sweet potatoes.

THE PLANTS

APPLE
Malus pumila
MAY-lus PEW-mi-lah

Deciduous Fruit Tree—Sun
Ht. 8'–20' Spread 15'–20'
Spacing 15'–30'

HABIT Pink and white spring flowers after the new foliage has emerged. Long-lived, productive, and relatively easy fruit tree to grow in Texas.

CULTURE Needs well-drained healthy soil. Fertilize following the Basic Organic Program and spray every two weeks during the growing season with Garrett Juice. Pick and store apples in dry, cool locations. Eat as soon as possible.

PROBLEMS Cotton root rot, brown rot, aphids, and various other insect and disease pests. Fire blight is a problem on some varieties. Building beneficial life in the soil is the answer to most of these troubles. Garrett Juice plus additives helps, and cornmeal in the soil at 20 lbs. per 1,000 sq. ft. is important.

NOTES Anna in early summer, but it may suffer frost damage in northern part of Texas. Dorsett Golden in late spring, but it may suffer frost damage in northern part of the state. Fuji in early fall—ugly but delicious. Golden Delicious in late summer. Molly's Delicious in midsummer, Braeburn in fall. Gala in summer through fall. Granny Smith in early fall. Holland is easy to grow, but the taste isn't much.

APRICOT
Prunus armeniaca
PROO-nus ar-men-ee-AH-ka

Deciduous Fruit Tree—Sun
Ht. 15'–20' Spread 15'–20'
Spacing 20'–25'

HABIT Easy-to-grow tree, but the fruit production is another matter. The early-blooming habit often causes a loss of fruit because of late freezes.

CULTURE Normal maintenance program using the Basic Organic Program. Eat fruit soon or store in a cool, dry place at 32°–40°. Will keep about two weeks.

PROBLEMS Brown rot, cotton root rot, plum curculio, birds, and squirrels. Treat soil with cornmeal at 20 lbs. per 1,000 sq. ft.

NOTES 'Bryan,' 'Blenheim,' 'Hungarian,' and 'Moorpark.' 'Manchurian' may be the best choice; 'Mongolian' is the worst. Beautiful little tree for the landscape, but not a good high-production fruit tree for the orchard.

Apple

Globe Artichoke

Arugula

Asparagus

ARTICHOKE, GLOBE
Cynara scolymus
si-NAH-ra SKO-li-mus

Perennial—Sun/Afternoon Shade
Ht. 3'–4' Spread 2'–3'
Spacing 2½'–3'

HABIT   Grows easily in warm to hot weather. It can stand only a few degrees below freezing. Shoots die to the ground and rot after one year's growth.

CULTURE   Roots can be dug, stored inside, and kept cool and dry. Brush away the soil and store in burlap bags. Suckers and roots can be potted and held indoors over the winter. Protect from cold weather after planted in the garden. Excellent drainage is needed. After the last harvest, cut the stems off at or below the soil surface. Cut buds when the size of a small fist by cutting 2" below the bottom of the bud. Eat while fresh.

PROBLEMS   Snails, slugs, caterpillars, and several diseases.

NOTES   Can be a helpful source of nectar for beneficial insects and can be used as an ornamental background plant. Annual in northern part of the state.

ARUGULA
Eruca vesicaria (subspecies: *sativa*)
e-RUE-ka ves-ee-CAR-ee-ah

Annual—Full Sun/Part Shade
Ht. 8"–36" Spread 18"
Spacing 12"

HABIT   Small, creamy yellow, four-petaled blossoms flecked with brown on tall stalks. Arugula has a rosette growth habit.

CULTURE   Needs moist, well-drained soil. Reseeds readily.

HARVEST   Pick the young leaves and use fresh for best flavor and food value.

PROBLEMS   Bolts quickly in warm weather. Harlequin bugs, caterpillars, flea beetles.

NOTES   Digestive aid—any bitter plant is a digestive aid. Stimulates the taste buds, contains lots of vitamins, green salad ingredient. Peppery and nutty taste—some say a butter taste. Really bitter after it has flowered.

ASPARAGUS
Asparagus officinalis
uh-SPARE-a-gus oh-fih-sih-NAY-lis

Perennial—Full Sun
Ht. 4'–5' Spread 6' and greater
Spacing 18"–24"

HABIT   Fernlike growth, red berries on female plants. Shoots come up from rhizomes. Late winter (usually February) division or crowns.

CULTURE   Best planting method is to prepare beds as usual with heavy amounts of compost, lava sand, sugar, organic fertilizer, or manure. Plant crowns (roots) in 3'–4' beds in late winter. Asparagus can also be grown from seed. Plant seeds 1" deep and 3" apart after soaking for 24 hours in liquid seaweed. Move to permanent beds when seedlings are about 12" tall.

HARVEST   Break off spears when 6"–8" tall as they emerge in early summer. Don't harvest many, if any, of the shoots the first year. You can harvest the first year without hurting future years' yields by planting year-old crowns. Store shoots at 32°–40° for 2–4 weeks.

PROBLEMS   Overwatering can cause crown rot and loss of new or established plants. Crown rot, spider mites, slugs, snails, cutworms, and other fungal diseases.

NOTES   'Mary' and 'Martha Washington,' 'Ben Franklin,' 'Jumbo Jim,' 'Jersey Gem,' 'UC 157,' 'Jersey Knight,' and 'Jersey Giant.' Cold weather helps produce larger shoots. Asparagus production is directly related to beneficial fungi in the root systems. Male plants produce more spears; females (with red berries) produce larger spears but have a higher mortality rate.

AVOCADO

Persea americana is cold tender and will only survive the winter in the southern tip of Texas. It can be grown easily from seed, but then a lot of people ask what to do with it after it is grown. You have three choices: (1) build a tall greenhouse, (2) move to Brownsville, or (3) toss it in the compost pile and plant an adapted plant.

BEANS

Phaseolus spp.
fa-SEE-o-lus

Annual—Full Sun
Ht. 18" to 8' Spread 18"–8'
Spacing 6" to 36"

HABIT Low-bush to high-climbing types. Beans are warm-season legumes that have deep-growing roots.

CULTURE Don't usually need heavy fertilization. Additional plantings can be made every 10–14 days for a longer harvest season.

PLANTING For spring, plant seed after all danger of frost. For fall crop, plant seed 12 to 14 weeks before the first average frost. In general, plant lima beans from April 1 to June 15 and July 1 to August 15. Plant seed ½"–1" deep about 1"–2" apart.

HARVEST 55–70 days after planting. Most bush beans mature in about eight weeks; climbers take 10–14 days longer. Green beans should be picked when the pods are young and tender and the seeds are still immature and soft. Beans for shells shouldn't be picked until they are full size and starting to change color. Avoid picking the beans when the foliage is wet.

Lima Beans

Beets

PROBLEMS   Planting too early when the weather is still cool is a problem. Aphids, garden fleahoppers, cutworms, stink bugs, and spider mites. There is evidence that all diseases, including viruses, can be controlled by applying cornmeal at 20 lbs. per 1,000 sq. ft. Root knot nematodes can be controlled by tilling citrus pulp into the soil prior to planting.

NOTES   Sulfur is a common organic pesticide used on beans, but it will burn the foliage of cucurbits like squash and cucumbers. There is some indication that garlic can be phytotoxic to all legumes. Boron toxicity is definitely a problem.

OTHER BEAN CROPS

Asparagus or yard-long beans   These produce beans up to 2' in length. They are climbing southern pea-type plants that need to be trellised. Oriental intensive gardeners love these beans.

Broad beans, fava beans, horse beans   These are all names for basically the same large beans (actually vetches) that like cool weather and are best grown as a fall crop. These beans require the same conditions and culture as bush beans. They can be picked and used as green, shelled, or dry beans.

Mung beans   These beans can be planted in succession for multicrops. Like black-eyed peas, they like the hot weather.

Soybeans   Warm-season bush beans, these beans should be treated like limas but need a longer growing season of about 120 days. They can be used as green, shelled, or dry beans. Very nutritious beans, unless they have been genetically altered.

BEETS
Beta vulgaris
BAY-ta vul-GAH-ris

Annual—Sun/Part Shade
Ht. 7"–12" Spread 6"
Spacing 3"–5½"

HABIT   Rosette of foliage out of a swollen root.

CULTURE   Well-drained healthy soil. Beets do best in raised flat-topped rows. The seed can be planted closely, but should be thinned to 3" for the final spacing. Beet seed can be planted in single rows, multiple rows, or broadcast on top of the beds or hills. Tops of beds should be 16"–20" wide. Plant seed ½"–1" deep; 1" seed depth is too deep in heavy soils. Thin the seedling to 3" for best production.

HARVEST   About eight weeks after planting (50–80 days). Harvest the foliage for salads and to cook as greens when it is young and tender. Harvest bulbs when they are 3"–4". Store 10–12 weeks at 32°–40°.

PROBLEMS   Nematodes, wireworms, grubworms, cutworms, flea beetles, leaf diseases, and boron deficiencies.

NOTES   'Pacemaker II,' 'Detroit Dark Red,' 'Chiogga,' and 'Red Ace.' Beets don't like low-pH soils. When thinning the young plants, the tops can be used cooked as greens or raw in salads.

Blueberry

Blackberry

BLACKBERRY
Rubus spp.
RUBE-us

Perennial—Full Sun/Light Shade
Ht. 3'–5' Spread: Far and wide
Spacing: 'Arapaho' and 'Navaho' 1'
okay; others 2'–3' in rows or 8'–15'
apart in hills; 'Doyle' 7' okay

HABIT   Bushy, wild-growing perennial. Some with thorns, some thornless.

CULTURE   Easy to grow in almost any soil. Two-year-old canes bloom and produce fruit and then die after the fruit has matured. Prune the old canes out after harvesting because they will never produce again. Do not do any winter pruning because the buds are formed in September.

HARVEST   Harvest the berries as they ripen and turn dark purple. Eat right away or store in the refrigerator at 32°–40° for about two weeks max. Harvest the leaves and use fresh in herb teas.

PROBLEMS   Double blossom (rosette), anthracnose, redneck cane borer. Aggressive spreading characteristic.

NOTES   'Doyle' is thornless and the most productive choice. 'Comanche,' 'Humble,' 'Brison,' 'Choctaw,' 'Navaho,' 'Womack,' and 'Rosborough' are also good. It's best to avoid 'Gem,' 'Lawton,' 'Young,' 'Barpen,' 'Fluit,' and the old thornless varieties. 'Arapaho' and 'Navaho' are good thornless varieties. The best raspberry for Texas is 'Doman Red' and should only be grown in sandy acid soils.

BLUEBERRY
Vaccinium spp.
va-KEEN-ee-um

Deciduous Shrub—Fall/Late Winter
Ht. 3'–10' Spread 3'–10'
Spacing 6'–12'

HABIT   Bushy deciduous shrubs with white spring flowers and purple berries. Shallow, fibrous roots, similar to azaleas. Plants mature in seven to eight years.

CULTURE   Plant bare-rooted or container-grown plants from fall to late winter. Blueberries need acidic soils with a pH no higher than 5.5. They benefit from cross pollination, so use at least three varieties in every planting. Drying out will ruin plants quickly.

HARVEST   Berries turn blue weeks before they are ripe. They ripen over a 2–5-week period. The best method is to taste some to see if they are ready. Ripe fruit is plump, has a slight softness, and will fall off the plant easily. Pick and eat fresh or store in the refrigerator at 32°–40°. Will keep for about two weeks.

Broccoli (Malcolm Beck)

Brussels Sprouts (Malcolm Beck)

PROBLEMS No major pests. Poor soil conditions are the only major problem.

NOTES The artificial products can easily burn plants, especially when young. For more information, see www.blueberry.org.

BROCCOLI

Brassica oleracea var. *italica*
BRASS-ih-kah o-le-RAH-see-ah i-TAL-ih-kah

Biennial—Full Sun/Light Shade
Ht. 12"–24" Spread 12"–24"
Spacing 12"–24", although 15" is ideal

HABIT Leafy vegetable with large flower heads. Leaves and flower heads are edible.

CULTURE For the spring garden, plant seed weeks before last average frost. Start indoors or in a cold frame around mid January. Plant transplants in early spring; broccoli can tolerate and actually likes light frost. For the fall garden, plant 10–12 weeks before first frost. Plant ¼"–½" deep. Press surface lightly but firmly with a board or flat trowel. When the fifth leaf emerges, transplant seedlings to 4" pots to hold until planted in the garden. Set transplants just below the first set of leaves. Continue fertilizing after the first harvest to encourage the secondary heads. Likes moisture and plenty of fertilizer. Fertilize when the heads begin to form and are about the size of a fifty-cent piece. Use half a handful of organic fertilizer around each plant.

HARVEST Cut heads 50–80 days from transplants. Harvest heads when they are about two-thirds of their potential size, when they are large but still firm. Cut above side buds, which will continue to mature into heads that can be harvested later. When the yellow flowers start to open, they get tough. Eat right away or store in the refrigerator at 32°-40° for 1–2 weeks.

PROBLEMS Aphids, harlequin bugs, cutworms, green worms, flea beetles, loopers, and boron deficiency.

BRUSSELS SPROUTS

Brassica oleracea var. *gemmifera*
BRASS-ih-kah o-le-RAH-see-ah jem-MIF-er-rah

Biennial, grown as Annual—Sun/Part Shade
Ht. 12"–18" Spread 12"–18"
Spacing 14"–18", single rows, 18" on center

HABIT Cool-season vegetable. Best as a fall crop.

CULTURE Plant so they can mature during cool temperatures, usually 55°–65° or cooler. Plant in late winter for a spring crop and in late summer, 8–10 weeks before the first frost, for a fall crop. Set transplants after the first set of true leaves appears. Plant seeds ¼" in the soil. Cover the plants with shade cloth when first planted in the summer. Keep the soil moist as the sprouts begin to form or they will be small and deformed. Remove the lower leaves only if they yellow or wither. Side-dress Brussels sprouts after harvesting the first small marble-size sprouts. Use about half a handful of fertilizer around each plant. Supports are sometimes needed when the plants get to be 10"–14" tall.

HARVEST Harvest 90–110 days from seed, 65–75 days from transplant. Plant sprouts form near ground level and produce in about two months. Sprouts are mature and ready for harvest when 1"–2" in diameter. Pull down with a twisting motion to harvest. Store mature sprouts in cool, dry place and eat soon after harvest.

PROBLEMS Aphids, black rot, cabbage loopers, and imported cabbage worms.

NOTES 'Prince,' 'Marvel,' 'Jade,' and 'Cross' are good varieties.

Cabbage

Cantaloupe

Cantaloupe male (left) and female (right)
flowers

CABBAGE

Brassica oleracea var. *capitata*
BRASS-ih-kah o-le-RAH-see-ah kah-pi-TAY-ta

Biennial, grown as an Annual—
Sun/Part Shade
Ht. 12"–24" Spread 12"–18"
Spacing 8"–18"; double rows, 12"
on center; 14"–18" is ideal

HABIT A cool-weather leafy vegetable grown as an annual that has edible
foliage and flowers. Cabbage is smooth and head-forming or savory (crinkled).
Head shape ranges from flat to pointed.

CULTURE Likes cool weather and moist, healthy soil. For spring crop, plant 2–4
weeks before last frost. For fall, 10–12 weeks before first frost. Use transplants
and set just below the first set of leaves. Plant seed indoors or in cold frame in
mid January. Plant ¼" deep. Keep the soil around plants mulched well. Add
compost tea and organic fertilizer to the soil when the inner leaves begin to
cup and start to form heads. Best time to fertilize cabbage is when heads start
to form.

HARVEST 60–120 days to harvest. Cabbage matures best at 60°–65°. Expect
about 10–20 heads per 10' of double row. Store in the refrigerator or eat right
after harvest. Harvest the young leaves of Chinese cabbage anytime. When
mature, the leaves and stems can be used for soups and stir-frying. Can be
stored 4–8 weeks at 32°–40°.

PROBLEMS Cabbage looper, imported cabbage worm, aphids, harlequin bugs,
flea beetles, and splitting heads caused by uneven moisture.

NOTES Chinese cabbage is best planted in flats and then planted into the
garden soil in early spring or late summer.

CANTALOUPE

Cucumis melo
KEW-kew-mis MEL-oh

Annual—Full Sun
Ht. 6'–8' on trellis or cage, 6"–8"
on the ground Spread 6'–10'
Spacing 3'–6', row spacing 4'–6'

HABIT Climbing or crawling vine with yellow flowers and delicious fruit.

CULTURE For spring, plant after all danger of frost. For fall, plant 12–14 weeks
before first frost. Plant 4–5 seeds ½"–1" in hills every 18"–24" on center in
rows. Thin down to the two strongest seedlings per hill. Needs healthy, well-
drained soil and full sun. To conserve space, grow cantaloupe on trellises or
cages. Cut back on irrigation as the melons mature.

HARVEST 60–90 days after planting. The melons will slip easily from the vines
when mature. Fruit on trellises may need to be supported to prevent damage
when they fall away. After the fruit is ripe, store it above 45°. Will keep
1–4 weeks.

PROBLEMS Poor flavor due to excess soil moisture. Powdery mildew, root knot
nematodes, aphids, cucumber beetles, squash bugs, flea beetles, and garden
fleahoppers. Lack of pollination and soil-borne diseases can also cause trouble.

CARROT

Daucus carota
DAW-kus ka-ROT-a

Biennial, grown as an Annual—
Sun/Light Shade
Ht. 8"–12" Spread: The tops will
spread 8"–12"
Spacing 3–4 seeds per inch

HABIT Ferny top growth and large, showy white flowers.

CULTURE Soft, healthy soil and moderate fertility. If the roots hit rock or hard
spots in the soil, the carrots will be deformed. Too much fertilizer will

encourage top growth instead of roots. Plant seed in late winter (3–4 weeks before last average frost) for an early summer crop and in midsummer (8–10 weeks before first average frost) for a fall/winter crop. Seed should be broadcast on top of the soil and then gently watered in. Seed can be planted in single rows, double rows, or broadcast. Water often with a light mist until seedlings emerge, but don't water too heavily or too often. Final spacing of 2"–4" on center. Wide rows are best. Thin the carrot seedlings to 12 plants per square foot. Eat the small ones that are removed. Keep plants mulched as they grow. They like cool weather and will grow all winter in these conditions. Mulch the top of roots to prevent "greening." Maintain even soil-moisture level as carrots mature. Root length is made the first week, then enlargement happens.

HARVEST   Dig the roots anytime they are of edible size. Eat fresh or store in the refrigerator. They can also be stored in the winter by leaving them in the ground. Carrots increase in sweetness and food value in cold weather. They can also be stored in the refrigerator at 32°–40° for about ten weeks or more.

PROBLEMS   Grubworms, wire worms, cutworms, snails, slugs, and pillbugs. Other pests include nematodes, bacterial diseases, rabbits, and armadillos. Lack of flavor can be caused by moisture stress, high temperature during maturity, or lack of trace minerals in the soil.

CAULIFLOWER
Brassica oleracea var. *botrytis*
BRASS-ih-kah o-le-RAH-see-ah bo-TRY-tis

Biennial, grown as an Annual—
Full Sun
Ht. 12"–24" Spread 15"–24"
Spacing 14"–16"

HABIT   This is the most difficult crucifer to grow. Of all the cabbage family, it is the least tolerant of freezing weather and hot summers. It has a relatively shallow root system.

CULTURE   Cool temperatures are needed for large, high-quality heads. Even soil moisture is needed to avoid "buttoning," or small heads.

HARVEST   Harvest tender greens anytime. Harvest heads when they are full and firm and about 6"–8" in diameter. They can be kept 2–4 weeks at 32°–40°.

PROBLEMS   Temperature extremes are damaging. Pests include cabbage loopers, aphids, imported cabbage worms, cutworms, and harlequin bugs. Avoid odd-looking or woody transplants.

NOTES   'Snow Crown' and 'Snow King' are two good varieties.

Left: Carrots; right: Cauliflower (Malcolm Beck)

Celery

Citrus

Kale

CELERY
Apium graveolens
A-pee-um gra-vay-OH-lenz

Biennial, grown as an Annual—
Sun/Part Shade
Ht. 12"–15" Spread 8"–10"
Spacing 8"–12"

HABIT   Upright, leafy vegetable with edible stalks. Hard to grow. Bitter taste
results from high temperature and lack of trace minerals in the soil.
CULTURE   Needs cool temperatures for success. Celery is cold hardy but will
freeze during harsh winters. Use transplants for the home garden. For fall,
plant 8–12-week-old transplants 14–16 weeks before the first average frost.
Sow seed in late winter in flats in organic potting soil no more than ¼" deep.
Move seedlings to 4" pots when 1" tall. Avoid moisture stress to young plants.
HARVEST   90–120 days. Harvest 30–40 stalks per 10' of row and store in the
refrigerator.
PROBLEMS   Blackheart, which is a calcium deficiency, and boron deficiency.
NOTES   Celeriac, also called knob celery, is one-half celery and one-half lettuce.

CITRUS
Citrus spp.
SIT-rus

Tropical Evergreen Trees—Full Sun
Ht. 8'–20' Spread 8'–20'
Spacing 10'–20'

HABIT   Fragrant flowers in spring followed by decorative and delicious fruit.
Glossy evergreen foliage. Generally, in Texas, citrus will only bear fruit on the
spring bloom.
CULTURE   Plant anytime, as long as protected from freezing weather. Best to plant
in warm soil and warm weather in the spring. Plant all citrus high, with the graft
union well above the soil line. Citrus needs little or no pruning; in fact, pruning
is detrimental to fruit production. Homeowners can grow citrus in pots. All the
citrus species can be grown in the far southern part of the state.
HARVEST   Stem should be cut, not pulled. Harvest the fruit in late summer
when mature and store in a cool place. Eating the fruit fresh from the tree is,
of course, best. The flowers that form in the summer can be harvested and
eaten any time. Fruit will store on the tree. After it has ripened and been
removed from the tree, store above 50°; will keep 2–6 weeks.
PROBLEMS   Soil and root diseases. Freeze damage in most of the state.
NOTES   The peelings of citrus are used to flavor food and drinks. Citrus flowers,
especially orange and lemon, are edible and good in teas. Also, the rinds of
organically grown citrus are sweet and can be eaten. But make sure the fruit is
organically grown because the pesticides collect in the rind.

COLLARDS AND KALE
Brassica oleracea var. *acephala*
BRASS-ih-kah o-le-RAH-see-ah ah-CEH-fa-la

Biennial, grown as an Annual—
Sun/Part Shade
Ht. 12"–24"
Spacing 10"–14"; rows should be
about 36" on center

HABIT   Cool-weather leafy vegetables.
CULTURE   Collard greens need cool weather and loose, well-drained, healthy soil
and have normal water and fertility requirements. For spring, plant 4–6 weeks
before the last average frost. For fall, plant 6–8 weeks before the first average
frost. Collard greens that mature in cool weather will have the best flavor. If
color is desired from the kale, don't overfertilize.
HARVEST   Harvest young leaves as needed for cooking. Flavor is better after a
frost. Can be stored up to three weeks at 32°–40°.

Corn

Cucumber

PROBLEMS   Cutworms, aphids, harlequin bugs, downy mildew, garden fleahoppers, loopers, and boron deficiency.

NOTES   Kale is one of the best winter-color plants. Both plants, especially the collards, do well from seed because they develop a deeper root system than transplants.

CORN
Zea mays var. *saccharata*
ZEE-ah MAYS sack-ah-RAY-ta

Annual—Full Sun
Spacing: In hills of 4–6 plants
3'–4' apart, or in rows 3' apart

HABIT   Fast-growing grasslike food crop.

CULTURE   Corn needs loose, healthy, well-drained soils. In the spring, plant corn after danger of frost and when the soil is 60° or warmer. Use 3–4 seeds per foot of row and plant 1½" deep. Make sure young seedlings don't suffer from lack of water. Thin seedlings to 10"–12" apart. Seed can be started in a greenhouse and transplanted outside later for the earliest possible corn. For a fall crop, plant 80–90 days before the first average frost date. Fertilizer helps to make good ears.

HARVEST   When corn silks have turned brown and withered (about 18–24 days after the first silks appear) and the ears are full. Best technique to tell if the corn is ready is to pull the husks back and look at or taste the corn. Pull the ears downward and twist off the stalks. This limits damage to plants and ears. For the best flavor, eat the ears as soon as possible. If necessary, put in bags and store in the refrigerator for up to three weeks at 32°–40°.

PROBLEMS   Poorly filled ears result from poor pollination. To avoid this, don't plant long single or double rows. Instead, plant in blocks, hills, or three or more rows. Downy mildew, mosaic virus, and other diseases.

NOTES   Some gardeners recommend planting when the full moon is near. That would be the second quarter. Others recommend the first quarter. Corn tastes better and is better for you if not overcooked; trace minerals are cooked and leached away.

CUCUMBER
Cucumis sativus
KEW-kew-mis sa-TEE-vus

Annual—Full Sun
Ht. 6'–8'
Spacing 15"–18" in rows,
2–3 plants per hill

HABIT   Vining plant that climbs by tendrils. Makes a good-looking decorative vine. Male and female yellow flowers. Females have swollen immature fruit behind the flower.

CULTURE   It is best to grow cucumbers in cages or on trellises to save space. For spring, plant seed after all danger of frost. For fall, plant seed 12–14 weeks before the average first frost. Plant seed ½"–1" deep after treating with seaweed, vinegar, or other biostimulant. Optimum temperature range is 65°–95°. Transplants can also be used. For cucumbers, even moisture is important to prevent misshapen fruit.

HARVEST   Plan to get 8–12 cucumbers per plant. Harvest when the fruit is the desired size. Small fruit are more tender than larger ones. If not eaten right away, store in a cool place; will keep 2–4 weeks.

PROBLEMS   Poor flavor is caused by too much soil moisture or not enough available trace minerals in the soil. Powdery mildew, leaf miners, aphids, squash bugs, and cucumber beetles. Yield will be reduced if mature fruit is left on the vine too long.

Eggplant

Fig

EGGPLANT
Solanum melongena
so-LAH-num me-lon-ZHEE-na

Perennial, grown as an Annual—
Full Sun
Ht. 18"–24"
Spacing 2½' rows, 3' on center,
plants 15"–18" apart

HABIT   Large, fuzzy leaves; thick stems; open growth; fruit in several sizes and basically two colors: purple and white.

CULTURE   Plant in spring after all danger of frost. For fall, plant 100–120 days before the first average frost. Eggplant does not like cold weather. Use 7–8-week-old transplants that are about 5–6" tall for best results. Do not plant deeply; eggplant does not have the ability to root from stems. If starting from seed, plant ½" deep. It is best to grow in cages because the plants get floppy.

HARVEST   Harvest the fruit as it matures, 65–80 days from planting. Use a knife or pruning shears to avoid damage to plants. Store the fruit in a cool place or eat as soon as possible. Harvest when two-thirds full size to avoid toughness. Expect 7–20 fruit per plant.

PROBLEMS   Very sensitive to frost. Leaf miners, potato beetles, flea beetles, and spider mites.

NOTES   The small, thin Japanese varieties are the most tender and have the best flavor.

FIG
Ficus carica
FIE-cus CAR-ih-ka

Deciduous Fruit Tree—
Sun/Part Shade
Ht. 8'–10' Spread 10'–12'
Spacing 12'–20'

HABIT   'Celeste' is a large-growing tree with small, very sweet figs with tightly closed eyes. 'Brown Turkey' or 'Texas Everbearing' are both productive trees with medium-sized fruit.

CULTURE   Figs don't need much other than an organic program and continuous mulch on the root system. They will grow in all soils, but like healthy soils best. Need plenty of water. Heavy mulching is very important.

PROBLEMS   Nematodes can be a pest but can easily be controlled by working citrus pulp into the soil. Varieties with open eyes are subject to damage from the dried fruit beetle. Birds, raccoons, possums, and squirrels are also problems.

HARVEST   Harvest in summer as the fruit matures. Harvest as soon as figs have ripened; they will not continue to ripen after being harvested. They are not ripe if the sap is white. Excellent dried. Store at 32°–40° for 2–3 weeks.

NOTES   'Celeste,' 'Texas Everbearing,' 'Brown Turkey,' and 'Alma' are good varieties. Shriveled fruit may result from using the wrong variety or from hot, dry weather. Figs are parthenocarpic; they produce fruit without pollination.

Grape

Horseradish

Jicama

GARLIC   See Chapter 8 (Herbs)

GRAPE	Deciduous Vine—Full Sun
Vitis spp.	High-climbing and wide-spreading
VIE-tis	Spacing 8'–10'

HABIT   Fast-growing climbing vine for structures and support.

CULTURE   Relatively easy to grow in healthy soil. Plant in fall. Transplants in one-gallon cans are best for the homeowner.

HARVEST   Harvest the grapes when they are mature (taste sweet and the seeds are brown) and before the birds and other animals get them. Cut the clusters from vines—don't pull. Store ripe at 32°–40° for 4–6 weeks. Leaves are best harvested when young and tender.

PROBLEMS   Grasshoppers, caterpillars, and various diseases.

NOTES   Grapes function as a good landscape vine as well as a food crop. Muscadines (*V. rotundifolia*) need sandy soil. Our native wild Mustang (*V. landicans*) is best for jams and jellies.

HORSERADISH	Hardy Perennial—
Armoracia rusticana	Full Sun/Part Shade
arm-o-RAY-ce-ah rus-ti-CAN-ah	Ht. 24"–40" Spread 12"–18"
	Spacing: Divisions 1' apart in rows 3'–4' apart

HABIT   Leafy perennial that spreads quickly with long, variously cut leaves. Looks like a big lettuce.

CULTURE   Deep, healthy soil is best for the production of large, thick roots. Plant root cuttings in spring or fall. Put the root pieces in the soil with the small end down and the large end 2"–4" below the soil level.

HARVEST   Fall is the best time to harvest. Use a spading fork to carefully dig the roots. Pick and use leaves for salad anytime, but the young spring growth is the most tender and tasty. Roots can be left stored in the ground for several months.

PROBLEMS   Various leaf-eating insect pests and slugs and snails.

JICAMA	Tropical Annual Legume—Sun
Pachyrrhizus erosus	Ht. 3'–4' Spread 4'–5'
pah-key-RISE-us eh-RO-sus	Spacing 8'–10'

HABIT   Vigorous spreading, bushy vine that has heart-shaped leaves, blue or white flowers, and lima-bean-like pods on fully developed plants.

CULTURE   Easy to grow in well-drained, healthy soil. Plant the beans in the spring in rows 2'–3' apart, with plants 8"–10" on center. Use the basic fertilization schedule and remove flowers from young plants to encourage the expansion of roots, the edible part of the plant.

HARVEST   Like potatoes, jicama may be harvested at any time during root development, although miniature roots have tender skin.

PROBLEMS   The usual caterpillars and beetles attack the foliage at times.

NOTES   Native to Mexico and northern Central America. Common name is pronounced HICK-a-ma.

Jujube

Kohlrabi

Leek

JUJUBE
Ziziphus spp.
ZIZ-ih-fuss

Deciduous Fruit Tree—Sun
Ht. 25'–30' Spread 15'–30'
Spacing 20'–30'

HABIT   Clusters of small yellow flowers in early summer. Shiny, edible, datelike purple-brown fruit in fall. Branches and twigs are spiny, gnarled, zigzagged (hence the name). Glossy, dark green leaves.

CULTURE   Slow to moderate growth in almost any soil.

USES   Unique shade tree. Edible and medicinal fruit that tastes like dried apples.

PROBLEMS   Can spread by root sprouts and seeds to become a rather annoying pest.

KOHLRABI
Brassica oleracea var. *gongylodes*
BRASS-ih-kah o-le-RAH-see-ah gon-gi-LOW-deez

Biennial—Full Sun
Ht. 10"–12" Spread 10"–12"
Spacing 6"–10"

HABIT   Fast-growing, cool-season turniplike bulb that forms above the ground and has leaves growing from it. It's actually an enlarged stem.

CULTURE   Similar to broccoli. Likes large amounts of organic matter. Best in raised beds, rows, or hills. Drought tolerant.

HARVEST   Harvest the leaves anytime and eat fresh in salads or cook as greens. Harvest the bulbs when they are 2"–3" or slightly larger. Fall crops can be harvested at a larger size. Will keep more than six weeks at 32°–40°.

PROBLEMS   Bulbs get woody in hot weather; small seedlings dry out during establishment. Tough bulbs can result from stress.

LEEK
Allium scorodoprasum
A-lee-um score-ro-do-PRAY-sum

Perennial—Full Sun/Light Shade
Ht. 18"–36" Spread 8"–10"
Spacing 4"–6"

HABIT   Leeks are related to and look like giant green onions with very tall, dark green flat leaves.

CULTURE   Same as for onions and garlic. Healthy soil and a basic, organic program. Plant the large bulbs in the fall for harvest in the early summer. They can also be planted in late summer for harvest in the winter and early spring. Plant the bulbs as deep as twice their diameter. Plant seed about ½" deep. Cover the seed with a thin layer of compost. Transplants work well if you can find them. Let the soil stay on the dry side as the plants mature.

HARVEST   In the early summer when the plant has matured but before the leaves start to brown and before the weather turns hot. Harvest the entire plant and either eat as soon as possible or store in the refrigerator at 32°–40°. Will last 8–10 weeks.

PROBLEMS   Few problems if any other than slugs and snails occasionally.

NOTES   Like onions and garlic, leeks are among some of the most healthy foods.

LETTUCE

Lactuca sativa
lac-TWO-cah sa-TEE-vah

Annual—Sun/Part Shade
Ht. 12"–18" Spread 12"–18"
Spacing 6"–12"

HABIT   Leafy, cool-season vegetable. For the best quality, lettuce needs to mature during cool temperatures.

CULTURE   Thrives in healthy soil. For spring, plant seeds 2–4 weeks before the last average frost. For fall, 8–10 weeks before the first average frost. For best production, use a succession of plantings. Broadcast seed or plant in rows on top of the soil. Seeds need light to germinate. When the seedlings have 2–3 leaves, thin to 2" on center; later thin to 8"–10". The small plants that are removed are excellent for use in salads, or eat them fresh in the garden. Avoid having lettuce mature in hot weather to avoid bitterness and bolting.

HARVEST   Harvest small thinning plants anytime. Harvest leaves before they mature, 25–70 days from planting. Lettuce can be cut and allowed to grow again. Cut leaves can be stored at 32°–40° for 1–3 weeks.

PROBLEMS   Cutworms, loopers, aphids, slugs, snails, flea beetles, and garden fleahoppers.

NOTES   High source of silica. The leaf-type lettuces are the easiest to grow. Lettuce and carrot seeds are the most difficult seeds to sprout. The slightest crust will stop them.

MUSTARD GREENS

Brassica juncea
BRASS-ih-kah JUHN-see-ah

Annual—Full Sun/Part Shade
Ht. 12"–24" Spread 6"–12"
Spacing 6"–8"

HABIT   Leafy, cool-season vegetable that can be cooked or eaten raw. It is cold hardy down to about 20°. Can usually be grown all winter in most of Texas.

CULTURE   Easy to grow in any healthy soil. Mustard likes lots of organic matter and raised rows to increase the drainage. For spring, plant seeds 3–6 weeks before the average last frost. For fall, plant 6–8 weeks before the first average frost. Plant seeds in rows or by broadcasting on top of the soil and 1" apart. Tamp the seed into the soil after sowing.

HARVEST   Harvest after 30–70 days by the cut-and-come-again technique or by removing the entire plant and planting additional seed. Greens are usable at any size. Young leaves are best for salads and fresh eating. Older leaves should be cooked. Harvest the seed when the pods turn brown. Young seedpods and small yellow flowers are also edible. Can be stored at 32°–40° for 1–3 weeks.

PROBLEMS   Aphids, flea beetles, cabbage loopers, harlequin bugs.

NOTES   *B. hirta* is white mustard; *B. nigra* is black mustard. Their seeds are used to make table mustard. *B. juncea* is brown mustard. Black mustard seed is the hottest.

241

Onion

Okra

OKRA

Annual—Full Sun

Hibiscus esculentus

Ht. 8'–15' Spread 5'–6'

hi-BIS-kus ess-kew-LEN-tus

Spacing: Thin seedlings to 6"–9", rows 3'–4' apart

HABIT   Upright growth that's aggressive after the soil has warmed in the spring. Large leaves, edible pods and yellow flowers, spiny stems.

CULTURE   Enjoys hot weather and is easy to grow (if you control the root knot nematodes with citrus) in healthy, well-drained soil. Plant seeds in the spring after all danger of frost. The best time is when the soil is between 75° and 90°. Soaking the seed in water for 24 hours before planting speeds germination. Adding a couple of tablespoons of seaweed or vinegar works even better. Sow seeds at 4–5 per foot of row and ½"–¾" deep.

HARVEST   Harvest the young pods daily. Pods should be about 3"–5" long. Once they get large and tough, they are no longer edible. They can usually be harvested 50–70 days after planting, 4–6 days after the first flower blooms. Store if necessary in the refrigerator, but be sure to eat the pods fresh. Expect about 20–30 pods per plant. Harvest daily or at least every other day over a long harvest season. Leaving pods on the plant to mature shuts down new pod formations.

PROBLEMS   Aphids, fire ants, stink bugs, nematodes, fungal diseases, cotton root rot. Curled or crooked pods are usually caused by insects like aphids or stink bugs.

ONION

Biennial, grown as an Annual—Sun/Light Shade

Allium cepa

A-lee-um SEE-pa

Ht. 8"–30" Spread 8"–12"

Spacing 1" apart for seeds, 2"–8" apart for sets

HABIT   Cool-season bulb that has dark green straplike foliage. Onions are related to lilies. They have round clusters of small flowers on hard stems.

CULTURE   Plant onions in raised rows for best results. Soil should be healthy and well drained. Onions have small root systems, so put the fertilizer close to plants and be sure to keep the soil moist—not too wet, just moist. For spring, plant seeds 3–4 weeks before the average last frost. For fall, plant seeds 8–10 weeks before the average first frost. Broadcast seed or plant in rows ¼"–½" deep. The small bulbs or sets should be planted 1" deep in rows. Plant transplants in shallow garden soil in the winter or very early spring. When using transplants, choose plants only ½" in diameter or less. During hard freezes, small onions can be covered with loose hay or floating row cover. Another method of starting onion seeds in the fall is to plant them in pots. Bulbs are made with energy stored in the green leaves, so the greener the tops, the bigger the bulbs.

HARVEST Harvest the green onions (scallions) at any time. Harvest the bulbs when the bulbs have swollen and the tops have died back. Sets usually take 35–45 days; seeds take 85–200 days. Some varieties of onions can be stored by leaving them in the garden soil. When removed from the soil, store bulbs in a cool, dry place. They will keep for months.

PROBLEMS Damping-off, slugs, snails, and cutworms.

NOTES Leeks are big onions that are often mistakenly called elephant garlic. All alliums are good eating and good for you.

Papaya

Pawpaw

PAPAYA
Carica papaya
KAR-ih-cah pah-PIE-yah

Tropical Fruit Tree—Sun
Ht. 8'–10' Spread 5'–6'
Spacing 4'–6'

HABIT Straight trunks, crown of very large, deeply cut leaves on long stems. Fruit on female plants. Both male and female plants are needed for fruit production. Papaya plants have the ability to change sex. Fruit production is best when plants are started from seed in the winter and set outside in beds after the last frost.

CULTURE The better the beds, the better papayas grow.

USES Tropical effect, fruit production in the southern half of the state.

PROBLEMS Can't take any frost. Primarily used as an ornamental in most of Texas.

NOTES Best to start new plants every year rather than trying to overwinter established plants in a greenhouse.

PAWPAW (Custard Apple)
Asimina triloba
ah-SIM-in-ah tri-LOBE-ah

Deciduous Fruit Tree—Shade/Part Shade
Ht. 15'–30' Spread 15'–20'
Spacing 10'–15'

HABIT Purplish-green flowers in April. Fruit is 3"–5", banana-shaped, and green when young, brown or black when mature; edible in the fall.

CULTURE Large fan-shaped leaves turn yellow in the fall. Young shoots and leaves are covered with rusty down. Seed is slow to germinate; plant in fall for germination the next spring. Can also be started from cuttings or layering.

HARVEST Pick when fruit is ripe—in late summer. The outside will be coppery brown and the inside creamy yellow. For sweet taste, keep fruit in cold storage until fully ripe.

PROBLEMS Leaf-eating ants. Hard to transplant large specimens; however, small plants are fairly easy.

NOTES Native to the deep acid soils of East Texas.

Peach

PEA (English Pea)

Pisum sativum
PEE-sum sa-TEE-vum

Annual—Full Sun
Ht. 2'–6' Spread 2'–6'
Spacing 2'–3', rows 30"–48" apart

HABIT Legume with small orchidlike flowers, followed by edible pods. Peas
    need support to climb.
CULTURE Peas are a cool-season annual and like moist, cool soil. For spring,
    plant seed 4–6 weeks before the last average frost. For fall, plant seed 8–10
    weeks prior to the first average frost. Plant seeds (peas) 1½" deep.
HARVEST Harvest the pods when they are young and tender, usually between
    50 and 80 days. Plants will start to bloom and grow pods after about 50 days.
    Harvest the first pods about 20 days after the blooms. It's best to eat them
    right away, but if not, store them in the refrigerator at 32°–40° for up to two
    weeks. English peas should be shelled just prior to being cooked.
PROBLEMS Chlorosis, cutworms.
NOTES These cool-season peas are the true peas. The southern peas include
    black-eyed, crowder, and purple hull; they are actually beans.

PEACH

Prunus persica
PROO-nus PURR-si-cah

Deciduous Fruit Tree—Full Sun
Ht. 15' Spread 15'
Spacing 25'–30'

HABIT Small tree with early spring flowers and summer fruit.
CULTURE The peach tree is one of the hardest-to-grow fruit trees in Texas.
    They require lots of tender loving care. Plant in spring or fall using transplants
    that are balled and burlapped, bare-rooted, or container-grown. Can be grown
    from seed, but the fruit probably won't be very good.
HARVEST Harvest the fruit when slightly soft to the touch and ripe. Eat
    immediately or store in a cool, dry place.
PROBLEMS Most of the disease problems can be minimized with the Basic
    Organic Program.

PEANUT (Goober Pea)
Arachis hypogaea
A-ra-kiss hi-po-JEE-ah

Annual— Full Sun
Ht. 15"–20" Spread 15"–20"
Spacing 10"–15"

HABIT Low-growing annual legume with a central upright stem. Peanuts have yellow or white flowers and underground pods that form on the roots. The pods contain the edible peanut.

CULTURE Peanuts need sandy soil, moderate moisture, and a long growing season. They are heavy feeders.

HARVEST Dig peanuts in late summer or early fall and let them air-dry before storing in a cool, dry place.

PROBLEMS Insects generally are not too much of a problem. Keep night-lights away from peanut plantings.

NOTES A good place to learn more about peanuts in Texas is the Texas A&M research station in Stephenville.

PEAR
Pyrus pyrifolia
PIE-rus pie-rah-FOL-ee-ah

Deciduous Fruit Tree—Full Sun
Ht. 15'–25' Spread 15'
Spacing 15'–20'

HABIT Upright-growing fruit tree with white flowers in the spring and summer fruit.

CULTURE This is one of the easiest fruit trees to grow in Texas. Needs less pruning than plums and peaches. Plant in the spring or fall. Balled and burlapped, bare-rooted, or container-grown transplants are all used, but containers are the best choice. Can be grown from seed, but the fruit probably won't be very good.

HARVEST Harvest the fruit in summer when slightly soft to the touch and ripe. Eat as soon as possible or store in a cold, dry place.

PROBLEMS Avoid fire blight by cutting back on the nitrogen fertilizer. Avoid planting Bartlett.

Below left: Black Peanut; below right: Pear

PECAN

Carya illinoinensis

CARE-ee-ah ill-ih-noy-NEN-sis

Deciduous Nut Tree—Full Sun
Ht. 80'–100' Spread 80'–100'
Spacing 80'–100'

HABIT Large-growing, graceful tree with medium green compound leaves, wonderful fruit in the form of pecans, and so-so yellow fall color.

CULTURE Plant year-round from containers, bare-rooted in the winter.

HARVEST Pick up pecans as they drop in the fall. Sometimes shaking or thrashing the trees is necessary to loosen the nuts from the tree. Nuts can be stored in a dry, cool place and for a longer time, shelled or unshelled, in the freezer.

NOTES Best are natives and hybrids like 'Caddo' and 'Kanza.' See Chapter 2 (Trees) for additional information.

PEPPERS

Capsicum spp.

CAP-see-cum

Perennial, grown as an Annual—
Full Sun/Shade
Ht. 12"–6' Spread 18"–36"
Spacing 18"–24"

HABIT This is a nightshade vegetable that varies greatly in size and heat of peppers.

CULTURE Easy to grow in most any healthy soil. Plant in spring after all danger of frost, about two weeks after tomatoes are planted. In fall, plant about 2½ months before first average frost. Peppers transplant easily and that is the most common method, although they can be grown easily from seed. Peppers are very sensitive to fertilizer. They need it in small doses only at bloom time. Will grow and produce in sun or shade.

HARVEST Harvest 60–100 days from seed, sooner for transplants. Don't break peppers from the plant. Cut them off to prevent damage to the stems and the rest of the plant. Peppers can be stored in a cool, dry place for a good long time, but they are best eaten fresh.

PROBLEMS Sunburn on the fruit can be avoided by planting in afternoon shade. Leaf miners, nematodes, spider mites, diseases.

NOTES Peppers make lovely ornamental landscape plants. The small fruiting varieties can be used as potted plants, and the chile pequín and chiltepíns will perennialize in North Texas under an organic program.

Habanero Peppers

Japanese Persimmon

PERSIMMON

Diospyros spp.

Dye-OSS-pear-os

Deciduous Fruit Tree—Full Sun

Ht. 60' Spread 30'

Spacing 20'–40'

HABIT   Tall-growing fruit and shade tree, with insignificant flowers; large, shiny leaves; and small pink to yellow 1" fruit in the fall. Dark, heavily fissured bark. Really good-looking tree. Oriental persimmons are much smaller trees, but have larger fruit.

CULTURE   Easy to grow in almost any soil. Plant anytime of the year if from a container, but fall is the best time. Transplants of container-grown trees grow best. Bare-rooted plants can be planted in the fall and winter.

HARVEST   The fruit ripens in the fall and has its best flavor when it easily releases from the tree. The fruit will often be sour until after the first frost, so harvest after the first freeze for the best taste. Eat immediately because persimmons don't store well.

PROBLEMS   Primary insect pest is the webworm.

NOTES   Other common names are common persimmon and Eastern persimmon. *D. texana* is the smaller-growing and small-fruited Texas native persimmon. *D. kaki* is the Japanese species. Varieties include 'Eureka,' 'Hachiya,' 'Tane-nashi,' 'Tamopan,' 'Fuyu,' 'Fuyugaki,' and 'Izu.'

PLUM

Prunus salicinia

PROO-nus sa-LICK-ih-nah

Deciduous Fruit Tree—Full Sun

Ht. 20' Spread 15'–20'

Spacing 20'–25'

HABIT   Small upright to spreading deciduous tree. Pink to white spring flowers are followed by summer fruit.

CULTURE   One of the easier-to-grow fruit trees—except in white rock. Plant bare-rooted plants in fall, but container-grown plants can be planted year-round. Also started from cuttings and graphs.

HARVEST   Harvest the flowers when in bloom and the fruit in the summer. Plums are ripe when they take on a deeper red color and are slightly soft to the touch. Pick fruit and eat fresh or store in a cool, dry place.

PROBLEMS   Diseases such as bacterial stem canker and brown rot; borers, plum curculio, and aphids.

NOTES   Rabbits love the shoots pruned from this and other fruit trees.

247

Potato

Pumpkin

POTATO

Solanum tuberosum
so-LAH-num tew-be-RO-sum

Perennial, grown as an Annual—
Full Sun
Ht. 18"–24" Spread 24"–36"
Spacing 8"–16" between pieces in
rows, 36" between rows

HABIT   Leafy vegetables that sometimes flower in cool weather, potatoes are tubers, which are actually modified stems, not roots. The tubers will tend to swell out of the soil. When they do, the sunlight hits them, and they turn green and will give you a tummy ache. Keep them covered with soil or mulch.

CULTURE   Fertilize fairly heavily when planting rather than doing a lot of side-dressing later. Keep the soil slightly moist. Many gardeners plant on Washington's birthday (used to be February 22). Others plant potatoes as early as January. Potato shoots can be frozen back without much damage to the crop. Official planting dates for spring are 2–3 weeks before last frost; for fall, 12–16 weeks before first frost. Plant the entire seed potato.

HARVEST   Harvest after 90–120 days, when the foliage starts to turn brown or, even better, just before the foliage starts to turn. Dig and eat as new potatoes as soon as they are large enough. Foliage needs to turn completely brown or the potatoes won't store well. Cure potatoes in a dark place above 50° and then store for as long as six months at 40°–48°.

PROBLEMS   Colorado potato beetles, flea beetles, garden fleahoppers, aphids, nematodes, wireworms, root fungi, leaf fungi.

NOTES   The best part of the potato is the skin, but unless you use a totally organic program, don't eat it.

PUMPKIN

Cucurbita pepo
kew-KUR-bi-tah PEEP-o

Annual—Full Sun
Ht. 12'–15' Spread 200 sq. ft.
Spacing 2'–6'

HABIT   Large stems and foliage, large yellow flowers. Pumpkins and squash are similar; the main difference is the stem. Pumpkin stems are tough and angular, while squash stems are round and more tender. Pumpkins have large root systems.

CULTURE   Pumpkins grow best in loose, coarse-textured soils and have normal water requirements. They can be planted anytime after the last frost, but to time your planting for Thanksgiving and Halloween, you have to do a little planning. If the variety needs 100 days to mature, pick the harvest date and count back 100 days or a few more for a cushion. Plant the seeds after all danger of frost and when the soil temperature is at least 70°. Use 4–6 seeds every 6' in rows about 8' apart, and plant about 1½" deep in the soil and a little deeper in sandy soil.

HARVEST   Pick pumpkins 85–160 days after planting, when they are the size and color you need. Always leave a 2"–4" stem stub. For winter storage, the skin should be hard. They will store up to six months at 45°–50°.

PROBLEMS   Poor pollination can be solved by encouraging biodiversity, especially bees and other beneficial insects.

Radish

'Texas Pink Eye' Southern Pea

RADISH
Raphanus sativus
RA-fa-nus sa-TEE-vus

Annual/Biennial, grown as an
Annual—Sun/Part Shade
Ht. 3"–12" Spread 4"–6"
Spacing 1"–4"

HABIT   Very fast-growing annual vegetable. The swollen root of the plant is the
edible part.

CULTURE   Radishes like cool soil and need moderate amounts of water and
fertilizer. For spring, plant seeds 4–6 weeks before the last average frost. For fall,
plant seeds 6–8 weeks before first average frost. They grow so fast, they can
almost be planted anytime. Broadcast or plant seeds in rows ½" deep. Use 3–4
seeds per inch and then thin the stand about 3–4 days after emergence.

HARVEST   20–35 days after planting. Some of the winter types take longer. Best
to eat radishes soon after harvesting. Store them if needed in the refrigerator.
An ice bath prior to storing helps.

PROBLEMS   Slugs, snails, cutworms, wireworms, nematodes, flea beetles, and
aphids.

NOTES   Radishes are the fastest of all the edible plants to grow and an excellent
choice to get children started in gardening.

RHUBARB
Many say that rhubarb can't be grown in Texas. If you want to give it a try, rhubarb is planted from seed or root divisions. Use the same timing as for horseradish, and don't harvest any stalks until the second growing season. It is a cold-
hardy perennial, but it has a tough time with our hot summers.

SOUTHERN PEA
Vigna sinensis
VIG-na si-NEN-sis

Annual—Full Sun
Ht.: Varies greatly
Spread: Varies greatly
Spacing: Bush-type 4"–6",
vining type 8"

HABIT   Warm-weather vegetable. Southern peas are either bush-type plants or
climbers.

CULTURE   Relatively easy to grow. Peas germinate poorly in cool soil, so don't
get in a hurry. Plant after the last frost in the spring and after the soil has
warmed to 70°. Fall crops are planted 90–120 days before the first average
frost. For best results, plant seeds (peas) in raised beds, 16"–24" wide and
36"–48" apart. Treat the seed with seaweed and rhizobia bacteria (nitrogen-
fixing bacteria). There should be enough moisture in the soil for germination.
Put seeds into furrows 1½" deep in sand or 1" in clay. Sow at 4–5 per foot of
row and cover with garden soil. Thin to 4"–8" when 3"–4" tall.

HARVEST   Harvest as snap peas when they are young, as green mature peas
once the color starts to change on the beans, and wait for full maturity for
harvesting dry peas. They will store best and the longest as dry, mature peas.
Snaps and green matures should be stored in the refrigerator if not eaten
right away.

PROBLEMS   Iron chlorosis, aphids, weevils, stink bugs, thrips, nematodes.

NOTES   Avoid seed that has been treated with toxic fungicides. They are often
pink in color. 'Big Red Ripper' is the most delicious of all southern peas.
'Texas Pink Eye' is an easy-to-grow pea from Texas A&M—a good one
to try.

Malabar Spinach

SPINACH

Spinacia oleracea
spee-NAH-kee-ah o-le-RAH-see-ah

Annual—Sun/Part Shade
Ht. 8"–12" Spread 8"–12"
Spacing 3"–8"

HABIT   Spinach is a relatively shallow-rooted, cool-season leafy vegetable that bolts easily in warm weather and warm soil.

CULTURE   Spinach likes temperatures between 50° and 60° and doesn't like highly acid soils. Crowded conditions cause stemming and poor-quality plants. For the spring garden, plant 4–6 weeks before the last average frost; for the fall garden, plant 8–10 weeks before the first average frost. Broadcast the seed or plant ⅛"–¾" deep in rows 4"–6" apart. Soaking the seeds overnight is helpful. Tamp the soil lightly after installing the seeds.

HARVEST   Harvest the foliage after 40–70 days, before the weather turns hot and as soon as the leaves are an edible size. Small leaves are more tender. Smooth-leaf types are thought to be best for canning; the crinkled-leaf (savory) types are best for fresh use. Eat right away or store in the refrigerator for up to two weeks at 32°–40°.

PROBLEMS   Flea beetles, aphids, cutworms, loopers, greenworms, and spider mites are controlled with the Basic Organic Program. Bolting can be avoided by growing in cool weather.

SPINACH, MALABAR

Basella alba
bah-SELL-ah ALL-ba

Twining Vine—Sun/Part Shade
Ht. 8'–20' Spread 8'–20'
Spacing 6'–8', but one or two plants is enough

HABIT   Succulent dark green vine with brightly distinctive red stems and leaf veins. Fast-growing and aggressive.

CULTURE   Easy to grow in any well-drained soil. Requires normal amounts of water and fertilizer. Plant in spring after the last frost, using seeds, cuttings, or transplants. Very easy to germinate from seed.

HARVEST   Pick the young, tender leaves and use fresh or store at 32°–40° for up to two weeks.

PROBLEMS   Spreads by seed and can become a pest, although the seedlings pull up easily if you get them early.

SPINACH, NEW ZEALAND

Tetragonia tetragonioides
teh-trah-GO-nee-ah teh-trah-go-nee-OY-deez

Annual—Full Sun/Part Shade
Ht. 2' Spread 3'
Spacing 12"–24"

HABIT   Vegetable that grows and produces well in the summer months. Tastes like regular spinach, but milder. Very sensitive to frost, but will produce well until the first hard frost.

CULTURE   This spinach likes more fertilizer than regular spinach. Pinch out the growing tips of plants to encourage wide branching and leaf production. Plant about the same time you plant okra and black-eyed peas. Weather and soil must be warm for germination. Transplant or seed. Plant 3–4 seeds ½"–¾" deep every 12". Seeds should be soaked before planting.

HARVEST   Anytime during the summer growing season. This spinach matures in about 55 days. Cut and store in the refrigerator prior to using.

PROBLEMS   Few if any pest problems, though some slugs and snails.

Yellow Straight Neck Summer Squash

Tatume Squash

Strawberry (Malcolm Beck)

SQUASH
Cucurbita spp.
kew-KUR-bi-tah

Annual—Full Sun
High-climbing or wide-spreading
(bush form)
Spacing: Hills or rows 4'–5' apart,
plants 24" to 6'

HABIT   Squash is a big, dramatic-leafed annual vegetable that varies greatly in growth characteristics. It is fast-growing and has several problems.

CULTURE   Plant in well-prepared, healthy soil. For spring, plant after all danger of frost. For fall, plant 12–14 weeks before the first average frost. Butternut will split and leak if planted in spring. Seed is the most common method, but squash can also be started from transplants. Plant 3–5 seeds per hill about ½"–1" deep.

HARVEST   In summer, harvest usually after 42–70 days; in winter, 80–120 days. Squash can be a very early crop if started in pots and transplanted. Harvest summer squash anytime the fruit is large enough to eat; the young fruit are delicious. Summer squash can be stored a short time in cool, dry places. Winter squash should only be harvested after it has totally matured. It has a longer storage life. Cut it from the vine only after the skin has hardened.

PROBLEMS   Garden fleahoppers, flea beetles, cucumber beetles, aphids, squash bugs, caterpillars, nematodes, powdery mildew, viruses, and other diseases.

STRAWBERRIES
Fragaria virginiana
fra-GAH-ree-ah ver-gin-ee-AN-ah

Short-lived Perennial—Full Sun
Ht. 6"–8" Spread 12"–18"
Spacing 12"–18"

HABIT   Low-spreading fruit crop with white flowers that grows by spreading runners.

CULTURE   Needs well-drained, highly organic soils. Raised beds are best. Matted row or perennial beds should be planted in the winter (December–February). Strawberries are harvested about 16 months later in April or May. Annuals are planted in the fall (early November) and harvested the next spring (February–April). Use transplants only.

HARVEST   Usually it is not recommended to allow the fruit to develop the first year, but I say, eat any you can get. Harvest whenever the fruit is red all over and ripe. After ripe, store in the refrigerator at 32°–40°, but strawberries don't last long, so eat them quick. They might last 1–5 days.

PROBLEMS   Slugs, snails, spider mites, various soil-borne diseases.

NOTES   Best perennials (matted row) include 'Sunrise,' 'Pocahontas,' 'Cardinal,' and 'Allstar.' Best annuals include 'Sequoia,' 'Chandler,' 'Fresno,' 'Tiogo,' 'Tangi,' and 'Douglas.' Strawberries are known to have cancer-fighting capabilities.

Sweet Potato

Swiss Chard

SWEET POTATOES
Ipomoea batatas
eye-po-MAY-ah ba-TAH-tas

Perennial, grown as an Annual—
Full Sun
Ht. 12"–15" Spread: Wide-spreading
Spacing 10"–12"

HABIT Fast-growing vining vegetable that has good-looking foliage.

CULTURE Sweet potatoes do the best in sandy acid soils, but will grow pretty well in all soils. Fairly drought tolerant once established. Plant after all danger of frost is gone and the soil temperature is about 70°, in general, April 5–June 31. About 40 days prior to the targeted planting date, place sweet potato seed roots on their sides in moist sand. Cover with a mix of sand and compost. Maintain at a temperature of about 80°. Water to keep the mix moist. After the "slips" appear, add more mix. When the slips reach a height of 8"–10", remove them with a twist and plant soon after. The ideal slips have 5–6 leaves, a stocky stem, and are 8"–10" long.

HARVEST Harvest anytime once they have reached a usable size, usually after 100–150 days. Expect 2–3 lbs. of potatoes per plant after the second month of growth and 60 or more pounds from a 15' row. Harvest the roots when the soil is on the dry side to avoid rotting. Do it whenever the potatoes are big enough to eat and before temperatures have fallen below 50°. Sweet potatoes can be left in the ground until needed.

PROBLEMS Sweet potato weevils, root knot nematodes, various diseases. Stunted plants from cold weather can be prevented by not planting too early. To avoid diseases, don't overwater. Misshapen roots also result from overwatering.

NOTES Sweet potato vines have been used to smother nutgrass, and they make a good summer ornamental ground cover.

SWISS CHARD
Beta vulgaris cicla
BAY-ta vul-GAH-ris KICK-la

Annual—Full Sun/Part Shade
Ht. 18"–24" Spread 18"
Spacing 18" rows, 12" apart or closer

HABIT Swiss chard or chard is a relative of the beet and has similar habits and needs. Chard is a beet without a bottom.

CULTURE Chard likes cool temperatures but tolerates some hot weather. Culture is about the same as for beets. For spring, plant the seed 3–4 weeks before the last average frost; for fall, plant 6–8 weeks before the first frost average date. Broadcast seed or plant in rows ½"–¾" deep.

HARVEST Use cut-and-come-again harvest on the foliage whenever it is large enough—after 55–65 days throughout the growing season. Swiss chard does not store well. Eat fresh. Cool quickly after harvest if storage is necessary. Chard can be harvested after the outer leaves are 4"–5" long. For the best flavor, wait at least 60 days.

PROBLEMS Aphids, flea beetles.

NOTES Chard can be eaten fresh in salads or cooked like other greens.

Wild Currant Tomatoes

'Super Fantastic' Tomato

Turnip (Malcolm Beck)

TOMATOES
Lycopersicum esculentum
lie-ko-PER-si-kum es-kew-LEN-tum

Tender Perennial—Full Sun
Ht. 3'–15' Spread 3'–15'
Spacing 3'–4'

HABIT Succulent upright to spreading perennial that functions as an annual in Texas for two reasons: one, it freezes easily, and two, it plays out with age as it develops insect and disease problems. Two types of plants exist: bush (determinate) and vining (indeterminate).

CULTURE Plant in well-prepared soil with lots of compost, lava sand, rock phosphate, and organic fertilizer. In sandy soil, add high-calcium lime. In alkaline soil, add Texas greensand. For transplants, use the following schedule: plant after all danger of frost in the spring and 12–14 weeks before the first average frost in the fall. Plant transplants by laying the plant down sideways or planting deeply. Tomatoes are able to root from the stems. The sideways method is best in heavier clay soils. If you start your tomatoes from seed, here's the plan. Plant the seeds indoors in organic potting soil, ¼"–½" deep, in a well-lit or greenhouse condition. They will germinate in 5–14 days at about 68°–85°. Keep the seedlings cool and in bright light to keep them from getting spindly.

HARVEST Harvest in summer when the fruit starts to ripen and turn red, usually 55–90 days after planting. Picking the tomatoes as the color first starts to change will help prevent birds, squirrels, and other critters from eating the fruit before you get it, and the fruit will continue to ripen indoors. Expect 5–20 lbs. per plant. For the best taste, pick the tomatoes after they have ripened on the vine and store indoors in a dry, cool place, not in the refrigerator.

PROBLEMS Southern blight, tomato pinworm, blossom end rot, aphids, spider mites, garden fleahoppers, hornworms.

NOTES Tomatoes do not like evening temperatures above 75°. They are pollinated by the wind—not by bees. Try the tiny wild currant tomatoes. They are very easy to grow, even in pots, and are delicious. Kids love 'em.

TURNIPS AND RUTABAGAS
Turnip—*Brassica rapa*;
Rutabaga—*Brassica napus*
BRASS-ih-kah RAY-pa; NAY-pus

Biennial, grown as an Annual—
Sun/Part Shade
Ht. 8"–15" Spread 8"–10"
Spacing 2" apart for greens,
4" apart for roots

HABIT Turnips are a leafy vegetable with a swollen, edible root. They mature during cool temperatures. Rutabagas are similar, but have a longer growing season and do best when planted for fall harvest.

CULTURE Prepare soil with the standard ingredients: compost, lava sand, organic fertilizer, and Texas greensand in alkaline soils. Use high-calcium lime in sandy acid soils. For spring, plant seed 4–8 weeks before frost. For fall, plant seed 6–8 weeks before first average frost. Broadcast or plant seed ¼"–½" deep in rows. Maintain even soil moisture level, especially as the plants mature.

HARVEST For turnips, harvest greens in 30 days, roots in 45–60 days; for rutabagas, harvest greens in 40 days and roots 75–100 days after seeding. Turnip greens, even the small ones removed during thinning, can be used in salads. They can be harvested by the cut-and-come-again method or by removal of the whole plant. Store the turnips at 32°–40° for up to 12 weeks. The greens will only last a few days.

PROBLEMS Grubworms and wire worms are the most troublesome pests, along with loopers and caterpillars.

NOTES Rutabaga greens are not normally eaten, due to their toughness.

WALNUT   See Chapter 2 (Trees)

WATERMELON
Citrullus vulgaris
sit-RUL-us vul-GAIR-iss

Annual—Full Sun
Ht. 20' or more
Spacing: Plants 4'–10',
rows 6' apart

HABIT   Watermelon is a vining plant with small yellow flowers and large stems and leaves. It is deep-rooted and drought tolerant. The fruit is either yellow or red.

CULTURE   Watermelon loves sandy soil but will grow in any soil. Plant in spring after all danger of frost is over and soil temperature is at least 70°, in general, April 1–30 and July 10–31. Directly plant the seed ¾"–1" deep. Use 3–4 seeds per spot, hill, or hole. Thin down to the two strongest and most vigorous seedlings. Pinch the unwanted ones off at the ground so the remaining roots won't be damaged.

HARVEST   Harvest in 75–100 days, when the melons are ripe. Using transplants instead of seeds can shorten the development time by about ten days. Harvest when the tendril nearest the fruit has completely turned dry and brown, or the second one out is brown, or thump it—mature fruit has a deep, dull sound. The ground spot should be an off-yellow and rough to the touch. Will store for 2–4 weeks.

ORGANIC PECAN AND FRUIT TREE PROGRAM

Pecan trees and fruit trees can be grown organically, and no, you don't have to spray toxic pesticides. For best results, plant adapted small-nut varieties like 'Caddo,' 'Kanza,' and the native pecans. Plant the trees in wide, rough-sided or square holes (not small, round holes, as some believe), backfill with soil from the hole (no amendments), settle the soil with water (no tamping), add a 1" layer of lava sand and compost mix, and finish with a 3"–5" layer of coarse-textured native cedar mulch. Do not stake the tree, wrap the trunk, or cut back the top. Very little pruning is needed or recommended. Mechanical aeration of the root zone of existing trees is beneficial, but tilling, disking, or plowing destroys feeder roots and should never be done. Pecans should never have bare soil under them. The root zone should be covered with mulches or native grasses and legumes year-round.

Feeding Schedule
ROUND 1:   February 1–15—organic fertilizer @ 20 lbs./1,000 sq. ft., lava sand or other volcanic sand @ 80 lbs./1,000 sq. ft., decomposed granite @ 80 lbs./1,000 sq. ft., and horticultural cornmeal @ 20 lbs./1,000 sq. ft.

ROUND 2:   June 1–15—organic fertilizer @ 10 lbs./1,000 sq. ft. and Texas greensand @ 40–80 lbs./1,000 sq. ft. or soft rock phosphate at the same rate if in acid soils.

ROUND 3:   September 15–30—organic fertilizer @ 10 lbs./1,000 sq. ft., and sul-po-mag @ 20 lbs./1,000 sq. ft.

Note: Once soil health has been achieved, Round 3 can be omitted. Rock powders are optional after the first three years.

Large pecan orchards can use livestock manure or compost at 1–2 tons/ acre per year along with establishing green manure cover crops. Lava sand and other rock powders can be applied any time of the year. Foliar-feed with Garrett Juice twice monthly.

Pest Control Program
Add the following to Garrett Juice and spray as needed.

Garlic tea   Spray at 1/4 cup/gallon of water or per label directions
Orange oil or d-limonene   Spray at 1 oz./gallon of water as a spray or 2 oz./ gallon of water as a drench
Potassium bicarbonate   Spray at 1 rounded tablespoon/gallon of water for diseases
Liquid biostimulants   Use per label directions
Neem products   Use per label directions for serious pest problems
Fish emulsion   Spray at 1–2 oz./gallon of water for additional nutrients

Spray Schedule
1st spraying at pink bud
2nd spraying after flowers have fallen
3rd spraying about June 15th
4th spraying during last week in August

The first two sprayings should contain Garrett Juice and garlic tea. Use additional sprayings as time and budget allow. For best results, spray every two weeks, but do at least once a month.

Insect Release
Trichogramma wasps   Weekly releases of 10,000–20,000 eggs per acre or residential lot for three weeks starting at bud break
Green lacewings   Release 4,000 eggs per acre or residential lot weekly for one month
Ladybugs   Release 1,500–2,000 adult beetles per 1,000 sq. ft. at the first sign of shiny honeydew on foliage

FRUIT VARIETIES FOR TEXAS

Zone 1

Apple—Gala, Granny Smith, Holland, Jerseymac, Prime Gold, Red Chief, Smoothee, Starkrimson Red Delicious, Starkspur Golden Delicious, Top Red
Apricot—Bryan, Hungarian, Moorpark, Wilson
Blackberry—Brazos, Rosborough, Womack
Cherry, Sour—Montmorency
Figs—Celeste, Texas Everbearing
Peach—Bicentennial, Denman, Jefferson, Milam, Ranger, Redglobe, Sentinel, Springold, Surecrop
Pear—Ayers, Kieffer, LeConte, Madness, Maxine, Moonglow, Orient, Surecrop
Plum—Allred, Bruce, Methley, Morris, Ozark Premier
Strawberry—Cardinal, Sunrise

Zone 2

Apple—Holland, Jerseymac, Molly's Delicious, Prime Gold, Red Chief,
  Smoothee, Starkrimson Red Delicious, Starkspur Golden Delicious, Top Red
Apricot—Bryan, Hungarian, Moorpark, Wilson
Blackberry—Brazos, Rosborough
Figs—Celeste, Texas Everbearing
Peach—Bicentennial, Denman, Dixieland, Frank, Harvester, Jefferson, Loring,
  Milam, Range, Redglobe, Redskin, Sentinel, Springold
Pear—Asian, Ayers, Garber, Kieffer, LeConte, Maxine, Moonglow, Orient, Zyers
Persimmon—Eureka, Hachiya, Izu
Plum—Allred, Bruce, Methley, Morris, Ozark Premier
Strawberry—Cardinal, Sunrise

Zone 3

Apple—Holland, Jerseymac, Molly's Delicious, Ozark Gold, Starkrimson Red
  Delicious, Starkspur Golden Delicious
Apricot—Bryan, Hungarian, Moorpark, Wilson
Blackberry—Brazos, Rosborough

FRUIT VARIETIES FOR TEXAS

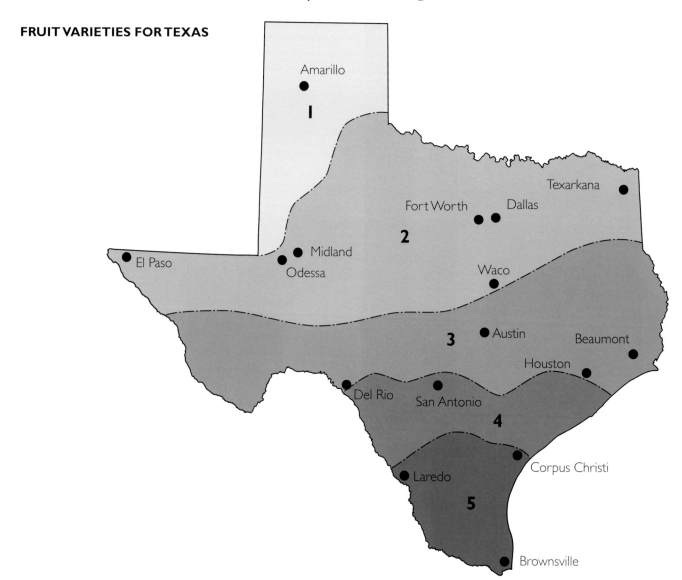

Figs—Celeste, Texas Everbearing
Peach—Bicentennial, Dixieland, Frank, Harvester, Jefferson, June Gold, Loring, Milam, Redglobe, Redskin, Sentinel, Springold, Summergold
Pear—Asian, Ayers, Garber, Kieffer, LeConte, Maxine, Monterrey, Moonglow, Orient
Persimmon—Fuyu
Plum—Allred, Bruce, Methley, Morris, Ozark Premier
Strawberry—Cardinal, Sequoia, Sunrise, Tangi

Zone 4

Apple—Anna, Dorsett Golden, Erin Shemer, Molly's Delicious
Apricot—Blenheim, Royal
Blackberry—Brazos, Rosborough
Citrus, Cold-Hardy—Changsha Tangerine, Kumquat, Meyer Lemon, Rustic Limequat, Satsuma
Figs—Alma, Celeste, Texas Everbearing
Peach—Bicentennial, Dixieland, Harvester June Gold, La Feliciana, Loring, Redskin, Rio Grande, Sam Houston, Sentinel, Springold
Pear—Kieffer, LeConte, Monterrey, Moonglow, Orient
Persimmon—Fuyu
Plum—Allred, Bruce, Methley, Santa Rosa
Strawberry—Douglas, Sequoia, Tangi, Tioga

Zone 5

Apple—Anna, Dorsett Golden, Erin Shemer
Apricot—Blenheim, Royal
Blackberry—Brazos, Brison, Rosborough
Citrus, Cold-Hardy—(Acid Citrus): Calamondin, Eustis Limequat, Kumquat, Meyer Lemon; (Mandarin Types): Changsha Tangerine, Clementine, Orlando, Satsuma; (Oranges): Hamlin, Marrs, Navel
Figs—Alma, Celeste
Peach—EarliGrande, Early Amber, Floridabelle, McRed, Rio Grande, Sam Houston, Sun Red
Pear—Fanstil, Kieffer, LeConte, Monterrey, Orient, Pineapple
Persimmon—Tamopan, Tanerashi
Plum—Bruce, Methley, Santa Rosa
Strawberry—Douglas, Sequoia, Tangi, Tioga

GRAPE AND PECAN VARIETIES FOR TEXAS

Region A

Grape—Black Spanish, Carman, Champanel, Favorite, Golden Muscat, Herbemont
Pecan—Cheyenne, Mohawk, Pawnee, Shawnee, Shoshoni, and natives

Region B

Grape—Black Spanish, Carman, Champanel, Favorite, Golden Muscat, Herbemont; Vinifera: Barbera, Chenin Blanc, Emerald Riesling, Ruby Cabernet, Thompson Seedless
Pecan—Cheyenne, Mohawk, Tejas, Western, Wichita

Region C

Grape—Black Spanish, Carman, Champanel, Favorite, Golden Muscat, Herbemont
Pecan—Caddo, Cheyenne, Choctaw, Kiowa, Mohawk, Shawnee, Sioux, Western, Wichita

Region D

Grape—Black Spanish, Carman, Champanel, Favorite, Flame, Golden Muscat, Herbemont, Reliance
Pecan—Caddo, Cape Fear, Cheyenne, Kanza, Osage, Shawnee, and natives

Region E

Blueberry—Briteblue, Delite, Garden Blue, Tifblue, Woodard
Grape—Black Spanish, Carman, Champanel, Favorite, Golden Muscat, Herbemont; Muscadine: Carlos, Cowart, Fry, Higgins, Jumbo, Magnolia, Regal
Pecan—Caddo, Cape Fear, Cheyenne, Choctaw, Desirable, Kanza, Shawnee, and natives

GRAPE AND PECAN VARIETIES FOR TEXAS

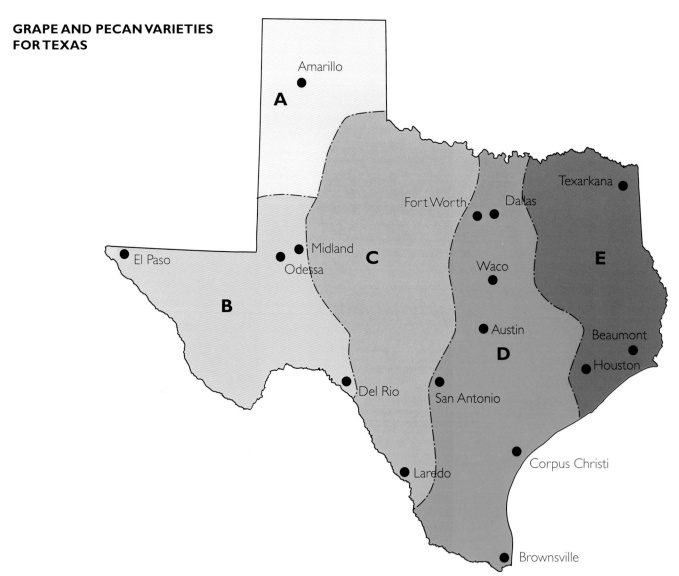

HOW TO PRUNE FRUITS AND NUTS

Apples
Prune to create limbs growing at 45° angles for best production. Do not remove large amounts of structure.

Apricots
Remove dead, diseased, inward-growing, and crossing limbs only.

Blackberries
Remove fruiting canes to the ground immediately after harvest. Keep other canes pruned to 36"–48".

Blueberries
Prune away low limbs near the soil and vigorous upright shoots. Keep the center of bushes open.

Grapes
Train grape vines to horizontal wire trellises and remove 80 to 90 percent of the top growth of mature vines each winter. To avoid overcropping, thin three-year-old vines to 10–12 clusters, five-year-old vines to 15–25 clusters, and mature vines to 40–80 clusters.

Nuts
Pecans and walnuts do not need to be thinned. Remove dead wood, limbs that are rubbing, and limbs that are a physical problem.

Peaches
Prune to create three main branches grown out at 45° angles to the ground. Remove about 40 to 50 percent of the total branching, including all gray two-year-old shoots. Fruit only bears on one-year-old red shoots.

Pears
Prune to create 45°-angled limbs. Remove dead, diseased, and inward-growing branches. Do not remove more than 20 percent of the bearing wood.

Plums
Prune to allow for as many 45°-angled limbs as possible and remove 20 to 30 percent of the total branching.

STRUCTURES FOR CLIMBING VEGETABLE PLANTS

One trick to increase productivity is to use structures for climbing vegetables. These structures are easy to make yourself. (1) Concrete-reinforcing wire mesh is the best material for making tomato cages. Many other vegetables can also be grown vertically in these structures. (2) A teepee trellis can be made from bamboo poles or metal rods. This structure is particularly good for growing beans, peas, cucumbers, and other climbing vegetables. (3) Chicken wire, chain-link fencing, or welded wire fabric mounted vertically and attached to metal or wooden stakes is another good structure for climbing peas and beans. (4) A barrel trellis can be made using a single metal rod or bamboo pole in the center, with string or wire connecting the top of the pole to the inside edge of the barrel. (5) The Japanese ring is another unique planting device. The ring can be made of welded wire or reinforcing wire and should be placed on well-prepared and raised soil. It should be 3'–5' tall and filled with compost. Tomato, squash, pepper, or other plants should be planted

1

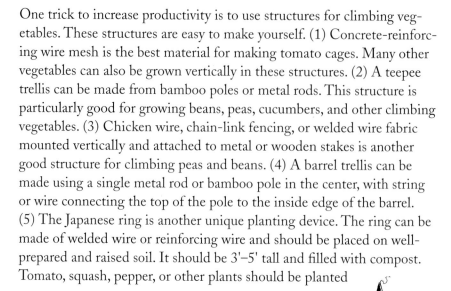

2

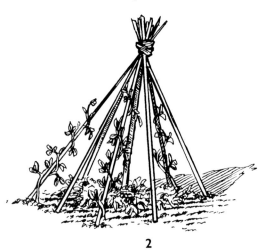

3

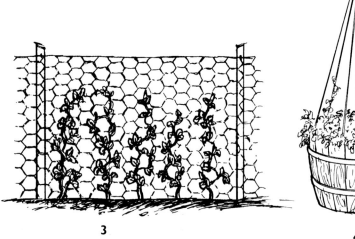

4

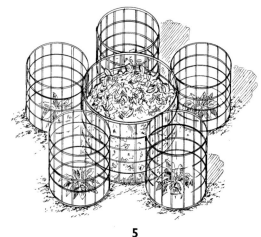

5

in additional rings attached to the outside of the big ring and spaced approximately 24" on center. The diameter of the ring can range from 2' to 4'. The plants can be staked, wired to the Japanese ring, or have their own individual rings. The plants are irrigated by watering the compost in the center ring. The water traveling through the compost carries natural fertilizer to the plants at each watering. The ring can also be recessed into the soil and filled with compost.

Vegetables are heavy feeders and do best when extra amounts of humus are available. High-quality compost, which is at least 20 percent manure, and earthworm castings are the best sources of humus in this case. Raise the planting area by building flat-topped hills or rows. The raised bed created by either technique improves drainage and soil aeration. Don't forget how important oxygen is to the root system.

COMMON GREEN MANURE CROPS

Alfalfa

Deep-rooted legume grown throughout the United States. This crop does well in all but very sandy, clay, acid, or poorly drained soils. Apply lime if the pH is 6 or below and add phosphate rock. Inoculate the seed with rhizobia bacteria when growing alfalfa for the first time. Sow seed in the spring to the north and east and in late summer elsewhere at 20–30 lbs. of seed per acre or 1–2 lbs. per 1,000 sq. ft. Alfalfa has high protein and high nitrogen content. It also contains calcium, magnesium, potassium, and many trace minerals. If cotton root rot appears, take the alfalfa out and use other annual winter legumes.

Alsike clover

Legume grown mostly in the northern states. This clover prefers fairly heavy, fertile loams, but does better on wet, acid soil than most clovers. Sow 6–10 lbs. of seed per acre in the spring, or in the early fall in the South. Use ½–1 lb. per 1,000 sq. ft.

Alyce clover

Legume grown in the extreme southern regions. It prefers sandy or clay loams with good drainage. Sow in late spring, 15–20 lbs. of scarified seed per acre. It is a summer-growing clover.

Austrian peas

Legume and winter crop for warmer climates. It prefers well-drained soils. Sow at 15 lbs. per acre or 2–5 oz. per 1,000 sq. ft.

Barley

Nonlegume grown in the north. It requires rich, loamy soil and does not perform well in acidic or sandy soil. In colder climates, sow winter varieties; elsewhere, sow spring varieties at 1½ bushels per acre.

Black medic

Legume grown throughout the United States. Very closely related to alfalfa, black medic is a vigorous grower on reasonably fertile nonacid soils. Sow 7–15 lbs. of scarified, inoculated seed. In the north, sow seed in spring; in the South, plant in the fall. It needs ample calcium in the soil.

Buckwheat

Nonlegume grown mostly in the northeast. It is one of the best choices for re-building poor or acid soils. It has an enormous, vigorous root system and is a good bee plant. Plant seed when the ground has warmed in late spring or early summer. Sow 2 bushels per acre or 2–3 lbs. per 1,000 sq. ft.

Cowpea

Legume and a good soil builder because its powerful roots crack hardpans. Inoculate the seed when planting it the first time. Sow seed as soon as the soil is well warmed, broadcasting 80–100 lbs. or sowing 20 lbs. in 3' rows. Grows very quickly.

Crimson clover

Winter legume that does well on almost any fairly good soil, but likes sandy soil best. On poor soil, grow cowpeas first for a preliminary buildup. Sow 30–40 lbs. of unhulled seed or 15–20 lbs. of hulled seed in fall. Hard-seeded strains volunteer from year to year in the South.

Hairy indigo

Summer legume grown in the South. Will tolerate a moderately poor sandy soil and will make a very tall, thick stand. Sow in early spring, 6–10 lbs. broadcast, 3–5 lbs. if drilled.

Hubam

Winter legume for Austin and the South for fall planting only, at 10–30 lbs. per acre. It will grow to 8' tall in calcium-rich soils.

Lespedeza

Legume grown in the South and as far north as Michigan in all types of soil. The northern species *L. cuneata* is particularly good for poor, sour soils. In the spring, sow 30–40 lbs. of seed per acre. Fertilize with phosphate rock. Many varieties are available.

Millet

Nonlegume grown in arid regions of the South and Southwest. Does better on poor soil than many other forage or green manure crops. It is usually planted thickly at about 35 lbs. of seed per acre. Many varieties are available.

Oats

Nonlegume widely grown throughout North America. Oats can be grown on almost any soil, provided the climate is cool and moist. Winter oats are only suited to very mild winters. In the spring, sow 2–3 bushels of seed per acre.

Persian clover

Winter legume grown in the southern and Pacific states. This clover prefers heavy, moist soils. Sow 5–8 lbs. of seed per acre in the fall.

Rape

Nonlegume that is a good cover for short growing periods in summer. Sow at 5–8 oz. per 1,000 sq. ft. Excellent for grazing. Should be used more.

Red clover

Legume grown in most areas, but is most useful in the north. This cover will thrive in any well-drained soil rich in phosphorus. Its decay is of exceptional benefit to crops that succeed it. Sow seed early in the spring; 15 lbs. of seed per acre is adequate, 4–8 oz. per 1,000 sq. ft.

Rye (cereal or elbon rye)

Nonlegume widely grown in the northeast. Rye tolerates many soil types, even very poor ones. It is easily cultivated and adaptable to any cool, dry climate. Recommended for nematode control when planted as a cover crop in gardens. Plant at 5–7 lbs. per 1,000 sq. ft.

Ryegrass

Nonlegume planted in the late summer or fall. Good plant for soil building and for crowding out nutgrass. Plant at 7–10 lbs. per 1,000 sq. ft. Primarily for use on lawn grasses.

Soybeans

Summer legume grown throughout North America. Soybeans thrive in nearly all kinds of soil. They can stand considerable drought. Use late-maturing varieties for best green manure results. Sow 60–100 lbs. per acre, spring to midsummer. For best results, inoculate the seed. Use 2–3 lbs. per 1,000 sq. ft.

Sudangrass

Nonlegume grown in all parts of the United States. Sudangrass tolerates any soil except wet. It is a very fast grower and therefore excellent for quick organic-matter production. In late spring, broadcast 40–50 lbs. of seed per acre, 2–3 lbs. per 1,000 sq. ft.

Sweet clover

Legume grown in all parts of the United States in just about any soil. Plants are especially adept at utilizing rock fertilizers and are excellent honey plants. Sow 15 lbs. of scarified seed to the acre, ½–1 lb. per 1,000 sq. ft. in fall or early spring. A fast-growing annual, white sweet clover can be turned under in the fall. Other varieties have their biggest roots in the spring of the second year, so turn them under then. Also sold as 'Hubam' and 'Madrid.' A great soil builder. It is a tall-growing clover.

Velvet beans

Legume grown in the South. One of the best crops for sandy, poor soils. Plants produce roots 30' long, vines up to 50' long. Sow seed in warm spring at 100 lbs. per acre broadcast, or 25–30 lbs. in wide rows.

Vetches

Legumes with varieties for all areas. Grow in any reasonably fertile soil with ample moisture. Hairy vetch does well in any soil and is the most winter-hardy variety. Hungarian is good for wet soils in areas having mild winters. In the north, sow seed in spring; elsewhere, in the fall. Depending on the variety, 30–60 lbs. will plant one acre.

Weeds

Whenever weeds do not steal needed plant food and moisture, they can be used as green manures to produce humus as well as to help make minerals available and conserve nitrogen.

Wheat

Nonlegume grown throughout North America. Wheat prefers a fairly fertile soil with a pH of about 6.4. Broadcast 1½ bushels per acre in the fall.

Winter Cover Crops

The best winter cover crops are rye, wheat, oats, ryegrass, hairy vetch, and other legumes. All may be sown from mid August to mid October so they will be well established before the frosts begin. During winter, they hold the soil in place and prevent erosion. Winter cover crops usually feature large fibrous root systems that add organic matter to garden soil when plowed or spaded under in the spring. They are mostly used as green manure. The seeds of grasses and legumes should be mixed together 50/50. Shallow-rooted grasses take nitrogen and moisture from the shallow soil. Legumes have deep roots and take nutrients and moisture from deep in the soil.

'Yuchi,' arrowleaf clover

A winter annual legume native to the Mediterranean. It is one of the best forages and produces the most tonnage of forage per acre.

VEGETABLE
PLANTING CHART

Plant	How Deep to Plant	From Seed Planting to Pickling
Beans, Bush	2"	60 days
Beans, Lima	1"	60–80 days
Beans, Pole	2"	60 days
Beets	1"	60 days
Broccoli	½"	70 days
Brussels Sprouts	½"	90 days
Cabbage	½"	50–100 days
Carrots	½"	70 days
Cauliflower	½"	45–70 days
Celery	½"	110 days
Collard Greens	½"	50–60 days
Corn	2"	70–100 days
Cucumbers	1"	50–60 days
Eggplants	½"	50–80 days
Lettuce	½"	40–60 days
Melons	1"	60–90 days
Mustard Greens	½"	30–35 days
Onions	1"	40–50 days
Parsnips	½"	90–100 days
Peas	1"	60–90 days
Peppers	½"	60–90 days
Radishes	½"	20–25 days
Spinach	½"	40–50 days
Squash, Summer	1"	40–60 days
Squash, Winter	1"	50–100 days
Tomatoes	½"	50–80 days
Turnip Greens	½"	40–50 days

For vegetable varieties, check with your local county agent, the local growers, or the *Texas Organic Vegetable Gardening Book* by Garrett and Beck.

Herbs

Purple Coneflower

In my broad definition, herbs are any plants that have a use other than providing beauty or some landscape requirement. Based on that definition, most plants could be considered herbs, but this chapter covers plants that are classically considered herbs.

BED PREP, PLANTING, MAINTENANCE

Herbs aren't fussy about space—many of the herb species can be planted in pots, window boxes, or tiny garden beds. Use 2" or 4" transplant pots for annuals and perennials and set them out in well-prepared soil. Prepare beds by tilling or forking the following amendments into the existing soil to a depth of 6"–8". The quantities are based on 1,000 sq. ft.

80 lbs. lava sand
50 lbs. corn or corn/bran product
40 lbs. Texas greensand (replace with high-calcium lime in acid soils)
5 lbs. dry molasses
3–5" quality finished compost
1" earthworm castings (optional)

Some gardeners like to loosen the soil to a depth of 12" prior to adding the amendments. The cooler parts of the year are the best times to install new plants, but herbs can be planted year-round in most of Texas.

When planting during the heat of summer, it is critical to soak the root balls of transplants in water before installing them. Add a tablespoon of seaweed or Garrett Juice per gallon of water and let the plants sit in the water until thoroughly soaked, then plant in moist beds. The root ball should be sopping wet and dripping before it goes into the moist soil.

Avoid working in beds that are sloppy wet, but never plant transplants in dry beds and never plant dry root balls. If you do, expect sick plants, lots of transplant shock and poor plant growth. After planting, the beds should be mulched with at least 1"–2" of organic mulch such as compost or shredded tree trimmings. Herbs that are sensitive to wet soil—such as rosemary, lavender, and sage—should be mulched only lightly.

Fertilize twice a year, at the most, with gentle organic fertilizer such as earthworm castings, alfalfa meal, cornmeal, or other natural fertilizers. Herbs in general do not like high fertility.

For medicinal uses of these plants, see *Herbs for Texas* by Garrett and Brannam.

THE PLANTS

ALFALFA
Medicago sativa
med-ih-CAY-go sa-TEE-va

Perennial Legume—Full Sun
Ht. 30" Spread 12"–18"
Spacing 6"–10"

HABIT Deep-rooted, cool-season, broadleaf perennial. Foliage has three leaflets. Purple flowers in spring and early summer, followed by spiraling seedpods.
CULTURE Plant from seed in the fall.
HARVEST Leaves and sprouts should be eaten fresh. Seed should be harvested when mature and stored in glass.
USES Leaves and sprouted seed are used in salads, on sandwiches, in teas, and in health drinks.
PROBLEMS Cotton root rot is a major concern. Blister beetles, leafhoppers, and aphids are sometimes pests.
NOTES Winter ground cover for large areas. Excellent nursery plant for beneficial insects. Alfalfa can be grown in containers or even flats for the production of alfalfa sprouts.

ALLSPICE
Pimenta dioica
pa-MINT-ta dee-oh-EE-ka

Tropical Tree—Full Sun
Ht. 30' Spread 15'–20'
Spacing: One is enough

HABIT Small greenish white flowers followed by dark brown to black berries that look like peppercorns. Small tropical evergreen tree. Aromatic bark, leaves, berries, and bunches of flowers.
CULTURE Needs well-prepared, healthy soil. Must be treated as a tropical and protected in the winter except in the most southern part of the state.
HARVEST Berries are gathered when mature but still green.
USES Flavor food, sweeten dishes with its peppery taste. Leaves can be used in teas. Warming medicine, greenhouse or container plant. Berries are eaten as a breath sweetener.
PROBLEMS Freezes in all parts of Texas except the southern tip of the state.
NOTES Seed sold in grocery stores has probably been heat-treated and will not be viable.

Alfalfa

Allspice

Giant Aloe Vera

ALOE VERA
Aloe vera or *Aloe barbadensis*
AL-low VER-a, AL-low bar-ba-DEN-sis

Tender Perennial—Full Sun
Ht. 35' Spread 24"
Spacing: Use individually or in clusters

HABIT Thick, succulent leaves in a rosette. Flower stems range in size from very short to over 20'.

CULTURE One of the easiest plants to grow. Needs well-drained soil and does best in full sun, but adapts surprisingly well to shade. Easy to grow in containers or in beds.

HARVEST Cut lower leaves off and use the gel and juice directly.

USES Flowers are edible. It's hard to decide whether to enjoy seeing them or eating them. Sticky gel is applied topically to skin abrasions, sunburn, insect bites, poison ivy rashes, and burns. Container plant.

PROBLEMS Sunburn in full sun if abruptly moved from indoors. Bacterial diseases in wet soil.

NOTES Even if you aren't a gardener, keep an aloe plant in your kitchen to use on burns and cuts. To apply, simply cut a leaf off the plant and squeeze the gel onto the wound. For more serious burns or cuts, you can slit open the leaf lengthwise and apply it as a poultice. Can be grown as a potted plant even in low-light areas. I have several indoors at all times.

ANGELICA
Angelica archangelica
an-GEL-ee-kah arc-an-GEL-ee-kah

Biennial—Shade
Ht. 6' Spread 2'
Spacing 2'

HABIT Taprooted, three-year biennial with large umbels of greenish white flowers. After the third year, it seeds and dies. Bright green compound leaves 2–3' long. Reseeds easily. All parts of the plants are fragrant.

CULTURE Likes shade and is easy to grow. Needs plenty of water. Needs well-prepared and well-drained beds.

HARVEST Harvest stems in May or June, leaves before flowering, roots in autumn, and seeds after maturing.

USES Young shoots can be used in salads. Second-year stems can be cooked and used like celery. Background foliage plant in shade gardens.

PROBLEMS Hard to establish in much of Texas because it does not like summer heat.

NOTES Juice of the plant should never come into contact with the eyes. Dried roots keep for years.

Angelica

Anise

ANISE
Pimpinella anisum
pimp-ah-NELL-ah ah-NEE-sum

Annual—Full Sun
Ht. 18"–24" Spread 12"
Spacing 2"–4"

HABIT   Umbels of tiny white flowers followed by seeds. White flowers resemble those of a large Queen Anne's lace. Looks like a very large, coarse carrot. Leaves are rounded and toothed when young but become feathery like coriander as plant matures.

CULTURE   Cool-weather plant that will bolt in hot weather. Easy to grow from seed. Needs rich, well-drained soil and must be protected from strong winds because the thin stems are fragile.

HARVEST   Gather the seeds when they begin to turn brown and store them in glass containers.

USES   Leaves are good in salad. Seeds are used in cooking and baking breads, cakes, and pastries. You can also make a tea from the seeds.

PROBLEMS   None serious.

NOTES   When taken in large amounts, it can be toxic, so use it carefully.

Anise Hyssop

ANISE HYSSOP
Agastache foeniculum
ah-guh-STAH-she fee-NIK-yew-lum

Herbaceous Perennial—Sun/
Part Shade
Ht. 24"–36" Spread 12"–18"
Spacing 18"–24"

HABIT   Purple, rose, or mauve flower spikes in summer. Upright plant with triangular, anise-scented leaves and nectar-loaded flower spikes; self-sows readily.

CULTURE   Easy to grow. Tolerant of moist soils but does best in well-prepared, well-drained beds. Prefers morning sun. Cut back when it gets tall and floppy.

HARVEST   Pick and dry the flowers as they bloom. Harvest leaves anytime. Flowers can also be used fresh.

USES   Leaves and flowers are excellent for tea. Flowers are good in salads. Sip a cup of tea with a meal to help prevent gas and bloating. Perennial garden. Fragrant plant, attracts bees and produces excellent honey. Good for potpourri and arrangements. An easy-care herb with many uses and a sweet fragrance. It should be a part of all tea and fragrance gardens.

PROBLEMS   None serious.

NOTES   Good-looking plant for the perennial garden or border.

African Blue Basil

BASIL
Ocimum basilicum
OH-see-mum ba-SEE-li-kum

Annual—Full Sun
Ht. 24"–36" Spread 18"
Spacing 12"–18"

HABIT   Highly aromatic square stems, soft leaves. Dark purple to pale green, serrated or smooth, glossy or crinkly. Flowers range from white to purple.

CULTURE   Fairly easy to grow in healthy beds. Must be planted outdoors after all threat of frost is gone. Likes the hot weather.

HARVEST   Basil freezes beautifully and keeps its lovely green color, too, but it's best to use fresh.

USES   Salads, vegetables, vinegars, oils, butter for seasoning, and fragrance. Probably the most popular culinary herb. Use it in teas and eat it fresh.

PROBLEMS   Caterpillars, very susceptible to frost.

NOTES   Tea made from basil is reported to be a good insect repellent.

BAY (Sweet Bay)

Laurus nobilis
LAR-us NO-bi-lis

Tender Evergreen Shrub—
Sun/Part Shade
Ht. 50' in warmer climates, under 8'
in northern part of state Spread 5'–20'
Spacing 5'–10'

HABIT   Upright evergreen shrub with small creamy flowers in late spring,
followed by shiny black berries.
CULTURE   Easy to grow in almost any situation. Does well in pots or in beds.
Needs some protection against harsh winter winds in the northern half of
Texas.
USES   Flavoring for many foods and teas. Container plant, potpourri, wreaths.
Fruit oil is used in making soap. Cut foliage is good for indoor arrangements.
PROBLEMS   Few other than freeze damage in severe winters.
HARVEST   Collect the evergreen leaves year-round and use fresh or store the
dried leaves in glass containers.
NOTES   Mine has been outdoors for over 15 years and is over 15' tall.

BORAGE

Borago officinalis
bo-RA-go oh-fih-sih-NAY-lis

Annual—Sun/Part Shade
Ht. 18"–24" Spread 12"–24"
Spacing 18"

HABIT   Fast-growing, fuzzy leaves, beautiful small bluish purple flowers. Leaves
are 6"–8" long. Stems, leaves, and flower buds are covered with silvery hairs.
Flowers are bright bluish purple, five-petaled, and star-shaped with cones of
black anthers.
CULTURE   Loves dry soil and full sun but can tolerate some shade. Has a long,
fleshy taproot and does not transplant easily. Gets floppy if not staked or cut
back frequently.
HARVEST   Collect the leaves when young and tender, the flowers while in
bloom, and the seeds after they have matured.
USES   Cucumber flavor. Vinegars and cooling teas. Flowers can be used as a
garnish or candied or frozen into ice cubes to add an interesting touch to
punches and other iced drinks. Leaves can be boiled and eaten. Young leaves
and flowers can be used in salads. Good-looking decorative annual. Excellent
plant for attracting bees.
PROBLEMS   Grasshoppers, chlorosis in poor soil.
NOTES   Sepals of the flowers are not edible.

Bay

Borage

Cardoon

Catmint

Catnip

CARDOON
Cynara cardunculus
SIN-ah-ra car-DUN-kew-lus

Tender Herbaceous Perennial—
Full Sun
Ht. 6'–8' Spread 4'–5'
Spacing 3'–4'

HABIT   Large, dramatic plant that should normally be treated as an annual. Huge gray-green, deeply cut, fuzzy leaves. Forms dramatic purple flowers that resemble thistle.

CULTURE   Likes deep, moist soil during the growing season, but will rot in wet soil in the winter.

HARVEST   Harvest the leaf stalks as needed and use fresh.

USES   Add leaf stalks to soups and stews. Dramatic or decorative specimen or a backdrop plant for larger herb gardens.

PROBLEMS   Can't stand wet feet. Grows very large, not suitable for small herb gardens.

NOTES   Mice like the seed, so be careful with the propagation location. Cardoon is a very close relative of the edible globe artichoke.

CATNIP
Nepeta cataria
NAY-peh-tah ke-TAH-ree-ah

Perennial—Full Sun/Dappled Shade
Ht. 18"–24" Spread 36"–48"
Spacing 12"–18"

HABIT   Catnip has gray-green foliage and bushy growth. Catmint is a woodier and more compact plant with tiny gray leaves. Catnip has a hot peppery flavor.

CULTURE   Easy to grow but does best in healthy, well-prepared soil. Keep it cut back and don't allow it to flower. Trim back hard when the plant gets floppy.

HARVEST   Harvest and dry foliage before it flowers.

USES   Tall, gray-leafed ground cover. Toys for cats. Repels insects.

PROBLEMS   Cats go nutty for it. They can also eat it all up before it has a chance to grow or bloom.

NOTES   *N. mussinii* is catmint. Cats are not as attracted to it as they are to catnip.

271

Chamomile

Chaya

CHAMOMILE
Chamaemelum nobile
ka-mee-MAY-lum NO-bee-lay

Annual—Full Sun/Dappled Shade
Ht. 18" Spread 36"
Spacing 12"

HABIT   White flowers with a yellow, cone-shaped center. Delicate fernlike foliage and small white daisylike flowers.

CULTURE   Easy to grow in well-drained soil.

HARVEST   Cut the flowers when in full bloom, dry and store in a cool place. The fresh flowers are more potent and make a delicious tea during the growing season.

USES   Social tea and children's tea, sleep-inducing tea.

PROBLEMS   Caterpillars and slugs.

CHAYA (Spinach Tree)
Cnidoscolus chayamansa
ny-DOS-co-lus chi-ah-MAN-sah

Tropical—Sun
Ht. 7'–15' Spread 3'–5'
Spacing: Don't need but one

HABIT   Clusters of white flowers about 3" in diameter. Blooms intermittently throughout summer. Upright fast growth. Likes rich fertile soil and ample moisture. Dark green leathery leaves are lobed like castor bean leaves but are smaller.

CULTURE   Easy to grow and not too fussy about soil type. Low fertilizer requirements.

HARVEST   Pick leaves fresh in the summer and cook.

USES   Cook as spinach and use in quiche or soups. Contains up to 33 percent protein. Makes an attractive summer foliage plant.

PROBLEMS   Will sometimes freeze outdoors in Texas winters. Leaves can be toxic until cooked.

NOTES   Several U.S. herbalists consider it dangerous to eat.

Chervil

Chicory

Endive

Garlic Chives

CHERVIL (Gourmet Parsley)   Annual—Part Shade
Anthriscus cerefolium   Ht. 24" Spread 6"
an-THRIS-kus kay-ree-FOE-lee-um   Spacing 6"–12"

HABIT   Umbels of tiny white flowers in early summer. Leafy annual herb that readily self-seeds. Branched hollow stems and bright green, finely textured leaves that look like Italian parsley.
CULTURE   Likes cool weather and partial shade; can tolerate some frost. Will bolt during the first warm days of spring.
HARVEST   Harvest anytime. Best to use fresh from the garden.
USES   Use like parsley in salads, soups, sauces, and garnishes. Flavor has a hint of licorice.
PROBLEMS   None serious.

CHICORY   Perennial—Full Sun
Cichorium intybus   Ht. 36" Spread 18"–24"
ki-KO-ree-um IN-tew-bus   Spacing 18"

HABIT   Lots of pretty, light blue flowers with fluted petals in summer. Related to sunflowers and grows like endive. Each bloom lasts only until noon.
CULTURE   Easy to grow. Tolerates drought, likes cool weather. Start seed early. Does well in alkaline soil.
HARVEST   Use the leaves fresh. Split the root to dry.
USES   Root is steamed as a vegetable or roasted and mixed with coffee to counteract its stimulant effect or substituted for coffee. Summer flowers.
PROBLEMS   Weedy looking.
NOTES   Chicory works as a biological sponge to soak up excess nitrogen and other nutrients from the soil.

CHIVES   Hardy Perennial—Sun/Part Shade
Allium schoenoprasum—Onion Chives   Ht. 12"–18" Spread 6"–12"
AL-lee-um skoyn-o-PRAH-sum   Spacing 6"–12"
Allium tuberosum—Garlic Chives
AL-lee-um tew-bah-ROE-sum

HABIT   Onion chives have pink or purple flowers in spring or early summer. Garlic chives have white flowers and bloom in late summer. Garlic chives have flat leaves; onion chives have hollow round leaves. Clumps should last four to five years before dividing.
CULTURE   Very easy to grow in most any soil and needs little fertilizer.
HARVEST   Cut and use fresh or dry for soup mixtures. Harvest by pinching off at the base to prevent unsightly brown stubs. Cut just before use to preserve the vitamins, aroma, and flavor.
USES   Seasoning for butters, salads, soups, and other foods. Leaves used for vinegars and breads. Cut the flowers off when growing the plant for culinary use. Especially good on baked potatoes and in scrambled eggs. Flowers can be added to salads, and they make a beautiful salad vinegar that is rosy red. Good border or window-box plant.
PROBLEMS   None serious. Wet soil can cause root disease. Occasional slug and snail damage.

273

Comfrey

Coriander

Creosote Bush

COMFREY (Knitbone)
Symphytum officinale
sim-FI-tum oh-fih-sih-NAY-lee

Perennial—Part Shade/Full Sun
Ht. 24"–36" Spread 36"–48" or more
Spacing 24"–36"

HABIT Deep-rooted, tough, spreading perennial. Large bristly leaves 8"–18" long, with light blue, pink, or red bell-like flowers in spring and summer.

CULTURE Very easy to grow. Needs ample water, but that's about it. Will do better in healthy soil and grows best in locations with morning sun and afternoon shade.

HARVEST Cut and use leaves and stems anytime.

USES Should not be taken internally. Topical treatment of rashes, scrapes, and especially insect bites and stings. Handsome coarse-textured specimen perennial for the landscape. Old leaves are excellent for the compost pile.

PROBLEMS Can be invasive. Roots are tenacious and, once established, difficult to dig up. Small pieces will generate new plants.

NOTES In short, comfrey is a very powerful and important herb that shouldn't be overused or misused.

CORIANDER (Cilantro)
Coriandrum sativum
ko-ree-AN-drum sa-TEE-vum

Annual—Full Sun or/Morning
Sun/Afternoon Shade
Ht. 18"–24" Spread 18"–24"
Spacing 12"–15"

HABIT Entire plant is pungently aromatic. Original leaves are flat and wide, resembling Italian parsley; they become feathery as white or mauve flowers appear with umbrella-shaped clusters of round seeds.

CULTURE Very easy to grow from seed in any well-drained soil. Likes lots of compost and other organic amendments.

HARVEST Cut and use the foliage anytime. Collect the seeds when they mature and turn brown.

USES Coriander is also good for preventing or relieving indigestion. Also said to help remove mercury from the body. The seed is the most powerful part of the plant.

PROBLEMS Weevils may attack dried seeds. Store with bay leaves.

NOTES Attracts beneficial insects and deters harmful ones with its strong odor.

CREOSOTE BUSH
(Chaparral, Greasewood)
Larrea tridentata
LA-ree-ah tri-den-TAH-dah

Evergreen—Full Sun
Ht. 3'–10' Spread 8'–10'
Spacing 3'–5'

HABIT Twisted gray stems with small, strongly scented, resinous leaves. Beautiful yellow dime-size flowers cover the plant in the spring followed by pea-size, fuzzy, reddish white fruit. Distinctive fragrance after a rain. It is a bushy plant with small, olive green leaves and an open appearance.

CULTURE Easy to grow in acid conditions in loose, well-drained soils. Cannot tolerate wet soil. Extremely drought tolerant.

USES Considered an anti-cancer plant. Good ornamental plant that has a strong fragrance after a rain.

HARVEST Harvest twigs and leaves; dry and store in a cool place.

PROBLEMS Galls on water-stressed plants. Pest control is rarely needed. Considered unsafe by some experts.

NOTES Hard to propagate from cuttings and extremely difficult to transplant. Nothing will grow under it. This plant is also listed in some books as *L. divaricata* and *L. mexicana*. Native to the southwestern deserts.

Dill

Cuban Oregano

CUBAN OREGANO

Coleus amboinicus
KO-lee-us am-BOYNE-ah-cuss

Tender Perennial—Sun/Part Shade
Ht. 18"–36" Spread 18"
Spacing 12"

HABIT   Pale purple flowers. Plants and seeds are not easy to locate, but they are easy to grow.

CULTURE   Grow it in partial shade and well-drained soil and keep it moist. Likes well-prepared soil and does well in containers.

HARVEST   Use fresh.

USES   It has the taste of a cross between regular oregano and camphor. Colorful annual bedding plant, especially in borders. Does well in pots and hanging baskets.

PROBLEMS   Few except freeze damage; will not stand most Texas winters.

NOTES   Its green-and-white leaves do not sport any of the red and yellow coloring normally associated with coleuses.

DILL

Anethum graveolens
a-NAY-thum gra-vay-OH-lenz

Annual—Full Sun
Ht. 24"–36" Spread 12"–24"
Spacing 12"

HABIT   Yellow, umbrella-shaped flower heads produce small oval-shaped seeds, which are delicious. Upright growth, hollow stalk. Foliage is aromatic, feathery, fernlike plumes, bluish-green when young, then dark green.

CULTURE   Easy to grow in healthy soil. Needs protection from strong winds.

HARVEST   Cut and gather the leaves to use fresh—dill doesn't save well. As the seeds turn brown, cut off the tops of plant and hang upside down in a paper bag to catch the seed.

USES   Gives dill pickles their distinctive taste. Foliage and seeds are excellent for salads, breads, baked potatoes, soups, and butters. Use fresh leaves in green beans and with fish. Good condiment for refried beans or any bean dish, as well as fish, greens, and spinach. Add dill seed or leaves to tuna salad, tartar sauce, or salmon croquettes. Rub onto pork roast, add a pinch to steamed carrots. Tea made from the seed or leaves promotes sleep and reduces nervousness. The seeds aid digestion.

PROBLEMS   Caterpillars of the swallowtail butterfly cause damage. Butterflies are worth a little damage, so share. Strong winds can blow tall plant over.

Epazote

Fennel

Feverfew

EPAZOTE (Jerusalem Oak)
Chenopodium ambrosioides
chin-no-PO-dee-um am-bros-ee-OY-deez

Short-lived Perennial or Annual—
Full Sun/Part Shade
Ht. 6' Spread 3'
Spacing: One plant is enough

HABIT   Summer flowers are small greenish balls. Looks and grows like a weed. Has pungent, spear-shaped, deeply toothed leaves.
CULTURE   Needs no fertilizer and very little water. Once established, it will come back from seed forever except in thick mulch.
HARVEST   Use the leaves fresh anytime. Harvest the seed when mature. Dry both leaves and seed and keep in a cool place.
USES   Leaves are used to flavor Mexican food and to marinate meats and flavor a wide range of dishes. Add 2 teaspoons of leaves to the bean pot for the last ten minutes of cooking to take gas out of the beans.
PROBLEMS   Can spread and take over. Weedy looking.

FENNEL (Sweet Fennel)
Foeniculum vulgare
fee-NIK-ew-lum vul-GAR-ree

Annual/Tender Perennial—
Full Sun/Part Shade
Ht. 3'–6' Spread 2'
Spacing 18"–24"

HABIT   Yellow umbels of flowers followed by aromatic seeds. Looks like bright green or bronze dill, with finely cut feathery foliage, hollow stems, a subtle anise or licorice scent, and golden seed heads or umbels, but it grows taller than dill. Sweet fennel has green foliage. Bronze fennel (*F. vulgare* var. *purpureum*) has copper-tinged to purplish foliage.
CULTURE   Easy to grow in healthy soil. One of the easiest to grow of all herbs.
HARVEST   Harvest mature seeds and store in a dry glass container. Collect and use the leaves before the plant flowers.
USES   Liquors, chicken broth, and salads. Excellent for flavoring fish. Stalks are edible when young. Use the fresh foliage in salads and the dry seeds in breads. Eat or make tea from the crushed seed. Seed sweetens breath. Bronze fennel is the most attractive for landscape use.
PROBLEMS   Swallowtail butterflies—but just plant enough fennel for them *and* for you. If there are too many caterpillars on your plants, pick some of them off.

FEVERFEW
Chrysanthemum parthenium
kris-ANTH-ee-mum par-THIN-ee-um

Annual/Short-lived Perennial—
Full Sun/Part Shade
Ht. 9"–24" Spread 12"
Spacing 12"

HABIT   White flowers with yellow centers from summer into fall. Erect, compact growth. White and yellow forms available. Soft, light green, serrated leaves.
CULTURE   Easy to grow in any well-drained soil. Will self-sow easily. Feverfew needs moist soil for best results.
HARVEST   Cut, dry, and store leaves and flowers in glass containers. Harvest the leaves before the flowers form. Pick the flowers just before they open, and hang them upside down to dry.
USES   Tea from the flowers alleviates migraine headaches and muscular tension. Good in the perennial garden and in containers. Dry flowers for potpourri, dried arrangements, or wreaths.
PROBLEMS   Can scorch in full sun. Likes morning sun and afternoon shade best.

Garlic

GARLIC

Allium sativum
AL-lee-um sa-TEE-vum

Perennial Bulb—Sun/Dappled Shade
Ht. 48" Spread 6"
Spacing 4"–6"

HABIT Some garlic has twisting and serpentine flower heads that are very decorative. Others have straight flower shoots, and some have no flowers at all. Flat, straplike, gray-green leaves, underground bulbs with many cloves.

CULTURE Plant cloves in the fall. Purchase big, healthy bulbs (organically grown if possible) and break them apart into cloves. Each clove should be planted 3"–4" apart and about 1" deep in clay soils, 2" deep in sandy soils. It's best to place the pointed end up, although garlic seems to grow fine if the cloves are sideways. After planting the cloves, cover the planting area with about 2" of mulch. A little frost burn to the foliage tips is normal. During hard freezes, the plants can be covered with hay or floating row cover for protection, but that's usually unnecessary. For larger bulbs, cut off the flowering stems as they emerge from the foliage.

HARVEST When the tips of the leaves first begin to turn yellow in early summer, the bulbs are ready for harvest. Don't wait until the entire top is brown; energy and food value is used up as the foliage deteriorates. Dig out gently with a turning fork. Cut the tops off or tie or braid them and hang in the garage or a partially shaded place to dry. Store in a cool, dry area. Use your garlic freely, but save some of the larger bulbs for the next year's planting.

USES Garlic leaves and cloves are great for eating and for seasoning vegetables, meats, sauces, gravies, soups, and just about anything else. Try the young leaves in scrambled eggs and garlic powder on most any meat dish. Garlic is taken for the prevention and treatment of colds and bronchitis. It is also said to help in treating lead poisoning, normalizing blood pressure, killing bacteria (it's a natural antibiotic), and detoxifying blood. It's a beautiful ornamental plant or a nice addition to mass plantings or interspersed in the perennial or rose garden. Deters many insect pests. Spraying with garlic tea works as well as toxic chemicals in getting rid of flying adult mosquitoes. Garlic tea sprayed on plant foliage prior to heavy insect infestations works as a powerful repellent to most problem insects and many diseases. Significant fungicidal powers.

PROBLEMS Few if any except occasional slug nibbles. Overwatering can rot the bulbs.

NOTES Garlic is one of the world's most health-giving foods, an important medicinal herb, a key ingredient in homemade insect spray, and a good-looking landscape plant. Giant garlic, or elephant garlic (*A. scorodoprasum*), has a milder flavor than true garlic and produces a fist-size bulb. It is actually a leek, but its culture is the same. Society garlic (*Tulbaghia violacea*) has narrow foliage and beautiful purple flowers in summer.

Germander

Ginger

Planting ginger

Gotu Kola

GERMANDER

Teucrium spp.
TOO-kree-um

Evergreen Perennial—Full Sun
Ht. 24" Spread 6"–12"
Spacing 6"–12"

HABIT Whorls of purple-pink flowers in summer. Small evergreen shrub with faintly aromatic leaves. It may also be clipped into a border or low perennial hedge.

CULTURE Easy to grow, no particular cultural requirements. Propagate by seeds, cuttings, or divisions. Likes to be sheared.

HARVEST Green foliage can be harvested anytime to use with cut flowers indoors.

USES Used almost exclusively as a landscape plant. Dark green attractive hedge or border. Fragrant foliage. Used in knot gardens. Excellent cut foliage for use in interior arrangements.

PROBLEMS None I've seen.

GINGER

Zingiber officinale
ZING-gi-ber oh-fih-sih-NAY-lee

Tender Perennial—Part Shade
Ht. 6' Spread 1'–2'
Spacing 12"–18"

HABIT Fragrant yellow-purple flowers in late summer or early fall. Upright, jointed stems similar to bamboo.

CULTURE Easy to grow. Heavy feeders. Some ornamental gingers will tolerate temperatures in the low 20s without serious damage. If grown in containers, they need plenty of light. Cut back ornamental gingers in the late fall and allow them to rest through the winter. Mature plants may be dug up and divided.

HARVEST Dig up the rhizomes in the late summer or fall (before the temperature drops below 50°) and store in a cool place. Ginger does not store well frozen; it becomes stringy and tough.

USES For making teas and flavoring many foods, including vegetables, meats, and desserts. The roots of all gingers are edible. Flowers of ginger can be eaten raw or cooked and are sometimes used to make gingerbread and gingersnaps. Ginger has been taken to promote circulation of the blood and to treat respiratory problems, voice problems, nausea, and motion sickness. It's also a strong antioxidant. Some people chew a small piece every day. Excellent container and greenhouse plant.

PROBLEMS Subject to wind damage if not protected. Freezes easily in northern half of the state.

GOTU KOLA

Centella asiatica
sin-TELL-la a-she-AT-tee-ka

Tender Perennial Ground Cover—
Shade/Part Shade
Ht. 4"–6" Spread 18"–36"
Spacing 12"–18"

HABIT Tiny maroon flowers at nodes produce even tinier seed that will self-sow. You'll probably never notice the blooms. Slow-growing ground cover that spreads like mint, but not as aggressively.

CULTURE Likes moist soil. Leaves are rounded and scalloped, closely resembling ground ivy or gill ivy. Freezes in the northern half of Texas.

HARVEST Harvest the leaves year-round; use fresh or after drying.

USES Gotu kola is considered a longevity herb and brain food. Temporary ground cover in shady areas. Good in hanging baskets.

PROBLEMS Sunburn, slugs. Will freeze in most parts of Texas.

NOTES Needs shade and moist, fertilized soil.

Hoja Santa

Hoja Santa under Ginkgo

HOJA SANTA

Piper auritum
PIE-per aw-REE-tum

Herbaceous Perennial—
Full Sun/Shade
Ht. 8'–10' Spread 6'–8'
Spacing 3'–8'

HABIT   Flowers are interesting cylindrical white spikes that bloom all summer. Hoja santa is a herbaceous or semi-woody herb that sprouts from the ground with many shoots. It has large, velvety, heart-shaped leaves that are often 10" or more in length.

CULTURE   Really easy to grow. Be sure you want it.

HARVEST   Pick the large leaves as needed and use fresh, or store dry or frozen if needed for the winter.

USES   Leaves can be used to flavor dishes and to wrap various fillers of meat, fish, and vegetables. Hoja santa has a distinctive root beer taste and is a popular ingredient in Guatemalan and Mexican food. Research shows that eating large quantities of hoja santa is not healthy, so use it in moderation.

PROBLEMS   Hail and high winds will damage the large leaves. May freeze out in the northern part of the state. Completely perennial as far north as the Dallas/Fort Worth area.

NOTES   *P. methysticum* (kava-kava) is a closely related herb that is used as a calming tea. Both this plant and hoja santa should not be overused.

HOREHOUND (Houndsbane)

Marrubium vulgare
ma-RUE-bi-um vul-GAR-ee

Perennial—Full Sun
Ht. 12"–14" Spread 18"–24"
Spacing 12"

HABIT   Clusters of small white flowers followed by many small seeds that germinate freely. Bushy and woody, with fuzzy, gray-green, wrinkled, and veiny leaves. Hardy but sometimes weedy looking.

CULTURE   Easy to grow, even in poor soil. It tolerates drought, so it's good for arid areas.

HARVEST   Harvest and dry leaves and stems anytime, but preferably before the flowers form. Use fresh, or store in glass containers in a cool, dry place.

USES   Use the leaves and stems to make teas, syrups, and tinctures. Drink the tea for respiratory problems. Good ground cover for dry areas. A gardening tea made from soaking the leaves in water has been used to control canker-worms and other insect pests.

PROBLEMS   Overwatering will kill it. Can become invasive.

Horehound

Hyssop

Kudzu

HYSSOP
Hyssopus officinalis
hi-SOAP-us oh-fih-sih-NAY-lis

Hardy Perennial—Sun
Ht. 24" Spread 18"
Spacing 12"

HABIT   Blue, white, or pink flower spikes from summer to fall. Flowers and foliage have musky odor. Shrubby evergreen herb with pointed, dark green leaves and small flowers that have a range of color. Slow-growing and upright.
CULTURE   Prefers dry, slightly alkaline conditions. Cut back to stimulate bushy growth. Can be kept clipped to 8"–12". Best to replant every four or five years.
HARVEST   Store dry leaves in glass containers. Use fresh leaves for best results.
USES   Flowers and leaves are edible and used in teas and sweet dishes. Attracts beneficial insects like bees and butterflies. Primarily grown as an ornamental.
PROBLEMS   Few other than minor insect problems occasionally.

JUJUBE   See Chapter 7 (Fruits, Nuts, and Vegetables)

KUDZU
Pueraria lobata
pew-RARE-ee-ah lo-BAH-ta

Deciduous Ground Cover/Vine—
Full Sun
High-climbing and wide-spreading
Spacing 3'–10'

HABIT   Perennial vine with high-climbing, spreading stems. Extremely fast-growing and aggressive, spreading by underground runners. Leaves are on hard, slender, hairy stems. Each leaf has three dark green leaflets that are 3"–6" long.
CULTURE   Extremely easy to grow.
HARVEST   Harvest the leaves anytime. The roots should be dug in the fall and winter. The ground root should be stored in a cool, dry place and in glass containers if possible.
USES   Kudzu is used in many Japanese-style dishes, including sauces, gravies, soups, salads, vegetables, rice, desserts, and drinks. Fast-growing ground cover for large problem areas, especially those subject to erosion. Terrific source of protein. Kudzu is a legume and a nitrogen fixer for the soil. Superior crop for grazing animals.
PROBLEMS   Root knot nematodes, blackleg fungus, mosaic virus, invasiveness.
NOTES   Kudzu has done great damage to forests in the South. That's the result of mismanagement. All that is needed to eliminate the weed aspect of the plant is to allow any kind of grazing animals into the stands. They'll inhale it.

Lavender

LAVENDER
Lavandula spp.
la-VAN-dew-la

Evergreen Perennial—
Full Sun/Part Shade
Ht. 24"–36" Spread 36"–48"
Spacing 18"–24"

HABIT Spikes of fragrant lavender-blue flowers in summer. Narrow, gray-green foliage, aromatic lavender-blue flowers on narrow stalks in spring and intermittently throughout the summer. Shrubby overall growth.

CULTURE Excellent drainage is a must. English lavender is the easiest to grow.

HARVEST Harvest leaves anytime. Harvest flowers early—when they first come into bloom. Dry and store in glass containers.

USES Use in cooking as you would use rosemary. Teas should be made from the flowers and leaves. Perennial garden, border plants, specimen plants. Beautiful perennial for the landscape.

PROBLEMS Overwatering or damp weather causes lots of trouble for lavender. Even normal rainfall can rot the roots and kill the plant unless the drainage is excellent.

NOTES English lavender (*L. angustifolia*) has smooth-edged leaves. French lavender (*L. dentata*) has a serrated leaf. Spanish lavender (*L. stoechas*) has gray leaves and flat, purple blooms with broad, flat-topped clusters of flowers instead of a spike. The pink- and white-flowering varieties are not recommended.

LEMON BALM (Melissa)
Melissa officinalis
me-LISS-ah oh-fih-sih-NAY-lis

Perennial—Part Shade
Ht. 20"–24" Spread 24"–48"
Spacing 18"–24"

HABIT Small white flowers clustered along the stem in summer. Bushy, spreading herb with heart-shaped, mintlike, lemon-scented leaves with scalloped edges.

CULTURE Likes loose, well-drained soil, little fertilizer, and occasional light feedings of compost. Overfertilization produces large leaves with little fragrance. Cut back often to maintain thick, compact plants.

HARVEST Harvest the foliage anytime and use fresh if possible. Can be dried or frozen, but not without a loss in scent and flavor.

USES Good tea plant. Contains lots of vitamin C and is one of the longevity herbs. Good for digestion, nausea, headaches, and depression. Attractive in shady areas of the landscape, but be careful—it will spread aggressively. Good honey plant. Use it in potpourri and flower arrangements, too. A good garnish for dessert, fruit, and tossed salads.

PROBLEMS Spider mites during hot and humid summers. Don't overwater.

NOTES *Melissa* is from the Greek word for "bee," indicating the plant's ability to attract these insects.

Lemon Balm

Lemon Verbena

Lemongrass

LEMONGRASS

Cymbopogon citratus

sim-bo-PO-gon si-TRA-tus

Tender Perennial—Full Sun
Ht. 30"–36" Spread 30"–36"
Spacing 30"–36"

HABIT   Aromatic clump grass with bulbous stems. Upright growth similar to
   pampas grass. Strongly lemon-scented foliage.

CULTURE   Freezes easily in North Texas but can live through mild winters under
   heavy mulch after being cut back. Needs excellent drainage. Some gardeners
   cut it back in midseason to stimulate new growth. Cut it back drastically in
   early winter and mulch, or lift out the clump to winter indoors in a container.

HARVEST   Use fresh, or store dry or frozen pieces of leaves or stalks for winter
   use. It's just as flavorful dried or frozen as it is fresh. Store in glass containers if
   possible.

USES   Teas, stir-fry dishes. Use the stalks to make vinegar or chop the stalks for
   salads and Oriental and Mexican dishes. Good in pots and as a summer accent
   plant.

PROBLEMS   Freeze damage, rust on leaves if overwatered.

NOTES   Leaves must be broken to release the lemony fragrance. The blades can
   be rubbed in an upward direction but never downward, as the leaves can
   cut you.

LEMON VERBENA

Aloysia triphylla (syn. *Lippia citriodora*)

a-lo-ISS-ee-a tri-FILL-la

Tender Perennial—Full Sun/
Light Shade
Ht. 3'–4' Spread 3'
Spacing 18"–24"

HABIT   Loose clusters of fragrant, pale purple flowers that are not very spectacular. Usually blooms in late summer. Open-growing shrublike herb with woody
   stems. Leaves are narrow, pointed, rough-textured, lemon-scented, and from
   1" to 3" long; they grow in whorls of three or four. Somewhat scraggly with
   long, limber branches. Freezes easily in the northern half of the state.

CULTURE   Needs well-prepared, well-drained soil. Will only perennialize in the
   southern part of the state.

HARVEST   Pick leaves and dry anytime during the summer. They can also be
   frozen, but the fresh leaves are best.

USES   Marvelous flavor for any meat and great in teas, jellies, and sherbet. Good
   for other desserts and sweet dishes. Has lots of vitamin C. Nice in mixed
   plantings. Chartreuse leaves contrast with the darker greens of other plants.

PROBLEMS   Spider mites, whiteflies, aphids, and worms if not grown in totally
   organic conditions.

Lovage

Sweet Marjoram

Peppermint

LOVAGE
Levisticum officinale
Le-VIS-ti-kum oh-fih-sih-NAY-lee

Tender Perennial—Part Shade
Ht. 3'–5' Spread 2'
Spacing 12"–18"

HABIT   Umbels or flat clusters of small yellow-green flowers, followed by many aromatic seeds. Leaves are large, dark green, deeply cut and divided, and celery-scented with yellow stems.
CULTURE   Easy to grow in any healthy, well-drained soil. Likes lots of manure compost and cool weather.
HARVEST   Harvest leaves anytime. Pick leaves just before bloom. Dig roots in the fall.
USES   Use like celery, which it resembles in appearance and taste. Use tender young leaves in soups, stews, and salads, or nibble on it fresh out of the garden. Use the seed crushed or whole. Cook with cabbage, add to soups and salads. Good salt substitute.
PROBLEMS   Cutworms, caterpillars. Hot weather and afternoon sun will burn the foliage. Not totally winter hardy.

MARJORAM (Sweet Marjoram)
Origanum marjorana
o-ree-GAH-num mar-jo-RAH-na

Perennial—Full Sun
Ht. 10"–15" Spread 18"–24"
Spacing 18"–24"

HABIT   Tiny budlike mauve-pink flowers, sometimes purple or white, but it's best not to let the plant bloom.
CULTURE   Easy to grow in any well-drained soil. They have tough, trailing stems and require a minimum of fertilizer and care.
HARVEST   Cut, dry, and store in a cool place.
USES   Italian food, vegetables, salads, meats, fish, eggs, and vinaigrettes. Border plant and ground cover. Marjoram is used in potpourri, perfumes, and bath products. The seed heads make great winter feed for wild birds. The flowers attract butterflies and bees.
PROBLEMS   Few if any.

MINT
Mentha spp.
MEN-tha

Perennial—Full Sun/Afternoon Shade
Ht. 1'–3' Spread unlimited
Spacing 1'–2'

HABIT   Aggressively spreading plant. Highly aromatic leaves on square stems are round, oval, or slightly pointed; smooth or wrinkly; and slightly serrated on their edges.
CULTURE   Very easy to grow. Like moist soils. Go easy on the fertilizer for best flavor.
HARVEST   Cut and use fresh, dry and store in glass containers, or freeze and store in plastic. It's always best to use mints fresh.
USES   Used to flavor all kinds of foods, especially green peas, salads, desserts, and drinks. Mints are best taken in teas. Ground cover in areas of wet soil.
PROBLEMS   Some chewing insects but none serious. Whiteflies and aphids occasionally. Most mints are aggressive spreaders and hard to keep under control.
NOTES   Divided into two groups according to fragrance: the spearmints (*M. spicata*) and the peppermints (*M. piperita*).

MONARDA (Bee Balm)   See Chapter 5 (Annuals and Perennials)

Mullein

Sweet Myrtle

Oregano

MULLEIN (Old Man's Flannel)
Verbascum thapsus
ver-BAS-kum THAP-sus

Hardy Biennial—Full Sun
Ht. 6'–7' Spread 12"–18"
Spacing: One here and one there or about 3' apart

HABIT Yellow, white, or purple flowers on tall spikes that form the second year; only a rosette of low leaves grows the first year. Large, fuzzy gray leaves; upright growth; yellow, white, or purple flowers.

CULTURE Treat like a wildflower—this native plant is very easy to grow in most any soil.

HARVEST Harvest leaves anytime; harvest flowers when they first open.

USES Tea ingredient. Flowers are sweet, leaves are bitter, but both are aromatic. Use in the wildflower garden or as a dramatic background plant.

PROBLEMS Leaf-chewing insects create cosmetic damage only.

NOTES Plant in a well-drained area in full sun and forget about it. You will pretty much have it from now on. Don't harvest this or any other herb from the roadside because of environmental pollution.

MYRTLE (Sweet Myrtle)
Myrtus communis
MUR-tus kom-EW-nis

Hardy Evergreen Shrub—
Full Sun/Part Shade
Ht. 15' Spread 6'–8'
Spacing 1'

HABIT Small, aromatic, glossy dark green foliage. Bushy and slow-growing. Beautiful when in bloom. Sweet-scented leaves and flowers.

CULTURE Can be grown in containers or beds that have been prepared well with compost and volcanic rock powders.

HARVEST Pick flowers while in full bloom and store in glass containers with tight-fitting lids in a dark place.

USES Flower buds and berries can be used in sweet dishes, the leaves in meat dishes. Attractive in containers. Can be pruned into topiaries. Good edging plant in the landscape and in knot gardens.

PROBLEMS Few if any; can freeze in the northern part of the state.

NOTES Good little plant that should be used more.

OREGANO
Origanum vulgare
o-ree-GAH-num vul-GAR-ee

Evergreen Perennial—Full Sun/
Part Shade
Ht. 8"–30" Spread 15"–30"
Spacing 18"

HABIT White to purple summer flowers followed by tiny seed. Very winter hardy and drought resistant. Sprawling, low-growing plant. Slightly woody stems. Leaves are oval to elliptical in shape, generally slightly hairy underneath, and have an aromatic scent.

CULTURE One of the easiest herbs to grow but does best in healthy soil.

HARVEST Harvest the leaves anytime. Stores well and is easy to dry. Best to use the leaves fresh from the garden.

USES Used in Greek and Italian food and especially in dishes with tomatoes, chili powder, and many other foods. Known as the pizza herb. Excellent herb tea ingredient. Chopped oregano is also good in scrambled eggs. Greek oregano makes a good evergreen ground cover. Flowers of all oreganos are interesting.

PROBLEMS Very few.

Patchouli

NOTES   Oregano seems to help deter insect pests. When taking the tea, inhale the vapors while drinking. Oregano has a stronger taste and aroma than the closely related marjoram.

PARSLEY
Petroselinum crispum
pet-ro-see-LY-num KRIS-pum

Biennial—Full Morning Sun/
Afternoon Shade
Ht. 12" Spread 8"–12"
Spacing 12"

HABIT   Umbels of white flowers followed by aromatic seeds. Italian parsley (*P. crispum* var. *neapolitanum*) has flat, glossy, dark green leaves resembling those of celery and grows to 1½'. Curly parsley (*P. crispum*) grows to 10" in height.
CULTURE   Slow to germinate from seed. Easy culture from transplants. Likes cool weather and moist, well-drained soil. Cut seed heads off to maintain compact growth.
HARVEST   Harvest whenever the foliage is present. Store by freezing if necessary. Parsley can be cut like a cut flower and stored in water in the refrigerator for a time; however, it grows well almost year-round here in Texas.
USES   Italian parsley has a better flavor for cooking, especially when fresh. Use in salads, vegetables, soups, and garnishes. Chop just before using and add to food at the last minute to preserve vitamins and minerals. Don't cook parsley—it destroys the vitamins and much of the food value. Curly parsley makes an excellent landscape border plant.
PROBLEMS   Parsleyworm, which becomes the beautiful swallowtail butterfly, spider mites, and aphids.

PATCHOULI
Pogostemon cablin
po-GOS-tah-mon CAB-lin

Tender Perennial—Partial to
Heavy Shade
Ht. 3'–4' Spread 2'–3'
Spacing 2'

HABIT   White flowers on spikes, but don't let the plant bloom. The leaves are the main feature of the herb. Upright, shrubby.
CULTURE   Easy to grow. Needs hot weather and likes sun as well as shade. Roots easily from semi-woody cuttings taken in fall or winter. Plant in well-prepared soil and apply water and fertilizer in moderation.
HARVEST   Harvest leaves anytime, dry and store in glass containers. Use the leaves fresh if possible.
USES   Pleasant planting for partially shaded areas. Foliage has an interesting texture. Fragrance in the garden.
PROBLEMS   Slugs, snails, and pillbugs sometimes.

Below left: Italian Parsley;
below right: Curly Parsley

PERILLA (Beefsteak Plant)
Perilla frutescens
pa-RIL-ah fru-TESS-enz

Annual—Full Sun
Ht. 36" Spread 36"
Spacing 6"–12"

HABIT   Purplish flowers, dark burgundy, purple, or green leaves. Small black seeds on decorative seedpods. Vigorous, easy-to-grow annual with a growth habit similar to that of coleus and basil. Often mistakenly called opal basil and black coleus.

CULTURE   Grows in most any soil and needs only a moderate amount of fertilizer and water.

HARVEST   Harvest and use the leaves anytime during the growing season. The leaves can also be dried and stored in glass containers.

USES   Leaves are used as an ingredient in salads and a flavoring for beefsteak. The purple variety is especially attractive in the border or color garden. Looks good with gray plants like wormwood or Texas sage.

PROBLEMS   Will reseed and spread to become a problem.

ROSELLE
Hibiscus sabdariffa
hi-BIS-kus sab-da-RIFF-ah

Annual—Full Sun
Ht. 4'–12' Spread 4'–8'
Spacing 2'–3'

HABIT   Yellow and maroon hibiscus-like flowers in October or later. Annual shrub that resembles okra and has yellow-petaled flowers that drop off, leaving protective sepals that swell into a succulent fruit.

CULTURE   Easy to grow in healthy soil. Use ample soil amendments, including orange peeling and pulp to control nematodes.

HARVEST   Cut flowers throughout the blooming period, dry, and store in glass containers in a cool place.

USES   The young leaves can be cooked or eaten raw. Use it in the landscape and in pots just like any other hibiscus. Flower buds are used to make red zinger tea.

PROBLEMS   The plant dies after pods are produced. Subject to nematodes and poor drainage.

NOTES   *H. acetosella* is a short-lived perennial called false roselle. It looks like a red maple seedling with maroon, maple-shaped leaves.

Below left: Perilla; below right: Roselle

Rosemary   Rue

ROSEMARY
Rosmarinus officinalis
roz-mah-RINE-us oh-fih-sih-NAY-lis

Evergreen—Full Sun/Part Shade
Ht. 12"–60" Spread 48"
Spacing 12"–18"

HABIT Very fragrant leaves; light blue, pink, or white flowers bloom intermittently throughout the year. Sometimes the plants are very showy. Rosemary is
an upright-growing shrub, but creeping varieties are also available. The edible
leaves resemble short, thick pine needles. The foliage is velvety and resinous to
the touch.

CULTURE Likes alkaline soil but will grow in any soil. Although full sun is ideal,
rosemary will tolerate a considerable amount of shade under tall trees. Provide
excellent drainage and avoid overwatering and underwatering.

HARVEST Harvest the foliage and flowers anytime, dry and store in airtight
containers. Use fresh green cuttings if possible.

USES Indispensable in cooking beef, wild game, and meats of all kinds. Delicious in breads, vinegars, butters, and teas. Good as a ground cover and in pots
and hanging baskets. Rub on your dog's fur after baths to help repel fleas.

PROBLEMS Freeze damage, spider mites, wet feet.

NOTES 'Arp' has a reputation for tolerating frost, but it seems to be somewhat
overblown. All forms seem to be cold tolerant in most of Texas—if grown
under an organic program.

RUE
Ruta graveolens
ROO-ta gra-vay-OH-lenz

Evergreen Perennial—Full Sun
Ht. 24"–36" Spread 36"
Spacing 12"–18"

HABIT Small yellow flowers followed by seed. Sprawling growth habit—will
sometimes fall over. Lacy, blue-green foliage. Good winter plant. Prune to
control its spread.

CULTURE Needs good soil. Do the bed prep right.

HARVEST Harvest seedpods for dried arrangements.

USES Not recommended as a cooking herb, mainly because it's a toxic plant.
Beautiful in the landscape, especially in the winter. Some gardeners use it to
repel cats. Can also be used to raise certain butterflies.

PROBLEMS Handling it, especially in the summer, will cause a skin rash in many
people that can be severe.

NOTES The leaves of the plant can cause serious dermatitis in sensitive indi-
viduals, so be sure to wear gloves and use care when handling or working
around rue.

Sage—golden and variegated

Salad Burnet

Sambac Jasmine

SAGE
Salvia officinalis
SAL-vee-ah oh-fih-sih-NAY-lis

Hardy Perennial—Sun/Part Shade
Ht. 24" Spread 18"
Spacing 18"–24"

HABIT   Purple spikes followed by small round seeds. Upright to sprawling character. Grows to 24" or taller and has rough gray leaves.

CULTURE   Beautiful purple flowers, but it's best to keep them from blooming. Cut established plants back severely in the early spring. This helps to prevent crown rot disease and dieback. The cuttings can be rooted. Sage is easy to grow from seed.

HARVEST   Harvest anytime but try to avoid heavy harvesting during the first year. Store dry in a tightly sealed glass jar.

USES   Cook with beans, potatoes, breads, vegetables, meats, dressings, gravies, eggs, potatoes, and beans. Makes a decent container plant. Use the leaves to line the bottom of a bowl or basket for storing tomatoes and other vegetables.

PROBLEMS   Too much water will knock it out from crown rot.

NOTES   For the most flavorful leaves, don't let it bloom. The dried leaves can become carcinogenic due to the high levels of volatile oils, so use fresh or within six months after drying.

SALAD BURNET
Sanguisorba minor
sang-gwi-SOR-ba MY-nor

Short-lived Perennial—Full Sun
Ht. 12" Spread 12"
Spacing 12"–18"

HABIT   Grows in a rosette clump with arching stems and small, round, ugly reddish flowers. Small, round, toothed blue-green leaves with a cucumber taste.

CULTURE   Easy to grow and likes cool weather. Evergreen unless the winter is severe. Undemanding when grown in healthy soil with organic techniques.

HARVEST   Harvest and use fresh or dry. For the best flavor, gather before flowers form.

USES   Provides cucumber flavor for salads, vinegars, butters, asparagus, celery, beans, mushrooms, potato salad, and other dishes. Low border plant. Good plant for containers.

PROBLEMS   Occasional pillbugs. Doesn't do well in the severe summer heat.

SAMBAC JASMINE
Jasminum sambac
yas-MEE-num SAM-bac

Tender Perennial—Full Sun/
Part Shade
Ht. 6' Spread 3'–6'
Spacing 3'–4'

HABIT   Continuous show all summer of fragrant white flowers that last only one day. Vining growth. Prune tips of the shoots to keep the plant compact and bushy.

CULTURE   Needs healthy, well-drained, rich organic soil.

HARVEST   Harvest flowers while in full bloom. They can be dried for later use or used fresh.

USES   Flowers make a delicious tea. Also used steeped in coffee, to sweeten desserts, and to give fragrance to beverages. Potpourri. Good container plant.

PROBLEMS   Freeze damage in the northern two-thirds of the state.

Savory

Scented Geranium

SAVORY

Satureja hortensis—SUMMER SAVORY
sat-ew-RAY-ah hor-TEN-sis
Satureja montana—WINTER SAVORY
sat-ew-RAY-ah mon-TAN-ah

Annual—Full Sun
Ht. 8"–12" Spread 20"
Spacing 12"

HABIT Blooms are white-to-lilac whorls of small star-shaped flowers. Compact, low, and spreading. Summer savory is more upright, with small, aromatic, dark green leaves, and grows a little taller. Winter savory is stiffer, woody, and evergreen.
CULTURE Needs healthy, fertile soil.
HARVEST Harvest the foliage anytime during the growing season. Since winter savory is an evergreen, it can be snipped anytime. Summer savory dies out during hot summers and should be harvested in early summer.
USES Savory is one of the best seasonings for beans—especially green beans. Also good with other vegetables and poultry. Chew the leaves or just add to foods as a seasoning. Makes a good border plant, widely used in knot gardens.
PROBLEMS Spider mites, especially on summer savory.
NOTES Bees and other beneficial insects love this herb when it is in flower. Winter savory is a better choice for the Texas climate.

SCENTED GERANIUM

Pelargonium spp.
pell-ar-GO-nee-um

Tender Perennial—Full Sun/
Moderate Shade
Ht. 18"–36" Spread 12"–18"
Spacing 12"–18"

HABIT Small, fragrant flowers followed by black seeds. Tender perennial that has interesting leaves with various shapes, textures, and fragrances.
CULTURE Easy to grow in most well-prepared garden soils or potting soils. Overfertilization ruins the strong fragrances.
HARVEST Gather leaves when green, dry in the shade. Use dried leaves for teas, fresh green leaves for everything else. Fresh leaves can also be used for teas.
USES Rose geranium is especially good for herb teas, sherbets, and cakes. *P. crispum* has small variegated leaves that don't go limp in hot tea. Good addition to the landscape for fragrance.
PROBLEMS None usually. Mealybugs if the plant undergoes stress.
NOTES Dominant fragrances of the most common types: *P. crispum* (lemon), *P. denticulatum* (pine), *P. fragrans* (nutmeg), *P. graveolens* (rose), *P. nervosum* (lime), *P. odoratissimum* (apple), *P. scabrum* (apricot), *P. tomentosum* (peppermint). There are more than seventy different varieties.

Stevia

Southernwood

SOUTHERNWOOD
Artemisia abrotanum
ar-tay-MEEZ-ee-ah a-BROT-an-um

Hardy Perennial—Full Sun
Ht. 3'–4' Spread 4'–5'
Spacing 2'–3'

HABIT   Small yellow flowers in late summer. Shrubby evergreen with soft, feathery, threadlike gray-green foliage that is silky to the touch. Very fragrant, smells much like a tangerine.

CULTURE   Not too fussy about soil conditions. Cut back in the spring to encourage new compact growth.

HARVEST   Cut the foliage and dry anytime during the summer.

USES   A tall ground cover in the landscape. Good companion plant for roses. Grows well in containers. Place among clothes to repel moths.

PROBLEMS   Gets leggy unless pruned back annually.

NOTES   Good for the fragrance garden.

STEVIA (Sweet Herb)
Stevia rebaudiana
STEE-vee-ah re-bah-dee-AN-ah

Tropical Annual—Full Sun/
Part Shade
Ht. 24"–36" Spread 24"–36"
Spacing 15"–18"

HABIT   Very small white flowers in the summer. Stevia grows wild in Central and South America but should be treated as an annual in Texas.

CULTURE   Fairly easy to grow here unless you overwater it or forget to water it at all. When it gets floppy, cut back by about 50 percent. It will become more compact, and you'll still have plenty to use.

HARVEST   Collect and use the leaves fresh as needed. The leaves and stems can also be dried, ground into a powder, and stored in glass containers.

USES   Herbal substitute for sugar. Stevia is a sensible replacement for Aspartame and saccharin. Stevia is a homely plant.

PROBLEMS   Rots if overwatered or grown without excellent drainage.

Sweet Annie

Sweet Herb

Sweet Marigold

SWEET ANNIE
Artemisia annua
ar-tay-MEEZ-ee-ah AN-you-ah

Annual—Sun
Ht. 8' Spread 4'
Spacing 3' apart or more

HABIT   Tiny ball-shaped, yellow-green flowers that produce lots of seed. A tall-growing annual with feathery, very fragrant foliage. The green stems are sometimes red in the fall. Although an annual, the plant seeds out in the fall and returns the next spring unless heavy mulch is used around the plant.

CULTURE   Very easy to grow in any soil.

HARVEST   Use the stems in wreaths, dried arrangements, and potpourri.

USES   Historically used as a tea to treat fevers, colds, jaundice, dysentery, malaria, and skin disorders. Very toxic, so use only topically. Background plant worth growing for fragrance. Dried arrangements and potpourri.

PROBLEMS   Can spread invasively from seed. Mulching the soil usually stops the problem.

SWEET HERB (Lippia)
Lippia dulcis
LIP-ee-ah DOOL-sis

Tender Perennial—Sun/Part Shade
Ht. 3"–6" Spread 12"–18"
Spacing 12"

HABIT   Sweet herb has small, white, cylindrical summer flowers. Will perennialize in the southern half of the state.

CULTURE   Very easy to grow in various soils. Normal fertilizer and water requirements. Don't overdo either or the sweetness will be diminished.

HARVEST   Harvest the leaves and use anytime. They can also be frozen or dried and stored in glass containers.

USES   Leaves are used as a sugar substitute in foods and drinks. Considerably sweeter than sugar. Interesting low border plant or ground cover.

PROBLEMS   Sometimes develops chlorosis, a trace mineral deficiency, but can be treated with earthworm castings and Texas greensand. A mix of rock powders, including volcanic material, will also help the condition.

NOTES   *Lippia* is a better-looking plant, but *Stevia* is the better sugar substitute.

SWEET MARIGOLD
(Mexican Mint Marigold)
Tagetes lucida (syn. *Tagetes florida*)
ta-JET-teez LOO-see-da

Perennial to Evergreen—
Full Sun/Part Shade
Ht. 18"–24" Spread 24"–36"
Spacing 12"–18"

HABIT   Yellow or golden marigold-like flowers, followed by black seeds. Upright, clumping. Flowers in late summer to early fall. Strong anise scent. Glossy lance-shaped leaves.

CULTURE   Likes loose, well-drained soil. Best in morning sun and afternoon shade. Very easy to grow from seed. Cut back to maintain compact look. Needs plenty of water and moderate fertilization.

HARVEST   Harvest the foliage anytime to use fresh or to dry and store in glass containers. It's best to use fresh green foliage during the growing season.

USES   Use the flowers in salads and as a garnish. Use the foliage to season any kind of meat, poultry, fish, and eggs. Use fresh—it loses its flavor when dried. You don't need much—this herb is very strong. Potpourri and dried arrangements.

PROBLEMS   Mealybugs and spittlebugs, which may burrow in emerging leaves during high humidity. Some spider mite damage possible during hot months.

NOTES   Mexican mint marigold is a terrible name. I don't know how it got started, but this plant has no relation to mint. Sweet marigold is probably the best name.

Sweet Woodruff

Tansy

Tarragon

SWEET WOODRUFF
Galium odoratum,
also known as *Asperula odorata*
GAY-lee-um o-doe-RAH-tum

Perennial—Shade/Part Shade

Ht. 6"–12" Spread 12"
Spacing 12"–15"

HABIT   Clusters of tiny white spring flowers. Spreading, low-growing whorls of pointed leaves on square stems. Spreads by stolons.
CULTURE   Needs abundant moisture and well-drained, healthy soil with plenty of organic matter. Divide plants in the spring. Cover with thick mulch (2"–3") in winter.
HARVEST   Harvest foliage anytime during the growing season. Leaves contain the blood thinner coumadin.
USES   Do not eat. A shade-loving ground cover. Potpourri, fragrance for the garden, insect repellent. Its scent gets stronger as the leaves dry.
PROBLEMS   Heat leads to stress and pest problems. Healthy soil with lots of compost and rock powders is very important.

TANSY
Tanacetum vulgare
Tan-ah-SEE-tum vul-GAR-ree

Perennial—Sun/Part Shade
Ht. 3'–4' Spread 3'–6'
Spacing 18"–24"

HABIT   Yellow buttonlike flowers in late summer that are long-lasting on the plant. Can become invasive, very sprawling if not kept trimmed. Opens up in the shade. Drought tolerant. Evergreen foliage has a camphor fragrance.
CULTURE   Easy in any soil but likes plenty of room.
HARVEST   Harvest the leaves anytime, the flowers when in full bloom.
USES   Native Americans crushed the leaves and rubbed on the skin to prevent insect bites. Use around doorways to repel flies. Excellent ant, flea, and fly repellent. The dried root is more powerful than the foliage, but you must kill the plant to use it. Sprinkle chopped, crushed foliage on ants. The dried flowers are pretty in wreaths.
PROBLEMS   Can be as aggressively invasive as mint and allelopathic to other plants.

TARRAGON
Artemisia dracunculus
ar-tay-MEEZ-ee-ah dra-KUN-kew-lus

Hardy Perennial—Full Sun/
Part Shade
Ht. 24" Spread 18"
Spacing 15"

HABIT   Tarragon has rare and insignificant yellowish flowers that rarely open fully. Seeds are even rarer. A wild-looking, many-branched perennial that tends to have a sprawling nature. It has narrow, dark green leaves and is very cold tolerant.
CULTURE   Does best in well-prepared soil. When it becomes woody, cut it back to the ground.
HARVEST   Pick foliage fresh and use immediately or cut the stems and hang in a cool, dry place. When the leaves are dry, store in glass containers.
USES   Leaves have a peppery, anise, or licorice taste and are used to season all kinds of foods: fish, chicken, butter, and breads. Use in salads and casseroles. A tea made from the leaves stimulates the appetite. A really ugly plant.
PROBLEMS   Too much water will kill it. Heavy feeder. Winter hardy if kept somewhat dry. Rats seem to enjoy eating it.
NOTES   Appears to be in a permanent state of wilt.

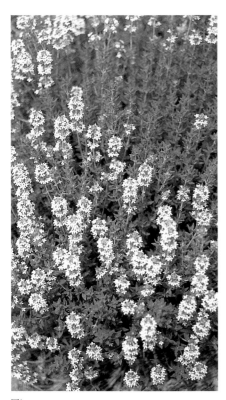

Thyme

THYME
Thymus spp.
TIME-us

Perennial—Full Sun
Ht. 3"–12" (creeping), 15"–18" (common) Spread 18"–36" (creeping), 15"–18" (common)
Spacing 12"–24"

HABIT   Tiny starlike flowers bloom throughout the spring and summer in shades from crimson to pink or white. Small, slightly pointed leaves, ⅛"–¼" in length, highly aromatic, ranging from glossy dark green to woolly silver or variegated green and gold. Woody stems. Upright and prostrate varieties are available. Hardy to below 0°.

CULTURE   Likes well-drained soils and full sun. If not kept pruned, branches become very woody and are easily split by wind or animals.

HARVEST   Harvest anytime during the growing season just before the plant blooms. Cut off entire stems and store dried or frozen.

USES   Thyme is used to flavor many foods and teas. Good border plant and low-growing ground cover for the landscape. Stepping on the edges of the plant along garden paths produces a wonderful fragrance. Good for bonsai planting.

PROBLEMS   Susceptible to root rot, crown rot, and fungal disease when grown in unhealthy soil, especially if poorly drained, too heavy, or watered too much.

NOTES   Thymes are notorious cross-pollinators, like the mints, and new hybrids pop up every year. The seeds are tiny—there are about 170,000 seeds per ounce. Seeds stay viable for three to four years.

Above: Elfin Thyme; below: Creeping Thyme

TURMERIC
Curcuma domestica
KUR-kew-ma doe-MESS-tee-ka

Tender Perennial—Full Sun
Ht. 24"–30" Spread 18"–24"
Spacing 24"

HABIT   Interesting yellow flowers with pink bracts in summer. A tropical herb that looks like ginger or a small banana plant and has exotic yellow and purple flowers. Leaves are large, 6"–8" wide, with a maroon band on both sides of the midrib. Aromatic rhizomes. Grows in clumps and tends to spread.

CULTURE   Grows best in healthy soil.

HARVEST   Dig and store the bright orange roots in late summer or fall.

USES   Flavors pickles, rice, and soups. Use as an annual for interesting texture and dramatic flowers. Ornamental potted plant, yellow dye plant.

PROBLEMS   Freezes if not protected. Few if any insect problems.

NOTES   Turmeric is a tender ginger.

Vetiver

Watercress

Wormwood

VETIVER
Vetiveria zizanioides
vet-ah-VER-ee-ah ziz-an-ee-OY-deez

Perennial—Sun
Ht. 5'–6' Spread 2'–3'
Spacing 2'–3'

HABIT I've never seen any flowers, but it supposedly has plumes. Decorative grass with plumes similar to those of a small pampas grass. Fragrant plant with a deep, tenacious root system.
CULTURE Vetiver needs plenty of sun and moist, rich, well-prepared soil.
HARVEST Harvest the roots in the fall.
USES Makes a fine accent plant in the landscape and can help control soil erosion. Fragrance plant. Roots are very fragrant and used in potpourri. The powdered root is said to repel clothes moths.
PROBLEMS None serious.
NOTES It is a cousin of the familiar pampas grass but not as showy. Reported to repel termites.

WATERCRESS (Indian Cress)
Nasturtium officinale
nas-TUR-she-um oh-fih-sih-NAY-lee

Hardy Perennial—Full Sun/
Part Shade
Ht. 2"–24" Spread: Creeper
Spacing 12"

HABIT Tiny white insignificant flowers. Small, rounded, smooth green leaves.
CULTURE Grows easily, as roots form at every joint. Plant seed in moist soil or let divisions root in water. For best results, cover sprouts until root system is established.
HARVEST Harvest leaves and use fresh.
USES Watercress is used in salads, soups, and sandwiches. It's delicious raw. Bog plant. Can be grown in containers.
PROBLEMS Needs lots of water.
NOTES Watercress is not related to the common nasturtium (*Tropaeolum majus*).

WORMWOOD
Artemisia absinthium
ar-tay-MEEZ-ee-ah ab-SIN-thee-um

Perennial Subshrub—Full Sun/
Part Shade
Ht. 36"–48" Spread 24"–36"
Spacing 18"–24"

HABIT Yellowish green flowers in midsummer. Fast-growing, very pungent, upright to sprawling, extremely aromatic foliage. Leaf color is silvery when young but darkens to pale green with age. Can be invasive.
CULTURE Easy to grow in most any soil. Cut back in the fall or early spring to prevent a leggy look.
HARVEST Cut the foliage anytime and use fresh or hang upside down to dry. Store in a cool place.
USES A bitter herb. Makes a good border plant and provides color contrast in the garden. Used as an insect repellent for fleas, ticks, and moths. Good in wreaths.
PROBLEMS Leggy and untidy if not kept trimmed.
NOTES The essential oil of wormwood is very dangerous. The toxic substance absinthium will leach out of the leaves of wormwood and will inhibit the growth of nearby plants.

NOTE: Read *Herbs for Texas* by Garrett and Brannam for more details on these and other medicinal and culinary herbs.

CHAPTER 9

Pest Management

Getting rid of all the bugs, beetles, slugs, snails, and other bothersome critters in the farm, garden, or landscape is impossible. It's also a bad idea, because most of these living organisms are beneficial. Insects usually do a great job of controlling themselves if we don't foul up the balance by spraying toxic pesticides, using harsh salt fertilizers, or watering too much or too little. Even the insects we would classify as harmful, such as aphids, are helpful in their own way. They attack plants that are in stress from soil problems, from unusual climate, or from poor plant selection. In doing so, they help to eliminate unfit plants.

Diseases are primarily microorganisms that are out of balance. Reestablishing the balance is the key to control. Toxic chemical pesticides not only don't do that, they make the situation worse by killing the beneficial microorganisms. The terms *germs, bacteria,* and *fungus* conjure up negative thoughts. They should, however, be considered negative only if they are out of balance.

INSECTS

Insect Life Cycles

A *complete* life cycle or metamorphosis is the type of insect development that has four distinct stages: egg, larva, pupa, and adult. Insects with this development include mosquitoes, wasps, flies, beetles, green lacewings, and ladybugs. An *incomplete* life cycle is a gradual metamorphosis. It is a type of insect development with no prolonged resting or pupal stage. Its three stages are egg, nymph, and adult. Insects with this type of metamorphosis include silverfish and the true bugs, like stink bugs, boxelder bugs, minute pirate bugs, and squash bugs. Instars are the immature forms of incomplete insects.

Some animals we call insects really aren't. These insectlike critters include spiders, mites, and galls. Galls aren't even animals; they are plant growths that are caused by fungi or insects. Insect galls are the most common. Mites and spiders are different from insects in that they have eight legs instead of six. These critters are included in the book because they are so similar to insects and because of their economic importance and influence on the balance of life.

Biological Control of Insect Pests

Bacillus thuringiensis 'Kurstaki'—This bacterial insecticide provides effective control of tent caterpillars, gypsy moths, cabbage loopers, tomato hornworms, and other leaf-feeding caterpillars. It is harmless to humans, animals, and beneficial insects.

Bacillus thuringiensis 'Israelensis'—This bacterial insecticide controls mosquitoes and black fly larvae very quickly and effectively. It is harmless to humans, animals, and beneficial insects. There is also a new formulation of the Bt (strain H-14) that is highly effective for the control of the fungus gnat larvae. It can be used as a drench or in overhead irrigation systems. For light infestations, it can be mixed and sprayed.

For more information on organic insect control, see Malcolm Beck and Howard Garrett's *Texas Bug Book*.

Photos by the author unless otherwise noted.

THE BUGS

Giant Bark Aphids

Aphid

Armyworm

APHIDS

Very small, pear-shaped insects that attach themselves to leaves and stems.

FEEDING HABITS   Aphids normally feed in groups on leaves or stems. They pierce foliage or tender stems and suck plant juices, causing leaf curling and stunted growth. The digested sap is secreted as the honeydew commonly seen shining on foliage. Some feed on roots.

ECONOMIC IMPORTANCE   Aphids reduce the health of stressed plants even further, roll or turn foliage yellow (reducing photosynthesis), and ultimately kill plants. On the positive side, they help to eliminate unfit plants. Some aphids are vectors of disease organisms like viruses.

NATURAL CONTROL   Plant adapted varieties and encourage natural biodiversity, healthy plants, and beneficial insects such as ladybugs, green lacewings, hover flies, praying mantids, and brachonid wasps. Avoid feeding plants heavy amounts of nitrogen.

ORGANIC CONTROL   Strong blasts of water, garlic-pepper tea, liquid seaweed, and the release of ladybugs and green lacewings. Citrus oil spray can be used for heavy infestations. Biological sprays are also now available.

ARMYWORMS

1½" caterpillars with stripes down the side of the body.

FEEDING HABITS   Feed mostly in the spring and early summer on small grains, stems, and foliage. Especially fond of corn, millet, and bluegrass but will also eat other grasses such as bentgrass and Bermudagrass.

ECONOMIC IMPORTANCE   Destructive to plant foliage and entire plants, especially young seedlings.

NATURAL CONTROL   Parasitic wasps such as trichogramma, parasitic flies, and ground beetles.

ORGANIC CONTROL   *Bacillus thuringiensis* products, citrus and neem products.

Asp

Assassin Bug

Bagworm

ASPS (Puss Caterpillars)
Painful stinging caterpillars that grow up to be moths.

FEEDING HABITS   Larvae feed mainly on deciduous trees and shrubs. They usually don't do a lot of damage.
ECONOMIC IMPORTANCE   Dangerous stings, especially for youngsters.
NATURAL CONTROL   Predatory flies and wasps.
ORGANIC CONTROL   *Bacillus thuringiensis* products.

ASSASSIN BUGS
(Beneficial) Insects that range widely in size and color.

FEEDING HABITS   Eat adults, nymphs, and larvae of many plant-eating insects. Like to eat troublesome insects, from mosquitoes to large beetles. Favorite foods include aphids, leafhoppers, beetle larvae, caterpillars, and small flying insects.
ECONOMIC IMPORTANCE   Control many troublesome plant-eating insects.
NATURAL CONTROL   Spiders and themselves. The young feed on each other.
ORGANIC CONTROL   None needed, highly beneficial.

BAGWORMS
Worms that spend most of their lives in brown bags attached to trees.

FEEDING HABITS   Eat foliage, starting on the upper part of the plant. They live in and feed on willow, cedar, cypress, some pines, box elder, locust, sycamore, maple, sumac, persimmon, and other ornamentals and fruit trees.
ECONOMIC IMPORTANCE   Defoliation of ornamental plants.
NATURAL CONTROL   Wasps, birds, and several insect parasites and predators.
ORGANIC CONTROL   *Bacillus thuringiensis* or orange oil products sprayed in the spring. Handpicking the rest of the year is by far the best technique.

BORERS

The larvae of long-horned beetles and insect pests that generate a huge amount of bad advice. The organiphobes used to recommend lindane, then they switched to Dursban. Now that those two toxic chemicals have been banned, the current chemical recommendation is synthetic pyrethroids. The only problem with all those toxic bits of advice is that they do absolutely no good for the tree. They don't address the real problem—plant stress. Borers only attack trees that are in serious stress. Eliminate the stress and the borers go away. Real problems include poor tree choice in the first place, too much or too little water, too much or the wrong kind of fertilizer, fill soil on the root system, herbicides, or other toxic chemicals. What works is to treat the active borers with Tree Trunk Goop (see Appendix) or beneficial nematodes and apply the Sick Tree Treatment.

Some in the landscaping industry still recommend wrapping tree trunks, especially red oaks, with paper or other materials. The supposed reason is to prevent borer beetle invasion. Not only does this not prevent insects, it actually gives them a more comfortable environment. The wrapping also creates weak bark, just like a bandage left on a wound too long, and it provides an excellent habitat for disease pathogens to grow and cause problems. Others say that the wrapping is to prevent sun scald on trunks. This rarely is a concern on healthy, properly grown trees, but if necessary use a whitewash of 50 percent white latex paint and 50 percent water. The tree will grow the paint away and the bark can gently readapt to the sunlight. The International Society of Arboriculture, the Texas Forest Service, and the Dirt Doctor all agree—wrapping trunks is a bad idea.

BOXELDER BUGS

Black-and-red true bugs that are mostly a nuisance.

FEEDING HABITS   Feed mainly on the seeds of female box elder and other heavily seeded trees. They will also eat seed, foliage, and flowers of ornamental plants and orchard crops. Injury is usually minimal.

ECONOMIC IMPORTANCE   Little if any.

NATURAL CONTROL   Birds and lizards.

ORGANIC CONTROL   Citrus oil or a mixture of manure tea, molasses, and citrus oil will kill them, but it really isn't necessary. Neem products are also effective on heavy infestations.

Boxelder Bug

Bumblebee on Vitex

Monarch Butterflues

Question Mark Butterfly

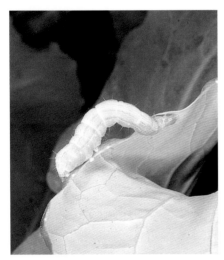

Cabbage Looper (Malcolm Beck)

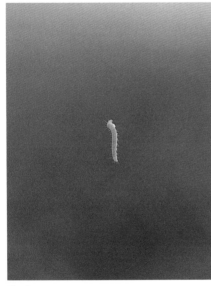

Cankerworm

BUMBLE BEES
Important beneficial pollinators.

FEEDING HABITS   Worker bees feed on the nectar of many flowering plants.
ECONOMIC IMPORTANCE   Pollination of ornamental and food crops; however, they are less effective than honeybees.
NATURAL CONTROL   Birds, wasps, and praying mantids.
ORGANIC CONTROL   If necessary, can be controlled with soapy water or citrus products or repelled with hot pepper products.

BUTTERFLIES
Beneficial to the eyes.

FEEDING HABITS   Adults eat nectar from flowers.
ECONOMIC IMPORTANCE   Pollination, diversity, and garden beauty.
NATURAL CONTROL   Wasps, birds, lizards, and predatory flies.
ORGANIC CONTROL   *Bacillus thuringiensis* sprays if really necessary.

CABBAGE LOOPERS
Caterpillars that eat holes in our plants.

FEEDING HABITS   Larvae eat lots of holes in green leaves.
ECONOMIC IMPORTANCE   Destruction of food-crop foliage.
NATURAL CONTROL   Trichogramma wasps, birds, paper wasps, and yellow jackets. Loopers are usually controlled by natural diseases and parasites; these function effectively only in an organic program.
ORGANIC CONTROL   *Bacillus thuringiensis* products.

CANKERWORMS
Small caterpillars that attack trees in the spring.

FEEDING HABITS   Larvae feed on tree and shrub foliage. They drop down on silk threads to evade predators, then go back and eat some more when danger has passed. Why? Guess they are still hungry.
ECONOMIC IMPORTANCE   Can defoliate broadleaf trees.
NATURAL CONTROL   Trichogramma wasps, birds, and lizards.
ORGANIC CONTROL   Band trunks with sticky material in late winter during egg-laying time. Caution: don't put sticky material directly on the trunk. It will girdle the tree. Put the material on a paper band. Spray with *Bacillus thuringiensis* products as a last resort.

Carpenter Ant

Centipede

CARPENTER ANTS
Large ants that do damage creating their homes.

FEEDING HABITS   Dead and live insects, plant sap, honeydew from other insects, pollen, seed.
ECONOMIC IMPORTANCE   Wood and structural damage; help to break down organic matter.
NATURAL CONTROL   Beneficial nematodes, birds, and lizards.
ORGANIC CONTROL   Boric acid products indoors; citrus products, diatomaceous earth, beneficial nematodes.

CARPENTER BEES
Pest bees that drill holes in our exposed wood structures.

FEEDING HABITS   Adults feed on nectar and pollen, larvae feed on "bee bread" made of pollen and honey.
ECONOMIC IMPORTANCE   Pollination of flowers, especially passion flowers. Also important for pollinating fruits and vegetables.
NATURAL CONTROL   Birds and microorganisms.
ORGANIC CONTROL   Paint the wood or use wood stain. Treat the wood with castor oil, hot pepper mix, or citrus oil products.

CENTIPEDES
(Beneficial and Pest)

FEEDING HABITS   Feed on small insects, including roaches, clothes moths, and house flies, and sometimes plant roots. House centipedes are predaceous; garden centipedes eat plant roots.
ECONOMIC IMPORTANCE   They have a bite about as powerful as a bee sting, but a bite is rare. They feed on slugs, grubs, worms, cockroaches, ants, and flies, and are considered beneficial around the house.
NATURAL CONTROL   Insectivorous animals.
ORGANIC CONTROL   None needed. They are actually beneficial. If they become a nuisance indoors, vacuum them up.

CHIGGERS
Tiny beasts that make your skin itch.

FEEDING HABITS   Nymphs attach to skin of various animals to feed.
ECONOMIC IMPORTANCE   Cause severe itching and small reddish welts on skin.
NATURAL CONTROL   Increased soil moisture. Some researchers say chiggers have no natural enemies. That may be true, but the imported fire ants will certainly eliminate them.
ORGANIC CONTROL   Sulfur dust is a good repellent. So is lemon mint, also called horsemint (*Monarda citriodora*). Take a hot, soapy bath to remove larvae. Stop the itching with baking soda, vinegar, aloe vera, or comfrey juice.

Chinch Bug

Cicada and Cicada Killer

Cockroaches in boric acid/sugar trap

Colorado Potato Beetle (Malcolm Beck)

CHINCH BUGS
Turf pest that only attacks weak grass.

FEEDING HABITS   Feed the most in summer and early fall. They suck the juice from grass leaves through needlelike beaks. They inject a toxic saliva into the plant that causes wilting. Most damage is caused by the nymphs and shows up in circular patterns. They like hot conditions and stressed turf.

ECONOMIC IMPORTANCE   Turf damage. Foliage turns yellow, then brown, and then dies. Almost never a problem in well-maintained turf.

NATURAL CONTROL   Healthy soil and turf. When weather turns cool in the fall, a beneficial fungus called *Beauveria* spp. moves in and kills these pests. It appears as a grayish cottony mass of fungal hyphae. Keep lawns moist and don't overfertilize. Bigeyed bugs are a natural enemy.

ORGANIC CONTROL   Diatomaceous earth and compost, manure tea, molasses, and citrus oil spray.

CICADAS
Loudmouth insects in your trees in the summer.

FEEDING HABITS   Nymphs feed on tree roots.

ECONOMIC IMPORTANCE   Cause little major plant damage. Most serious damage comes from the egg-laying slits in the bark of small branches, which cause tip growth to die.

NATURAL CONTROL   Cicada killers.

ORGANIC CONTROL   We know of no effective techniques yet. There are never enough of them in any one place.

COCKROACHES
Embarrassed people call them water bugs.

FEEDING HABITS   Will eat any kind of food left accessible. They are attracted into houses for food crumbs and water.

ECONOMIC IMPORTANCE   Ruins foodstuff. Most cockroaches live outside and help to decay organic matter. Believed to spread disease, but contrary to popular opinion, they rarely if ever spread human disease.

NATURAL CONTROL   Gecko lizards, scorpions, and beneficial nematodes. Freezing temperatures will kill some species.

ORGANIC CONTROL   Boric acid products, baking soda soap, and sugar baits. Caulking the cracks and crevices, and setting out moist sponges with beneficial nematodes.

COLORADO POTATO BEETLES
The bane of potatoes.

FEEDING HABITS   Adult beetles and larvae feed on plant leaves.

ECONOMIC IMPORTANCE   Food-crop destruction.

NATURAL CONTROL   Ground beetles, assassin bugs, and giant wheel bugs.

ORGANIC CONTROL   *Bacillus thuringiensis* 'San Diego'

Corn Earworm

CORN EARWORMS

Good to find—they mean the corn cob is nontoxic.

FEEDING HABITS   Larvae eat the foliage and buds of many crops such as tomatoes, beans, cotton bolls, lettuce crowns. They enter the corn ears at the tip, eat the kernels at the end, and leave masses of moist castings that cause mold to form. They enter the stem end of tomatoes. Called tomato fruitworm when eating tomatoes. The larvae are cannibalistic if they run into one of their own.

ECONOMIC IMPORTANCE   A cosmetic problem for home gardeners. Not seriously damaging to corn crops, but considered one of the most destructive pests to other agricultural crops.

NATURAL CONTROL   Tachinid flies, trichogramma wasps, and naturally occurring *Bacillus thuringiensis*. Bats, birds, and other insectivorous animals.

ORGANIC CONTROL   *Bacillus thuringiensis* products for serious infestations. A drop of mineral oil on top of each ear after silks have wilted. Apply beneficial nematodes to the soil. Organic, healthy corn plants are bothered less, and early plantings are damaged less than late plantings.

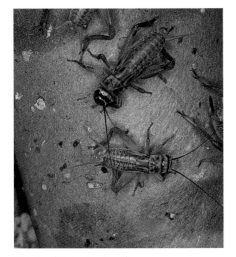

Cricket (Malcolm Beck)

CRICKETS

Easy to kill with orange oil products.

FEEDING HABITS   Eat several kinds of plants, especially long sprouts. Indoors they can damage wool, cotton, silk, synthetic fabrics, carpets, rugs, and furs. They also like food scraps; leather and rubber; beans, cucumbers, melons, squash, and tomatoes.

ECONOMIC IMPORTANCE   Keep people awake at night.

NATURAL CONTROL   Birds and naturally occurring microbes.

ORGANIC CONTROL   *Nosema locustae* products, diatomaceous earth, and orange oil. Boric acid products that contain attractant bait are also effective indoors.

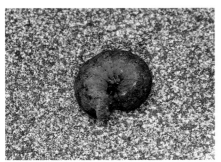

Cutworm

CUTWORMS

Nasty little beasts that hide in the ground.

FEEDING HABITS   Cut off young seedlings at ground level. Some will climb up plants and chew foliage as armyworms do.

ECONOMIC IMPORTANCE   Several species of cutworms can damage small grains, tomatoes, peppers, eggplant, and cabbage.

NATURAL CONTROL   Trichogramma wasps, birds, frogs, fire ants, and beneficial nematodes. Plant big, healthy transplants.

ORGANIC CONTROL   Cutworm collars around plants. Diatomaceous earth or fireplace ashes around plants. *Bacillus thuringiensis* products mixed with moist bran and molasses around plants. Release beneficial nematodes. During daylight hours, scratch the soil around damaged or cut-off plants and heavily water the soil. The cutworms will float out, and then you can step on them or feed them to the chickens. Crushed red pepper and cedar flakes will also help.

Dragonfly

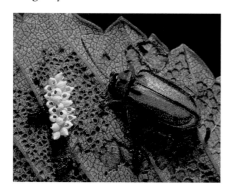
Elm Leaf Beetle (Max Bagley)

DRAGONFLIES
My favorite beneficial insect.

FEEDING HABITS   Hunting behavior is called "hawking." They eat several flying pest insects, including house flies, gnats, and mosquitoes. They will sometimes eat old, weak, slow honeybees and other sick beneficials. Can eat as many as 300 mosquitoes a day.

ECONOMIC IMPORTANCE   Beneficial insect.

NATURAL CONTROL   Birds.

ORGANIC CONTROL   None needed. Enjoy their beauty and insect control.

ELM LEAF BEETLES
Only attack lousy trees.

FEEDING HABITS   Larvae eat green tissue from the surface of leaves. Adults eat holes in elm tree leaves and cause a skeletonized look.

ECONOMIC IMPORTANCE   Disfigure elm trees; will sometimes come into the house and be a nuisance. Extremely destructive to ill-adapted elm trees.

NATURAL CONTROL   Birds. Don't plant Siberian elms, and cut down the ones you have.

ORGANIC CONTROL   *Bacillus thuringiensis* 'San Diego.'

FIRE ANTS
Chemical pesticides created the problem—organics is the solution.

FEEDING HABITS   Omnivorous, will feed on almost any animal or plant. They eat other insects, oils, sugars, and young seedlings and saplings.

ECONOMIC IMPORTANCE   Tremendous economic problem due to electrical device damage. They also kill baby animals. They do have a beneficial side, however. They eat ticks, chiggers, termites, boll weevils, garden fleahoppers, cotton bollworms, pink bollworms, tobacco budworms, pecan weevils, hickory shuckworms, flies, fleas, cockroaches, and corn earworms. They are a beneficial predator in controlled numbers.

NATURAL CONTROL   Lizards, birds, other insects, and microorganisms.

ORGANIC CONTROL   Garden-Ville Auntie Fuego, beneficial nematodes, and diatomaceous earth. Beneficial microorganisms in the compost tea and in the gut of nematodes seem to be doing the actual control. Diatomaceous earth on dry days or a mixture of compost tea, molasses, and citrus oil any time. Many gardeners report good results with instant grits and other instant breakfast cereals. Spraying products that contain molasses helps keep them away. Applying ground-up orange and grapefruit rinds to the mounds is another excellent control.

FIREFLIES
Beautiful and beneficial.

FEEDING HABITS   Firefly adults don't eat much of anything, but larvae are carnivorous. They eat other insects, snails, and slugs.

NATURAL ENEMIES   Man—with chemical sprays.

CONTROL   None needed—beneficial.

FLEAS
Easily controlled with organics.

FEEDING HABITS   Larvae feed on dry blood of fleas, mice, rats, and other animals, excreta, and other organic matter. Adults feed on fresh blood.

ECONOMIC IMPORTANCE   Easy to control with organic techniques; expensive pest. Can cause severe skin problems for dogs and cats. Flea allergy is the most common skin disease of pets. Fleas can transmit tapeworms.

NATURAL CONTROL   Keep sites clean and animals healthy. Beneficial nematodes and fire ants.

ORGANIC CONTROL   Beneficial nematodes and citrus products. Flea control requires a comprehensive program. Use banana stalks under decks. The most effective flea control device is the vacuum cleaner, which will remove flea eggs, flea larvae, and flea food. Put towels down where pets lie, and wash those towels weekly. Use diatomaceous earth.

Below left: Fire Ants (Texas Department of Agriculture); below right: Firefly or Lightning Bug (Max Bagley)

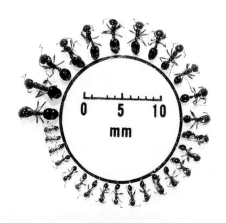

Fourlined Plant Bug

Wooly Oak Gall (Malcolm Beck)

Gall on Red Oak

Galls

FLY PARASITES
One of the beneficial wasps.

FEEDING HABITS   Larvae feed on developing flies in the larva and soft pupa stages. Adults draw fluid from fly pupae.

ECONOMIC IMPORTANCE   Controlling flies and keeping them from becoming a big nuisance.

NATURAL CONTROL   They serve as their own control, as they reduce the population of their host.

ORGANIC CONTROL   None needed.

FOURLINED PLANT BUGS
Beautiful but nasty little beast.

FEEDING HABITS   White or dark spots appear on upper sides of leaves where these bugs have sucked juice. When severe, the entire leaf will wither and drop. The spots look more like a fungus disease than insect damage. They especially like mints, monarda, sage, comfrey, and oregano.

ECONOMIC IMPORTANCE   Cosmetic damage early in the growing season. They are rarely present after it gets hot.

NATURAL CONTROL   Birds, assassin bugs, and other insectivorous animals.

ORGANIC CONTROL   Treat before the insects mature with any orange oil–based spray such as Garden-Ville Auntie Fuego or GreenSense Soil Drench. Dust with natural diatomaceous earth.

FUNGUS GNATS
Stop watering so much.

FEEDING HABITS   Larvae eat fungal matter and decaying organic matter. They will also do some damage to plant roots and stems.

ECONOMIC IMPORTANCE   Can damage plant roots but are more of an irritation than anything.

NATURAL CONTROL   *Bacillus thuringiensis* 'Israelensis.' Water potted plants and courtyards less often.

ORGANIC CONTROL   Neem or citrus oil products. Cornmeal will kill the algae that the gnats are feeding on. Caution: Do not use neem products that contain piperonyl butoxide (PBO).

GALLS
Ugly but only a sign.

FEEDING HABITS   Wasp, fly, or aphid gall insects "sting" a plant, which causes a growth that the insect uses as a home for its young. The gall serves as a shelter and food supply.

ECONOMIC IMPORTANCE   Although unsightly, most are not considered very damaging. Tannic acid from galls has been used for centuries to tan skins of animals. Many galls contain materials that make the finest inks and dyes. Some galls contain products that have been used in medicine since the fifth century B.C.

NATURAL CONTROL   Biodiversity.

ORGANIC CONTROL   None needed, although healthy plants seem to have fewer galls.

Giant Wheel Bug (Malcolm Beck)

Grasshopper

Ground Beetle (Malcolm Beck)

GIANT WHEEL BUGS
Big beneficial friends.

FEEDING HABITS   Insect eaters; suck juices from many troublesome insects such as moths, squash bugs, cucumber beetles, and webworms.
ECONOMIC IMPORTANCE   Beneficial insects that feed on several pest insects.
CONTROL   None needed.

GRASSHOPPERS
The hardest insect to control.

FEEDING HABITS   Nymphs and especially the adults chew foliage of many crops. Nymphs like grass.
ECONOMIC IMPORTANCE   Can destroy crops in a hurry.
NATURAL CONTROL   Natural enemies such as blister beetles, ground beetles, predatory flies, parasitic flies, and especially birds. Beneficial fungi that inhabit healthy soil.
ORGANIC CONTROL   Floating row cover or biological controls such as *Nosema locustae* or *Beauvaria bassiana*. Garlic-pepper tea. All-purpose flour from the grocery store works as well. A mixture of molasses, compost tea, and citrus oil also works. Build soil health and mulch bare soil. Drench soil with neem products.

GROUND BEETLES
If running around on the ground, leave 'em alone.

FEEDING HABITS   Both larvae and adults eat caterpillars; Colorado potato beetles; larvae, pupae, and eggs of root maggots and flies; larvae of imported cabbage worms; diamondback moths; cutworm and cabbage loopers; aphids; asparagus beetles; slugs; flea beetles; and snails. Come to think of it, they feed on many of our most noxious insects.
ECONOMIC IMPORTANCE   Control of many troublesome pests.
CONTROL   None needed. These are very beneficial insects.

Harlequin Bug

Hoverfly

Honeybees (*Agricultural Research* magazine, USDA)

HARLEQUIN BUGS
Their job is to take out expended plants.

FEEDING HABITS   Both the nymphs and adults feed heavily on all members of the cabbage family, causing light splotches, shriveling, and deformity.
ECONOMIC IMPORTANCE   Can destroy a garden in a hurry.
NATURAL CONTROL   Biodiversity. Plant in the proper season—the fall. Encourage birds. Plant "trap" crops of mustard, turnip greens, and the like.
ORGANIC CONTROL   Spray with manure compost tea, seaweed, molasses, vinegar, and citrus oil.

HONEYBEES
Our most important pollinators.

FEEDING HABITS   Workers feed on nectar and honey and gather pollen. Larvae feed on honey and royal jelly.
ECONOMIC IMPORTANCE   Honey production and pollination of many ornamental and food crops.
NATURAL CONTROL   Mites and the unnatural synthetic pesticides. Sevin is one of the worst pesticide choices left on the market. It is extremely toxic to bees.
ORGANIC CONTROL   None needed.

HOVER FLIES
Looks like a bee but can't sting.

FEEDING HABITS   Adults are attracted to and feed on the nectar and pollen of many flowers. Larvae are predators on aphids, caterpillars, mealybugs, scale, thrips, corn borders, and corn earworms. They especially like small flat flowers such as carrots, Queen Anne's lace, horseradish, and wild mustard. They can often be seen on roses. The grublike green larvae love aphids. They hold them up and suck their juices as if drinking soda from a bottle and then toss the dry skin aside. They eat about one aphid per minute.
ECONOMIC IMPORTANCE   Larvae are effective predators of aphids and other troublesome insects. The hover fly hurriedly floats from flower to flower, drinking nectar. By doing so, they are excellent pollinators, which we now need, since so many of our honeybees are being destroyed.
CONTROL   None needed.

Adult June Beetle

Lace Bugs (Max Bagley)

Above: Lacewing adult; below left: Lacewing larva (Malcolm Beck); below right: Lacewing eggs (Malcolm Beck)

JUNE BEETLES
Grubworm parents.

FEEDING HABITS   Larvae feed on plant roots or decaying organic matter. Feeding decreases as soil temperatures decrease in the fall when the grubs migrate deeper into the soil. Adult beetles chew leaves at night but are not highly destructive.

ECONOMIC IMPORTANCE   Can cause reduced plant production and even plant loss. Damaging to lawns. Grubs are rarely a problem for organically maintained gardens with healthy, biologically alive soil.

NATURAL CONTROL   Grow nectar and pollen plants to attract native predators and parasites. Beneficial nematodes, cats, skunks, opossums, armadillos, raccoons, foxes, coyotes, and other insectivorous animals.

ORGANIC CONTROL   Beneficial nematodes, compost, sugar, and light traps for adults. Milky spore disease does not seem to work on our Texas grubs. *Heterohabditis* nematodes seem to be the most effective nematodes for grubworms.

LACE BUGS
Delicate but damaging insects.

FEEDING HABITS   Suck sap from underside of leaves using piercing, sucking mouthparts. Damage appears on leaf surfaces as pale brown or yellow specks.

ECONOMIC IMPORTANCE   Damage to foliage can make nursery plants unmarketable. The mottling of the leaf surface can severely reduce photosynthesis.

NATURAL CONTROL   Provide proper irrigation and other care to maintain plant health. Encourage beneficial insects and microbial activity.

ORGANIC CONTROL   Horticultural oil, citrus oil, and molasses. Neem and biological products containing beneficial fungi. Garden-Ville Fire Auntie Fuego formula.

LACEWINGS
Beautiful and beneficial.

FEEDING HABITS   Larvae, or "aphid lions," feed on aphids, thrips, mites, mealybugs, scale, whiteflies, eggs of leafhoppers, moths, cabbage loopers, corn earworms, Colorado potato beetles, asparagus beetles, leaf miners, and several other small caterpillars and beetle larvae. Developing larvae eat from 100 to 600 aphids a day.

ECONOMIC IMPORTANCE   Control of many troublesome insects. One of the most important beneficial insects.

CONTROL   None needed; should always be encouraged.

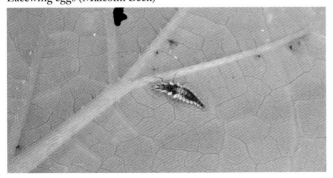

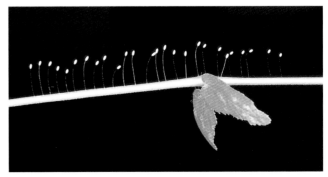

Lady Beetle pupa

Lady Beetle adult and larva

Lady Beetle larva pupating

LADY BEETLES (Ladybugs)
Even organiphobes admit their value.

FEEDING HABITS   Feed on aphids, mites, and other soft-bodied insect pests. Unfortunately, the imported Asian or harmonia lady beetles like the taste of ripe plums and peaches and will eat the fruit if something else provides an opening.

ECONOMIC IMPORTANCE   Great control of aphids and other small troublesome insect pests. Can be stored in refrigerator for several weeks. Release about 1,500 beetles per 1,000 sq. ft. in the home garden.

NATURAL CONTROL   Very few enemies. They don't taste good. You don't believe it? Try one.

ORGANIC CONTROL   None needed; should be encouraged.

LEAFCUTTING BEES
Cosmetic damage pest.

FEEDING HABITS   Eat pollen and nectar from many flowers.

ECONOMIC IMPORTANCE   Important plant pollinators and should not be killed. Troublesome around machine shops because they will plug up any exposed pipes. Mechanics have learned to tape over the ends of pipes, fuel lines, and other openings.

NATURAL CONTROL   Good biodiversity will keep them from being too abundant. Birds, praying mantids, and lizards.

ORGANIC CONTROL   None needed in most cases—their damage is only cosmetic.

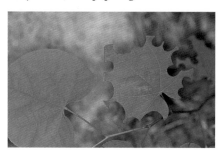

Leafcutting Bee damage

Leafhopper

Leafminer

Longlegged Fly

Millipede

LEAFHOPPERS
Minimal damage pest.

FEEDING HABITS   Adults and nymphs suck juices from stems and undersides of leaves, causing a mottled look.

ECONOMIC IMPORTANCE   Toxic saliva can cause stunted leaf growth or warty, crinkled, or rolled edges. Some are vectors of plant disease.

NATURAL CONTROL   Maintain healthy plants. Protect natural enemies such as parasitic wasps and flies, damselbugs, minute pirate bugs, lady beetles, lacewings, and spiders. Birds, frogs, lizards, and insectivorous insects.

ORGANIC CONTROL   Strong blasts of water and citrus oil products. Horticultural oil for heavy infestations.

LEAFMINERS
Minor pests.

FEEDING HABITS   Larvae tunnel through leaf tissue, leaving unsightly trails.

ECONOMIC IMPORTANCE   Can destroy seedlings but cause only a cosmetic problem on mature plants.

NATURAL CONTROL   Leafminers have many natural enemies such as hummingbirds. *Dacnusa sibirica* is a parasitic wasp specific to some leafminers. Beneficial nematodes will attack the pupae in the soil.

ORGANIC CONTROL   Floating row cover on vegetable crops. Neem products or citrus oil products.

LONGLEGGED FLIES
Aptly named beneficials.

FEEDING HABITS   Adults capture and eat many small soft-bodied troublesome insects.

ECONOMIC IMPORTANCE   Adults are effective predators of mosquito larvae and many other soft-bodied insects.

NATURAL CONTROL   Lizards and birds.

ORGANIC CONTROL   None needed.

MILLIPEDES
Mostly beneficial—so don't kill them.

FEEDING HABITS   Feed mostly on decaying organic matter. Will sometimes damage seedlings, especially in damp soils. Some millipedes are predators and eat small insects. Some millipedes will eat plant roots, but for the most part they are beneficial, breaking down organic matter.

ECONOMIC IMPORTANCE   Beneficial in breaking down organic matter, but will eat fruit that rests on the ground—such as strawberries and tomatoes.

NATURAL CONTROL   Mulch bare soil to keep low-growing fruit off the soil. Maintain biodiversity.

ORGANIC CONTROL   Dry soil out with wood ashes or diatomaceous earth. Drench soil with citrus tea if millipedes become a problem.

Mud Dauber (Malcolm Beck)

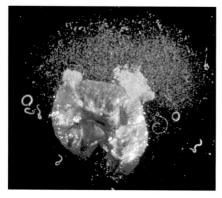

Biosafe Beneficial Nematodes attacking grubworm

Paper Wasps (Malcolm Beck)

MOSQUITOES
Easy to control with organic techniques.

FEEDING HABITS   Females suck blood of animals. Males occasionally eat nectar and honeydew.

ECONOMIC IMPORTANCE   Serious disease vectors.

NATURAL CONTROL   Mosquito-eating fish; predators such as bats, purple martins, hummingbirds, damselflies, aquatic beetles, spiders, predatory mites, and dragonflies.

ORGANIC CONTROL   Habitat drainage. Spray or treatment of stagnant water with *Bacillus thuringiensis* 'Israelensis.' Spray for adult infestations with garlic-pepper tea, Garrett Juice plus citrus oil, and Garden-Ville Auntie Fuego. To avoid being bitten by mosquitoes, use essential oil of lavender to mask the human odors that attract mosquitoes. Several herbal repellents are now available. Vanilla extract either dabbed on full strength or mixed with water and sprayed is usually effective. Toxic chemical sprays such as pyrethroids do more harm than good.

MUD DAUBERS (Dirt Daubers)
Very beneficial—try to live with them.

FEEDING HABITS   Female adults hunt and paralyze spiders, crickets, cicadas, flies, and leafhoppers. Before sealing each egg cell, she drops a spider in to feed the larva later. Adults like flowers and feed on nectar and pollen.

ECONOMIC IMPORTANCE   Control of spiders, especially black widows.

NATURAL CONTROL   Birds and spiders.

ORGANIC CONTROL   None needed.

NEMATODES
Good Guys and Bad Guys.

FEEDING HABITS   Troublesome nematodes feed on many vegetable and ornamental plants. Feeding causes lesions and galls on roots and stimulates excessive branching. Beneficial nematodes feed on grubs, roaches, and termites.

ECONOMIC IMPORTANCE   Plant-attacking nematodes reduce plant vigor, stunt growth, and cause death. Beneficial nematodes give important control of grubs, roaches, termites, fleas, ticks, and other troublesome pests.

NATURAL CONTROL   Harmful nematodes are controlled primarily through healthy biodiverse soil containing beneficial fungi.

PAPER WASPS
Beneficial even though they sting.

FEEDING HABITS   Wasp larvae are carnivorous and are fed moth and butterfly larvae that are chewed up by the adult wasp workers.

ECONOMIC IMPORTANCE   Control of several troublesome caterpillars of moths and butterflies.

NATURAL CONTROL   Spiders. Splash water on nest to knock wasps off, then move nest to higher but similar location in the shade. Don't try this if you're allergic to wasp stings or if you are chicken!

ORGANIC CONTROL   Soapy water or citrus oil products if the nest is in a problem area. Do this only as a last resort—these insects are very beneficial.

Pecan Nut Casebearer damage

Sowbug

Praying Mantis

PEACH TREE BORERS
Control with the Basic Organic Program.

FEEDING HABITS   Borers chew inner bark of lower tree trunk. Mass of gummy sawdust appears at base of trees.
ECONOMIC IMPORTANCE   Damage to tree trunks. Vectors of wilt fungi and other diseases.
NATURAL CONTROL   Healthy soil, compost, thick mulch over root system. Ichneumon and other predatory wasps.
ORGANIC CONTROL   Tobacco dust (snuff) or sticky tape around base of tree. Squirt beneficial nematodes into holes. Treat soil with beneficial nematodes. Paint tree trunks with Garrett Goop.

PECAN NUT CASEBEARERS
A few are helpful.

FEEDING HABITS   Damage is done in early spring, just after pollination.
ECONOMIC IMPORTANCE   Damage to pecan crops can range from a very light thinning, 10 percent or so, to a loss of 80 or 90 percent of the entire crop.
NATURAL CONTROL   Trichogramma wasps and other beneficial insects.
ORGANIC CONTROL   *Bacillus thuringiensis* sprays.

PILLBUGS AND SOWBUGS (Roly Poly Bugs)
Helpful and harmful.

FEEDING HABITS   Feed mostly on decaying organic matter but can be severe plant pests, especially on young seedlings.
ECONOMIC IMPORTANCE   Beneficial to the breakdown of natural organic matter, but they obviously get tired of eating dead brown stuff sometimes and attack plants.
NATURAL CONTROL   Let beds dry out between waterings.
ORGANIC CONTROL   Dust hot red pepper powder around plants. Dilute with diatomaceous earth for economy; sprinkle it around young seedlings. Put an apple core or some brewer's yeast in a glass (plastic is safer) countersunk into the soil. Cover it with a dish or pot. Spray with concentrated citrus oil. Add molasses and manure tea for even better results. Coffee grounds on top of mulch also help.

PRAYING MANTISES
Interesting beneficial that is fun to watch.

FEEDING HABITS   Nymphs and adults feed on aphids, beetles, bugs, leafhoppers, flies, bees, caterpillars, wasps, butterflies, and anything else that ventures by, including small animals like lizards and snakes—also each other.
ECONOMIC IMPORTANCE   Questionable. They are interesting insects but undependable for control of problem insects.
NATURAL CONTROL   Various insect parasites.
ORGANIC CONTROL   None needed.

Praying Mantis egg case

Euonymus Scale (*Agricultural Research* magazine, USDA)

Slugs (Malcolm Beck)

Snail

Soft Brown Scale

SCALE INSECTS

Stationary insects that suck the juice from leaves and stems.

FEEDING HABITS   Scales suck plant sap through piercing, sucking mouthparts. Will attack many ornamental and food crops.

ECONOMIC IMPORTANCE   Can do severe damage by reducing vigor and stressing plants. Serious citrus pest.

NATURAL CONTROL   Twicestabbed, lindorus, and vedalia lady beetles; parasitic aphids; parasitic wasps; healthy plants.

ORGANIC CONTROL   Dormant oil in winter, horticultural oil year-round, and citrus oil products in the growing season.

SLUGS, SNAILS

Organic controls work best.

FEEDING HABITS   Slugs and snails feed primarily on decaying organic matter, but they also have a taste for your best ornamental and vegetable plants. They feed at night (although on damp drizzly days they will stay out all day) and will climb trees or eat on the ground. They like to eat fungi, lichens, green foliage, worms, centipedes, insects, animal feces, carrion, and other slugs.

ECONOMIC IMPORTANCE   Very destructive to many garden plants and food crops. The decollate snail is predatory and helps to control plant-eating snails, although there is some worry that it will destroy the balance of native snails— but we doubt it.

NATURAL CONTROL   Maintain permanent stands of clover and mulches to favor ground beetles and rove beetles (which eat slugs). Centipedes also eat slug eggs. Other predators include small mammals, snakes, frogs, toads, lizards, birds, and carnivorous beetles. In the insect world, their biggest enemy is the larva of the lightning bug.

ORGANIC CONTROL   Dust dry hot pepper in problem areas—it works great. Mix with diatomaceous earth for economy. Coarse-textured, crushed hot pepper like that used on pizza is best. Citrus oil spray works well, and coffee grounds sprinkled on top of the mulch also helps. Cedar mulches are also important.

Spider Mites

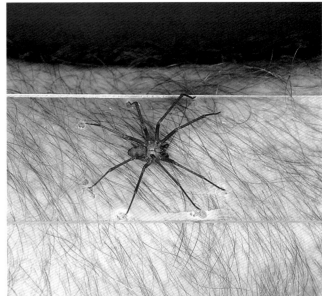

Brown Recluse Spider

Argiope Spider

SPIDER MITES
Tiny plant juice–sucking critters.

FEEDING HABITS   Both nymphs and adults pierce plant cells and suck juice.
   They feed on fruit, foliage, and roots. Infested leaves turn silvery or yellow,
   then curl and are covered with a fine web.
ECONOMIC IMPORTANCE   Serious damage to food crops and ornamentals.
NATURAL CONTROL   Predatory spider mites, ladybugs, minute pirate bugs,
   thrips, lacewings, and lady beetles. Address the cause of the plant stress.
   Mites attack only sick plants that can't pull up water properly.
ORGANIC CONTROL   Spraying just about anything every three days for nine
   days will get rid of them. Garlic-pepper tea and seaweed mix is one of the
   best sprays. Citrus oil sprays and seaweed sprays are also effective.

SPIDERS
Extremely beneficial critters.

FEEDING HABITS   Paralyze prey with venom and feed on insects and other
   small animals.
ECONOMIC IMPORTANCE   Spiders are highly beneficial because they feed on
   many troublesome insects. Black widows and brown recluses are the only
   poisonous spiders, and they are very dangerous ones.
NATURAL CONTROL   Mud daubers and other wasps. See Mud Daubers.
ORGANIC CONTROL   If a problem, knock the webs down with a broom. If they
   have to be killed, use soapy water or citrus. Vacuum thoroughly and often.
   Eliminate other insects—the spiders' food source. All but the black widows
   and brown recluses are totally beneficial. *Note:* See the medical device for
   treatment of poisonous bites explained in the Appendix of the *Texas Bug
   Book.*

Squash Bug nymphs

Squash Vine Borer larva

SQUASH BUGS
Hard-to-control vegetable crop pest.

FEEDING HABITS   Adults and nymphs suck plant juices, causing foliage to wilt, blacken, and die.

ECONOMIC IMPORTANCE   Can destroy crops in the cucurbit family.

NATURAL CONTROL   Parasitic flies, spiders, assassin bugs, birds, and snakes. Interplant luffa gourds.

ORGANIC CONTROL   Crush the copper-colored eggs when found on the backs of leaves. Handpick the first adults to appear in the spring. Plant lots of flowers for pollen and nectar to attract predatory flies. Cover seedlings with floating row cover and hand-pollinate. Spray compost tea, molasses, or citrus oil for serious infestations. Dust plants with whole wheat flour.

SQUASH VINE BORERS
Tough-to-control pests.

FEEDING HABITS   Larvae (borers) enter the base of the stem in early summer, causing a greenish grass, and leading to wilting and death. They will also feed on fruit of cucumbers, gourds, melons, pumpkins, and squash.

ECONOMIC IMPORTANCE   Destruction of squash plants.

NATURAL CONTROL   Plant more than just a few plants. Plant early and promote vigorous growth. Plant cucurbits with more solid stems, such as butternut and winter squash. Beneficial nematodes. Interplant luffa gourds.

ORGANIC CONTROL   Slit the stem and remove the border. Pile soil over the damaged stalk. Some say injecting *Bacillus thuringiensis* or beneficial nematodes into the stalk with a syringe works. Both methods are a lot of trouble. Cover plants with floating row cover. Spray base of plants with pyrethrum or citrus oil products regularly. Spray plants with a Bt product when yellow flowers first bloom. Check the base of stems often to remove the reddish eggs before they hatch. Treat soil with beneficial nematodes.

STINK BUGS
Some are actually beneficial—meat eaters.

FEEDING HABITS   Adults and nymphs suck juice from flowers, fruit, seed, and leaves. Leaves wilt, turn brown, or have discolored spots. Fruit is scarred and sometimes "cat-faced." Pods sometimes drop, and seed can be deformed. Although most are sapsuckers, several species suck the blood of caterpillars, beetles, and other pests.

ECONOMIC IMPORTANCE   Cosmetic and sometimes serious damage to food crops and ornamental plants.

NATURAL CONTROL   Parasitic wasps and tachinid flies.

ORGANIC CONTROL   Handpick the bugs and crush the eggs; spray organic pesticides as a last resort. Use citrus oil sprays for heavy infestations.

Below left: beneficial Stink Bug; below right: pest Stink Bug

Tachinid Fly

Texas Leafcutting Ant (Malcolm Beck)

Forest Tent Caterpillar

Tent Caterpillar

TACHINID FLIES
Parasitic flies.

FEEDING HABITS   Larvae feed on caterpillars, beetles, fly larvae, true bugs, corn borers, corn earworms, imported cabbage worms, cabbage loopers, potato stem borers, cutworms, armyworms, Mexican bean beetles, Colorado potato beetles, stink bugs, squash bugs, tarnished plant bugs, cucumber beetles, sawflies, and grasshoppers. Adults feed on pollen, nectar, and honeydew or sometimes aphids and leafhoppers.

ECONOMIC IMPORTANCE   Help to control many troublesome insects. Tachinid larvae destroy the eggs of many pest insects, including caterpillars, beetles, true bugs, flies, crickets, grasshoppers, and katydids.

NATURAL CONTROL   Birds and lizards.

ORGANIC CONTROL   None needed—extremely beneficial insect.

TENT CATERPILLARS
Caterpillars that usually form tents, though forest tent caterpillars do not.

FEEDING HABITS   Larvae feed on the foliage of trees and can completely defoliate the plants.

ECONOMIC IMPORTANCE   Will defoliate and stress deciduous trees.

NATURAL CONTROL   Birds, parasitic flies, and wasps. Plant nectar and pollen plants to attract them.

ORGANIC CONTROL   Prune branches with tents and destroy. Spray caterpillars while young with Garden-Ville Auntie Fuego sprays or catch them in sticky tree bands. Release trichogramma wasps in the spring. Spray citrus oil products. Spray *Bacillus thuringiensis* product as a last resort.

TEXAS LEAFCUTTING ANTS
Devastating foliage-stripping insect.

FEEDING HABITS   Feed on fungus that grows on the compost pile made in the mound. The ants use all kinds of plant materials to make the compost piles. Howard's listeners report that these ants even use the berries and leaves of mistletoe.

ECONOMIC IMPORTANCE   Leafcutting ants will defoliate and kill food and ornamental plants. One of the most difficult ants to control.

NATURAL CONTROL   Lizards and birds love to eat 'em. Thick mulch around all plants helps. Beneficial nematodes help control all pests that live in the ground.

ORGANIC CONTROL   Treat the mounds with Garden-Ville Auntie Fuego. Citrus baits and beneficial nematodes are also effective.

THRIPS
Small flower-spoiling insects.

FEEDING HABITS   Adults and nymphs rasp and suck the juice from plant cells and cause silvery speckles or streaks on leaves. Flowers turn brown on the edges and don't open properly. Thrips will attack many different kinds of plants.

ECONOMIC IMPORTANCE   Causes reduced plant production and ruins flowers. A serious onion pest. Damage can cause decrease in bulb size. Spreads viruses.

NATURAL CONTROL   Bigeyed bugs are the most important natural control, along with minute pirate bugs, lacewings, and lady beetles. Heavy rainfall also helps. Nematodes applied in water drenches will control species that pupate in the soil. Excellent control of thrips on roses.

ORGANIC CONTROL   Spray with horticultural oil or neem products when necessary or release predatory mites or pirate bugs. Garlic tea and seaweed sprays are very effective. Cover plants with row-cover material.

TICKS
Hard-to-control bloodsuckers.

FEEDING HABITS   Suck blood of warm-blooded animals.

ECONOMIC IMPORTANCE   Vectors of several diseases.

NATURAL CONTROL   Cut brush and weeds. Wear protective clothing. Keep interiors well cleaned and vacuumed, fill cracks with steel wool or copper mesh. Ticks have few natural enemies other than fire ants.

ORGANIC CONTROL   Dust with diatomaceous earth and pyrethrum for severe infestations. Keep out mice. Stock firewood away from the house. Locate bird feeders away from the house. Spray with citrus oil or d-limonene products. Apply beneficial nematodes.

Thrips damage

Tick (Malcolm Beck)

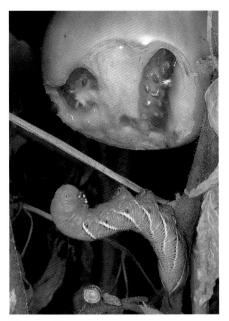

Tobacco Hornworm

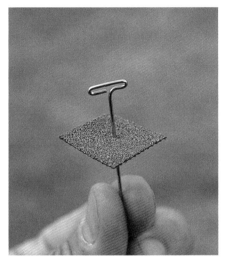

Trichogramma Wasp

TOBACCO HORNWORMS
Big worms that are easy to pick off.

FEEDING HABITS   Caterpillars eat foliage—mostly at night. Moths sip nectar from flowers at dusk.

ECONOMIC IMPORTANCE   Can defoliate plants overnight. These moths are important for the pollination of deep-throated flowers and night bloomers.

NATURAL CONTROL   Parasitic wasps, brachonid wasps, birds, skunks, and lizards. Trichogramma wasps parasitize the eggs.

ORGANIC CONTROL   Handpicking. *Bacillus thuringiensis* products will kill them, but spraying for these pests is a waste of time and money.

TOMATO HORNWORMS
Big worms that are easy to pick off.

FEEDING HABITS   Caterpillars feed mostly at night on foliage of nightshade plants like tobacco and tomato. Moths sip nectar from flowers.

ECONOMIC IMPORTANCE   Can defoliate plants overnight. The adult with its long proboscis is necessary to pollinate deep-throated flowers and night bloomers.

NATURAL CONTROL   Birds, parasitic wasps, and brachonid wasps attack the worms. Trichogramma wasps attack the eggs.

ORGANIC CONTROL   Handpick caterpillars. Spray *Bacillus thuringiensis* products as a last resort only. Release lady beetles and lacewings to attack eggs.

TRICHOGRAMMA WASPS
Beneficial little wasps that don't sting.

FEEDING HABITS   Little is known about the feeding habits of the adult wasps.

ECONOMIC IMPORTANCE   Very effective control of many troublesome pests in the landscape and in agriculture.

NATURAL CONTROL   These parasitoids are reared and shipped as larvae or pupae within the eggs of an alternate host.

ORGANIC CONTROL   None needed—highly beneficial. There are approximately 3,000 moth eggs on the 1-inch card in the photo. An adult wasp emerges from each egg. The females then fly off to parasitize other moth eggs, preventing them from hatching into pest caterpillars.

TWIG GIRDLERS
Cosmetic damage only to terminal growth of the tree.

FEEDING HABITS   Females feed on the cambium layer as they cut the stems to allow the laid eggs to fall to the ground. I have no idea what the males are up to!

ECONOMIC IMPORTANCE   Relatively little—just a curiosity.

NATURAL CONTROL   Birds and ichneumon wasps.

ORGANIC CONTROL   Compost fallen twigs; the composting process will take care of the larvae.

Walking Stick

Fall Webworm

Webworm

Whiteflies

WALKING STICKS
Fascinating and sometimes very destructive.

FEEDING HABITS   Plant feeders, mostly at night. Can defoliate trees, but it's rare.

ECONOMIC IMPORTANCE   Usually not significant but can explode to cause severe plant damage.

NATURAL CONTROL   Parasitic wasps, flies, and birds.

ORGANIC CONTROL   Hand removal. They make interesting pets and are harmless to humans. Plant oil products can be effective.

WEBWORMS
Caterpillars with ugly homes.

FEEDING HABITS   Larvae eat outer foliage of trees, especially pecans. They eat fast and furiously and create an ugly mess in the foliage of trees.

ECONOMIC IMPORTANCE   Cosmetic damage to trees. Complete defoliation can badly stress trees.

NATURAL CONTROL   Protect the wasps, the birds, and the assassin bugs because they eat webworms.

ORGANIC CONTROL   Spray *Bacillus thuringiensis* products, always at dusk, as a last resort. Use one tablespoon of molasses per gallon of spray. Catch larvae in sticky tree bands.

WHITEFLIES
Easily controlled with seaweed spray.

FEEDING HABITS   Nymphs and adults suck plant juices and weaken plants. They especially like plants in the tomato and squash families.

ECONOMIC IMPORTANCE   Heavy infestations weaken plants and spread viral diseases.

NATURAL CONTROL   Native parasitic wasps, lacewings, lady beetles, and pirate bugs. Beneficial fungus called *Beauvaria bassiana*.

ORGANIC CONTROL   Spray garlic tea or garlic-pepper tea and seaweed. Release the parasitic wasp *Encarsia formosa* indoors. A spray mix of manure compost, molasses, and citrus oil works very well.

BENEFICIAL INSECTS: HABITATS AND BENEFITS

Assassin bug Flowering plants of ornamentals and food crops
Controls aphids, Colorado potato beetles, small flying insects, caterpillars, leaf-hoppers, Mexican bean beetles

Bee Beehives and flowers
Pollinates flowers, produces honey

Damsel bug Vegetation of all kinds
Controls aphids, caterpillars, thrips, plant bugs, leafhoppers, treehoppers

Damselfly Ponds, pools, water features
Controls mosquitoes, gnats, other flying insects

Dragonfly Ponds, pools, water features
Controls mosquitoes, gnats, other flying insects

Giant wheel bug Shrubs, trees
Controls moths, squash bugs, cucumber beetles, caterpillars

Ground beetle Drainage ditches, rock gardens, ornamental and vegetable gardens, greenhouses
Controls aphids, flea beetles, cabbage worms, slugs, cutworms, garden leafhoppers

Hover fly Herbs, flowers
Controls caterpillars, thrips, corn earworms, aphids, mealybugs, scale, leafhoppers

Ichneumon wasp Woodlots, flowers
Controls caterpillars, beetles, moths, borers

Lacewing Fencerows, woodlots, night lights
Controls aphids, scale, thrips, mites, mealybugs, whiteflies, moths, loopers, beetles, leafminers

Lady beetle Hedgerows, leaf litter, gardens, wildflowers, other protected places
Controls aphids, Colorado potato beetle eggs, spider mites

Longlegged fly Ornamental and vegetable gardens
Controls many small, soft-bodied insects

Minute pirate bug Pollen and nectar plants
Controls caterpillars, thrips, mites, aphids

Mud dauber Flowering plants, food crops, barns and garages
Controls spiders, crickets, cicadas, flies, leafhoppers

Praying mantis Wooded areas, grass strips, fencerows, vines
Controls aphids, beetles, leafhoppers, caterpillars, flies, and wasps

Spider Beehives, wood scraps, fencerows, gardens
Controls many insect pests

Spined soldier bug Vegetable garden
Controls borers, moths, caterpillars, beetles

Tachinid fly Herbs, flowers
Controls cutworms, stink bugs, beetles, corn borers, squash bugs, caterpillars, cabbage worms, sawflies, grasshoppers

Wasp Orchards, vegetable gardens, ornamental gardens
Controls casebearers, caterpillars, and corn earworms

PLANTS THAT ATTRACT BENEFICIAL INSECTS

Alyssum—hover flies, lacewings, pirate bugs, tachinid flies, wasps
Caraway—hover flies, lacewings, tachinid flies, true bugs, wasps
Coreopsis—bees, hover flies, lacewings, lady beetles, wasps
Coriander—hover flies, pirate bugs, tachinid flies, wasps
Cosmos—hover flies, lacewings, lady beetles, pirate bugs, wasps
Goldenrod—bees, bigeyed bugs, lady beetles, soldier beetles, wasps
Lantana—bees, hover flies, wasps
Liatris—bees, true bugs, wasps
Roses—bees, hover flies, wasps
Sunflowers—hover flies, lady beetles, wasps
Tansy—bees, hover flies, lady beetles, pirate bugs, wasps
Yarrow—bees, hover flies, pirate bugs, wasps

BENEFICIAL INSECT RELEASE SCHEDULE

Quantities given are for each acre or residential lot.

April–May
Release trichogramma wasps at 10,000–20,000 eggs weekly for six weeks. Begin releases when tree leaves start to emerge.
April
Release green lacewings at 2,000–4,000 eggs weekly for four weeks.
Release lady beetles as needed on aphid-infested plants. Use 2,000 bugs per 1,000 sq. ft.
May–September
Release green lacewings at 1,000–2,000 eggs every two weeks.

SOURCES OF BENEFICIAL BUGS

A-1 Unique Insect Control—5504 Sperry Drive, Citrus Heights, CA 95621, (916) 961-7945, Fax (916) 967-7082, www.a-1unique.com
American Insectaries, Inc.—30805 Rodriguez Road, Escondido, CA 92026, (760) 751-1436, Fax (760) 749-7061
Arbico—P.O. Box 4247, Tucson, AZ 85738, (800) 827-2847
Beneficial Insectary—14751 Oak Run Road, Oak Run, CA 96069, (530) 472-3715
Beneficial Insect Co.—244 Forest Street, Fort Mill, SC 29715, (803) 547-2301
BioAg Supply—710 South Columbia, Plainview, TX 79072, (806) 293-5861, Fax (806) 293-0712, (800) 746-9900
Bio Crop Care—P.O. Box 87, Mathis, TX 78368, (800) 233-4914, info@biofac.com

BioLogic—Springtown Road, P.O. Box 177, Willow Hill, PA 17271,
    (717) 349-2789

Buena Biosystems—P.O. Box 4008, Ventura, CA 93007, (805) 525-2525

Gulf Coast Biotic Technology—72 West Oaks, Huntsville, TX 77340,
    (800) 524-1958

Harmony Farm Supply—P.O. Box 460, Graton, CA 95444, (707) 823-9125

Hydro-Gardens, Inc.—P.O. Box 25845, Colorado Springs, CO 80936,
    (800) 634-6362

Kunafin Trichogramma Industries—Route 1, Box 39, Quemado, TX 78877,
    (800) 832-1113, Fax (830) 757-1468

M&R Durango—P.O. Box 886, Bayfield, CO 81122, (800) 526-4075

Mellinger's Nursery—2310 W. South Range Road, North Lima, OH 44452,
    (800) 321-7444

New Earth, Inc.—9810 Taylorsville Rd., Louisville, KY 40299,
    (502) 261-0005

N-VIRO Products, Ltd.—610 Walnut Ave., Bohemia, NY 11716,
    (516) 567-2628

Oxnard Pest Control Association—632 Pacific Ave., P.O. Box 1187,
    Oxnard, CA 93032, (805) 483-1024, Fax (805) 487-6867

Peaceful Valley Farm Supply—P.O. Box 2209, Grass Valley, CA 95945,
    (916) 272-4769

Planet Natural—P.O. Box 3146, Bozeman, MT 59772, (406) 587-5891,
    (800) 289-6656

Rincon-Vitova Insectaries, Inc.—P.O. Box 1555, Ventura, CA 93022,
    (805) 643-5407, (800) 248-2847

Tri-Cal Biosystems—P.O. Box 1327, Hollister, CA 95024, (408) 637-0195

Worm's Way, Inc.—3151 South Highway 446, Bloomington, IN 47401,
    (800) 274-9676

DISEASES AND OTHER AILMENTS

Plant diseases are usually caused by four major types of living organisms: fungi, bacteria, viruses, and pathogenic nematodes. Diseases are an imbalance of microorganisms and are sometimes hard to identify, since the results of infection are more visible than the organisms themselves.

All organic products help control disease. When soil is healthy, there is a never-ending microscopic war being waged between the good and bad microorganisms, and the good guys usually win. Disease problems are simply situations where the microorganisms have gotten out of balance. If allowed to do so, the good guys will control the bad guys. When pathogens are brought into their proper proportions, they are no longer troublesome. In most cases, they become beneficial at that point.

Drainage is a key ingredient for the prevention of diseases. Beds or tree pits that hold water and don't drain properly are the ideal breeding place for disease organisms.

As with insects, spraying for diseases is only treating symptoms, not the major problem. The primary cause of the real problem is usually related to the soil and the root system. It is therefore critical to improve drainage, increase air circulation, add organic material, and stimulate and protect the living organisms in the soil. Here are some of the most common diseases and other harmful conditions.

Anthracnose

Fungal disease that attacks and turns sycamores and other trees brown. Not normally fatal. Spray Garrett Juice plus garlic tea on emerging new foliage in early spring. Apply the Sick Tree Treatment. Sprays of potassium bicarbonate, garlic, and neem are also effective. Avoid planting ill-adapted trees. It also attacks beans and ornamentals. The foliage turns a tan color overnight. Potassium bicarbonate sprayed on the plant as leaves emerge in the spring will sometimes help. The best cure is soil improvement and selection of adapted plants.

Bacterial Blight

A plant disease that causes dark green water spots that turn brown and may die, leaving a hole in the leaves of tomatoes, plums, and several ornamentals. Spots on leaves are usually geometrical and located between the leaf veins. Control includes creating biologically healthy soil. Drenching the soil with neem can also help. Hydrogen peroxide and Consan 20 are also effective.

Bacterial Leaf Scorch

A fatal disease of sycamores and other plants. It causes a browning between the veins of the leaves. It kills limbs from the tips and progresses down the branch quickly. Often incorrectly diagnosed as anthracnose. Apply the Sick Tree Treatment.

Black Spot

Common name of fungal leaf spot that attacks the foliage of plants such as roses. There is usually a yellow halo around the dark spot, then the entire leaf turns yellow and ultimately dies. Best controls include selection of resistant plants and the use of Garrett Juice plus potassium bicarbonate. Severe cases cause leaves to drop. Plant resistant cultivars, and compost all dropped leaves and trimmings. Mulch bare soil to prevent dirt and spores from being splashed up onto plants. Apply horticultural cornmeal to the soil and spray Garrett Juice with potassium bicarbonate. Spray with compost tea and cornmeal juice.

Black Spot

Brown Patch in St. Augustine

Brown Patch

Chlorosis—maybe iron deficiency, maybe not. Trace mineral deficiencies in general can cause this symptom.

Blight

When plants suffer from blight, leaves and infected branches suddenly wither, stop growing, die, and may rot. Drench the soil with neem. See also Early Blight and Fire Blight.

Brown Patch

Cool-weather fungal disease of St. Augustinegrass. Brown leaves pull loose easily from the runners. Small spots in lawn grow into large circles or free forms that look bad and weaken the turf but rarely kill the grass. Potassium bicarbonate is a curative spray; soil health, drainage, and low nitrogen input are the best preventatives. Apply cornmeal at 20 lbs. per 1,000 sq. ft.

Canker

A stress-related disease of trees and shrubs that causes decay of the bark and wood. Cankers have to start with a wound through the bark. Fungicides do not work on this disease. Hypoxolyn canker is a common disease of certain oaks, such as stressed post oaks, especially after droughts or long rainy seasons. The brown spores rub off easily, and the bark sloughs off the trunks. No treatment is necessary other than improving the immune system of the tree. This is the number-one disease seen on post oaks. The stress leading to this disease is often caused by herbicide treatment to the root zone. Look for cracks, sunken areas, or raised areas of dead or abnormal tissue on woody stems. Cankers ooze sometimes and can girdle shoots or trunks, causing the plant above the canker to wilt and die. Blights and canker diebacks look quite similar. Cold-injury symptoms can look like or lead to the development of cankers. Healthy soil and plants are the best solution. Use Garrett Goop on the injured spots, improve the environmental conditions, and apply the Sick Tree Treatment.

Chlorosis

A condition caused in various plants by trace mineral deficiency. Iron scarcity is usually blamed, but the cause can be the lack of several trace minerals or magnesium. To cure—improve trace mineral availability by applying greensand, humate, Volcanite, or Earth's Fortune organic fertilizer and by foliar feeding. One of the most effective products is Medina Air/Ground Treatment. After minerals are applied, spread a natural mulch for continued control.

Construction Damage

Construction activity causes compaction of the soil, which squeezes out oxygen and kills beneficial microbes and root hairs of trees and other plants. Prevent it—don't allow it—use physical barriers. Build strong fences so contractors cannot access the root zone.

Cotton Root Rot

A fungal disease common in alkaline soils that attacks poorly adapted plants. The best preventative is healthy soil with a balance of nutrients and soil biology. Adding sulfur to the soil at 5 lbs. per 1,000 sq. ft. annually will help. Do annual soil tests and stop when enough sulfur is in the soil. Products that contain sodium will sometimes help. Cornmeal and living organism products will also help. The Sick Tree Treatment is the best solution. In no-till agriculture, the organic content comes up. Cotton root rot is a disease created by humans, since the application of chemicals destroyed the soil and humus. Apply compost, rock powders, and humates.

Damping-Off on lavender

Downy Mildew on tomato plant

Sick Red Tip Photinia

Curly Top

A viral disease that attacks vegetable crops such as tomatoes. To prevent, control the aphids that spread the disease. Use shiny material such as silver mylar under plants. Drench soil with neem product. Spray with Garrett Juice plus garlic tea.

Damping-Off

Fungal disease of emerging seedlings. Small plants fall over as if burned at the ground line. A disease caused by a number of fungi, mainly *Pythium, Rhizoctonia,* and *Phytophthora.* The symptoms include decay of seeds prior to germination, rot of seedlings before emergence from the root medium, and development of stem rot at the soil line after emergence. The collapse of seedlings at or just below soil level is usually caused by bad handling, overcrowding, or poor drainage. Mix cornmeal into the planting mix or dust the surface of the soil after germination with the cornmeal.

Downy Mildew

Fungal disease that attacks fruits, vegetables, flowers, and grasses. Symptom is a white to purple downy growth, usually on the underside of leaves and along stems, which turns black with age. Upper leaf surfaces become pale. It can overwinter on infected plant parts and remain viable in the soil for several years. It is spread by wind and rain and in seeds. To control, thoroughly compost infected leaves that have fallen and apply cornmeal to the soil surface. Spray with Garrett Juice plus cornmeal juice.

Early Blight

A fungal disease that primarily infects ornamental plants, vegetables, tomatoes, potatoes, and peppers. Brown to black spots form and enlarge on lower leaves, developing concentric rings like a target. Heavily infected leaves dry up and die as spots grow together. Targetlike, sunken spots will sometimes develop on tomato branches and stems. Both fruits and tubers can also develop dark, sunken spots. Control this disease by planting resistant cultivars and soaking seed in a disinfecting solution such as a hydrogen peroxide mixture before planting. Spray plants with compost tea, and treat soil with cornmeal products. Spray cornmeal juice.

Entomosporium Leaf Spot

A fungal disease of photinia, hawthorns, and other related plants. It primarily hits large monoculture plantings and is most active in spring and fall. It shows up on the foliage as round, dark purple spots. It can be controlled by improving soil conditions and avoiding susceptible plants. Potassium bicarbonate spray or cornmeal juice will stop the spotting on the leaves if caught early. Try to avoid watering the foliage. Improving the health of the root system with aeration, compost, and rock powder is the long-range cure. Products containing alfalfa will also help. Use the Sick Tree Treatment for ultimate control. Spraying toxic chemical fungicides is a total waste of time and money.

Fungal Leaf Spot on photinia

Fungal Leaf Spot on red oak

Fire Blight on pear tree

Herbicide damage on yaupon

Fire Blight

A bacterial disease of plants in the rose family in which blossoms, new shoots, twigs, and limbs die back as though they have been burned. Leaves usually remain attached but often turn black or dark brown. Prune back to healthy tissue and disinfect pruning tools with hydrogen peroxide. At first sign of disease, spray plants with Garrett Juice plus garlic or neem. Consan 20 and agricultural streptomycin are also effective controls. Kocide 101 is a copper-based fungicide often recommended. Some consider this organic, but I don't. The best recommendation is to spray Garrett Juice plus garlic, treat the soil with horticultural cornmeal, apply the Sick Tree Treatment, and reduce the nitrogen fertilizer. High-nitrogen synthetic fertilizers are the primary cause of this disease.

Fungal Diseases

Fungi are the microbes that are the easiest to see with the naked eye. They are sometimes seen as round or free-form shapes on plant foliage. Downy mildew grows from within a plant and sends out branches through the stomata to create pale patches on leaves. Powdery mildew lives on the leaf surface and sends hollow tubes into the plants. Rust fungi are named for the reddish color of their pustules. Leaf spot fungi cause yellow-green spots with black exterior rings. Soil-inhabiting fungi cause damping-off, which kills small seedlings. Many fungi are encouraged by constant moisture on foliage. All fungal problems can be controlled with adapted plants, cornmeal products, and Garrett Juice. Other effective tools include potassium bicarbonate, baking soda, milk, and neem.

Fungal Leaf Spot

See Entomosporium Leaf Spot.

Fusarium and Verticillium Wilt

Fungal diseases that attack a wide range of flowers, vegetables, fruits, and ornamentals. Plants wilt and usually turn yellow. To control, plant resistant cultivars and treat with cornmeal products. Remove affected branches and thoroughly compost them or the entire plants. Spray with Garrett Juice plus potassium bicarbonate or cornmeal juice.

Gray Leaf Spot

A disease of St. Augustinegrass that forms gray vertical spots on the grass blades. A light baking soda spray is the best curative. Prevent by improving soil health, applying cornmeal, and spraying Garrett Juice.

Herbicide Damage

Most, if not all, of the toxic chemical herbicides can cause plant problems. Contact killers and the pre-emergents can kill the beneficial fungi and the feeder roots of trees as well as foliage. Symptoms can look similar to oak wilt. That may be exactly what we are seeing in some oak wilt areas. Detox the soil with Garrett Juice and orange oil. To save trees and shrubs, use the Sick Tree Treatment after applying an activated-carbon product like NORIT.

Herbicide damage from spraying the Asian jasmine with Roundup

Iron deficiency on photinia

Juniper dieback

Mistletoe

Mistletoe on cedar elm

Iron Deficiency

A nutrient deficiency that causes leaves to turn yellow with the veins remaining green. In an advanced stage, the leaves are totally yellow, and then dead. Treat with Texas greensand and compost or the entire Sick Tree Treatment. Insufficient iron in plants is characterized by striped, yellow, or colorless areas on young leaves. The growth of new shoots is affected, and plant tissues may die. Lack of other trace minerals can also cause this problem. Magnesium deficiency, for example, looks identical and is more common.

Juniper Dieback

Fungal disease of cedars and junipers. Also called twig dieback. Spores look like a yellow worm oozing out. Treat by pick-pruning and mulching. Spray Garrett Juice plus potassium bicarbonate. Best solution: stop planting ill-adapted junipers.

Leaf Spots

A cosmetic disease of oaks and elms. No control is needed. Many different fungi can cause spots on the leaves, but most of them are of little consequence. A typical spot has a definite edge and often has a darker border. When lots of spots are present, they can grow together and become a blight or a blotch. Fungal spots are usually round or free-form in shape.

Lichen

Lichen is a growth seen on rocks and the trunks of trees that is actually two plants. Commonly growing in flat greenish, gray, brown, yellow, or black patches, lichen consists of algae and fungi that live together in a symbiotic relationship. The fungi absorb and conserve moisture and provide shelter. The algae conduct photosynthesis, growing and providing protein for the fungus.

Lightning Damage

If your tree gets hit by lightning, keep your fingers crossed. Install lightning protection to prevent future damage. There are two kinds of lightning damage. When the lightning travels along the outside of the tree in the rainwater, bark is knocked off but damage is usually minimal. If the lightning goes through the center of the tree, the bark is blown off and the tree is a goner. For the former, apply the Sick Tree Treatment.

Mistletoe

Tree parasite that primarily attacks sick, stressed trees. Physical removal and soil health is the long-term control. Remove entire infested limbs where practical. Apply black pruning paint to large wounds and apply the Sick Tree Treatment. This is the only case where I recommend the use of pruning paint. In most cases, it prevents growth and hurts the plant. In this case, it helps prevent the regrowth of the mistletoe.

Molds

Fungi that have a powdery or woolly appearance on the surface of the infected part. Botrytis thrives in moist conditions and is often seen on dropped flower petals or overripe fruit. Look for a thick gray mold or water-soaked spots on petals, leaves, or stems. It first infects dead or dying tissue, so removing faded flowers and blighted buds or shoots helps control the problem. Peonies, tulips, and lilies are sensitive in wet weather. Remove and compost infected material. Space, prune, and support plants to encourage good air movement. Spray plants with Garrett Juice plus potassium bicarbonate or cornmeal juice.

Oak Leaf Blister on live oak

Root Knot Nematodes on tomato roots

Nematodes

Root knot nematodes are plant-damaging, microscopic, unsegmented, parasitic worms. Some are harmful, and some are beneficial. Some nematodes attack plant roots and greatly reduce production. Nematode-invasion symptoms include wilt, reduced growth, lack of vigor, and other problems. Control measures involve crop rotation, enriching the soil with compost, and planting pest-free stock. Liquid biostimulants help. Citrus pulp and sesame tilled into the soil prior to planting have shown good results. A few types are barely visible to the naked eye. Larvae that hatch from eggs molt several times before maturing to adults. Troublesome nematodes puncture plant cell walls, inject saliva, and suck out the cell's contents. Some species move from plant to plant in water or on garden tools; others attach themselves permanently to one root. Some nematodes cause excessive branching of roots, rotted roots, or enlarged lumps on roots. Other nematodes simply reduce the size of root systems. Carrots and other root crop plants will be stunted or have yellowed leaves, and roots may be distorted or have swollen areas. Legumes are supposed to have swellings on their roots that are caused by nitrogen-fixing bacteria. The difference is that the bacteria nodules are attached to the outside of the root. Nematodes swell from the inside.

Tilling orange peelings into the soil is often the most effective control. Till or fork citrus pulp into soil prior to planting, or gently work it into the root zone of existing plants. Stimulate soil biology with compost, organic fertilizers, and microbe stimulators. Cedar flakes used in the mulch of outdoor gardens and as the floor material in greenhouses repel nematodes effectively.

Oak Leaf Blister

A rare disease that needs no control. It usually results from a heavy rainy season. Leaves change from light green to a light brown dry blister and this only happens in isolated spots on the tree.

Oak Wilt veinal necrosis on live oak (Texas Department of Agriculture)

Oak Wilt fungal mat on red oak (Texas Department of Agriculture)

Crack over Oak Wilt fungal mat on red oak (Texas Department of Agriculture)

Oak Wilt

A disease of the vascular system of oak trees that is transmitted through the air by insects and through the root system of neighboring trees by natural grafting. Apply the Sick Tree Treatment—see Appendix. Oak wilt attacks red oaks and live oaks, especially when they occur in large monocultures and are treated with synthetic fertilizers and pesticides. The disease on red oaks shows up first as greasy green leaves that then turn brown, starting on the ends; this change is usually seen on one limb at a time. Live oak leaves have veinal necrosis (brown veins and green in between). Some leaves will be dead on the end half. Red oaks have sweet-smelling fungal mats on the trunks. Dutch elm disease is closely related. I do not recommend injecting fungicides into trees, and I don't recommend removing trees that are near sick trees. The chemical injection hurts the tree, wastes money, and doesn't address the real problem. This procedure has been pushed by Texas A&M and the Texas Forest Service for many years, but I have yet to hear anyone report that the fungicide injections have ever saved a single infected tree.

Biodiversity and soil health are the best deterrents. The disease is supposedly spread in the spring by a small beetle called nitidulid. There are probably many other possible vectors. Some people advise painting pruning cuts of live oak and red oak in the spring. I'm not so sure this is important. If you do, use Lac Balsam or natural shellac.

Peach Leaf Curl

A fungal disease of peaches, nectarines, and almonds that causes leaves to be puckered and pale or reddish at first, but later in the season they will turn pale green, shrivel, and drop off. The leaf's midrib doesn't grow, causing the leaves to become puckered and curled. This disease also causes deformed, thickened leaves and can affect the quality and quantity of the fruit crop. Fruit may have a reddish, irregular, rough surface, and the tree may have decreased fruit production. Spray Garrett Juice plus garlic tea in the late winter as the buds begin to swell and again in autumn when the leaves begin to fall.

Pecan Scab
See Scab

Phytophthora on periwinkles

Phytophthora on periwinkles

Powdery Mildew on phlox

Phytophthora

A common fungal disease in periwinkles that are being grown using synthetic fertilizers and pesticides. Beneficial microbes in healthy organic soil will normally keep this disease organism under control. Lilacs, rhododendrons, azaleas, and some hollies are sometimes infected by *Phytophthora* fungi. Plants suffer shoot dieback and develop stem cankers. Prune to remove infected branches and to increase air movement. Add compost and rock powders to the soil. In healthy soil, plants rarely have this problem. On peppers, potatoes, and tomatoes, *Phytophthora* infection is also known as late blight. The first symptom is water-soaked spots on the lower leaves or stems that enlarge and develop a white downy growth. Dark-colored blotches, sometimes like sunken lesions, penetrate the flesh of tubers. During a wet season, plants will rot and die. *Phytophthora* overwinter on underground parts and in plant debris. To control, compost all infected plants and tubers, presoak seed in a disinfecting solution such as hydrogen peroxide, and plant resistant cultivars. Sprays of potassium bicarbonate can help control outbreaks during wet weather. This is the disease that has greatly reduced the use of periwinkles as a bedding plant. Creating healthy soil through the use of compost, organic fertilizers, and rock powders will control the pathogen. Good drainage is critical. Horticultural cornmeal is effective on this disease. Wait to plant susceptible plants until the soil is warm in the early summer.

Pierce's Disease

A bacterial disease of grapes. It lives on but does not infect alfalfa, blackberries, cedar elm, grasses, red oaks, and willows. Leafhoppers are one of the main vectors. Management includes removal of host plants around vineyards and stimulation of beneficial microorganisms. This is a stress problem caused by pushing the plants with too much fertilizer and pesticides. It rarely happens in an organic program. Also called xylella. Treatment includes aerated compost tea and hydrogen peroxide.

Pine Tip Blight

A pine disease that forms black bumps on the needles. It resembles pine tip moth damage and can be controlled with the Sick Tree Treatment.

Potassium Deficiency

Potassium deficiency causes reduced vigor and poor plant growth. Frequently, the older leaves turn white and curl, later becoming bronzed. Severe deficiencies cause poorly developed root systems. To treat deficiencies, add rock, granite dust, wood ash, or other potassium-rich organic material to the compost and directly to the soil. Heavy consistent mulching also helps maintain the potassium supply.

Powdery Mildew

Fungal disease causing a white or gray powdery growth on the lower leaf surface and flower buds of zinnias, crape myrtles, many vegetables, phlox, lilac, melons, cucumbers, and many other plants. It is common during cool, humid, cloudy days. Leaves turn yellow on the top. Controls include baking soda spray, potassium bicarbonate, neem, garlic, and horticultural oil. Garrett Juice plus garlic tea is best for long-term results. Treat soil with horticultural cornmeal and use the entire Sick Tree Treatment for serious problems. This disease can cause long-term weakness when it occurs early in the growing season. This common fungal disease is increased by humidity but is actually deterred by water. Spray neem every seven days for severe cases.

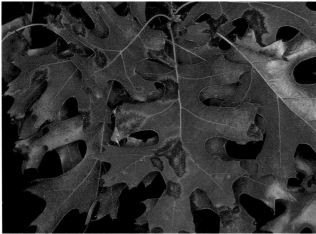

Red Oak Fungus

Rust on beans (*Agricultural Research*, USDA)

Sapsucker damage on ginkgo

Pecan Scab

Pythium

A fungal pathogen that's a water mold, soil inhabitant, and common cause of root rot and damping-off of seedlings. Horticultural cornmeal is the best treatment.

Red Oak Fungus

Fungal disease of red oak that happens primarily in humid, rainy weather and is mostly a cosmetic concern only. Make sure trees aren't planted too low and aren't being overwatered. Spray foliage with compost tea plus potassium bicarbonate or cornmeal juice.

Root and Stem Rot

These rots can usually be controlled with good drainage, good air circulation, and healthy soil. Plant healthy plants. Compost all infected plant material. Be careful to watch for physical injury, which may invite problems on woody plants. Treat soil with horticultural cornmeal.

Rust

Fungal disease that forms orange spots on the surface of foliage. Pustules form on the underside of leaves. This is mostly a cosmetic disease but can be treated with Garrett Juice mixed with garlic tea, potassium bicarbonate, or cornmeal juice. Rusts require two different plant species as hosts to complete their life cycle.

Sapsuckers

Beautiful birds that attack and severely damage stressed trees. Sick trees build up complex carbohydrates or sugars as a defense against their stressed condition. The birds can detect that condition and go after the sweet sap. Spray the trunks with garlic-pepper tea, apply the Sick Tree Treatment, and treat wounds with Garrett Goop.

Scab

Fungal disease that causes fruit, leaves, and tubers to develop areas of hardened and sometimes cracked tissue. Fruit scab can be a major problem on apples and peaches. Compost fallen leaves, prune to increase air movement, and spray during the growing season with cornmeal juice. Regular sprays of garlic and seaweed will also help. Compost tea is also beneficial, and horticultural cornmeal should be applied to the soil.

Smut on corn   Sooty Mold on orange tree

Slime Flux

Slime flux is the foul-smelling sap that oozes out of wounds in trunks of trees such as elm, maple, and birch. The sap ferments and produces chemicals that kill the bark. If the seepage continues over a period of a month or more, considerable injury and even death to the bark will occur. Apply Tree Trunk Goop to the wounds and then use the entire Sick Tree Treatment.

Slime Mold

Turf fungal disease that is mostly cosmetic. Slime mold spore masses coat the grass and look like cigarette ash on the surface of the blades. The spores can be easily wiped off. Remove the mold spores from the grass by rinsing with water during dry weather, or mowing and raking at any time. Baking soda spray or potassium bicarbonate will kill it. So will cornmeal.

Smut

Fungal diseases of grasses, grains, and corn. Corn smut attacks kernels, tassels, stalks, and leaves. Smut galls ripen, rupture, and release spores through the air to infect other plants and overwinter in the soil. Select resistant cultivars, remove and compost galls before they break open, and rotate crops.

Sooty Mold

Black fungal growth on the foliage of plants such as gardenias, crape myrtles, and other plants infested with aphids, scale, or whiteflies. Sooty mold is caused by the honeydew (excrement) of the insect pests. Best treatment is the release of beneficial insects to control the pest bugs. Also spray Garrett Juice plus garlic or garlic-pepper tea. Treat soil with horticultural cornmeal and use the entire Sick Tree Treatment.

St. Augustine Decline (SAD)

Virus common in St. Augustinegrass that causes a yellow mottling. The grass slowly dies away. The answer is to replace turf with a healthier grass and to plant a mix of native grass, wildflowers, and herbs.

Take-All Patch in St. Augustine

Virus disease

Take-All Patch (Bermuda Decline)

A disease that can attack several species of grass. It is caused by the fungus *Gaeumannomyces graminis* var. *graminis,* and is mostly found in St. Augustinegrass but can also cause problems in Bermudagrass. It is most active during the fall, winter, and spring, especially during moist weather. The first symptom is often yellow leaves and dark roots. Area of discolored and dying leaves will be circular to irregular in shape and up to 20' in diameter, and thinning occurs. Unlike brown patch, the leaves of take-all–infected plants do not easily separate from the plant when pulled. Stolons will often have discolored areas with brown to black roots. Regrowth of the grass into the affected area is often slow and unsuccessful because the new growth becomes infected. Controlling take-all patch is said to be difficult, but it isn't with organic techniques. Good surface and subsurface drainage is important. Cut back on watering and fertilizing. Use only organic fertilizers. If soil compaction exists, aeration will help to alleviate this condition and allow the grass to establish a deeper, more vigorous root system. Prevent take-all patch by maintaining healthy soil. Control the active disease by aeration, cornmeal and compost applications, and the Basic Organic Program.

Tree Decline

A generic term referring to a sick, declining tree. Not a specific disease but rather a compound result of one or more of the following: planting an ill-adapted tree, construction damage, drought, lightning strike, using synthetic fertilizers, chemical contamination, soil compaction, or other contributing factors.

Viruses

The smallest and most difficult to control of all microorganism pathogens. Plastic mulch reflects ultraviolet light that repels insects that carry various devastating diseases, including viral diseases. University research has shown that using silver-colored plastic mulch under tomatoes and other plants provides significant insect control. Although it may work, I don't really like it as much as natural mulch. Mosaic viruses destroy chlorophyll, causing leaf yellowing. Another virus blocks the plant's vascular system, restricting the flow of water and nutrients. Control usually involves eliminating infected plants. There is little that can be done to restore the health of a virus-infected plant. Viruses are transmitted by vegetative propagation, in seeds, on pollen, and on tools and gardeners' hands. Viruses are also transmitted by insects, mites, nematodes, and parasitic plants. Viruses slow plant growth and reduce yields. Infected leaves may deform and develop mottling, streaking, or ring-shaped spots. Purchase certified plants, control insects that spread viruses, and remove and thoroughly compost all infected plants.

Wet Wood

Bacterial wet wood shows up as oozing cell sap, a white frosty material that attracts insects. Increase the tree's health so it can wall off the problem area. Use the Sick Tree Treatment.

Wilt

When fungi or bacteria clog a plant's water-conducting or vascular system, they can cause permanent wilting and death. Wilt symptoms may resemble those of blights.

Wind Damage

Don't overprune. Remember that heavy pruning is weakening and detrimental to tree health. Pruning is done for your benefit, not the tree's benefit.

Wood Rot

These rots are usually the result of physical injury and normally don't kill healthy trees. Remove decaying or dead wood and treat the wound with Garrett Goop. Don't cut back into healthy tissue. That only spreads the decay. Don't use pruning paint—leave it exposed to air to speed healing.

Xylella

A xylem-limited disease or bacteria that plugs the vascular system of elms, oaks, sycamore, pecans, and other trees. It looks like heat stress damage and can easily be diagnosed by lab tests. This is the bacterial disease that is attacking oleanders. It is also called Pierce's disease, which attacks grape vines. Use the Sick Tree Treatment.

OTHER BEASTS IN THE GARDEN

Bats and Purple Martins

Bats in most regions can outnumber purple martins as much as one hundred to one. They also eat far more mosquitoes. They come up from their winter homes in Mexico about the same time the martins arrive in the spring, but they stay three to four months longer than the birds do. Purple martins are beautiful and their songs are pleasant, but they do little to control insect pests.

Bats, on the other hand, are important to the ecosystem, especially in insect control. One bat can eat about 600 mosquitoes and other night-flying insects per hour. Bats also help to pollinate flowers by feeding on plant nectar and pollen.

There are many misconceptions and outright falsehoods about bats. Bats aren't evil. They don't suck blood from your neck—the only blood-loving bats are the vampire bats that live in Latin America. Bats are interesting furry mammals with large wings.

Bats are intelligent, friendly, gentle, clean, and little if any health threat. They cause fewer incidents of rabies than do cats and dogs. More people die from dog attacks annually than have died in history from contact with bats. Because of the misunderstandings about these wonderfully helpful creatures, their populations have been dwindling all over the world.

Nectar-eating bats aid the pollination primarily of tropical fruits in warm regions but also of the agave plant from which tequila is made.

Anyone interested in receiving more information about our furry flying friends can write or call Bat Conservation International at P.O. Box 162603, Austin, Texas 78716, (512) 327-9721.

An excellent book on bats is *The Bat in My Pocket* by Amanda Lollar. This book and other educational information are available from the non-profit organization she runs called Bat World, located at 217 N. Oak, Mineral Wells, Texas 76067, (817) 325-3404.

Bat Houses

Bat houses work best in a location within 1,000 ft. of water. Insect populations will be higher around water. The houses should be oriented toward the east or southeast so they warm up quickly in the morning.

Armadillo trap with guide boards

Lava gravel mulch used to prevent squirrel digging

Hang them in an unobstructed spot, side of building or pole, 12' to 15' above the ground, but not too close to your living quarters because bat guano will accumulate underneath and it has a strongly sweet and powerful aroma. Bat guano is very high in nitrogen and great for your garden soil. An excellent publication on bat houses is *The Bat House Builders Handbook* by Merlin Tuttle and Donna L. Hensley. It is distributed by the University of Texas Press, P.O. Box 7819, Austin, Texas 78713-7819. Bat World in Mineral Wells also provides plans in exchange for a small donation and sells state-of-the-art bat houses.

Mice, Rabbits, Armadillos, Beavers, and Other Beasts
To discourage these animals, use Havahart Deer and Mice Repellent or other approved organic repellents. Live traps may also be used. Each case should be dealt with on an individual basis. Human hair and dog clippings from the groom shop will repel some of these critters. Hang in nylon bags or bury just under the soil surface.

Cats in Beds and Squirrels in Pots
Orange peelings have been reported to repel cats, but mulch is the solution. Mulch the soil with pointy material like sweetgum balls, rose or blackberry trimmings, or lava gravel. Lava gravel may be the best choice, but do not put plastic under it.

Deer
These are difficult animals to control, and electric fences are sometimes needed. We have received reports of success spraying garlic-pepper tea as a repellent. The commercial product Liquid Fence, although smelly, seems to work.

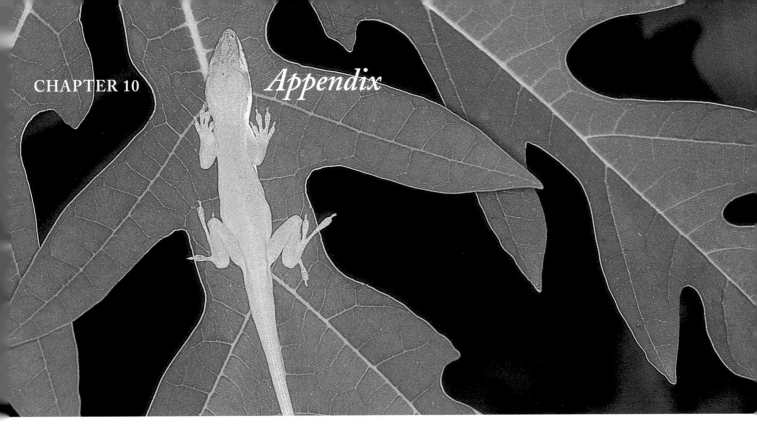

CHAPTER 10

Appendix

FORMULAS

Garrett Juice:

You can buy Garden-Ville Garrett Juice commercially or you can make your own. The concentrate formula is as follows:

1 gallon compost tea or liquid humate
1 pint liquid seaweed
1 pint apple cider vinegar
1 pint molasses

Note: For additional power, add corn juice (see below) and lava water (soak 1 cup lava sand in 1 gallon of water).

Use 1½ cups of concentrate per gallon of water.

Garrett Juice (Ready to Use)

1 gallon water
1 cup compost tea
1 oz. liquid seaweed
1 oz. apple cider vinegar
1 oz. molasses

Note: Be sure always to shake these products well before spraying to avoid burning plants.

Fire Ant Control Drench

Add 2 oz. of orange oil per gallon to the ready-to-use Garrett Juice formula. This mix can also be used as a general purpose insecticide spray.

Vinegar Herbicide

Full-strength vinegar (10%–20%)

2 oz. orange oil or d-limonene per gallon of vinegar

1 teaspoon liquid soap or other clean surfactant per gallon of vinegar

Note: Do not use products that contain glacial acetic acid. Use natural or ethyl-alcohol-based vinegars.

Garlic-Pepper Tea Insect Repellent

In a blender with water, liquefy two bulbs of garlic and two cayenne or habanero peppers. Strain away the solids. Pour the garlic-pepper juice into a one-gallon container. Fill the remaining volume with water to make one gallon of concentrate. Shake well before using and add ¼ cup of the concentrate to each gallon of water in the sprayer. To make garlic tea, simply omit the pepper and add another bulb of garlic. For additional power, add 1 oz. each of seaweed and molasses to each gallon. Always use plastic containers with loose-fitting lids for storage.

Sick Tree Treatment

First of all, make sure that your tree is not planted too low. If there is no root flare showing above the ground, chances are it's too low. Use a hard rake or hire an arborist to use an air spade to remove the excess soil above the actual top of the root ball. Expose the root flare and root ball top and leave the area dished with only shredded bark added. Now for the rest of the Sick Tree Treatment:

Trunk injections do more damage than good.

Tree Trunk Goop applied to damaged tree

1. Aerate the root zone heavily. Start between the dripline and the trunk and go far out beyond the dripline. A 7"–12" depth for the aeration holes is ideal, but any depth is beneficial. An alternative is to spray the root zone with a living organism product such as Bio-Inoculant or AgriGro.

2. Apply Texas greensand at about 40–80 lbs./1,000 sq. ft., lava sand at about 40–80 lbs./1,000 sq. ft., horticultural cornmeal at about 10–20 lbs./1,000 sq. ft., and sugar or dry molasses at about 5 lbs./1,000 sq. ft. Cornmeal is a natural disease fighter, and sugar is a carbon source to feed the microbes in the soil. A cornmeal, wheat bran, and molasses product from Alliance Milling can also be used.

3. Apply a 1" layer of compost followed by a 3"–5" layer of shredded native tree trimmings. Native cedar is the very best source for mulch.

4. Spray the foliage and soil monthly, or more often if possible, with Garrett Juice (see formula above). For large-scale farms and ranches, a onetime spraying is beneficial if the budget doesn't allow ongoing sprays. Adding garlic tea to the spray is also beneficial while the tree is in trouble.

5. Stop using high-nitrogen fertilizers and toxic chemical pesticides. The pesticides kill the beneficial nematodes and insects. The fake fertilizers are destructive to the important mycorrhizal fungi on the roots.

A premix of lava, greensand, and compost is now available from the organic suppliers. All you'll have to add is cornmeal and topdressing mulch.

Since the fungal mats form on red oaks only, not on live oaks, the live oak wood can be used for firewood without any worry of spreading the oak wilt disease. Red oak wood needs to be stacked in a sunny location and covered with clear plastic to form a greenhouse effect to kill the beetles and fungal mats. When oaks are shredded into mulch, the aeration kills the pathogens and eliminates the possibility of disease spread. That goes for all species.

Tree Trunk Goop

Mix equal parts of each of the following in water: soft rock phosphate, natural diatomaceous earth, and manure compost. Slop it on the trunk. *Note:* Fireplace ashes can be substituted for the soft rock phosphate. Replace it if rain or irrigation washes it off. For any physical damage to trunks, spray with hydrogen peroxide and then treat wounds with Tree Trunk Goop. If you don't have manure—use compost tea. Raw linseed oil can be added to make the material stay on the trunk much longer.

Notes

All foliar-feeding sprays should have a pH of 6.0 or less for best efficacy. Lower the high pH of water by adding vinegar.

GARDENING
BY THE MOON

Because weather is so unpredictable, some gardeners and even farmers of large acreage are fairly successful by letting the moon phases dictate when to plant. For example, if soil conditions permit, they always plant potatoes in the period between the third and seventh day after the full moon in February.

Even though some scientists still reject the notion of moon-sign planting, moon gardening makes the hobby still more fun. There is a good lunar gardening guide on the market, *Llewellyn's Moon Sign Book,* published annually. This book is useful for deciding planting dates, but it doesn't tell you about variety, seasons, soil types, and the many other things you need to know about vegetable growing. Maybe, just maybe, moon-sign planting can stack the odds in our favor in the when-to-plant gamble!

Here are the most common general recommendations:

SOIL TYPES

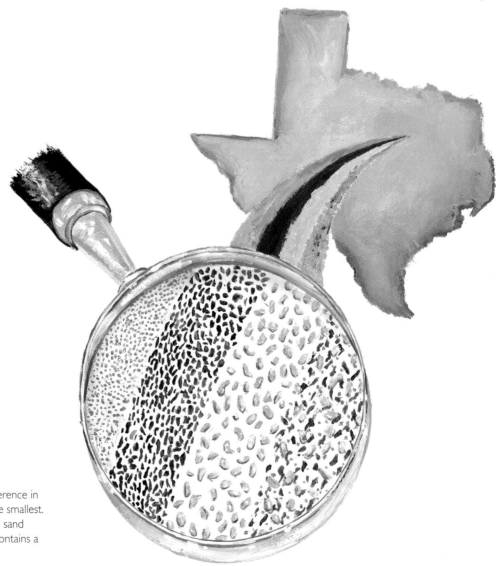

Close examination shows the difference in soil particle sizes. Clay particles are smallest. Silt particles are intermediate, and sand particles are coarsest. Loam soil contains a blend of all three sizes.

New moon to first quarter:
Plant the seeds of above-ground crops that have external seed. Plants in this
  category include asparagus, broccoli, Brussels sprouts, cabbage, cauliflower, strawberries, celery, grains, leeks, lettuce, parsley, and spinach. Pick
  the most appropriate sign for the specific crop: Cancer, Scorpio, Taurus,
  Libra, or Pisces.

First quarter to full moon:
Plant above-ground food crops and flowers that contain seed within a fruit
  or pod. This is the quarter for planting beans, melons, squash, cucumbers,
  tomatoes, grapes, and peppers. The best signs are Cancer, Scorpio, and
  Pisces, followed by Taurus, Capricorn, and Libra.

Full moon to last quarter:
Plant bulbs and root crops, along with biennials and perennials that need
  strong roots. Plants in this category include beets, carrots, turnips, garlic,
  onions, and radishes, and they do well when planted in Pisces, Taurus,
  Capricorn, or Libra.

Last quarter to new moon:
If you must plant, do so in a fruitful sign. It's better to spend time weeding,
  cultivating, and controlling pests in a barren sign.

AVERAGE FIRST FREEZE DATES—FALL

City	Date	City	Date
Amarillo	October 24	Kerrville	November 6
Austin	November 22	Lubbock	November 3
Corpus Christi	December 15	McAllen	December 8
Dallas	November 13	Port Arthur	November 16
El Paso	November 12	San Antonio	November 26
Galveston	December 25	Texarkana	November 11
Houston	December 11	Wichita Falls	November 11

AVERAGE LAST FREEZE DATES—SPRING

City	Date	City	Date
Amarillo	April 17	Kerrville	April 6
Austin	March 18	Lubbock	April 9
Corpus Christi	February 9	McAllen	February 9
Dallas	March 23	Port Arthur	March 11
El Paso	March 9	San Antonio	March 15
Galveston	January 24	Texarkana	March 21
Houston	February 14	Wichita Falls	March 27

**AVERAGE DATE OF
FIRST FROST**

**AVERAGE DATE
OF LAST FROST**

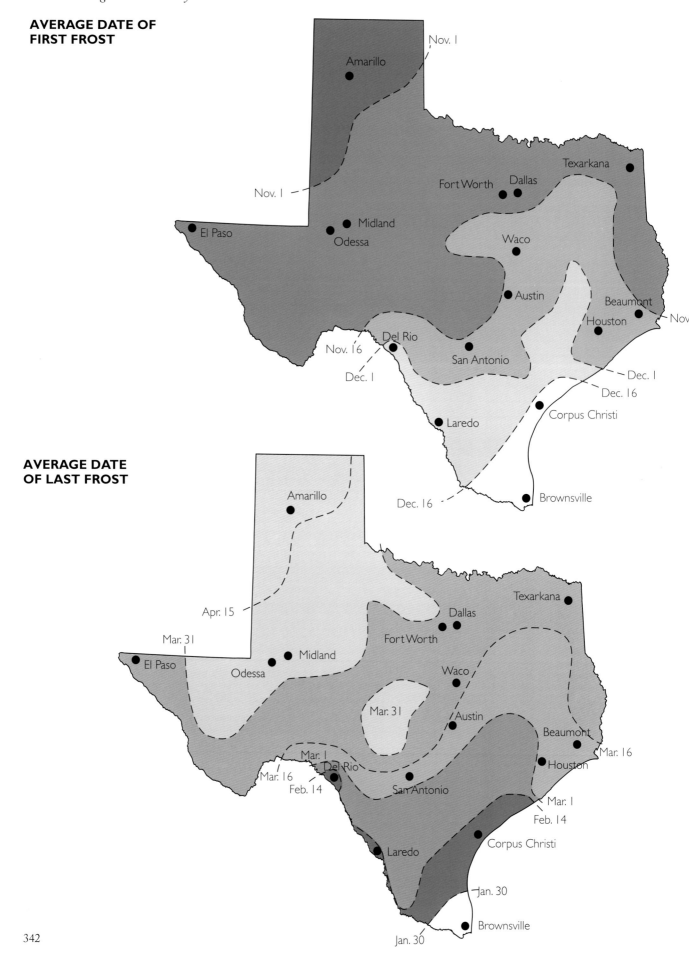

GARDENING REGIONS

RANGES OF AVERAGE MINUMUM TEMPERATURES

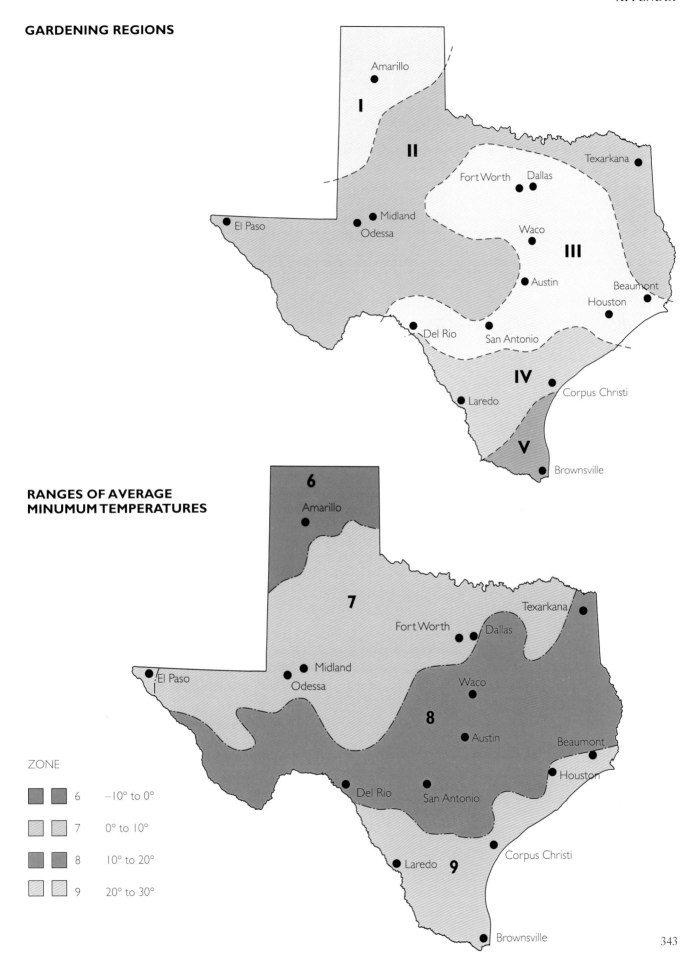

ZONE

	6	−10° to 0°
	7	0° to 10°
	8	10° to 20°
	9	20° to 30°

343

ORGANIC FERTILIZERS AND SOIL AMENDMENTS

Alfalfa Meal

Alfalfa provides many nutritional benefits not only for plant use but for soil organisms as well. One very important ingredient is tricontanol, a powerful plant growth regulator. It can be applied dry or made into alfalfa tea and sprayed directly on plants as a foliar fertilizer. Alfalfa is very high in nutrients, vitamins, and valuable minerals. It also includes sugars, starches, proteins, fiber, and 16 amino acids. Use at 10–20 lbs. per 1,000 sq. ft.

Alfalfa Tea

In a five-gallon bucket, put one cup of alfalfa meal. Fill bucket with water and let it sit overnight. The result will be a thick tea. Apply generously to the root area of shrubs and flowers or use as a foliar spray after straining. Watch out for the smell, but this is a powerful tool.

Alliance Cornmeal Soil Amendment

This blend of 60 percent wheat bran and 30 percent cornmeal with 10 percent molasses is used at 10–50 lbs./100 sq. ft. as a source of nutrients and organic matter, and provides cornmeal's natural disease control. It can be used as the primary bed-prep material or mixed with any of the commonly recommended additions. It is also an excellent mild organic fertilizer. This company also sells the horticultural cornmeal by itself as well as an algae control product and a compost starter product.

Bat Guano

All-purpose natural fertilizer containing major nutrients and many trace elements. The analysis will vary with the age of the guano. It has fungicidal qualities and has almost no chance of being contaminated with pesticides or chemicals. It is an excellent supplemental fertilizer for most plants, but especially flowers. Best to apply once or twice during the growing season. It looks mild but has as much as 10 percent nitrogen, so be careful not to overuse.

Bioform

Liquid products that contain fish, seaweed, molasses, and dry products that include poultry manure and other natural ingredients. Bioform 4-2-4, with 3 percent sulfur, is the totally organic product. Bioform 8-8-8 contains some urea. Bioform Dry 5-3-4, with 1 percent sulfur, is a powerful natural fertilizer. A 40 lb. bag covers approximately 2,000 sq. ft.

Bioinoculant

General term for any product that stimulates beneficial biological activity. Specific products include Bio-Inoculant, Earthworm.

Biosolids

The politically correct term for sewer sludge. Most cities produce this product. It is the best of all organic fertilizers if not contaminated and should be used more often. It is also the most maligned of all organic fertilizers. Many so-called organic gardeners think this is an unacceptable product. Truth is, it's the most tested and controlled fertilizer on the market. Yes, there's a possibility for it to contain heavy metals and pesticides. That's a contamination problem that should be stopped before it gets to the composted material. However, the levels of contaminants in biosolid compost are very low from the competent companies.

Biostimulants
These are liquid or dry formulations that contain either microorganisms or materials that stimulate the native microbes in the soil. Included in this category are AgriGro, Agrispon, Bioform, F-68, Bio-Inoculant, Earthworm Lawn and Garden, Medina, and Garrett Juice.

Blood Meal
Organic source of nitrogen and phosphorous. Good to use as a mix with cottonseed meal. It's expensive but good to use occasionally. Analysis can range from 12-1-1 to 11-0-0. Does have a strong odor.

Bluebonnet Farms
Line of organic fertilizers and soil amendments including corn gluten meal, horticultural cornmeal, and trace mineral products.

Bone Meal
Source of calcium and phosphorous recommended for bulbs, tomatoes, and other vegetables. Analysis will range from 2-12-0 to 4-12-0, with 2–5 percent calcium. Soft rock phosphate is better and cheaper.

Bovinite
A peat moss replacement product made from dairy cow manure by the Erath Earth compost company. It is a clean, nutrient-rich, and biologically active material that is produced by the action of a liquid-handling cyclone device.

Bradfield
Bradfield's natural fertilizers are alfalfa based and blended with animal protein, natural potassium sulfate potash, and molasses. Approximate analysis is 3-1-5. They should be used at the rate of 20–30 lbs. per 1,000 sq. ft. Most broadcast spreaders, set fully open, will dispense this fertilizer at approximately 10 lbs. per 1,000 sq. ft. per pass.

Cattle Manure
Manure is one of our greatest natural resources. It has to be handled properly and not overused in any one area. Using too much of anything can cause problems. Manure can be properly used in several ways. Cow manure is a good ingredient for the manufacture of compost or for use directly on agricultural fields. It should be composted prior to using in the home vegetable garden.

Cedar Flakes

Good for repelling chiggers and fleas and for lowering the pH of the soil. An excellent material to use on the floor of greenhouses. Cedar flakes are an excellent control for harmful nematodes.

Chelators

Chelated iron and other chelated nutrients are used when a direct dose of a particular nutrient is needed to quickly solve a deficiency. Chelated products are organic compounds with attached inorganic metal molecules, which are more available for plant use. Compost, humus, humic acid, and microorganisms have natural chelating properties.

Chicken Litter

Chicken litter is a good natural fertilizer high in nitrogen. Pelletized forms are better because they are not as dusty. Approximate analysis is 6-4-2. Unfortunately, commercial chickens are still being fed lots of unnatural things, including arsenic. Best to compost before using.

Coffee Grounds

Excellent low-pH soil amendment. Best to compost with other materials. Collect grounds at home and from your local restaurant or coffee shop and use in the compost pile or apply directly to the soil at 20–80 lbs. per 1,000 sq. ft.

Compost

The best fertilizer and the key to any organic program. It is Nature's own product, high in nutrients, humus, humic acid, and microorganisms. Compost has magical healing and growing powers and can be used successfully on any and all plants. Analysis will vary due to ingredients. Compost can be made at home or purchased commercially. The best composts are those made from a variety of organic material such as hay, sawdust, paunch manure, leaves, twigs, bark, wood chips, dead plants, food scraps, pecan hulls, grass clippings, and animal manure. The best manure to use is whatever is locally available: chicken, turkey, cattle, horse, rabbit, etc.

The best composts are those that are made from several ingredients. The ideal mixture is 80 percent vegetative matter and 20 percent animal waste. The best materials are those that you have on your own property. The second best materials are those that are locally available.

Even though there are many recipes for compost, it's almost impossible to foul up the compost-making process. For new gardens or planting beds, the composting can be done in the ground by tilling raw organic matter into the soil and covering the surface with mulch. To use this method effectively, it's best to do the work at least six months prior to planting. Composting in the ground, as the forest does, takes longer than composting in a pile. Remember that composting is more of an art than a science, and a little experimenting is good. There are many acceptable ways to build compost piles, but I find that the simplest systems are usually the best.

The best time to compost is whenever the raw materials are available. It's ideal to have compost piles working year-round. Choose a convenient site—some easily accessible utility area such as behind the garage or in the dog run. The compost pile can be located in sun or shade, and covers are not necessary. The most effective compost piles are made on a paved surface so that the liquid leachate can be caught and used as a fertilizer. When the pile is on the ground, the leachate is wasted, but the earthworms can enter the pile and help complete the natural degradation of the material. So both methods work.

Next, decide what kind of a container to use. I don't use a container at all; instead, I just pile the material on the ground or on a concrete slab. Containers are only helpful if you have limited space.

It's controversial whether dog and cat manure should be used in the compost pile, but here's my take. If it was once alive, it can and should go in the compost pile. I used to go along with the crowd and say not to use greasy cooked food from the kitchen. But then . . . Earth to Howard: if it can't go into the compost pile, then you shouldn't have been eating it!

Materials should be chopped into variously sized pieces and thoroughly mixed together. Compost piles that contain nothing but one particle size will not breathe properly. Layering the ingredients, as most books recommend, is unnecessary unless it will help to get the proportions right. After the first turning, the layers are jostled and gone. Green plant material contains water and nitrogen and will break down faster than dry, withered materials. Add some native soil (a couple of shovelfuls) to each pile to inoculate the pile with native soil microorganisms. To thrive, microorganisms need: (1) an energy source, which is any carbon material such as leaves or wood; (2) a nitrogen source, such as manure, green foliage, or organic fertilizers; and (3) vitamins, which are stored in most living tissue.

Watering the pile thoroughly is important and best done while mixing the original ingredients. The proper moisture level is between 40 to 50 percent, similar to the wetness of a squeezed-out sponge. Piles that are too wet will be anaerobic and not decay properly. Piles that are too dry won't compost properly or fast enough. Once you have gotten the pile evenly moist, it's easy to maintain. Add a little water during dry periods. If you have ants or other insects in your compost pile, it's usually too dry or sloppy wet.

Turning the pile is important. It keeps the mixture aerobic by helping oxygen penetrate the material. Turning also ensures that all the ingredients are exposed to the beneficial fungi, bacteria, and other microorganisms that work to decay the raw material into humus. It also assures that all the ingredients are exposed to the cleansing heat at the center of the pile. In a properly "cooking" compost pile, the heat of approximately 150° kills the weed seeds and harmful pathogens but stimulates the beneficial microorganisms. Don't be concerned if your pile heats for a while and then cools off—that's natural. The entire process takes anywhere from two months to a year, depending on how often the pile is turned. Piles with high levels of nitrogen will compost faster. If the ingredients contain a high percentage of wood chips, the process may take even longer. It's interesting that softwood sawdust or chips break down slower than hardwood materials.

Compost activators help the pile heat up and cook faster. Many specific products exist and work, although almost any organic fertilizer can be used as a compost activator at the rate of 3–4 lbs. per cubic yard of compost.

Compost has many uses. Partially completed compost makes an effective topdressing mulch for ornamental plants and food crops. It's easy to tell when the compost is finished and ready to use as a fertilizer and soil amendment. The original material will no longer be identifiable, the texture will be soft and crumbly, and the fragrance will be rich and earthy.

Compost can be used to fertilize grass areas, planting beds, vegetable gardens, and potted plants. It is the only organic material I recommend for the preparation of new planting beds. It is better than pine bark or peat moss because it's alive, it contains mineral nutrients, and it's loaded with beneficial microorganisms. Peat moss and pine bark are lifeless and have little nutrient value.

Corn Gluten Meal

Corn gluten meal is a natural weed-and-feed fertilizer. It should be broadcast in the spring before weed germination to prevent grassburs, crabgrass, and other annuals. For the cool-season or winter weeds, broadcast again before germination in the fall at 15–20 lbs. per 1,000 sq. ft. for the control of henbit, dandelions, annual bluegrass, and other winter weeds. It also serves as a powerful organic fertilizer, having about 9–10 percent nitrogen.

Cornmeal

A food product that when used on the soil or in bed preparation functions as a natural fungal disease control. Use it at 10–20 lbs. per 1,000 sq. ft. to prevent or cure brown patch in St. Augustine, damping-off disease, fungal leaf spot, and other fungal diseases. This natural fungicide is a mild fertilizer and disease fighter that should be used until your soil gets healthy. It has also been strongly reported to help human and animal fungal skin diseases when mixed with water and applied wet. See my web site, www.dirtdoctor.com, for details.

Cornmeal Juice (Corn Juice)

Natural fungicide spray made by soaking cornmeal in water. Put about a cup of horticultural cornmeal per gallon of water in a nylon bag and soak for at least an hour. Add the milky liquid to compost tea or Garrett Juice and spray plant foliage.

Cottonseed Meal

A natural fertilizer with an acid pH. Analysis will vary and ranges from 6-2-1 to 7-2-2 with trace elements. It does have an odor, but it is a good organic source of nitrogen. As of this printing, there is no good source of organically grown cottonseed meal—and that's a concern.

Diatomaceous Earth (DE)

Mostly used as an animal food supplement and pest control product, diatomaceous earth also has soil-amendment properties because it provides silica, iron, and a long list of trace elements. It can be used from 10 to 50 lbs. per 1,000 sq. ft.

Dillo Dirt

Austin compost product made of sewer sludge and wood chips. Excellent soil builder and organic fertilizer.

Earth's Fortune

A blend of very fine-textured volcanic ash and humate that can be mixed with water to spray on foliage or drench into the soil. The fine texture allows it to be used at low rates and provide strong increased plant growth. It can be mixed with Garrett Juice or other compost-tea sprays for great benefit to food and ornamental crops.

Earthworm Castings

An effective organic fertilizer that is high in bacteria, calcium, iron, magnesium, and sulfur as well as N-P-K and has over 60 trace minerals. Earthworm castings make an excellent ingredient in potting soil, in flats when germinating seed, and as an addition to each hole when planting vegetables, herbs, or small ornamentals. It is a gentle, sweet-smelling, and clean organic fertilizer. Excellent for house plants.

Epsom Salts

A synthetically made form of magnesium sulfate. Usually made from the action of sulfuric acid on magnesium oxide. A fast-acting source of magnesium and sulfur, it is acceptable in an organic program. Magnesium and sulfur are two commonly deficient elements in Texas soils. Epsom salts can be used in liquid sprays or drenches at 1 tablespoon per gallon or dry at 10–20 lbs. per 1,000 sq. ft. around ornamental plants and food crops.

Erath Earth

A line of compost and organic pest control products. Vovinite is their peat moss replacement product that is used in potting soils and compost mixes.

Texas Gardening the Natural Way

Fireplace Ashes

Ashes do have fertilizer and soil-building value if used properly. They are the concentrated mineral salts left from the burning of tree wood. Yes, they are strongly alkaline, but that's not as important as some will lead you to believe. They have high levels of sodium but also magnesium, phosphate, potash, iron, manganese, copper, sulfur, and boron. The proper way to use fireplace ashes is to mix them together with various carbon materials such as dry leaves, sawdust, and dry plant material. Even with this technique, don't overuse them.

Fish Emulsion

A concentrated liquid fish fertilizer for use directly in the soil or as a foliar feed. The analysis will range from 4-1-1 to 5-2-2. It is reported to be an effective insecticide. Good all-purpose spray when mixed with liquid kelp. Has an odor for about 24 hours—a pretty strong one, in fact—so be prepared.

Fish Meal

A natural fertilizer originally used in this country by Native Americans growing corn, although they used whole fish. Fish meal has a high analysis of approximately 8-12-2, but it is also stinky, so use with caution. Very good for flowering plants.

Garden-Ville Soil Food

Organic fertilizer made in San Antonio by compost maker Malcolm Beck. Approximate analysis is 6-2-2. This is an organic fertilizer for gardens and lawns containing bat guano, brewer's yeast, desert humate, Norwegian kelp, compost, fishmeal, meat and corn meal, molasses and langbeinite, cottonseed meal, blood meal, and alfalfa meal. Use at 20–30 lbs. per 1,000 sq. ft.

Garrett Juice

Garrett Juice is our primary foliar-feeding tool. It is also a subtly powerful liquid soil fertilizer as well. For foliar feeding, use it with water at 2–3 oz. per gallon and use on herbs, vegetables, ground covers, shrubs, vines, trees, turf grasses, and greenhouse plants. Garrett Juice is a blend of manure compost tea, seaweed, apple cider vinegar, and molasses. It can be used on plants of any age, but it's always best to spray any liquid materials during the cooler parts of the day. For soil treatment, the application rate can be doubled. Garrett Juice provides major nutrients, trace minerals, and other beneficial components.

Glauconite

See Texas Greensand

Granite Sand

Sandlike residue from the granite quarry or natural deposits. Excellent way to add minerals to planting beds. Much better than washed concrete sand. Contains 5 percent potash and many trace minerals. Also has para-magnetism. Decomposed granite from the Marble Falls area is great in potting soils and for bed preparation and can be used for walkways, drive-ways, and other areas where soft paving is desired. Can also be broadcast fertilizer-style to increase plant growth of all kinds.

GreenSense
A line of organic horticultural products, including soil amendments, fer-tilizers, and pest controls. Some are as follows: GreenSense all-purpose lawn and garden fertilizer (5-2-4) is an odor-free fertilizer made from composted dairy manure, cottonseed meal, corn gluten meal, and more.

Gypsum
This natural material is calcined sulfate and is an excellent source of cal-cium and sulfur. Gypsum also neutralizes plant toxins, removes sodium from the soil, and opens the soil structure to promote aeration and drain-age. Gypsum is approximately 23 percent calcium and 17 percent sulfate. It is not needed in high-calcium soils.

Horse Manure
Horse manure is higher in nitrogen than most other farm-animal ma-nures and is an excellent material to use for the manufacture of compost. Fresh manures should not be tilled directly into the soil unless they are applied a month before planting or composted first. Sheep manure has similar properties and uses.

Hou-Actinite
Biosolids compost made from Houston sewer sludge. Hou-Actinite is also an ingredient in several organic fertilizer blends.

Humate
Humate, or leonardite shale, is basically low-grade lignite coal and is an excellent source of carbon, humic acid, and trace minerals. Percentage of humic acid will vary. May be made into liquid form or used in the dry form.

Hu-more
A line of excellent organic products made from composted cow manure and alfalfa. Other products contain cotton burr compost. The compny also makes humus and alfalfa tea.

Hydrogen Peroxide
An oxidizing liquid for use on soil in diluted amounts. A dangerous prod-uct in concentrated forms. Very controversial and not highly recom-mended. Can be used to clean fruit before eating.

Kelp Meal
A dry fertilizer made from seaweed, with an approximate analysis of 1-0-8. It has lots of trace minerals and plant hormones, which stimulate

root growth and regulate plant growth. Seaweed also provides soil-conditioning substances, improves the crumb structure or tilth, and helps stimulate microorganisms.

Lava Sand

The sand-size and smaller waste material left from lava-gravel manufacturing. It is an excellent, highly paramagnetic soil-amendment material. It can be used in potting soils and bed preparation for all landscaping and food crops. You can use as much as you want for as long as you want. Finer-textured material would be even better if it was easily available. This is one of the most controversial products I recommend. All the hardheaded organiphobes have to do to see its power is—try it! Remember that the most productive soils in the world—found in Costa Rica, Hawaii, and parts of the West Coast and the Mediterranean—occur in places with a history of volcanic action and are almost solid lava.

Lime

A major calcium fertilizer, dolomitic lime contains 30–35 percent magnesium. High-calcium lime is preferred, because most low-calcium soils have plenty of magnesium. High-calcium lime is calcium carbonate.

Manure-based Compost

This is the basic building block of organics. It is the material we would find on an undisturbed forest floor. It acts as a gentle fertilizer by encouraging microbial action.

Medina

A line of liquid and dry products manufactured in Hondo, Texas. Products range from soil biostimulants to fertilizers. Medina Soil Activator is a stimulant, and HastaGro is a powerful organic-based fertilizer.

Milorganite

Sewer sludge fertilizer from Milwaukee. Has been widely used on golf courses. Many cities now make a similar product. Hou-Actinite is a biosolids product made in Houston.

Molasses

Sweet syrup that is a carbohydrate used as a soil amendment to feed and stimulate microorganisms. Contains sulfur, potash, and many trace minerals. Liquid molasses is primarily used in sprays. Dry molasses is used as an ingredient in organic fertilizers but is a powerful product by itself. Dry molasses is not solid dried molasses. It is an organic material, like rice hull bits, that has been sprayed with liquid molasses and dried. It is a powerful carbon source that really kicks up microbial activity and can be effective used at very low rates. Homeowners should use at 10 lbs. per 1,000 sq. ft.

Rabbit Manure

The average analysis of rabbit manure is around 2.5-1.5-5. Mixed with leaves, sawdust, straw, grass, and other vegetative materials, it makes an excellent compost. Can be used directly as a fertilizer without fear of burning plants. Llama and alpaca manures can also be used directly, without composting first.

Root Stimulators

This is a generic term that refers to mild fertilizers or any material that stimulates microbial activity and root growth. Liquid seaweed, vinegar, molasses, and compost tea also function as root stimulators. Most commercial root stimulators are simply liquid synthetic fertilizers and should not be used. Garrett Juice is a natural root stimulator.

Seaweed

Best used as a foliar spray. Excellent source of trace minerals. Should be used often. Contains hormones that stimulate root growth and branching. Many trace elements are found in seaweed in the proportions found in plants. Seaweed contains hormones and functions as a mild but effective insect control, especially for whiteflies and spider mites. It acts as a chelating agent, making other fertilizers and nutrients more available to the plants. Seaweed or kelp is available in liquid and in dry meals.

Sewer Sludge

See Biosolids

Soft Rock Phosphate

A mixture of fine particles of phosphate suspended in a clay base. Economic form of natural phosphorous and calcium. Unlike chemically made phosphates, soft rock phosphate is insoluble in water, will not leach away, and is therefore long lasting. It has 18 percent phosphorous and 15 percent calcium, as well as trace elements. Florida is the primary source.

Sulfur

A basic mineral often lacking in alkaline soils. Applying granulated sulfur at 5 lbs. per 1,000 sq. ft. twice annually can bring base saturation of calcium down and raise magnesium. Be careful not to breathe the dust, overapply, or use when planting seed. It can act as a pre-emergent herbicide. Sulfur dust is also used as a pesticide in some situations.

Sul-Po-Mag

A naturally occurring mineral containing 22 percent sulfur, 22 percent potash, and 11.1 percent magnesium. An excellent product for the organic program.

SuperThrive

A liquid product made from vitamins and hormones. It is a good supplement for flowering plants. Use three drops per gallon at each watering for best results. It can be mixed with other products.

Sustane

A manufactured fertilizer made from composted turkey manure and other natural materials. It is granulated, has some odor for 24–36 hours, and has shown to be an excellent product for soil improvement and re-duction of diseases.

Texas Greensand

A naturally deposited undersea sediment containing a mineral called glauconite, or iron potassium silicate. Mined from ancient seabeds, Texas greensand is an excellent source of iron and other trace minerals, with a normal analysis of about 0-1-5. It's best used with other fertilizers and organic materials. Contains 19–20 percent iron, so it can be a bit of a problem in soils with high levels of iron. Jersey greensand or high-calcium lime is a better choice for people with acid soils.

Turkey Manure

Turkey manure is a high-nitrogen product that is an excellent ingredient for compost making. It is too "hot" to use directly unless planting is delayed for several weeks.

Urine

This is a natural source of urea. Livestock urine is high in nitrogen and potassium, containing two-thirds of the nitrogen and four-fifths of the potassium voided by an animal. Use plenty of bedding to capture the urine. Soaked bedding or liquid can be applied at will to garden or field crops and pastures. Because urine is relatively concentrated, it should be applied sparingly and only in damp weather for best results.

Fertilization with urine alone can produce extra-fine growth of grasses and clover much earlier in the spring than other types of feeding. The elements in urine are more quickly available because they are in solution. Urine is also a good activator for converting crop residues to humus.

Volcanite

A Garden-Ville rock-mineral product made from a blend of lava sand, granite, zeolite, basalt, and Texas greensand. It can be mixed into beds under preparation or broadcast on the soil surface. Use from 10 to 80 lbs. per 1,000 sq. ft.

Zeolite

A natural volcanic material used to absorb odors, gases, and liquids and as an amendment for most soils. Zeolite originates from volcanic miner-als with unique characteristics. Its chemical structure classifies it as a hydrated aluminosilicate composed of hydrogen, oxygen, aluminum, and silicon arranged in an interconnecting lattice structure. Zeolite has the ability to absorb certain harmful or unwanted elements from soil, water, and air. An example of this is the removal of calcium from hard water. It has a strong affinity for certain heavy metals such as lead and chromium.

Zeolite works as a soil amendment by absorbing nutrients, especially ammonia, and then releasing them at a rate more beneficial to plant root development.

Zeolite can also be used for air and water purification, cat litter material, shoe deodorizer, animal-feed supplement, garage floor spill remover, cooler and refrigerator odor and moisture remover, animal stall odor and moisture remover, and soil amendment. Mix raw zeolite (powder or granular) into the soil for new bed preparation. Broadcast onto contaminated soil to detoxify. Rates can vary from 10 to 50 lbs. per 1,000 sq. ft. More than 50 lbs. won't hurt anything but is probably a waste of money. Zeolite has a very high cation exchange capacity (CEC). It helps fertilizer to be more efficient.

PEST CONTROL PRODUCTS

Antidesiccants

Also called antitranspirants, these products are made from pine oil and are nontoxic and biodegradable. They are sometimes used for the prevention of powdery mildew on roses and crape myrtles. They work by spreading a clear film over the leaves. Not highly recommended for use as fungicides. Best used to prevent plant foliage from drying out.

Bacillus thuringiensis (Bt)

Beneficial bacteria applied as a liquid spray or powder to kill caterpillars. Sold under a variety of names, such as Thuricide, Dipel, Bio-Worm. Use *Bacillus thuringiensis* 'Israelensis' (Bti) in water for mosquitoes. Use Garrett Juice or molasses with Bt for extra effect. Sugar in the molasses provides protein and keeps insect-killing bacteria alive on the foliage longer, even during rain. Encapsulated Bt products such as Foray are now on the market. They have a longer residual effect on plants.

Baking Soda

Mixed at the rate of 4 teaspoons per gallon of water, baking soda makes an excellent fungicide for black spot, powdery mildew, brown patch, and other fungal problems. Add one teaspoon of liquid soap or vegetable oil to the mix. Be careful to keep the spray on the foliage and not on the soil, as it can alter soil chemistry. Baking soda is composed of sodium and bicarbonate. Both are necessary in the soil, but only in very small amounts. Potassium bicarbonate is an even better choice because it's better for the soil.

Bordeaux Mix

A fungicide and insecticide usually made from copper sulfate and lime. Good for most foliar problems and an effective organic treatment for diseases on fruits, vegetables, shrubs, trees, and flowers, including anthracnose, botrytis, bacterial blight, peach leaf curl, and twig blight. Wet down decks and other hard surfaces before spraying. Some staining is possible.

Citrus Oil

Best to buy commercial orange oil, but you can make citrus oil by soaking citrus peelings in water. D-limolene should be mixed at 2 oz. per gallon of water. Add a tablespoon of molasses and a cup of compost tea for best insect pest control.

Compost Tea

Fill a container half full of compost and finish filling with water. Let the mix sit for 10–14 days, and then dilute and spray on the foliage of any and all plants that are regularly attacked by fungal pests. How to dilute the dark compost tea before using depends on the compost used. A rule of thumb is to dilute the leachate down to one part compost liquid to four to ten parts water. Be sure to strain the solids out with old pantyhose, cheesecloth, or row-cover material.

Copper

Traditional fungicide for powdery mildew, black spot, peach leaf curl, and other diseases. Copper is also an ingredient in Bordeaux mix. I no longer recommend any copper products. Several much less toxic choices are available for fungal control.

Corn Gluten Meal

This is a natural pre-emergent weed control and fertilizer with an analysis of 9.5-0.5-0.5. Corn gluten meal reduces the germination and establishment of troublesome annual weeds. It is available as a powder or in granular form. It is a byproduct of the corn milling process and commonly used in pet and livestock feed. It can be used in vegetable gardens as a fertilizer and can help with weed control, but be careful. It can damage the germination of your food crops started from seed. Use it only after your vegetable seeds are up and young plant roots are well established. It is a powerful fertilizer and will create large healthy weeds if applied after they germinate. It should be applied at 20 lbs. per 1,000 sq. ft. sometime around October 1 and March 1. An additional application can be made around June 1.

Cornmeal

This is a powerful disease-control material. Use at 20 lbs. per 1,000 sq. ft. or 200–800 lbs. per acre to add cellulose and stimulate the beneficial microorganism called *Trichoderma* that controls several disease pathogens such as *Rhizoctonia, Pythium, Fusarium, Phytophthora,* and others. It can also be used in pools and water features to control algae at 2 cups of cornmeal per 100 sq. ft. or 150 lbs. per acre.

Diatomaceous Earth (DE)

Natural diatomaceous earth is approximately 5 percent aluminum, 5 percent sodium, and 86 percent silicon. It is the skeletal remains of microscopic organisms (one-celled aquatic plants) that lived in seawater or freshwater lakes millions of years ago in the western United States. The broken skeletons have razor-sharp edges that scratch the exoskeleton of insects, causing them to desiccate and die. Apply using a dusting machine (manual or electrostatic), covering plants or lawn areas entirely. Be sure to use a dust mask when applying! DE is nonselective, so use sparingly. Breathing dusty material can cause lung problems. As a food supplement, use at 1 to 2 percent of the food volume for feeding pets or livestock. Never use swimming pool DE.

Dormant Oil
Long-standing organic treatment for scale and other overwintering insects. It is petroleum based and will kill beneficial insects, so use sparingly. It's recommended to spray dormant oil at temperatures between 40° and 80° when rain is not expected. It works by smothering the insects and their eggs. Effective against scale, aphids, spider mites, and others. Do not use sulfur as a fungicide without waiting 30 days after using dormant oil.

Floating Row Cover
Gardening fabrics designed to cover plants in moist greenhouse warmth while allowing water, light, and ventilation for proper plant respiration. These row-cover materials protect foliage from chewing insects, prevent harmful insects from laying eggs, and reduce diseases carried by pests. Birds, rabbits, and other animals are also discouraged from feeding on plants.

Garlic-Pepper Tea
An organic insect- and disease-control material made from the juice of garlic and hot peppers such as jalapeño, habanero, or cayenne. This is one of the few preventative controls that I recommend. However, its use should be limited because it will kill small beneficial insects. It is effective for both ornamental and food crops.

Lime Sulfur
A traditional organic fungicide (calcium polysulfide) for fruits, berries, roses, nuts, and ornamental plants. Spray plants as buds swell, but before they open. It is effective for powdery mildew, anthracnose, peach leaf curl, and brown rot. It also controls insects such as scale and mites. It can be phytotoxic, so I recommend other fungal controls.

Liquid Copper
A flowable formulation of copper salts for fungal control on roses, vegetables, fruits, and ornamentals. Used for control of powdery mildew, bacterial blights, and anthracnose, but is toxic to the soil when overused. I do not recommend any copper-based pesticides.

Nicotine Sulfate
An old-time organic pesticide used for the control of hard-to-kill insects. Although it is a quickly biodegradable product, it is dangerous to handle and should not be used.

Nosema locustae

A biological control for crickets and grasshoppers. It works the same way Bt works on caterpillars. It's applied as dry bait, then the insects eat the material, get sick, and are cannibalized by their friends. Charming, isn't it—but it works. Brand names include Nolo Bait, Grasshopper Attack, and Semispore.

Oils

There are now four types of spray oils: dormant, summer, horticultural, and vegetable.

Dormant oils are petroleum based, relatively free of impurities, and have been used as far back as 1880. Dormant oils have lower volatility and more insect-killing power than the other oils, but they can be more toxic to plants. These oils should only be used during the winter months when plants are dormant.

Summer oils, also petroleum based, are lighter, less poisonous to plants, more volatile, and less effective on insects. They can be used during the heat of summer on some hard-to-kill bugs.

Horticultural oils are the lightest and most pure petroleum oils. They can be used for spraying pecan trees and fruit trees, but they are also effective on shrubs and flowers that have scale or other insect infestations.

Vegetable oils are plant extracts. They are environmentally safe, degrade quickly by evaporation, fit into organic or integrated pest management programs, are nonpoisonous to the applicator, are noncorrosive to the spray equipment, and kill a wide range of insects. The state of Texas is also pushing toward vegetable oils. Drilling lubricants can no longer be petroleum oils.

Potassium Bicarbonate Fungicide

Mix 4 teaspoons (approximately 1 rounded tablespoon) of potassium bicarbonate with 1 teaspoon of liquid soap or other surfactant. Spray the foliage of plants afflicted with black spot, powdery mildew, brown patch, and other diseases. Baking soda at the same mixing rate can be used, but it is not as beneficial for plants and the soil.

Pyrethrum

Available in liquid or dry forms, pyrethrum will kill a wide range of insects, including aphids, beetles, leafhoppers, worms, caterpillars, and ants. It is short-lived and natural but toxic to animals. Pyrethrum is made from ground-up painted daisies (*Chrysanthemum cinerariaefolium*). Artificial substitutes, called pyrethroids, should definitely be avoided. Pyrethrin is the active natural ingredient in pyrethrum. Pyrethrum is an acceptable organic pesticide, but it is too toxic for me to recommend any longer. DDT is sprayed on the pyrethrum crops in Africa, so guess what you get along with your organic pesticide? I am especially opposed to products containing piperonyl butoxide (PBO).

Rotenone

Rotenone is dangerous if not handled carefully, but it is still considered by some to be an acceptable organic product. There are products available containing a combination of rotenone and pyrethrum. Rotenone is particularly dangerous to fish. I don't think we should ever use this material.

Sabadilla Dust

Made from the crushed seeds of a tropical lily, sabadilla dust is effective on some of the hard-to-kill garden pests such as thrips, cabbageworms, grasshoppers, loopers, leafhoppers, harlequin bugs, adult squash beetles, and cucumber beetles. This is a toxic and very hard-to-find material. I don't use it.

Soap

Nonphosphate liquid soaps and water mixed together into a spray make a good control for aphids and other small insects. Strong solutions can damage plant foliage, and even weak solutions can kill many of the microscopic beneficial insects, so use sparingly.

Sulfur

Finely ground sulfur is used by mixing with water or dusting on dry to control black spot, leaf spot, brown canker, rust, peach leaf curl, powdery mildew, and apple scab. Mix with liquid seaweed to enhance fungicidal properties. Sulfur will also control fleas, mites, thrips, and chiggers. To avoid leaf burn, do not use when temperature is 90° or above. Do not use on cucurbits such as cantaloupe, squash, cucumbers, and watermelon.

Tanglefoot

Spread on the bark of trees to control gypsy moths, canker worms, climbing cutworms, and ants. Made from natural gum resins, castor oil, and vegetable waxes. Can be used on tree trunks to discourage sapsucker damage.

Triple Action 20

Triple Action 20 is a synthetic fungicide, but it has extremely low toxicity and biodegrades very quickly. It is said to give excellent control of fire blight. Use at 1 teaspoon per gallon. It is also sold as Consan 20.

Vinegar

Vinegar can be an effective tool for controlling a few problem fire ant mounds. Pour it directly into the center of the mound. Use the strongest dilution available. Five percent and 10 percent vinegars are commonly available in the grocery store. Vinegar is an effective herbicide on a hot, sunny day, especially 20 percent food-grade vinegar. It's a nonselective herbicide, so be careful to keep it off your good plants.

Weed Fabric

Synthetic material sold supposedly to control weeds and conserve soil moisture. Not recommended. Use natural mulch in order to maintain the natural processes in the soil.

Yellow Sticky Traps

Nontoxic bright yellow cards that trap insects with their sticky coating. They are used to monitor insect populations. They are not very effective in greenhouses against whiteflies, even though some organiphobes still mention them as a control.

Zinc

A trace mineral that is an important fertilizer element for pecans and other crops. Will defoliate fruit trees if overused. It is not needed in acid soils or balanced soils. Spraying or applying raw zinc products to the soil regularly is not recommended. Zinc is a trace element found in most organic fertilizers.

HOUSE PLANTS

Plants for use inside the house or office can also be grown organically and will have far fewer problems under the natural program. Indoor plants provide an important benefit besides looking nice and softening spaces: they also help clean the air.

Potting soil for interior plants should be the same used for outdoor potted plants. The two best mulches for potted plants are shredded cedar and lava gravel.

The fertilizer program is simple. In fact, the two most common mistakes made with house plants are too much water and too much fertilizer. Adding a mild organic fertilizer once a year in the spring is usually plenty. Compost, earthworm castings, or compost tea, along with a one-time application of lava sand, is all I use. Use about ¼" of lava sand and gently work it into the soil.

Adding a tablespoon of apple cider vinegar per gallon of irrigation water will help keep your potted plants healthy and vibrant.

The easiest plants to grow tend to be the most effective at air purifying. My recommended list is as follows:

Bright Areas	Semi-Shade	Shadiest Areas
Aloe vera	Aglaonema	Aglaonema
Areca palm	Boston fern	Heart leaf philodendron
Bamboo palm	Corn plant dracaena	Red emerald philodendron
Christmas cactus	Croton	Pothos
Croton	Heart leaf philodendron	Sanseveria
Orchids	Pothos ivy	
Dieffenbachia	Janet Craig dracaena	
Lady palm	Shefflera	
Dwarf banana	Warneckii dracaena	
	Rubber plant	
	Spathiphyllum	
	Parlor palm	
	Spider plant	

An excellent book on the air-purifying properties of plants is *How to Grow Fresh Air* by Dr. B. C. Wolverton (Penguin Books, 1997).

POISONOUS PLANTS

Many poisonous plants exist and are commonly used in landscaping. The range of toxicity is great. Some toxic plants will just give you skin rashes or a stomachache rather than kill you. Children need to be taught which plants can be eaten and which are dangerous. It is best not to let them eat any plants without your approval and supervision.

Some of the commonly used toxic plants include azaleas, bluebonnet, boxwood, Carolina jessamine, castor bean, cherry laurel, chinaberry, Chinese tallow tree, coral bean, crocus, daffodils, English ivy, four o'clock, foxglove, hyacinth, iris, Japanese ligustrum, jimsonweed, lantana, larkspur, ligustrum, lilies, Mexican buckeye, milkweed, morning glory, nandina, oaks, oleander, periwinkle, pittosporum, red buckeye, sweet pea, Texas mountain laurel, wax ligustrum, wisteria, and yaupon holly.

Several good books and web sites on poisonous plants are available, and for a question about the toxicity of any plant, you can call the Poison Control Center at 1-800-222-1222.

Index

Ipomoea batatas, 252
Ipomoea fistulosa, 189
Ipomoea quamoclit, 141
Ipomoea spp., 149
Ipomopsis rubra, 202
Iris, 185
Iris spp., 185
Iron Cross vine, 141
Iron deficiency, 328
Irrigation, 16
Italian cypress, 50, 94
Italian jasmine, 118
Italian stone pine, 81
Ivy, Boston, 146
Ivy, English, 146
Ivy, fig, 146, 147
Ivy, Persian, 146
Ixora, 185
Ixora coccinea, 185

Japanese anemone, 161
Japanese aralia, 100
Japanese ardisia, 137
Japanese black pine, 82
Japanese holly fern, 112
Japanese honeysuckle, 144
Japanese katsura, 59
Japanese ligustrum, 119
Japanese maple, 62
Japanese photinia, 124
Japanese viburnum, 133
Japanese wisteria, 154
Japonica, 127
Jasmine, Asian, 147
Jasmine, Confederate, 147
Jasmine, Italian, 118
Jasmine, yellow, 147
Jasminum humile, 118
Jasminum nudiflorum, 118
Jasminum sambac, 288
Jatropha, 185
Jatropha integerima, 185
Java plant, 167
Jerusalem artichoke, 204
Jerusalem oak, 276
Jerusalem sage, 185
Jerusalem thorn, 78
Jessamine, Carolina, 138
Jicama, 239
Jimsonweed, 176
Johnny-jump-up, 191
Johnsongrass, 219
Jonquil, 173
Joseph's coat, 186
Juglans nigra, 90
Jujube, 240
June beetles, 309
Juniper, blue rug, 118
Juniper, creeping, 118
Juniper, Pfitzer, 118
Juniper, shore, 118

Juniper, Tam, 118
Juniper dieback, 328
Juniperus ashei, 45
Juniperus chinensis, 118
Juniperus conferta, 118
Juniperus horizontalis, 118
Juniperus sabina, 118
Juniperus virginiana, 45

Kale, 236
Katsura, 59
Kava-kava, 279
Kelp, 353
Kelp meal, 351
Kidneywood, 59
Knitbone, 274
Koelreuteria bipinnata, 55
Koelreuteria paniculata, 55
Kohlrabi, 240
Korean pittosporum, 125
Kudzu, 148, 280

Lablab purpureus, 145
Lacebark elm, 52
Lace bugs, 309
Lacevine, silver, 148
Lacewings, 309
Lacey oak, 69
Lactuca sativa, 241
Lady beetles, 310
Ladybugs, 310
Lagerstroemia faurei, 48
Lagerstroemia indica, 48
Lamb's ear, 186
Lamium, 148
Lamium maculatum, 148
Landscape design, 3
Langtry oak, 69
Lantana, 186
Lantana spp., 186
Larkspur, 187
Lathyrus odoratus, 205
Laurel oak, 75
Laurus nobilis, 270
Lavandula spp., 281
Lava sand, 95, 352
Lavender, 281
Lavender cotton, 128
Lawns, 211–225
Lazy daisy, 175
Leafcutting ants, 317
Leafcutting bees, 310
Leafhoppers, 311
Leafminers, 311
Leaf spot, 326, 328
Leather leaf mahonia, 120
Leek, 240
Lemonball tree, 54
Lemon balm, 281
Lemongrass, 282
Lemon mint, 189